EDGE OF ENGLAND

DEREK TURNER

Edge of England

Landfall in Lincolnshire

HURST & COMPANY, LONDON

First published in the United Kingdom in 2022 by
C. Hurst & Co. (Publishers) Ltd.,
New Wing, Somerset House, Strand, London, WC2R 1LA
© Derek Turner 2022
All rights reserved.
Printed in Great Britain by Bell and Bain Ltd, Glasgow

Distributed in the United States, Canada and Latin America
by Oxford University Press, 198 Madison Avenue, New York, NY 10016,
United States of America.

A Cataloguing-in-Publication data record for this book
is available from the British Library.

This book is printed using paper from registered sustainable
and managed sources.

ISBN: 9781787386983

www.hurstpublishers.com

CONTENTS

'A good prospect alone will ease melancholy'
— Robert Burton, *Anatomy of Melancholy*

'In the following pages, I have endeavoured to describe a dream,
partly of study, partly of adventure'
— George Borrow, *Lavengro*

To annalists, antiquarians, archivists, chorographers, chroniclers, dilettanti, folklorists and glossarians

ACKNOWLEDGEMENTS

The following people helped make this amorphous book a reality, by reading and commenting on parts or all of the text at different stages, and in other ways.

Eva and Nick Moore, for commenting on the Lincoln chapter. Dr Jack Cunningham, for giving me the benefit of his expertise on Robert Grosseteste and Lincoln diocesan history. Anthony Jennings, for insights about architecture and other matters. Dr Liam Guilar, who not only knows about Roman to early medieval Britain but scanned the text with acute poetical sensibility. Stuart Millson and Edward Parnell, who read it for both accuracy and evocation. John Lewis-Stempel, who knows about animals and farming, as well as English history. Dr Robert Stove, who read over the musical references. My brother, Dr Stephen Turner, who checked the mathematics and science sections. My father, Captain Derek Turner, who checked over the maritime references. Tony Lazell and Alan Mumby of Far Welter'd, who checked the dialect section. Dan Bell for his handsome map. Michael Dwyer of Hurst, who was wonderfully patient and tolerant, and made shrewd editorial decisions. Amanda and Guy, and other family and friends, who put up with long periods of greater than usual abstraction. Any remaining errors or interpretations are my own.

LIST OF ILLUSTRATIONS

(All photographs unless otherwise stated are © Derek Turner, 2022)

Map of Lincolnshire reproduced by kind permission of Dan Bell, © Dan Bell, 2022

SECTION ONE

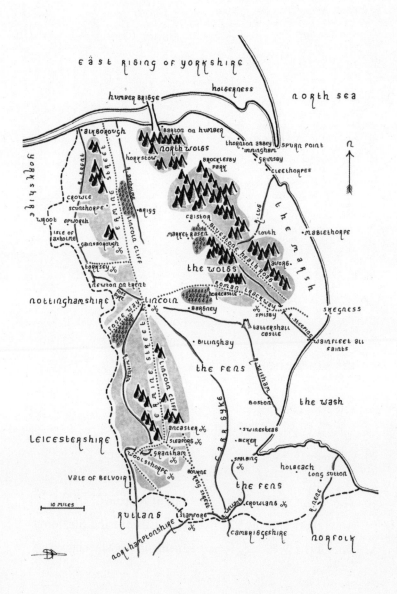

Map of Lincolnshire, © Dan Bell, 2022

PROLOGUE

LONDON TO LINCOLNSHIRE

'The grete tounes se we wane and wende'
—Chaucer, 'The Knight's Tale'

THE ROAD NORTH—FORAY INTO FENLAND—THE WALL OF THE
WOLDS—SIGHT OF THE SEA—THE OUTER MARSH—
THE LONELY HOUSE

Hard Christmas cold, half-awake humans, cats shoved into carriers, effects into cases, out into sodium-orange predawn, scrape the screen, reverse out, join the A2 exodus. Chaucer's road... But not for long, because we charge into the Blackwall Tunnel's castellated maw, and emerge north of the river, before we really come alive.

Up through the bleary East End—then Essex, Hertfordshire, Huntingdonshire—Eastern Counties Association, low-lying lands of Low Church sentiment and lazy rivers under frost and the winking overfliers of Stansted, paling and widening as a great sun climbs out of the earth, and we listen to Purcell's King

Arthur—his Cold Genius complaining wonderingly when he first rises over Britain,

What power art thou?
Who from below
Hast made me rise?
Unwillingly and slow
From beds of everlasting snow!

Baroque patriotism for a quiet country, with even the motorway empty. More motion now. Lorries appear, cars branch off in unglamorous directions—Harlow, Bishop's Stortford, Huntingdon, St Neot's.

Cambridge, M11 becomes A14, we see the Norman Cross. Peterborough—ring roads around unloveliness, and at the city's core Catherine of Aragon's empty tomb. To the east Flag Fen—Bronze Age boats, buildings and causeways, scraped posthole by posthole out of three-and-a-half millennia of mud by anatomists of ancient Anglia. Then—the county sign, our Rubicon—in 1999 still bearing a black-and-white Lincoln Imp, crude rendering of a crude carving high up in the medieval choir of the Cathedral forty miles away across Fens. Anglia joins the Home Counties and London in our past, and we are in the Midlands—indeterminate term for an indeterminate place, suddenly, excitingly substantial.

Keep on, keep on, through a cryogenic country—ice-greasy dykes, whited spears of last year's grass, nipped shoots of coming crops, breath-hanging sheep chewing moodily, dark clumps of clay, old willows, tractors and pick-ups, raised roads, linear red-brick villages, medieval church towers. The triangular bridge and Norman abbey arches of Crowland—founded by fevered Saxon saints, burned by Danes, landmark to Hereward the Wake, prosperous institution of Ingulf and Pseudo-Ingulf, dissolved by Reformers, scene of a Civil War siege. A void-spanning arc of

PROLOGUE

England—and part of its echoing soundtrack, the Abbey's peal of bells England's first.

The road unrolls itself into Holland. Sun shines upon our scenery but has no heat to spare. Lincolnshire seems brilliant and clear, save for miasmas emanating from ditches, drains, and dykes. Huge daffodil and tulip fields (a hare racing along a boundary), prosaic cabbages and sprouts, complacent Georgian and Victorian farms, sail-less windmills, ugly barns, cow-shit steaming to itself, unbending roads thundered by vegetable transporters. Spalding—castled by the Conqueror's standard-bearer, its vault-piercing church as wide as it is long, substantial merchants' houses lining the tidal Welland—first sense of the sea, just a few miles away and sometimes over the centuries far too close.

We see Boston's stupendous Stump—the sixteenth-century lantern tower of St Botolph's, golden-finialled guiding light for a swampy town, beacon for farers across the fens, welcome seamark for sailors creeping up from Hanseatic ports into the Haven, last sight of the old country for Pilgrim Fathers wanting a New World. Handsome houses along the Spilsby Road, villages along an Anglo-Saxon causeway traversing then-trembling marshes towards the first hills we've encountered.

Up the shoulder of one, in the complaining car. In the rear-view mirror, the Fens are a newly-painted Cubist dreamscape, concluding in the far-off coda of the Stump—its finials, I swear, still glinting from fourteen miles' distance. The Wolds loll lazily—richer than the more productive plain, at times almost aristocratic, with hidden halls and manor houses up treed driveways, and just outside Spilsby, the remaining gatepier of Eresby Hall, seat of the Willoughby d'Eresbys, a classical column fenced off against animals at the end of a leafless avenue. John Franklin would have known that vista—maybe imagined it at his bitter end, a scene from a temperate boyhood to set against his blasted waste.

Almost there, and accelerating. Up and down, up and down again, between fields known to Tennyson—more hares, a roe deer, a buzzard—hawthorn hedges, and Waterloo plantations standing to attention. We descend again and flick urgently through Alford, with its windmill, thatched houses, and plaque to Thomas Paine. The Wolds slump, like the seashore they were, into a blue-gold-grey and lonely vast—the Marsh, and beyond that the even greater illimitability of the North Sea, finally seen after so long sensed.

Another defining structure—St James' spire at Louth, one of the tallest in the country, inspiration for an insurrection, painted by Turner. We pass under its significant gnomon to see Trollopean streets through steamed-up windows—plum-red brick, Dutch gabling, wide doors, sash windows, butchers with unplucked pheasants hanging on hooks, greengrocer shops groaning with produce, market stallholders still busy but also starting to close up, calling cheerfully to the crowd and bantering between each other in terms heard here for centuries.

Due east along almost deserted roads between disconsolate dykes—cramped, excited, impatient, stiff. We shrink, or the sky grows—above, around and behind. Dizzying distances, space... Ahead, the sky looks biggest of all, whitening like a new world where we know it meets the sea, just beyond sand hills and salt marsh.

Even emptier roads branch off our Roman-straight B-route, little potholed carriageways not busy since the last war, when bomber crews whiled away tense hours and days by aerodrome control towers and Nissen huts. Ex-RAF housing—pinched farmworkers' cottages with plastic windows—caravans—grander houses—welcome coverts—a heron winding himself up out of a tiny waterway—little bridges—sluice gates—an old pumping station—ranks of dead reeds—a moorhen charging across frantically in front—old furrows in fields—bits of boats in gardens—more medieval churches, one with a picturesquely leaning tower—three shot carrion crows nailed futilely to a fence. Clouds clench, the sun falters. Then our road—*our road*—final potholes avoided or endured—brown thorny hedges itchy with sparrows—and finally, The House.

Dark-windowed, cold-chimneyed, damp greenness down the front, rotting windows, scuffed door, scrubby garden, dralon curtains. The door is difficult to open, and once inside, there is a deathly cold, smells of damp and drains, and mice. Naked bulbs dangle obscenely from above; those curtains hang from plastic tracks; the walls are dirty and pockmarked; the suspended ceiling in the main room has a pole punched in it.

The former owner has left several bags of household waste, old clothes, and a painting of her own production: a pink horse charging angrily across an unfeasible field, as if incensed by its clumsy execution. Under thick drifts of ash and sycamore leaves, the little back garden is mounded with solidified potters' clay— evidence of other artistry—and even more enigmatic lumps of concrete. Soot has fallen into the mean 1970s fireplace and spilled out onto the floor. We look at all this, the laden car, and each other, and wonder where to start.

ANOTHER COUNTRY

'Tow'rds Lincolnshire our Progresse layd'
—Michael Drayton, *Poly-Olbion*

LINCOLNSHIRE IN THE IMAGINATION—WETLANDS CULTURE—
ENGLAND'S UKRAINE—LAST RESORTS—CITY VERSUS COUNTY—
LINCOLNSHIRE IN REALITY

'Why Lincolnshire?' I was often asked. It was oddly hard to explain. It was a more difficult question to answer than 'Why not London?'

In the late 1990s, many Londoners talked about moving out. Unlike most of those many, we were looking in Lincolnshire.

Lincolnshire. The name resounded because it was so rarely heard—on the news, in conversation, in cultural references. I thought of this as an ancient oversight; the antiquarian topographies I enjoyed rarely bore 'Lincolnshire' on their spines, and only mentioned the place in passing. Shelves in second-hand bookshops creaked under the chorographical weight of Cornwall, Devon, Dorset, Kent, the Lakes, Norfolk, Somerset, even Middlesex—but almost never Lincolnshire. The county was often only mentioned in passing in books about eastern England, or whole-island itineraries. As one rare Lincolnshire historian admitted, 'It is hardly rash to say that the county, as a whole, excites less interest than any other in the mind of an average Englishman.'[1]

Perhaps it was because I was not an Englishman that I became increasingly intrigued.

The proverbial mentions of Lincolnshire I found were all disparaging, showing the county as decaying, boorishly rustic, and even a target of diabolical ire. There was a gnomic saw, derived from a sixteenth-century romance, *The Red Rose Knight*: 'Lincoln was, London is, and York shall be.' Lincolnshire music-making was laughed at; as Shakespeare's *Henry IV* (born in Old Bolingbroke, near Boston), repines 'I am as melancholy as a gib cat... or the drone of a Lincolnshire bagpipe.'[2]

There was a seventeenth-century saying: 'Lincolnshire, where hogs shit soap, and cows shit fire'—a reference to supposed Lincolnshire customs of washing with pig excrement, and burning dried cow-dung.[3] The scholar Thomas Greaves, who swapped college for a Lincolnshire rectory, wrote fastidiously of being in a place '*nec literis, nec artibus quisquam hic locus nisi rusticanis, atque sordidissimis*' (with no literature, no arts except of a rustic or sordid sort).[4]

An old colloquialism cast a dreadful shadow over the city, with bad-tempered looks long proverbially likened to the way 'the Devil looks over Lincoln' with 'a *torve* [stern, severe] and *tetrick* [sour; sullen] countenance.'[5] By the eighteenth century, even Lincolnshire's once much-demanded 'linsey' wool had fallen into disrepute, 'linsey-woolsey' becoming shorthand for a blend of linen and wool and hence by extension 'Vile; mean; of different and unsuitable parts.'[6] While all areas wax and wane over time, and rustics everywhere have always been the butt of scorn, there seemed to be an especially *redundant* quality to the county. As two of its rare advocates noted, 'There is a "goneness" about Lincolnshire that is difficult to capture in words.'[7]

It was unusual to meet people who knew Lincolnshire, or who had even been there, unless passing through some corner of it on their way to somewhere *à la mode*. When I asked a Cambridge-educated work colleague, a keen countryman who should have known better, what came into his head when he thought of Lincolnshire, he snorted in contemptuous amusement, and said, 'Cabbages!' Pressed, he thought for a moment and added, 'Flat as a billiard-table,' then started talking about Yorkshire. Others I asked were equally ill-informed, nonplussed even to be asked. The mere word could almost be a conversation killer. Lincolnshire started to look like a continent apart—a large, and largely blank, space, almost islanded by cold sea, great estuaries, soggy wastes, and a filigree of fenny waterways.

The chorographic connotations were admittedly few, and vague—farming, flatness, flooding, a cathedral, Lincoln Green, sad seaside resorts, Vikings, Bomber Command, Margaret Thatcher, old-school England—and almost nothing else. Lincolnshire was sparsely populated, with no big cities, so had proportionally fewer celebrants, let alone celebrities, than many other counties—but it seemed to be about more than relative emptiness. Lincolnshire appeared not the sort of place that encouraged lyricism, or nostalgia; it was somewhere people came from, not escaped to.

There was a sense that the whole county (with the exception of Lincoln Cathedral) was historically unexceptional, culturally marginal, predictable, boring and frequently ugly. Even the cathedral was mostly of interest to medievalists or tourists.

Lincolnshire was a blank, taken-for-granted space that post-war politics had largely sidestepped, almost completely circumvented by major transport routes.

It was neither South nor North, but Midlandian—an ill-defined, in-between transit zone lazily assumed to have no 'must-see' sights and little that was even interesting. Even the accent, on the very rare times it was heard, sounded halfway between Hull and Hunstanton. The most famous Lincolnshire native, Margaret Thatcher, had taken elocution lessons to rid herself of her accent, in favour of a strangulated version of RP (received pronunciation)—although sometimes dialect words would creep into her cut-and-thrust, as when she famously asked Labour frontbencher Denis Healey if he was too 'frit' to call an election.[8] The county was notable chiefly to agronomists and economists as a high-functioning English version of Ukraine, sometimes even called 'the bread-basket of England,' where steppe-sized harvesters combed squared fields between equally angular chicken sheds. It was a county very hard to comprehend.

Surely somewhere that had escaped the outside world's often unwelcome attentions must have distinctive qualities? Lincolnshire had been semi-forgotten, a *terra* near-*incognita* (if not necessarily always *firma*) starting less than a hundred miles from London. It was not the only unknown or underestimated piece of England, but it was the closest and the largest. *Lincolnshire.* The name beguiled with a sense of cleanliness and *space*—room to breathe, scope for the imagination.

* * *

Topography has long been against Lincolnshire—or for it, depending on perspective. Not all of Lincolnshire is level, and not all levels are the same anyway. But people who have never visited often assume it is a vast, featureless and possibly insalubrious plain. This matters, because there is a long-standing prejudice against level landscapes, particularly damp ones.

Since the onset of agricultural and city-based 'civilization,' marshlands have been marginal, and mires a metaphor for moral as well as physical confusion. Rulers plundered their clay, fish, fowl, reed, salt, samphire and willow, and cultivated crops and pastured animals in their drier corners, but they didn't live there. Nor did anyone else who didn't have to. For millennia, marshes have been, or at least have been popularly imagined to be places of doubtful solidity, of fevers and floods, and drownings and muds, fugitives and outlaws, unseen animals booming and creaking in deep reed beds, and unearthly will-o'-the-wisps tempting the unwary to quit the causeway.

Sir Gawain found himself lost in marsh, symbolising his inability to keep his dreadful appointment with the Green Knight. For John Donne, marshes were a murky halfway house between the soul's sparkling source and the body's bitter dissolution:

> Who would not bee affected to see a cleere and sweet River in the Morning, grow a kennell of muddy land water by noone, and condemned to the saltnesse of the Sea by night?[9]

John Bunyan's Christian strays into the Slough of Despond, and has to be saved by Help, who tells him,

> This miry slough is such a place as cannot be mended. It is the descent whither the scum and filth that attend conviction of sin do continually run.[10]

Marshes are places of drains, gases, 'pondlife,' 'scum,' sewers and stagnation. The German ethnomusicologist Marius Schneider, borrowing from Sumerian and other mythologies, saw marshes as places of 'decomposition of the spirit,' where the 'passive' elements (water and earth) fuse and rot without 'active' air and fire to invigorate them.[11]

Marshes were seen as purposeless places, where backwaters meandered towards muddy inconclusiveness. In psychoanalysis, swamps are symbols of the unconscious. Synonyms like bog, morass, and quagmire all carry similar connotations of dirt, dullness, and quaking uncertainty. *Beowulf*'s Grendel was a swamp-thing. That classic marshland shrub or tree, the willow, was a traditional symbol of mourning—'Let Wyllows wynde aboute my hed, a Wrethe for Wretches mete.'[12] In Tolkien's Old Forest, 'Old Man Willow' is the darkness at the forest's heart, ancient but filled with evergreen hate. In early nineteenth-century London, prostitutes were referred to as 'fens.'[13] Toilets have long been 'bogs,' RUC policemen once dreaded being posted to dangerous 'bog stations' like Crossmaglen—and their Catholic and Republican adversaries with much less reason still speak of supposedly slow-witted 'bogmen' (the English word *bog* comes from the Irish-Gaelic *bogach*, meaning 'soft ground'). Donald Trump was plumbing deep artesian sources when he bragged about 'draining the swamp.'

Wetlands are also notoriously unhealthy. For centuries the maze of slow-moving waterways ensured the prevalence of often dangerous fevers, either typhus or malaria. The connection between still waters and sweaty agues was registered by Caliban:

> All the infections that the sun sucks up / From bogs, fens, flats on Prosper fall and make him / By inch-meal a disease![14]

Lear, too, feared 'fen-sucked fogs' that 'fall and blister'.[15]

It was not until the nineteenth century that the role of insects—lice, mites and fleas for typhus, the *Anopheles* mosquito for malaria—was understood. The indigenous British strain of malaria was never the most lethal, and by 1800 was already abating, thanks to gradual shrinking of mosquito habitat, wider availability of quinine, and airier and lighter houses, and is presently absent. Malaria was a much more serious problem for colonialists in Africa and Asia, who had reason to be grateful for the anti-mosquito mesh they jokingly called 'Crowland sack.' Elegant *Anopheles* still whine along Lincolnshire's waterways, and lay eggs in our pond, which hatch into larvae with swivelling heads like Noh Theatre masks.[16]

'Yellowbellies,' the nickname for Lincolnshire natives, is said to derive from the hue of malaria victims who have been treated with opium, although there are other possible origins—the yellow *fleur-de-lis* on Lincoln's coat-of-arms; the canary of the Lincolnshire Regiment's uniform facings; the long, lemon coats worn by county coachmen; powder from mustard farming; dust from iron-stone quarrying, and yet others. In any case, locals long ago learned to live with this problem:

> The Fenmen ... counted little of the ague which attacked them, and was called 'the Bailiff of the Marshland'.[17]

Originally an insult, Yellowbelly has in recent years been affectionately co-opted into a Lincolnshire-wide pride, used alongside the colourful county flag adopted in 2005. But clearly such a nickname has historically only added to outsiders' vague sense of clammy discomfort.

Lincolnshire's boggy places were even further from London than those of the Thames Estuary, Cambridgeshire, or East Anglia, and distance lent disenchantment. In *The Sad Shepherd*, Ben Jonson located a witch's lair among the 'rotten mists' of the 'drowned land of Lincolnshire.' In *Peveril of the Peak*, Walter Scott's Roger Wildrake styled himself 'of Squattlesea Mere in the moist county of Lincoln.' *Bleak House*'s disconsolate Chesney Wold, where the rain was 'ever falling, drip, drip, drip, by day and by night' was in Lincolnshire. That novel's repellent lawyer, Mr Tulkinghorn, lived and was murdered at Lincoln's Inn in

London (named after the third Earl of Lincoln, who had a house there in Edward I's reign)—a place to Dickens emblematic of the floundering ambiguity and wallowing injustice of the English legal system.

Distaste for fenny places runs deep, but it also stems in part from the eighteenth- and nineteenth-century aestheticization of Nature, with its ironically studied distaste for 'artificiality' and emphasis on 'picturesque,' 'pleasing' and 'sublime' qualities—cliffs, forests, mountains, torrents, waterfalls, wilderness. Excitable writers and the jaded wealthy alike increasingly demanded ruggedly 'Gothick' vistas as backdrop for extravagant emotions, great houses, overblown stories and radical idealism.

Unemphatic, undulating countryside, like the Essex-Bedfordshire-Cambridgeshire-Huntingdonshire corridor that leads towards Lincolnshire, was unpoetic enough. But plashy, indeterminate places like the Fens, where the chief activities were agriculture and wildfowling, the inhabitants were supposedly boors, and altitudes could be measured in inches, were increasingly beneath notice. The only romantically 'Gothick' connection with Lincolnshire is tangential—Thomas Love Peacock's 1818 satire of the macabre taste in literature, *Nightmare Abbey*, a mansion 'in a highly picturesque state of semi-dilapidation,' looking onto 'a fine monotony of fens and windmills,' whose morose owner, Mr Glowry, associates only with equally misanthropic gentry and employs servants called Graves, Mattocks and Skellet, in a camp, damp atmosphere of eeriness and intrigue.

Some artists would remain appreciative of lowland fertility and placidity, as shown in Constable's representations of Suffolk, and, more directly, in the calm Lincolnshire pastorals of Peter De Wint (1784-1849), called 'golden hours eternised' by Edmund Blunden,[18] which derive from the Netherlandish tradition of landscape genre paintings emphasising light and rational order.

John Sell Cotman (1782-1842) also painted windmills at Crowland, and Joseph Crawhall (1861-1913) made dreamily impressionistic studies of Lincolnshire's pastureland. But visions of this half-complacent kind were often disregarded as emotionally and geographically uninteresting.

This prejudice persists. Mountains maintain their conventional, even clichéd, appeal to the emotions—celebrated in art, on programmes and biscuit tins. Where Wagnerians or the hospitality industry can offer dramatic dioramas, the Fens have only humorously-named 'Hills' a few feet higher than their surrounding fields; the hamlet of Willoughby Hills, near Boston, is 7 feet, 10 inches above mean sea level, which is only slightly higher than my cottage in the Marsh. Fine distinctions are inevitable in a landscape where inches can make the difference between existence and inundation, but they don't offer obvious atmosphere. Yet mountains can also be boring and even ugly— and mountainous vistas are only deceptively clear, and inevitably lack detail. While you can see the world from a height, to know it you need to descend. Appreciating lowlands requires a different set of spatial skills, a more intimate awareness.

The twentieth-century Lincolnshire enthusiast Maurice Wilmore Barley admits that seeing the beauty of England's lowlands 'requires a more lively eye than do the highlands.'[19] He cites Suffolk's George Crabbe, who also knew the southern Lincolnshire landscape:

...all that grows has grace; / All are appropriate — bog, and marsh, and fen, / Are only poor to undiscerning men.[20]

It would have been easier to love lowlands in Crabbe's time, or even Barley's. The Fens have always been ruthlessly exploited, but as late as the 1950s they were more varied than now—wetter, wilder, less pesticide-poisoned, with bungalows and caravans only just beginning to make their appearance. Since then, until very recently, there has been enormous rationalisation, expedited by technology—dykes being drained, piped or straightened, fields enlarged into practical prairies, hedges and trees uprooted, wildlife expelled, crops and livestock standardised, verges razored, old buildings removed or disfigured, the handmade red-brick, 'mud and stud' (the Lincolnshire equivalent of wattle and daub) and pantiled or thatched vernacular increasingly replaced by cheaper, easier-to-obtain materials. Farmers, of course, need to farm, and viably, but the resultant environment is frequently bleak. As the Boston-born Catholic poet Elizabeth Jennings (1926-2001) reflected uneasily,

Everything was too neat, and someone cares / In the wrong way... / Sickness for Eden was so strong.[21]

There are major differences between the Fens of the county's south, and the Marsh of its east. The Fens themselves vary greatly, for those who take the trouble to look. They are also frequently beautiful, and interesting. They are not even uniformly flat. But the worst aspects of the Fens exemplify Lincolnshire for many visitors, and deter others from deeper explorations. This is the part of the county most people are likely to see, when they pass through the county at all—and many will not see it in optimal circumstances, perhaps halfway through a long journey, trapped behind caravans or thundering vegetable lorries.

The Fens make little attempt to charm or cozen. Little or nothing is allowed to run riot, and imaginations are kept puritanically in check. They lack the sleekness of the South, the cachet of the Cotswolds, the half-timbered homeliness of Shropshire, the picturesqueness of the Dales or the Lakes. They are open to every wind in the winter, and even when softened by summer, many find their uncompromising planes and amphitheatrical skies disconcerting, or even desolating. The chapels, with their Spartan elevations, hint at sere and unforgiving creeds.

This is a hard-worked landscape, asserting order over disorder, large tranches of it drained, tamed, treeless—and those who coax their living from it are often too busy feeding the nation to think about history, and although notably law-abiding, are instinctively impatient with anything (wildlife protection, or planning permission, for example) that impedes their activities. They take the natural world for granted, just as Londoners take London's wonders for granted, and are accustomed to farming just the way their parents did. Unfortunately, those parents usually farmed in the 1950s-1970s, when intensive agriculture was coming into its own, with all its terrible consequences for the countryside.

Intensive farming and mass tourism interests, and sometimes too-close connections with councillors, have often ensured that planning controls were (are) lax or weakly enforced. Old farm outbuildings are often of little use to modern farmers, who have big machines to house, and chemicals or crops to store safely, and so they have often been swept away in favour of boxes of concrete and steel; although this is understandable, the net effects are regrettable. Farmers are generally too busy to worry about aesthetics. Older farmhouses are patched up on the cheap, or razed and rebuilt in blandly functional form during some period of prosperity. Although attitudes and practices are altering, still too many south Lincolnshire fields are regimented rectangles, unwelcoming to any growths except the uniform coloured and sized crop, inimical to wildlife with their slug pellets and sprays, and the dykes dividing them too often choked up with green scum—eutrophication caused by fertiliser run-off. Verges where wild flowers might cling on are mown unthinkingly by landowners, council workers or 'tidiness'-obsessed householders.

Side roads discourage exploration, even their longest, straightest stretches narrow, often bordered by deep dykes, and seriously uneven, their surfaces swooping in response to the rippling substrate. They have a tendency to dome in the middle, and flake away at the edges into holes and adverse cambers. Twentieth-century widening schemes did not take into account the roads' origins as sheep droves, the width of a few animals. The feet and hooves of centuries have compacted the central spines, but the newer margins always want to fall away to water. The harvesters, tractors and trailers that ply these backroads exacerbate the difficulties, repeatedly churning up the tarmac, difficult to overtake.

Farmers' jobs are dull, repetitive, strenuous and of course vitally important, so few would begrudge them chemical or technological aids. Some among the non-farming population are far more blameworthy, most often incomers who have come in search of 'country views' but inadvertently spoil them for others, ironically damaging the very thing they have come to find. Lincolnshire has more than its fair share of bungalows with plastic windows, caravan parks, garden centres and chicken farms. Is it so surprising that so many passing through shake their heads and tap the accelerator?

*   *   *

As well as scenery snobbery, Lincolnshire has long had a problem with class. William Camden described Fenlanders as,

> ...rude, uncivil, and envious to all others whom they call Upland-men ... as rough and uncultivated as the soil itself ... marching about on a sort of stilts like giants.[22]

One eighteenth-century versifier expressed his contempt for those who passed existences here:

The Goths were not so barbarous a Race
As the grim Rusticks of this motly Place,
Of Reason void, and Thought, whom Int'rest rules
Yet will be Knaves tho' Nature meant them Fools,

A strange half-humane and ungainly Brood
Their Speech uncouth, as are their Manners rude.[23]

More recently, Bernie Taupin, Elton John's Lincolnshire-born lyricist, said,

Lincolnshire is the Idaho of England—you were either going to drive a tractor for the rest of your life or head for the city to work in a factory.[24]

This comparison can be overdone, but from certain perspectives, Britain's farmers are culturally comparable to American Midwesterners, ridiculed as hicks or just regarded with incomprehension. To a culturally influential minority, the Fens are Britain's equivalent to America's 'Flyover Country'—almost blank spaces between places, inhabited by almost aliens, grasping 'gammon,' red-faced philistines out of touch with modern thinking. More mainstream people enjoy programmes about artisan cheese-making or rearing rare breeds in some rugged glen, but Fen farming is much less interesting or photogenic.

Traditionally, those outsiders who *did* go to Lincolnshire, on holiday or in retirement, were predominantly working-class white people, from the cities of the East Midlands and South Yorkshire. Middle-class Londoners who emphasised their liberal understanding simply didn't come much into contact with these groups, and accordingly often misunderstood them. Lincolnshire's strung-out resorts—Skegness, Ingoldmells, Chapel St Leonards, Mablethorpe and Cleethorpes—which had never had the same status as Aldeburgh, Brighton, Broadstairs or Scarborough anyway, were notoriously in long-term decline.

'Seaside towns' was a socioeconomic near-synonym for social deprivation—*cul-de-sac* coasts and 'last resorts' lacking proper education, jobs or opportunities.

It was difficult for some to understand why anyone wanted to go to such places, let alone go there more than once. Yet even in their mostly shabby state, they attracted large numbers of retirees, as well as loyal visitors returning each summer to a cheap (if no longer necessarily cheerful) ambience of amusement arcades, downmarket stores, and fast-food joints. The only respite from the chilly breezes outside lay in grim pubs serving lager and showing Sky Sports, and pier-end, or career-end, acts like Bernard Manning, Ken Dodd, Rod Hull & Emu, Seventies and Eighties pop retreads, pantomimes, former talent-show winners, and Butlin's redcoats.

The people who liked such places were fundamentally incomprehensible to some politicians, and a subset of opinion-makers, of the kind who made TV programmes, wrote newspaper columns or performed stand-up comedy. Tony Blair seemed instinctively out of sympathy with all shires (which had, of course, not voted Labour, even during the landslide of 1997), and was accused by country people of displaying arrogance as well as incompetence during the 2000 clash with farmers and hauliers over petrol prices, the foot-and-mouth epidemic of 2001, and the fox-hunting ban of 2004. While most Lincolnshire residents were neither hauliers nor livestock farmers, and never hunted—and although the government may not have been as incompetent or uncaring as was claimed—rural life was often affected adversely by actions that seemed motivated more by metropolitan ideals than practicality. Our newly-met neighbours shook their heads about London's real or supposed lack of understanding of what the countryside needed. Farmers who had never ridden to hounds, or even wanted to, plastered their pick-up trucks symbolically with stickers supporting fox-hunting, the so-called sport of 'toffs.'

Beyond the New Labour project, but linked to it, there were some who saw the people of Lincolnshire as worse than incomprehensible. From that perspective, they were also backward-looking, badly dressed, poorly educated, narrow-minded, obese, philistine, tattooed and probably racist. Seen from certain angles, the Cross of St George seemed to flap sinisterly above suitably monocultural fields—over a true-blue uncultured wasteland, full of complacency, exploitation, false consciousness and dangerous nationalism.

A clever 1997 BBC2 programme, *Double Dutch*, heaped irony like phosphates on the Fens as an English Deep South of brutal 'commercial primacy,' dark instincts and philistinism, an inbred 'open prison,' where 'hick has spoken unto hick, and white trash unto white trash.' The presenter had frequently justified fun at the expense of the Fens' no-nonsense nomenclature, *faux*-Dutch tulip fields, wind-filled bird-scarers, billowing plastic-sheeted crops, and Lincolnshire-style square dancing and stock-car racing.[25] There have been many less witty articles in the same vein, for example about Boston as incorrigibly unwelcoming[26] and the county as a whole as England's 'most racist.'[27] Sacha Baron Cohen's 2016 film *Grimsby* brought humour back to the stereotype, but his character Nobby, albeit well-meaning, was a feckless and stupid football hooligan.

Lincolnshire's already suspect sociocultural standing was compounded by being the *Heimat* of Margaret Thatcher, *fons et origo* of her deeply unfashionable philosophy. The intemperate hatred felt by so many for the Granthamian grocer's daughter was as much aesthetic as ideological—a vitriolic personalisation of a perennial disdain. The contumely piled on Thatcher's Methodist, Midland, patriotic, repressed, shop-keeping, upwardly mobile, Victorian values was an updated iteration of 'Court' and 'Country' divisions found in earlier conflicts, from Wat Tyler and Jack Cade via the Lincolnshire Rising and the disastrous resentments of the 1630s, up to the ongoing Brexit, Covid-19 and 'anti-woke' culture wars.

There were truths to be gleaned from the chaff of critique, and many unappealing aspects of this depiction of the provinces. But it was also clear that these views were gross caricatures that, rather than deterring me, spurred me on to explore further and meet some of these people for myself. This allegedly contemptible county had produced some of English history's most extraordinary and influential individuals. I found real histories of Lincolnshire, and discovered a whole substratum of Lincolnshire learning, ranging from enthusiastic local historians and proud churchwardens to world-leading scholars. Gradually, a huge county started to come into focus.

I discovered that the coast was not all, not even mostly, caravans; that the Wolds and other uplands were as beautiful and varied as any countryside in England; that the towns were attractively characterful, and the countryside between alive with wildlife and strewn with deserted villages and wonderfully impressive churches.

I also found out that the Fens could also be beautiful, and that even the least promising parts could be re-seen. I liked marshy places anyway, and the secret animals that lived there. One of my earliest memories was of seeing a water rail race across a Dublin path in the rain; I wouldn't see another for forty-five years, dashing across a Lincolnshire track like a coda to childhood. There were sights that stopped me in mid-step—some neat conjunction of dyke angles, some comfortably slumbering old house in a lush garden, tilting church towers, little red-brick bridges, hand-made sluice gates with dates, quietly humming pumping stations, embankments smothered in dandelions, Nonconformist graveyards whited with cow parsley, large swirls of fish in blossom-strewn brown waters, lumpily pollarded or coppiced old willows making surreal silhouettes or draggling their branch-tips in the dyke like some scene from Chinese mythology.

There were crossroads in the middle of nowhere pointing towards somewheres like Fishtoft, Little Steeping, Pode Hole, Toynton All Saints, Tumby Woodside and Wasp's Nest; 1960s tractors and trucks still in use; the blue darts of kingfishers; comically boxing or ineffably elegant hares; cock pheasants cocketing away at my approach, and barn owls pale and silent as steam in the failing light. Charles Kingsley (*Hereward the Wake*), Dorothy L Sayers (*The Nine Tailors*), John Gordon (*The Giant Under the Snow, The House on the Brink, The Fen Runners*), Graham Swift (*Waterland*) and Philip Pullman (*Northern Lights*) had found clarity here; could I?

Maps of old watercourses brought vanished landscapes imaginatively back from oblivion, the re-imposed blue lines life-giving like blood transfusions slaking the soil's and soul's thirst, conjuring a not quite obliterated domain. Lincolnshire people have dozens of terms for degrees of marsh, and size and type of watercourse, words that had become place names, suffused with proper noun poetry—counter, cut, deeping, delph, drain, fall, feit, fitties, fleet, goole, gowt, graft, gull, hag, holm, ing, outfall, river, sewer, turbary, wong, and yet more.[28] There had been twenty pools or deeps between Toynton and Boston alone that could be used if sailing to the sea, with names like Stickford Syke, Kealcote Syke, Rogger, Keal Cavern, Silver Pitt, Goodwin, Long Water, Silvergate Hole, Ardh Booxe, Swinam Lade, Goop Hole, Domine, Gass Water, and Hernholme—once flashing with life, now piped and gurgling cold in the dark, but I saw them in my sleep.

Former fen farmers led even harder lives than the farmers of today, but possibly they had been more stimulating—because they were so much closer to the clay, because what they did meant life or death, and something great could still be heard

17

rustling in the reeds. Even if the soils were claggy and clinging, and horizons ultimately unreachable, the skies were always open to the field-worker's imagination.

Lincolnshire people, like people everywhere, have often misused their environment, would probably have exhausted it long ago had they had the means, and must often have resented their lot. But some at least must have loved where they lived, finding a locus for patriotism in the disregarded plain, just as other English see *Jerusalem* in Barking or Huddersfield. A few must even have found something like contentment in the hard-to-find heart of the bog, like Confucian sages—or secrets, like the Stoics. Just maybe, I started to think, if *I* went to Lincolnshire, I might find understanding of my own—and a huge new side to England.

2

SHADOWS IN THE WATER

'Head with foot hath private amitie, /
And both with moons and tides'
—George Herbert, *Man*

BEFORE BRITAIN—DOGGERLAND—THE ANIMAL KINGDOM—
DYNAMIC SANDS—CREEKS AND POOLS—UNDERSEA

Warm waters, silvery with fish. A plesiosaur arrows near the surface of the sunlight zone, her outline constantly broken and remade by refracted glare. Crabs stalk across fine sand among ammonites and waving weeds, perhaps sometimes dimly conscious of her shifting shadow, unconsciously avoiding the bluer, colder abyss that stretches away to infinity just beyond their safer shelf.

It is an ideal element for this ideally evolved reptile, with abundant food, a pleasant temperature, and teasing tricks of light—a perfect place for this thing of grace, a perfect space to assuage her great hunger. Queen of the aquamarine, apex predator of her era, she speeds through the shallows with surety, maybe even seeing sport in following frantic fish and squid as they flee in panic towards the deeper, sapphire shades, silhouetting herself for a few seconds against the flooding light behind. That's too long. She isn't the apex after all.

Her progress stops suddenly. She shudders and her backbone breaks, as an even larger behemoth[1] grabs her at the base of her neck and twists. The silvered-blue shallows explode in brief but brutal frenzy, releasing a cloud of blood, bone fragments, bubbles and scales, while smaller things race for their lives. But then, instead of gorging, the brutal behemoth mysteriously goes, scudding back into blue immensity, its only trace in history tooth marks on the victim's bones as her carcass, broken but briefly held together by skin, subsides baggily to the sand, and the waiting crabs.

Darkness. Silence. Time beyond reckoning. Mass extinctions. Bone turns to stone. The sea cools and shrinks, the bed upheaves. Waters trickle away, continents shift, ice advances and retreats. The sea goes away, lands form for future naming. Darkness. Silence. Stillness. Then...

Far distant rumours, painfully slowly nearing—bangings, tremblings, judderings. Then suddenly close—life returning, metallic clinks, hammering. The layers are being pierced, the veil lifted. Voices! A last few spadefuls—and for the first time in 180 million years, light bursts upon the beast in the shape of nineteenth-century brickmakers, staring men bespattered with clay, calling to the foreman to come and see what they've found in Lincoln's ground.

The fossil is fished out of the pit and carted away by a very different kind of man, and the brickmakers watch them thoughtfully for a few moments, or share amused glances, before returning to their own back-breaking occupation. Their pit will one day itself become a fossil of the Anthropocene Age, its revealing gulfs filled up so a school can be built on top.

*   *   *

Human history is the thinnest of skins on evolution—a skin so thin we try to root it in rocks. Palaeolithic cave art was not just a record of events, but the laying of a claim upon the land—part protection of resources, part mystical bonding with a particular place. The evocative handprints seen in many sites are not just the imprints of individuals, but a kind of clutching at substance. The abstract signs and horned shamans that intermingle with the hunted animals, large-breasted women and spear-toting men suggest a confused but rich cosmology, where grim realities were alleviated by dreams of destiny.

Jacquetta Hawke's 1951 bestseller *A Land* was a brilliantly imagined response to the crowding modernity of the Festival of Britain—an unclassifiable evocation of global geology blended with British localism, biology with artistic impressions from prehistory via medieval poets to Henry Moore and John Piper. It was scorned by scholars, but unlike those desiccated specialists, Hawkes knew of the commonality between all generations and all living things, and an imaginative but profound connection between places and the people who live in them. She thought in epochs and grand themes, yet also wrote books as universal as UNESCO's *History of Mankind* and as insular as *The Archaeology of Jersey*.

She opens *A Land* by describing herself lying in her London back garden on a warm summer's night, feeling herself simultaneously pinned to specific soil, and wandering among speaking stars:

Now the two little globes of my eyes, unlit in the darkness, look up at their shining globes, and who shall say that we do not gaze at one another, affect one another?[2]

The monumental works of Henry Moore (a friend of Hawkes') seem to her to be as much calling archetypal forms out of the rock as original works of envisioning. His neo-primitivism was also somehow medievalism and modernity. It was a vision both archaic and as startlingly new as the South Bank's Festival architecture. She was one of the Festival of Britain's consultants, attuned to its aim of looking backwards and forwards at once. Abram Games' posters for the Festival 'incorporated heraldic imagery and angular geometry to create a modern portrait of the national character.'[3]

In 1951, the war was very recently won, and a gallant people were emerging blinking from long sacrifice into a richly deserved better tomorrow. There was a sparklingly new Health Service, slum-clearing and school-building programmes, and a nascent nuclear industry, parts of a greater national corporatism, and a sense of renewed purpose, in a country stewarded by people still widely seen as benevolent and wise. In those pre-Suez days, Britain could still see itself as an equal power with others, still holding onto much of its Empire, its totemic wartime leader back in Downing Street, and the emptiness of the Exchequer about to be relieved by a prolonged period of economic recovery. The following year, with a beautiful new monarch anointed according to ancient and mythic rites, saw the rise of an idea of 'New Elizabethans,' a lucky generation which, like the English of Elizabeth I, would extend themselves across the world to lay the foundations of a finer future.

Now, these things seem at best naively touching, at worst cynical machinations concealing multitudinous exploitations. Many point out the anomalies, inequities and inconsistences of all corporate identities. But strict rationality of this kind seems insufficient. If nations are mere 'imagined communities' with 'invented traditions,' as Benedict Anderson and Eric Hobsbawm believed, then to many people the imagination is preferable to the reality.[4] The stripping away of illusions can also have complex consequences, as Zbigniew Herbert reflected: 'The loss of memory by a nation is also a loss of its conscience.'[5] If nations are just notions, with no objective reality, then what can be said about even the most fanatically followed ideologies or the largest religions? We cling to what feels closest and most solid; if the world's tectonic plates are always moving, at any given moment they are also standing still.

*   *   *

Lincolnshire is frequently scanted by earth scientists. Much of the county is 'new' in geological terms, and still in flux—alluvial, flat, fenny, marshy, prone to flooding, crumbling into the ocean at its edges. William 'Strata' Smith's famously candy-striped pioneering geological maps of 1815 show the Lincolnshire littoral as a dispiritingly brown, boggy vastness.[6]

The exceptions are the Lincolnshire Wolds, a band of mostly chalk hills that extend through the centre of the county from the Humber to near Spilsby in the south, and from Alford in the east towards Lincoln and the rolling Kesteven uplands of the county's south. Near the county's capital, the country rises into the slender Lincoln Cliff of older Jurassic limestone, in which lurk the stunningly preserved fossils of plesiosaurs. The oldest human structures reflect the nearest materiality, switching abruptly from red-brick to honey-coloured stone. The most celebrated of these structures is Lincoln Cathedral, one of the few English cathedrals built from local stone, and which still owns the quarry on the city's Riseholme Road.

In recent decades, earth science interest has focused on Doggerland, the name given to the bed of the North Sea which until about 8,000 years ago was dry land, allowing foot passage between England and the continent. It was inhabited by our antecessors even before they became humans; 800,000-year-old footprints were briefly visible on Happisburgh beach in Norfolk in 2013, before being destroyed by the sea which had exposed them.[7]

Doggerland may later have had spiritual significance, as suggested by 'Seahenge,' the prehistoric, probably ritual, wooden circle salvaged from Holme-next-the-Sea in Norfolk in 1998, now in King's Lynn Museum. Doggerland was certainly worth hunting over, judging from the remains occasionally dredged up by oil prospectors and trawlers (*dogger* is a Dutch word for trawler)—a flint scraper, found in 450 feet of water off the Shetlands, mammoth and rhinoceros bone, arrow points, spearheads, lumps of peat from drowned moors. Although alternating, depending on climate, between tundra and temperate steppe, this was a fertile and varied environment, with lakes, reed beds, marshes, tree-crowned hills and gentle valleys. It was a basin for great rivers, some still extant—Humber, Ouse, Rhine, Thames, Tweed—others now scarcely remembered—Bytham, Urstrom—except by Deep Time thinkers, and trawlermen who claim to be able to sense ancient beds beneath their boats.

The stumps of trees that died thousands of years ago can occasionally be seen at the lowest tides on some stretches of the coast. These have long been objects of folkloric fascination—as long ago as the tenth century, there was talk of 'Noah's woods'— and even scientific interest. Lincolnshire's Sir Joseph Banks brought the exiled Portuguese philosopher-scientist José Francisco Correia da Serra to see the 'decayed trees' of Sutton-on-Sea (then Sutton-le-Marsh) in 1796. De Serra reported that there were a 'great number' of these trees on tiny islets, identified birch, fir and oak stumps and the roots of reeds, and collected holly and willow leaves. Most of the wood was decomposed, although some was still hard, even useful:

The people of the country have often found among them very sound pieces of timber, fit to be employed for several œconomical purposes.[8]

The islets he landed on, locally called 'huts,' have all gone now, victims of both coastal erosion and twentieth-century beach replenishment schemes, but some of da Serra's stumps are still *in situ*, brown-black rounded lumps encrusted with barnacles, festooned with dead crabs and surrounded by greasy mud, dreary but curiously captivating. Prone trunks can also be seen at Cleethorpes, and lumps roll up on beaches along the coast, especially after north-easterlies. These crumble easily when you pick them up, and if brought back to adorn the garden, soon flake into nothingness. When I can bring myself to burn any, it gives off a unique and delicate aroma, and crumbles to beautifully feathery, light-grey ash. Awareness of the beach's ancient arboreal nature underpins all explorations; I once found a washed-up builder's helmet, satisfyingly bearing the name of a company called Forest/Wave Navigation. Geography can be geomancy, and all the world is transient, as an eighth-century Irish poem reminds us:

> *Across ridges, the crest of*
> *A wood, your curragh sails:*
> *A forest, heavy with mast,*
> *Sleeps under your keel.*[9]

Long after the land-bridge was severed, higher ground would have protruded above the waves, like the Dogger Bank—towards the end only spasmodically visible, like the forlorn and slimy islets visited by Banks and da Serra. Now sand eels have taken the place of starlings, whales that of mammoths,[10] and the antediluvian happy hunting ground is reduced to vaguely redolent BBC Shipping Forecast sea area. The English east coast, once a western province of a vaster land, became a barrier and front line, with world-changing consequences. If Britain had never become an island, doubtless the history of the last 2,000 years would have been quite different. Lincolnshire can often seem like a landscape of loss, a place of amputation.

But this sense of impermanence adds to the county's allure. How we react to this undoubted ambience depends on personal outlook, but many find melancholy pleasure in the level and lonely expanses of the English east. When W. G. Sebald wrote 'The east stands for lost causes,'[11] he had Suffolk mostly in mind, but his sombre observation can be extended easily to the Lincolnshire littoral, with its exhausted estuaries, silted creeks, springy salt marsh, broad strands, glutinous mudflats, old sand dunes, and freshwater marsh. Climatic and topographic changeability have given rise to unique ecosystems that not even an overabundance of caravans can obscure.

In Deptford, we would see foxes, rats, sparrows, and almost nothing else, whereas from the moment we first turned the key in the cottage's scuffed and swollen door we were surrounded by living things, many of which I hadn't seen since my childhood, and many others previously known only from books.

The house's old bricks, pantiles and wood harboured life we only noticed by degrees—lichens and mosses on the roof and walls, impressively sized spiders, house mice in the kitchen, field mice in the garden, the bats in the attic, the minotaur beetles in our bedroom, the pallid centipedes in the compost, the jackdaws that nested in the chimney, the dunnocks, finches, robins, tits, yellowhammers and wrens, kestrels and buzzards, shrews that squealed in the under-grass, the minnows and moorhens that flashed or scuttled in the dyke across the little road.

The field between the house and the 1380s church threw up curlews, geese, hares, partridges, pheasants, swans, and weasels. The ash trees and sycamores beyond hosted a large rookery, and the church itself more bats, more spiders, and mason bees. Muntjac and roe deer hooves were printed precisely across our flowerbeds at nights, badgers snouted for worms, and moles upheaved mini-Wolds across our lawn. As we got to know the tiny garden, we identified many species of insect, some rare, and added to their tally by eschewing chemicals and tidiness, and cordoning off noticed nests. One older neighbour still used folk-names for the local fauna—busby bandy bee (ladybird), arrow-wiggle (earwig), pyewipe (lapwing), hedge betty (sparrow) and the onomatopoeic Billy Pick-cheese (blue tit).

The reeded waterways and 'unimproved' fields had even more to offer—barn owls, egrets, herons, kingfishers, snipe, water rails, water voles, rudd, perch, sticklebacks, tufted duck and, if you were lucky, pike—glimpsed loitering below if you peered carefully over a bridge parapet. Dipped nets would throw up water boatmen, pond skaters, whirligig beetles, caddis larvae, frog, newt and toad tadpoles, freshwater mussels and ramshorn snails, while damselflies and dragonflies zipped electrically in front, or dipped ovipositors in the lazy flow. Finding these felt like returning to a lost garden of childhood, and a certain quarry pond in the Wicklow mountains.

The local nature reserve had been established principally for the natterjack toad, which laid long pearl necklaces of eggs in shallow sweetwater ponds among seventh-century sand dunes. The toads are more often heard than seen—on some days surprisingly loud, a creaky pulsation audible from 100 yards away, as complacent a summation of the English summer as any Lords cricket crowd. Their domain was caught between fields and a gas storage complex, lit like a small futuristic city at night—the only major light pollution between Mablethorpe and Grimsby.[12] The first common crane I ever saw was flapping slowly over the terminal's chimneys, startlingly huge even at several hundred yards, as surreally outsized as Pink Floyd's pig over Battersea Power Station.

The rare-flowered, orchid-dotted, elder-, hazel-, and hawthorn-strewn dunes also held larger expanses of freshwater, the whole slender strip a magnet to endangered invertebrates and migrant birds, from avocets to wheatears. The most imposing of these avian migrants, and certainly the most obvious, were the hundreds and hundreds of geese, of several species, which opted to overwinter here—arriving in late September, with a magnificent declarative trumpeting, like Old Testament war trumpets or the serpentines of Vikings, and a powerful downbeating rush of pinion and crisp feather. They bring the nameless North with them, and take it when they go—and even more, the smell of open water, and exploration, and the passage of Time. 'The goose,' D. H. Lawrence rhapsodised, 'the bird that swims on the waters and thrusts its head deep into the flood of the Beginning and the End.'[13]

Best of all were the bitterns, secretive spirits of the swamps— the Irish poet's 'bittern that's shy and apart / And drinks in the marsh from the long bog-drain,'[14] their booming a medieval motif of desolation:

> *Down to a mareys faste by she ran—/*
> *Til she cam there, hir herte was a-fire—/*
> *And as a bitore bombleth in the mire.*[15]

Grass snakes slid across paths, tiny lizards hid under stones. Grasshoppers stridulated drily, amplified and echoed by the calls of grasshopper warblers—and black-and-scarlet burnet moths laid eggs on ragwort which hatched into oddly colour-clashing orange-and-black caterpillars. Tiny blue butterflies vied for proboscis space with painted ladies, peacocks, red admirals and skippers and, once, a Camberwell Beauty, flapping blackly along a thorny ride—a near mythical insect, long extinct in England, that evoked the lost Edwardian south London of Richard Church, or Henry Williamson's *Chronicles of Ancient Sunlight*—a civilisation of amateur naturalists, comfortable villas, Elgar, and long bicycle rides looking down on distance-blued Surrey. Even death could look lovely here; I remember a recently dead carrion crow, lying in a patch of sun beneath trees, intact and gleamingly black, studded with iridescent greenbottles, like a mislaid piece of Visigoth jewellery.

The pools among the willow-meads sometimes look oddly watchful, for the Australian poet Les Murray, 'skylights of a filled kingdom' whose absorptions 'may float up districts away.'[16] On windless winter days they reflect bare and motionless branches, their exposed roots stretching down like tentacles into the blackest of black waters. Clouds traverse their cold obsidian surface, troubled backdrop to your own reflection and whatever else, or whatever nothing, you seem to see. There are refractions here too, distortions as well as doppelgangers, as breezes play across all surfaces.

After heavy rain or high tides, temporary pools form out on the salt marsh, fleeting crystalline realms when grass stays briefly green underwater, like the underwater lands envisioned by Julian of Norwich, who dreamed of going,

> ...downe into the see-ground, and there I saw hill and dalis green, semand as it were moss-begrowne, with wrekke and gravel.[17]

There were pools between worlds in Lewis' Narnia, while Ted Hughes' 'Pike' was fished out of a pool at Conisbrough 'as deep as England.' The ardent seventeenth-century poet Thomas Traherne saw in such pools answers to enigmas of religion, existence of another universe:

> By walking men's reversèd Feet
> I chanc'd another World to meet;
> Thought it did not to View exceed
> A Phantasm, 'tis a World indeed,
> Where Skies beneath us shine

And Earth by Art divine
Another face presents below,
Where People's feet against Ours go.[18]

From the outer edges of the dunes rose that emblematic bird, Shelley, Meredith and Vaughan Williams' skylark, a great singing yet equally salvific for radical poet, psychological novelist and Great War-haunted composer. Closer to, the marram is thronged with rare beetles and flies, ladybirds that look like they've just flown in from some medieval margin, and stalking harvestmen, as green-brown and spindly as their grass. Burnet-moth caterpillars march determinedly in the wrong direction until restored to ragwort, and crashed bumble bees struggle clumsily in the fine and ever shifting sand. They clamber onto outstretched hands with alacrity, to buzz fatly for a while, before suddenly raising their unfeasible wings, after this rare respite from their lives of danger and toil.

West Doggerland extends even further east, incorporating a thick band of salt flats, like a last stand of the land. Out here, away from the defences of the dunes, even on mild days the wind can be cruel, racing in off the sea's grey-green geometry fresh from the north German plain. There are also artificial defences of the dunes—at intervals, concrete World War pillboxes, looking blankly onto the once German ocean, evidence of old tensions, and a belief some Hun might come.

In his 1903 novel *Riddle of the Sands,* which canalised existing anti-Prussian sentiment, Erskine Childers' hero uncovers a naval plot, with Wilhelmine warships lurking among the complicated sandbars of East Frisia, awaiting secret orders to descend on England—an invasive implication building on long-standing insular suspicion, from the landing of the Romans, via Saxons, Vikings, Normans and Napoleon up to Brexit.

All island nations are nervous of incursions, even if sometimes those arriving are also originators; the eleventh-century Irish *Leabhar Gabhála* ('Book of Invasions') simultaneously traces national origins to relatives of Noah, and bemoans the depredations of the Norse. Childers saw little inconsistency in being both defensive of England and an Irish nationalist (even a fanatical one), like many other Anglo-Irish Protestants chivalrously attached to a Romantic, 'Celtic' conception of a free and united Ireland. Childers was executed by the Irish Free State government in November 1922 for his IRA gun-running activities; his English public-school-educated eldest son, another Erskine, would become the fourth President of Ireland.

The clean openness draws birds of prey, and those who love them, just as eastern Essex appealed to John Baker and his *Peregrine*. Once, on its first flight, somebody's pet peregrine *x* saker falcon flew straight here from Barnsley, a hundred miles across England—only in the cool regretful evening to hop calmly onto this stranger's extended hand, its jesses still jingling, but its head hanging in tired regret at his escapade.

The salt marsh can also be perilous in itself, wide and capable of sudden inundation, with deep and tangling plants, and steep-sided, sticky creeks sometimes only seen when a redshank rises up from under your feet with its shrill and bubbling signal. Crabs sidle along greasy bottoms like seagoing spiders, ungainly, but infinitely more successful than any number of proud plesiosaurs.

At last, of course, come strand and sea, an ozoned zone at once alien and beguiling, dangerous and exhilarating. The sea commands in all its moods and phases, under full moon or sun, in scorching sun or freezing fog, under battering gales, great dragging curtains of rain and muffling snow—far out and unnaturally straight in summer, close to and terrifying in storm surges, when our broad familiar beach becomes a wilderness of waters, and drifting trunks are tossed like sticks.

Storms roll in trash and tribute—plastic bags and polystyrene, but also firewood, sea coal, fish crates from the Faroes, Dutch milk cartons, Polish vodka bottles, Spanish coffee jars, a plastic Buddha with a burnt-out light fitting, lifebelts, signs warning of quicksand or radioactive materials, boat and even house name plates, an intact angler-fish skeleton, the corpse of a Staffordshire bull terrier still wearing his collar, skulls of dolphins, dentures, the lid of a Grimsby Crematorium jar still bearing the name of its late lamented contents. A few finds are finely 'œconomical,' like the nineteenth-century teak ship's door with a porthole I found in a dune at Mablethorpe and ported home effortfully for rehanging.

This part of the coast is celebrated for seals, which have waxed plentiful since the once world-leading fishing industry has waned. In the autumn, they congregate close in by their hundreds, mating, suckling pups and bellowing at each other, attracting tourists from all over the Midlands. Their beautifully variegated skins show why sealskin was sought. Seemingly forgiving our atrocious treatment, they give an impression of benevolent intelligence; there are folk tales about seals that can become humans, or humans seals. They sometimes approach quiet swimmers, and curiously circle round—disconcerting, because large and massively at the elemental advantage. If you tread water, the braver or stupider ones get nearer still, occasionally allowing you to touch them before they charge away in fright. My Jack Russell once started barking at a seal bobbing a few feet off the shore—but hid behind me when her mate heaved up from under the surface and began to flop flabbily onto the beach, his eyes marbles, his mouth redly hissing and roaring. Even the smallest need to be respected; I once picked up a very young solitary pup, her eyes weeping pus, to take it to the sanctuary, and she bit my face with gusto.

Their ability to find food is extraordinary, because when we put our heads underwater, all we normally see is crazily dancing sand, as Doggerland restlessly reconfigures itself. Yet that food is sometimes superabundant. Once, in chest-deep water, I found myself among a storm of life—a boiling shoal of sand eels, with gulls and terns plucking them expertly from above, seals wreaking havoc around the edges, and finally a porpoise, black pig of the briny, oblivious to me as it curveted close by, before eventually chivvying the shoal away.

One plant clings incredibly to life hundreds of yards out from any other—a halophyte called marsh samphire, or glasswort, a sodium-filled succulent resembling a tiny pine tree. In oblique lights, the samphire strand could be Siberia seen from an aircraft. In the late summer, millions of gossamer spiders are blown out from the land, and swarm on the samphire stalks, the highest point in their world, to perish hopelessly when the tide returns. Once gathered for glass-making, today samphire is a delicacy for humans, while in winter its seeds are predated by passerines.

Looking landwards from the uttermost edge, feet in the frisping main, the great plain is not always a plain. It undulates and alters daily, dynamically humping up sand to make the land invisible from certain angles, taking it away the next day, and piling it somewhere else. Some sand comes from the sacrificial coast of Holderness, and more from central Doggerland, longshore drift broadening beaches along this fortunate stretch of the coast before starting to strip them away again from Mablethorpe, and all points south all the way to the Thames Estuary—with a brief respite at Gibraltar Point beyond Skegness, on the northernmost corner of the Wash.

Wide pools form and spread, and drain away through the grains. Foot-high 'cliffs' of compacted sand build up and flump soggily down again, over and over again, into swift-flowing temporary channels. Cockles and whelks, hermit crabs, flatfish fry, and shrimp are constantly being carried away or cast up to dinosaur-style disaster, like accelerated evolution. It feels like looking down from space at wildly sped-up epochs of the earth—like Blake, 'to see a World in a Grain of Sand'[19]—a world, like Borges' *The Book of Sand*, without beginning or end, beyond any quantification. Beneath bare feet, all is thrumming change, all substance charging away forever, vaguely dangerous, and ultimately unsteadying. Did it feel anything like this 800,000 years ago for the equally exposed hominids of Happisburgh?

Sand seems to stand as a metaphor for our existence, our constant coming together and drifting apart, our essential defencelessness, our gallantry and resilience. 'History,' said Heraclitus, 'is a child building a sandcastle by the sea, and that child is the whole majesty of man's power in the world.'[20]

3

THE BRACING COAST

'Where the broad ocean leans against the land'
—Oliver Goldsmith, *The Traveller*

THE WASH—SKEGNESS—WAINFLEET ALL SAINTS—
GUNBY—BOSTON—MABLETHORPE

The night I came to London to live, there was a storm over Camden Town. I remember standing outside the Tube station watching the war in the sky, filled with inchoate excitement, almost as if this display had been put on for *my* benefit. Sometimes it's hard not to ascribe personal significance to big weather, to believe the cosmos is somehow marking some major change in *your* circumstances. By satisfying coincidence, there was an even bigger storm on our first night in Lincolnshire.

If the pyrotechnics over north London had been impressive, they faded into inconsequentiality against this. There are no tall buildings here, no busy roads and hardly any streetlamps, and the tempest emptied itself immediately overhead. When the sheet lightning shook itself out across the empty field in front, it was a stupendous magnesium flare, making everything white, and the succeeding black was not just black but Vantablack, the most lightless of all shades—the earth 'without form and void' for a few seconds, until my eyes recovered—only to be temporarily blinded again by the following flash. When the thunder followed, the little house seemed to shudder, the cats dived behind the sofa, and the electricity went off. When the rain came, it was not something that could be viewed abstractly from a shop doorway, that gurgled in gutters, and made swishing noises under cars—but a battle formation that drilled into the earth, beat down the spikes of next year's silage, and turned the cottage front into a cataract.

In the country, weather becomes a factor in everything. Climate change can come down extremely quickly when out in huge unroofed spaces. I have been caught by cloudbursts in shelterless sixty-acre fields, and taken unawares in storms down on the lowest tideline, forced to run long squelchy, slippery distances back to the car, acutely conscious of being the tallest thing for several miles in any direction. I find myself looking often upwards; there is a Lincolnshire saying that 'a Fenman lives three-quarters of his life in the sky.' Nephelomancy—divination by clouds—could be the county's oldest religion. The city offers exciting experiences, but these are often abstract; the countryside connects you to tough physicality.

English country houses are proverbially cold and inconvenient, a long-standing *Punch* joke—and this comes home when rain courses through *your* roof, or frost forms on the *inside* of your windowpane. Most of the heat from the fires that blaze with such show in the hearth vanishes up the chimney. Sometimes days are made almost unendurable by a duvet of gull-grey cloud that squats sullenly over the coast, making the house as cheerless as a cloister, and depriving the garden of light. Greens and browns become grey-greens, grey-browns; our faces look grey, the food on our plates, even the finches on the birdseed outside. The only colour comes when a sparrowhawk flying below radar jump-jets over the wall, to snatch one of these, when for several seconds there is panic, and the whole world comes down to the acid yellow of her eye.

Naked branches claw the windows. The long grass all bends one way, the animals who live in it having sensibly decided to die at the end of summer, or lie latent in some deep place. Tall teasel leans right over, bowed by the blast, with goldfinches clinging grimly to its spiny stems as they extricate the seeds. The corrugated iron barns next door shake and squeak, and the cattle under cover low and moan by night and day, like dinosaurs calling from the primordial. A rope left hanging somewhere in the farmyard bangs and bangs repeatedly.

Inside the house, we wear multiple jumpers, long johns, fingerless gloves and boots, and vie with cats and dogs for space around the fire. It is impossible to wall out the natural world with distractions, because the electrical and broadband connections, never good, blink in and out and often go off for hours, as wires sway wildly in the vault. The stag weather vane swivels stiffly, moved by the world's violence—lifting gilt antlers in defiance, giving a rutting rattle to the sky. I find myself sitting and standing and sitting again, seeing pictures in the fire, trying to read, making desultory conversation, trying not to get annoyed by the nine-year-old's noise, coughing in the smoke that sometimes comes chummily down the chimney, and looking out a lot, in constantly dashed hopes of wind-drop and sunshine. It is too cold to go out, too cold to stay in. Low pressure glooms over the Marsh, and has come to stay. The wind sometimes really does whine, a squealing banshee trapped in the chimney, or an eldritch instrument sounding through earth and heaven.

After several days of wind, I stop pretending to work, put on even more clothes, and go out. At least I will be *moving*. Experience—and snobbishness—tell me this is no time for anoraks or baseball caps but 'proper' country clothes—the kind proper country people never wear. I pull on tweeds, sheepskin cap, wool scarf and leather gloves, and British Army boots. Because I *know* what it will be like as soon as I close the front door.

The moment I'm out I wish I hadn't been so rash. The wind really *does* snatch my breath—really *does* make the collar of my coat snap—really *does* bring water stinging to my eyes. But it then does something else. The house gave false promise of protection; out here, I am getting what I expect. The wind wicks away delusion, excuses, self-pity—and the stronger it is, the more it tries to bend me, the more stupid satisfaction there is in standing against it. Irritation evaporates; I feel something almost like *exaltation*.

The Jack Russells, so desperate to come, seem briefly to regret their decision, blinking at the gale, their stiff fur standing up, their ears flapping—and then a rabbit crosses the road, and they are away, like me, suddenly remembering they are animals among elements. Their fiercely uncomplicated joy is in some way mine, and everyone's: from wind-giddy children in school playgrounds to sailors pitching in a Force Ten far from shore. They come back filthy and wet from the ditch where they lost the rabbit—and deliriously happy, snapping playfully at each other, grinning sprites of the East Country.

Perverse pleasure increases. Rooks explode out of the rushing rookery. Wrens whir into hawthorns. A blackbird bounces across a sheep field. The sheep it bounces among, with their stained and tangled wool, watch me warily, their elongated pupils staying horizontal even when they lower their heads to eat—a disconcerting ability called cyclovergence, giving their eyes a wider field by admitting more light forwards and backwards. A little egret looks askance at me, opens his ivory wings and flaps away, powerful and slow. A barn owl out before his hour follows in the egret's wing-flaps, sparing a few seconds to give me an appalled gaze. A snipe prodding amongst lank vegetation zig-zags away. Seeing all these animals just getting on with existing, even in the teeth of the gale, makes me ashamed of earlier self-pity.

Even some humans are getting on uncomplainingly; a yellow Lindsey Marsh Drainage Board machine is moving along the dyke, its skeletal arm rising high in the bare air before plunging down into the ditch, to come up clenching a fistful of reeds and dirty mud to be dumped on the bank before the machine moves on, leaving behind slimy lines of black filth studded with reed roots and the shells of freshwater mussels, and a sloshing mess of Jeyes Fluid-hued water. The driver nods at the foolish walker. Proper country people don't go for walks. A neighbour in a passing tractor, who is *not* wearing 'proper' country clothes, smiles and lifts his hand in salute. The bell on the church tower tells the hour. It's later than I think, but isn't it always?

I ready myself as I walk down the track towards the final rise. There is a little shelter here, just below the ridge of the sandhills, although the topmost branches of the blackthorns are in a frantic tizzy. The metal clip on the halyard of the Army's warning flagpole goes *ding-ding-ding* against aluminium. A warning to the curious... I crest the ridge and battle onto the beach, my 'proper' clothes flapping around me like the cerements of William Ager, M. R. James's ghostly guardian of the lost East Anglian crown.

If the wind was bad around the house, seaward of the dunes it is a wild thing from Ultima Thule, shrieking into my face before passing to lay low all the east, and batter itself to death hours afterwards on some eastern outcrop of the Pennines. I gasp afresh, and the dogs blink in renewed surprise at this assault. The azure sea in which I have swum has become a dreadnought-grey and lead-white wilderness, a dazzle pattern of danger and roaring force. Waves tipped with Melville's horror-inducing 'Whiteness of the whale'[1] curl themselves up and over and smash incessantly, breaking and carrying millions of fragments of Doggerland. Theodor Storm's Frisians call the North Sea '*Blanker Hans*' ('White John'), the diminutive personal name only making the terrible *Blanker* seem even more palely impersonal. But it is not just white. The mud is becoming water; the flying foam is flecked with sand. Drifting wood is black with wet; rolling coal is blacker and shinier yet, except for the dead barnacles that cling to them like tiny extinct volcanoes. Gulls are ivory phantoms like Melville's albatrosses, scything or tumbling past, full of 'wonderment and pale dread.' The world is a Turner painting, and I'm just staffage.

The long and level strand I have seen silent and covered with ice floes and snow, even-striped under a sky as uniform as a Rothko, has become a battlefield, sodden with dead waves, and strewn with detritus and slime among the last-stand tussocks of grass. Drier sand is picked up and twists in tiny tornadoes, or gets propelled landward in knee-high abrading curtains which whip at my boots and make the poor dogs blink again. Their fur gets a coating of grit, their eyes are instantly kohl-rimmed; they shake their heads in dismissal, and chase each other in the absence of rabbits. But then there *is* a rabbit, or a roe deer, incongruous on any beach, but doubly so when sensible animals should be in shelter—and the dogs are off again, seemingly believing they're wolves, or hounds of the Wild Hunt.

Glaciers, winds and seas like this, and even worse, over æons funnelled tons of sand far inland, to make desolate heaths and sandy slopes for rabbits to burrow in, for the convenience of future carrot-growers and inconvenience of Cromwell's troops at Gainsborough—and along the eastern edge of the Lincoln Cliff fly in the face 'and shoes and pokkets' of the eighteenth-century antiquary William Stukeley. I have to hold onto that sheepskin hat as I venture out farther. Wind immediately forces its way down my neck, and between my cuffs and gloves. Even the Army boots start to succumb, hardly surprising after years of abuse.

But the discomfort doesn't matter when I get to the water's edge at last, and find the waves there almost as tall as me, and immeasurably more impressive. They are idiotically insistent, magnificent—belly-flopping, collapsing, colliding with each other and cross-currenting on the sand, outdoing, overtopping and undercutting each other with a vast sucking and susurration. The sea-longing comes over me as I stand in danger of getting carried away. Cockles and whelks are being cast like pearls at my feet. Dark birds are flying out there, only just above the water. Far off, a white ship stands well out to sea.

Herring gulls rolling past impale me with their eyes, and then I hear the seals, calling—*hoooo hoooo hooooooo*—one of the loneliest of sounds and most eerie, strangely audible even above the waters and wind. What can they be *doing* out here in these conditions, surely perilous even for them—and what are they saying to each other within the huge howling? Can they be *enjoying* themselves? I spot one, just beyond the biggest breakers, a black head like a dog's, lolling casually behind a crest and weight of water that would break me without trying. The dog-head disappears, and the beach feels even more lonely than before.

* * *

The eastern seaboard often elicits emotional intensity. In 1880, Algernon Swinburne visited Suffolk to view the site of Dunwich, Suffolk's famous sea-taken town. He was middle-aged, going deaf, and broken in health by what the *Dictionary of National Biography* calls 'imprudences.' But he found his excited youthful voice once more in the grand notion of the drowned town, and wondering what the fate of its many monasteries might signify for the future of Christianity. 'A land that is lonelier than ruin,' he rhapsodised, 'A sea that is stranger than death...' This was a frontline in a war without start or finish:

> *The waves are as ranks enrolled,*
> *Too close for the storm to sever:*
> *The fens lie naked and cold,*
> *But their heart fails utterly never:*
> *The lists are set from of old,*
> *And the warfare endureth for ever.*[2]

It is a venerable cliché to see the sea as terrifyingly meaningless— Psalm 130: 'Out of the deep have I called unto thee, O Lord'— and seashores as metaphors for ebbs and flows of emotion. Thirteen years before Swinburne, Matthew Arnold had famously gazed out from Dover Beach, and given himself over to despair, dwelling on the drying up of a 'Sea of Faith,' giving rise to a future of 'darkling plains' and meaningless suffering.[3] On any coast, especially a lonely one, we are daily reminded how small we are, how weak against this coldly thoughtless force that never stays still, that alters everything, undercuts everything, every minute, every day, every year.

But humility and melancholy are only two of many emotions that may be evoked by the sea's edge. Even Swinburne could hear lighter notes among the sea's running, see other shapes in its surfaces:

> *For the sea too seeks and rejoices,*
> *Gains and loses and gains,*
> *And the joy of her heart's own choice is*
> *As ours, and as ours are her pains:*
> *As the thoughts of our hearts are her voices,*
> *And as hers is the pulse of our veins.*[4]

Alfred Tennyson, who often holidayed in Mablethorpe as a boy, saw the coast in all its moods, or through all *his* moods:

> *Here often, when a child, I lay reclined:*
> *I took delight in this fair strand and free:*
> *Here stood the infant Ilion of my mind,*
> *And here the Grecian ships did seem to be.*
> *And here again I come and only find*
> *The drain-cut levels of the marshy lea,*
> *Gray sandbanks and pale sunsets, dreary wind,*
> *Dim shores, dense rains and heavy-clouded sea.*[5]

In 1827, the coast called imperiously to the young poet and his older brother Charles, who hired a carriage to dash from Louth to Mablethorpe to celebrate their first publication, *Poems by Two Brothers*. They swept to the beach and shouted their verses at the sea. The Tennyson *frères* were not far removed emotionally from the fantastical figure I once saw from far off on Mablethorpe beach, a man facing into a blistering easterly and *dancing*, capering, gyrating, turning and twisting grotesquely and wildly, a Corybant of the coast cavorting as if overcome by all that beauty and force.

* * *

The county's coastline can be divided into two zones. In the south is the huge and muddy maw of the Wash, from the Norfolk border to Gibraltar Point south of Skegness, extending its influence in a narrow crescent inland, taking in the towns of Long Sutton, Holbeach, Boston and Wainfleet All Saints. Further north is a long and gently curving strand, interspersed with mud and marsh, from Skegness to Cleethorpes, reaching inland to former seashores at the foot of the Wolds. If the Wash is a giant mouth, the Skegness to Cleethorpes section is an enormous eye seen from the side, or a convex mirror scattering light back at the continent.

Local terminology is as imprecise and sometimes interchangeable as the land and sea themselves, but generally the Wash is considered part of the Fens, while the section between Skegness and Cleethorpes belongs to the Marsh. The Fens section is generally more artificial in its appearance, more arable, more industrial, and less touristy (although busy tourist routes pass through). The Marsh half is drier, more varied, less raw-looking, traditionally wealthier, emphasising pasturage over arable farming, and since the twentieth century heavily dependent on tourism.

Their different characters are suggested by village nomenclature and distribution. Villages in the Fens are less likely to bear Viking names (they are mostly medieval), and are more clustered than those in the Marsh. Even parish boundaries hint at differing ages and degrees of solidity, with parishes in the Fens having comparatively narrow sea frontages and incorporating several kinds of soil, while those in the Marsh generally follow subtle geological divisions—the Middle Marsh's boulder clays, the Outer Marsh's coastal silts. But the whole coast shares a sense of being at an angle to the edge of England, trembling on the verge of vision.

One of the first houses we considered buying was at Gedney Drove End, perched on The Wash near Holbeach, whose chief selling point was that it offered spectacular sea views. We had told estate agents we wanted only to see old houses, which did not stop some of them trying to interest us in bungalows. This 1930s house was by our standards too new, and Art Deco not to our liking. But we allowed ourselves to be tempted into a viewing by the village's name, and (judging from the map) dramatic-looking location.

We had earlier been to Gedney church a few miles south, just one of the extraordinary churches to be seen along the A17 running east from Spalding into Norfolk—large, lovely, full of hard light, with homely touches, like the fourteenth-century door lock inscribed with 'Beware before, avyseth Johannes Pette,' and the jumble of medieval stained glass that somehow survived the Puritans, showing King Solomon with a red robe and golden crown. Richard Hakluyt (1552?–1616), author of 1589's *Principall Navigations, Voiages and Discoveries of the English Nation*, which Froude called 'the prose epic of the English nation' and was long standard reading for schoolboys, was vicar here once—a once hugely influential author, smelling the sea while he worked on his sermons, perhaps dwelling often on Psalm 107:

> They that go down to the sea in ships, that do business in great waters;
> These see the works of the LORD, and his wonders in the deep.

That area combines bleak windsweptness with fertility, and sinuous roads following the lines of old sea banks to tiny places with unexpected stories. Lutton was the birthplace of Richard Busby (1606–95), a zealous churchman and notoriously severe headmaster of Westminster School, who used to say his rod was the sieve that sifted the wheat of scholarship from the chaff.[6] The allegedly boorish county of Lincolnshire has produced many enlightened educators; Busby could not be accused of being enlightened, but he was renowned. He whipped the youthful John Dryden enthusiastically, which didn't deter the poet from sending his sons there. Uncompromising Royalist though Busby was, he also had so solid a scholarly reputation that he retained his headship right through the Civil War, at the heart of Parliamentarian London. His principles were incorruptible; when Charles II visited the school after Restoration, Busby asked to be excused from removing his hat in his presence, in case the boys thought the King a greater man than he.

When we got at last to the road's end at the Drove End, we realised immediately that having spectacular sea views was this house's *only* selling point. Those views were nevertheless not only worth seeing, but worth going to see.

Standing in the little back garden, looking northeast straight into an eye-watering wind, with a lurid winter sun and a very high tide, The Wash was illimitable—a huge silver sheet whipped into stiff tips by wind and tipped with cold orange. The sky was cloudless, the same silver-white as the water. This gave an effect of there being no horizon, strengthened because there were no boats anywhere to be seen. Turning east, the little cliffs of north Norfolk could be seen six or seven miles away—to the north, slightly further away, the lower lines of Lincolnshire—and to the northwest a very distant prospect of the Boston Stump, like a lantern in a waste. That day's tide must have been high indeed, because normally there are salt marshes to be seen, and mudflats braided by creeks and dotted with waders, but on that day there was only a narrow strip—almost as if a ship could have anchored close inshore. But no modern ship ever could.

Commercial shipping does however use The Wash, with ports at King's Lynn in Norfolk, and Boston and Sutton Bridge in Lincolnshire, but it is hazardous even to small craft with its almost complete lack of real shelter and constantly shifting depths. The Nene, Ouse, Welland and Witham and smaller waters debouching into the estuary are constantly washing down material, and The Wash's bucket shape tends to retain and bank it up. Sandbanks move and change in size, but they have perennial names and almost personalities. These names can be full of old bitterness and memories of ancient and ongoing dangers—Thief Sand, Blackguard Sand, Sunk Sands, Roaring Middle, Pandora. Does the Mare Tail flick to warn of a kick to come? Does Bulldog Sand not let go? Others just sound dispiriting—Clay Hole, Hook Hill, Westmark Knock. Is the Maccaroni (*sic*) Channel especially tortuous? Who were Peter Black, or Roger, or Scotman, or Styleman—all now just sands?

Presumably Seal Sand was a place seals once hauled up in numbers, to be harvested for their skins—an ancient activity that went on until 1978 and was only outlawed in 1999. Presumably the waters around Herring Hill were once an especially good place to search for the 'silver darlings,' on whom the east coast economy long subsisted? Walking here on a falling tide, we once found a puddle writhing with trapped and desperate herring and grabbed huge slimy handfuls for release. It felt like some small return for the centuries. Another sandbank is The Ants; perhaps there was an especially heavy fall of insects in some otherwise unremembered year, a memorable phenomenon of biomass that may have been seen as auspice or omen. We similarly find strange summer windfalls of invertebrates down by the shoreline, at imminent danger of death—ants, but also bees, butterflies, devil's coach horses, gossamer spiders and ladybirds—and sentimentally cram scores into bags or pockets or shoes, to be ported towards the relative safety of the land.

Norfolcian navigators negotiating Lynn Roads, Yellowbellies making for Boston Deeps, and Hanse captains bringing Lubeck wine to trade for wool (in cogs specially designed for Lincolnshire conditions—larger, with flat bottoms and detachable keels) had to know these things, had to see beneath surfaces, and place abstract markers on a featureless plain. From out in the middle of the estuary, the watercolour smudges of river mouths are marked only by tall poles or blocky little buildings, some military, all perilously situated—insubstantial, subtle and easily missed, even in good weather. Inevitably, sailors sometimes miscalculated, overpowered by currents, overtaken by fog, caught in creeks, mazed in marsh, snagged in subsurface Doggerland.

The churchyards between Wainfleet and Sutton Bridge are filled with named and nameless men who traced tricky courses and didn't always return to home ports.

This is not the kind of coast which attracts legends of fabulous shipwrecks, lost lands and sunken cities, as along the coasts of Cornwall, Ireland, Scotland and Wales. Some low-lying English seaboards *are* tinged with romance. Kent's Romney Marsh has Russell Thorndyke's *Dr Syn* stories; the Thames estuary countless tales, of which *Great Expectations* is only the most famous; Suffolk its Dunwich and Wild Man of Orford; Norfolk its 'Seahenge', and lost city of Shipden; Holderness its royal Ravenspur (and twenty-one other towns); the Dee and Mersey their mini-Atlantises; and Morecambe Bay, its history-haunted medieval Queen's Guide to the Sands. Due east of Lincolnshire, Theodor Storm has immortalised the Frisian coast for generations of Danish and German readers. But The Wash shuns romancing—despite continual use from the Bronze Age on, and huge changes of topography and other dramas in historical times, from ambitious reclamation schemes to disastrous storms. The Wash too has its lost towns, its submerged landscapes, its nervy relations with the sea, as suggested by a nineteenth-century folk rhyme:

> *When Dalproon stood*
> *Long Sutton was a wood.*
> *When Dalproon was washed down,*
> *Long Sutton became a town.*[7]

The Cross Keys Wash near Sutton can, however, lay claim to one long resonant tradition—the loss of the treasure of King John in 1216, just a week before the maligned 'Lackland' himself expired. This has been the source of enormous interest ever since, with the major contemporary accounts—Roger of Wendover's *Flores Historiarum*, Ralph of Coggeshall's *Chronicon*

Anglicanum, and Matthew Paris's *Chronica Majora*—differing on details, and further confused by conspiracy theories about Cistercian or Templar involvement, and the alleged poisoning of the monarch.

The Wash was then about a third larger than today, its coastline much less defined, and local knowledge was essential; there would be official Guides to Sutton Wash into the 1820s. According to the tradition, John's baggage train tried to cross the mouth of the Nene, then called the Wellstream, and was overtaken by the tide (the King had gone by a much longer but drier inland route). The treasure was supposedly an incalculable cache, the Crown Jewels of their time, symbolic of God's endorsement of John, and underwriting his battles against the barons and France. It was said to have included such redolent items as the crown and purple pallium of Empress Matilda, the 'Sword of Tristram' (supposedly the former property of the *Volk* hero), jewelled rings given by the Pope, phylacteries, reliquaries, thuribles, and literally hundreds of basins, collars, cups, dishes, rings, sceptres, swords, vestments and yet other things. So staggering a financial and symbolic loss—if it really happened, something doubted by sceptics like Charles R. Beard[8]—cannot have sweetened John's temperament during his final few fretful days as the dysenteric monarch sweated and vomited his way from Swineshead Abbey near Boston, where he spent that night, and Newark, where he died unlamented.

The margins of the Wash began to be reclaimed in Roman times, although the 'Roman Bank' that runs much of the way around is really medieval. By the time John's porters tried to cross, hundreds of acres of salt marsh had already been turned into what would later be called 'conquest' or 'dearbought' land. This process accelerated in the late medieval and early modern periods, with reverses during severe floods. In 1607, jurors at

Gedney explained why it was difficult for them to be accurate in their reckoning:

> ...the numbringe of the acres is a verie uncertaine thinge for us to doe for there wilbe some tymes a hundrethe acres of marshe ground: and within three howers space the best of it wilbe over-flowed with the sea above six foote deepe.[9]

The estuarial profile is altering still, with hundreds of acres accreting naturally since the 1940s.

Spasmodic searches for John's treasure, including a lengthy 1930s search funded by the Baltimore financier John Rawlings Henry Boone and involving the eminent archaeologist Sir Mortimer Wheeler, have been stymied by centuries of alterations to the course of the Nene, which have erased whatever landmarks there might have been. If John's treasure really was lost that day in the Wash, it is likely to remain lost forever. Perhaps it is more valuable as a symbol.

The present mouth of the Nene is marked by two matching markers from the 1830s, the East and West Bank Lighthouses. They were markers for shipping to and from Port Sutton Bridge, and a customs hailing-station. Port Sutton Bridge, which was opened in 1987, had an ill-starred predecessor. The first ship to attempt to enter the newly built dock in May 1881 found the water too shallow, and had to unload some of her cargo before proceeding. The following month, not long before the official opening, the ground around the dock began sinking, burying two traction engines and cracking the concrete walls. The scheme was abandoned swiftly, and the dock basin is now a golf course.

South is a swing bridge, carrying the A17. Hilaire Belloc found this then newish bridge to be half-open, 'a monstrous thing of iron' whose mechanism was being cleaned by a surly man (by implication an antithetical Low Church Protestant) 'with a little rag,' who ignored Belloc's questions about when he might be allowed to cross. Another employee was even ruder when Belloc persisted, asking him whether he could see somebody was cleaning the bridge.[10] South again, the Nene dwindles towards Wisbech, Cambridgeshire's sole port, its tidal action finally running out at Tydd Gote on the border, appropriately opposite Foul Anchor.

The East Bank Lighthouse was leased by the naturalist and painter Sir Peter Scott in 1933, using the proceeds from his first art exhibition to bring it back from dereliction. He used the building as a home and studio, and to keep captured geese. Scott often went wildfowling on The Wash—a challenging and time-consuming pastime, with wily prey and in frequently dangerous conditions. The Wash's wildfowling was highly lucrative for farmworkers, who could earn a week's wages with a brace of geese, and highly regarded as a sport by leisured Victorians and Edwardians. Mark Lemon, founding editor of the country sports magazine *The Field* (and *Punch*) was a Boston resident. Well into the 1970s, the sea walls would be lined with wildfowlers, and there is still wildfowling here, albeit strictly controlled. One brilliantly coloured winter sunset, I watched two fowlers and their dogs striding homewards with game bags across darkening salt flats, a scene from a Delft tile.

By the 1930s, Scott was having qualms. He was especially troubled by the idea that he was wounding many birds he didn't catch, and that these increasingly rare creatures were dying painfully and pointlessly. His freezing days of punt-gunning or stalking, and his hard-won knowledge of birds, boats and tides, were to prove useful when he went from shooting geese to catching them alive for study. His most successful technique was based on an old Fenland plover-netting method, the double Clap Net, in which a single net attached to two poles descended in seconds on the targets when a pegged rope was released suddenly.

He lived in the Lighthouse until called up in 1939, inspiring the American writer Paul Gallico, whose 1940 patriotic story *The Snow Goose: A Story of Dunkirk* features a thinly disguised Scott and a relocated East Bank Lighthouse. The artist resident dies heroically during the evacuation from Dunkirk but is magically eternised by a returning white bird. Gallico's choice of bird was poetic, but unrealistic—the real-life Snow Goose, *Anser caerulescens*, is a native of the high latitudes of North America—but Scott later would keep real ones in his collection. Scott had planned to return to the Nene after the war, except that in 1945 the sea wall was pushed further out in urgent search of extra farmland. The following year, he founded the Wildfowl & Wetlands Trust at Slimbridge on the Severn instead, but his former residence is still a beacon to conservationists.

*   *   *

In this flood-prone champaign, churches were navigation aids, often literally, always metaphorically—symbols of moral meaning, making sense of otherwise empty horizons. Builders and their patrons vied to distinguish their creations from others, set at two- or three-mile intervals along the road from Spalding to Wisbech.

Long Sutton's thirteenth-century spire looms above the final anchorages of the town's more reputable Georgian inhabitants. Gravestones bear the usual cherubim, funerary foliage, swags and urns, but also a sexton shown in life and as a skeleton, a thatcher's tools, and the name of the last Guide to The Wash. Perhaps the church's most striking stone is inside, a slab saying simply 'Alas, poor Bailey,' commemorating a local doctor murdered outside the town in 1795—the cursory inscription somehow conveying the accepting-plangent tone of Georgian regret. A less reputable inhabitant was Dick Turpin, who lived here under the alias of

John Palmer in the 1730s, using it as a base for sheep- and horse-stealing, and a convenient halfway house between his father's pub in Essex and Yorkshire, where he sold the horses he stole.

But all the churches display strong individualities, a corridor of roadside art—the separate tower and chancel at Sutton St James, Fleet's flying buttresses, Whaplode's monument to Sir Anthony Irby (whose 'unripe decease' in 1610 was the subject of a Phineas Fletcher poem), the huge candelabrum at Frampton, the towering Tudor font cover at Fosdyke. Moulton has a phenomenal Perpendicular tower—and the late Anglo-Saxon Elloe Stone, marking the meeting place of the Court of the Wapentake. The Wapentake was an administrative division in the Danelaw, from an Old Norse word *vápnatak*, meaning 'the taking of weapons.' The men assembled in these courts would clash weapons and shout to signify assent. This custom legendarily led to a misunderstanding at the coronation of the Conqueror, when the gathered *thegns* shouted to show their approval of his accession. William's Norman retinue, unacquainted with this custom, believed the Anglo-Saxons were revolting, and fires and scuffling broke out as the congregation fled, and the ceremony was concluded in a rush. William was said to have been left shaking in fright, and the incident was interpreted as an omen.

Cut into a windowsill in Leverton church is the 1597 signature of Henry Peacham, the rector's son, footnotable as author of 1622's *The Compleat Gentleman*, which outlined 'the most necessary and commendable qualities concerning minde or bodie that may be required in a noble gentleman.' Peacham's manual of manners matters oddly even now, because Samuel Johnson drew heavily on it for all the heraldic definitions in his *Dictionary*, the first systematic lexicon of our language. The tower at Surfleet has subsided 6 feet out of true, and looking up it from inside is dizzying, like being aboard a pitching ship. The church at Holbeach has a porch that would be at home in a Toyland castle, and the haunting tomb of Sir Humphrey Littlebury, who died during the Wars of the Roses. Littlebury lies in ornate armour, looking up prayerfully, his feet on a lion, his nose-smashed head pillowed startlingly on the head of another nose-smashed man wearing a netted hood—a representation of Sir Humphrey's helm, a false head to sit on top of his own for identification in battle, frowning down on foes, perhaps intended to be a fearsome Saracen.

Such things, and the enigmatic landscape in which they were set, were formative on Holbeach's best-known native, the antiquary William Stukeley (1687-1765). Stukeley's attorney father had demolished a medieval hospital in Holbeach; his son was far more conservative and romantic, the generation gap in reverse. William studied at a school inside the church's castled porch, on one occasion pausing on the narrow winding stairs to scratch his name on the wall—almost undiscoverable now among the spider-stalked darkness, a suitable fate, perhaps, for a man given to long thoughts. In 1756, Stukeley drew a radically nostalgic picture of his birthplace, reinstating a decorative plantation that had been cut down in 1747, by a Spalding man he calls 'a stupid penurious wretch.' The house was heedlessly obliterated in 1922.

Stukeley was an inquisitive and solitary child (despite having siblings), and clever with his hands. He went simpling (gathering medicinal herbs) with the town apothecary, carved sculptures, studied building techniques, made a flute and learned to play it. He also developed an early interest in drawing, surveying and topography. He drew maps all his life; his 1723 map of the *Parts of Holland, Lincolnshire* is still an invaluable resource as well as art object. He could see the magic of words, listening hungrily to traditional stories and combing the classics for English allegories; 'he found to his delight an epithet in Plutarch which could be applied to Whaplode Wood.'[11]

He went on to Cambridge, medical practices and vicarages in Grantham, Stamford and London, friendships with Halley, Newton, Warburton and Wren, founding membership of the Society of Antiquaries, and interests ranging from anatomy and botany to hermetic philosophy and numismatics. There was also abstruse controversy. The *Dictionary of National Biography*, arguably harshly, boils down an inquiring life to one mistake— 'To him was primarily due the error of supposing one Oriuna to have been the wife of [third century Roman Emperor in Britain and northern Gaul] Carausias, he having read Oriuna for Fortuna on a coin.'[12]

His work is full of magic and poetical fantasy, yet antiquarianism was a modern movement in its time, the first stirrings of a recognizable science of archaeology, albeit blended in with superstitions, and the perceived need to reconcile discoveries with Scripture. '[Stukeley's] passion for discovery made him one of the best contemporary observers of landscape and the soil.'[13] For the first time, students of history attempted to understand the functions and uses of buildings they had previously merely described, or ascribed to fantastical erectors. Stukeley and others saw 'the earth not just as a potential treasure-chest but as a repository of interpretable traces.'[14] The antiquarians dreamed, but they could also be highly practical.

Although antiquarianism (blended with Protestant providentialism) and even archaeology had started two centuries before, Stukeley was one of the earliest to take an organised interest in prehistory. He discovered the 'Avenue' leading towards the Avon at Stonehenge, and made a detailed ground plan of Avebury, untiringly delving in search of artefacts and recording what he found with precision. His drawings of those expeditions are charmingly evocative of hot afternoons fossicking among the roots of Britain, and learning for learning's sake. He argued passionately against the needless erasure of old buildings, and his accounts and drawings are sometimes the only record of structures like Arthur's O'on, a rare Roman building north of the Antonine Wall that was destroyed in the 1740s, and even his own house in Grantham. His fieldwork was always impelled by anxiety that the monuments would disappear. He watched locals breaking up monoliths at Avebury with horror:

> ...the barbarous massacre of a stone here with leavers and hammers, sledges and fire, is as terrible a sight as a Spanish Atto de fe ... the faggots, the smoak, the prongs, and squallor of the fellows looks like a knot of devils grilling the soul of a sinner.[15]

But he cut scholastic corners. In his 1724 *Itinerarium Curiosum*, he mentions 'a long and particular catalogue' of Roman coins, but felt it 'a nauseous formality to print 'em.' In his preface to 1740's *Stonehenge*, he admits,

> ...the method of writing, which I have chosen is a diffusive one, not pretending to a formal and stiff scholastic proof of everything I say, which would be odious and irksome to the reader, as well as myself.[16]

Careful spadework at Stonehenge and elsewhere was carried out against less careful assumptions. He ascribed the setting up of the stones to Druids, and envisioned Ancient Britons as noble savages of some kind, an 'oriental colony' arriving after Noah's flood, from whom the modern English had declined. 'Golden Age' nostalgia is at least as old as the Greeks, so Stukeley should be forgiven, and he was in any case working within a culture susceptible to such theories.

But he also saw Druidism as a precursor to (Anglican) Christianity, the 'aboriginal patriarchal religion.' Caught up in early 'Celticism'—he was instrumental in popularizing the word 'Celt'—he nicknamed himself Chyndonax, a supposed Gaulish Druid's name, and was called, or called himself, 'Archdruid.' Fellow historian Thomas Hearne shook his head sadly—'His friends think him crazy'—and he probably was, in part. He fell for the literary hoaxer Charles Bertram's forged *De Situ Britanniae*, a purported account of Roman antiquities by the real-life monk Richard of Cirencester. He battled bootlessly to reconcile the results of his painstaking fieldwork with Biblical chronology, classical lore and legendary Trojan origins against the advice of friends, and to the detriment of his reputation.

However, some of his work is also almost literally foundational of English archaeology, and his patriotic antiquarianism powerfully shaped the Romantic movement, and so English thought, for two centuries. It also percolates wistfully into current ideas about national identity:

> It is to Stukeley and his contemporaries that we owe so much of our unconscious attitude towards the history and landscape of our country to-day.[17]

* * *

Another Holbeacher who tried to make history was less successful. Sir Norman Angell (1872-1967) devoted a long and busy life trying to eliminate war forever. To say he was earnest would be understatement; at twelve, 'he discovered Mill's *Essay on Liberty* ... and for a long time considered it his prime source of intellectual excitement.'[18] A drily industrious destiny was set. Best-selling books like *Patriotism Under Three Flags: A Plea for Rationalism in Politics*, and *Europe's Optical Illusion* (in 1910 republished as *The Great Illusion*, from which Jean Renoir's 1937 anti-war film *La Grand Illusion* took its name) pounded home his message that armed aggression never paid, a doctrine so closely associated with him others called it 'Norman Angellism.'

In every one of the ensuing forty-one years, he published a new, painstaking, dull book, advocating a League of Nations, Free Trade, Liberal and Labour principles, national cooperation and collective defence against aggressors, especially Germany, Italy and Japan. In 1933, he received the Nobel Peace Prize. Considerable though his artillery may have been, obviously it was ultimately ineffective. Even the title of his 1951 autobiography, *After All,* has a tired tang. In his asceticism, evangelism, industry, respectability and seriousness, Angell stands for a certain type of eastern Englishman—a type by no means extinct. He also

> ...remains a thinker of note, and the most cogent exponent of a political rationalism which has the potential to underpin international relations in the interests of peace.[19]

*   *   *

To many people, Lincolnshire means Skegness, and Skegness means the British seaside holiday—to be precise, the English working-class seaside holiday. The town has been called both 'Nottingham-on-Sea,' and 'the Blackpool of the east.' But if it is a Blackpool, it is one with a tenth of the Lancashire resort's population, inconveniently far from major conurbations, at the end of a long and featureless road, and lacking distinctive architecture. There are no Winter Gardens in Skegness, or famous Illuminations, or Tower Ballroom, or trams—and the only political party ever to have held a national conference in the town was the United Kingdom Independence Party, in 2012. This was a rational choice for UKIP, judging from the Brexit referendum; it was also a defiant assertion of that party's unfashionability, its deliberate choice of the hinterland rather than the metropole.

Trains from Nottingham terminate at the little station, disgorging mostly East Midlanders to mingle around the statue of the Jolly Fisherman—the town's famous emblem, adopted from a 1908 Great Northern Railway poster showing him skipping along the sands above the slogan 'Skegness is SO bracing!' Cleethorpes, at the other end of the tourist strip, has a less original and frequently vandalised mascot, The Boy with the Leaking Boot, although it does possess a miniature railway and a pier. Mablethorpe has no railway and no pier, nor even a mascot. But it does have shades of Tennyson, while fans of *Brit Noir* may think of it as the out-of-season setting for Ted Lewis' 1980 novel *GBH*, in which a vicious criminal lies low out on the coast—fearing the police, but also revenge attacks, as in Lewis' more famous novel, *Jack Returns Home*, which became the 1971 film *Get Carter*.

Before the railway came in 1873, Skegness was populated by fishermen and their families, whose lives were probably generally lacking 'jollity.' There had been Roman activity hereabouts, with a road from Lincoln stretching at least to nearby Burgh-le-Marsh, and almost certainly onwards to the coast, and a ferry to Brancaster in Norfolk. It is speculated that there were forts, or at least fortlets, at Skegness and elsewhere, in a line all along to the Humber. Until 1422, Ingoldmells had lands referred to as 'Chesterland' or 'Casterland,' indicating the former presence of a fort. As one historian notes:

> It seems inconceivable that the coast opposite such an important settlement as the *colonia* at Lincoln would be unprotected.[20]

The coastline the Romans knew has changed completely. Skegness no longer even has a 'ness' (headland), and there are traditions of a major port called Wilegrip Haven whose site is three or four miles out at sea. In his *Itinerary* of 1535-43, John Leland reported,

> To Skegnesse sumtyme a great haven toune a 4 or 5 miles of. Mr Paynelle sayid onto me that he could prove that there was ons an haven and a towne waullid having also a castelle. The old toune is clene consumid, and eten up with the se, part of a chirch of it

stode a late. At low waters appere yet manifest tokens of old buildinges.[21]

It is impossible to visualise any structures out there now among the restless haze—except, that is, for the clustering offshore wind turbines which have materialised along the once empty horizons over the last ten years. On the church tower at Winthorpe, now part of 'Skeggie's' sprawl, are the marks of old high tides, 8 feet above today's ground—old fates, and maybe future ones, if some sea-rise predictions come true.

By the nineteenth century, the once 'waullid' town was a huddle of cottages, farms and sheds, and a few other buildings, with cockle boats and cobles drawn up on the sea-facing sands or mazy, marshy creeks. As well as the usual waterside occupations of fishing, reed-cutting and wildfowling, there was ferrying to the far side of The Wash, and 'free trade,' in the eighteenth century meaning of that term—smuggling to and from the continent. Small boats landed gin, snuff, sugar, tea and tobacco in the creeks to the east of the town, and 'owlers' carried the cargoes inland along drove roads, while a single excise officer from Boston tried vainly to intercept them. (Tom Paine, author of *The Rights of Man*, was briefly an excise officer at Alford.)

As well as being thankless, this could also be dangerous work. According to local tradition, the town's Vine Hotel long concealed a sinister secret—the skeleton of a murdered exciseman, identified by brass buttons bearing the royal insignia, found immured in the cellar during nineteenth-century renovations. The unquiet officer, some staff have sworn, moves things around in Rooms 8 and 23, and turns on radios when nobody's there. A lighter legend is that the Vine's garden is the early morning one into which Tennyson so famously invited Maud, 'For the black bat, Night, has flown.'[22]

Once the railway arrived, the foreshore's owner, the Earl of Scarbrough, threw himself into turning Skegness into a 'select' resort, building a pier, a church and laying out parks and tree-lined streets, which even now retain a sense of spaciousness and substance, at odds with much subsequent development. Scarbrough also paid for a new sea wall of limestone, as well as drains, gasworks, brickworks and sites for chapels and schools. The pier he funded (Gustav Holst played in its orchestra and composed while walking on the beach) was once England's fourth-longest, at 1,184 feet, but boats, fires, wartime contingencies, floods and storms all exerted a toll, and it now extends just 380 feet. (As of August 2021, there are plans to rebuild it.) There had been small-scale tourism in the eighteenth century, but now the masses could get here cheaply, easily and quickly. The town's permanent population quadrupled between 1850 and 1900, from 500 to about 2,000.

In 1922, the town council finally purchased the foreshore, and set about making it brashly raw, with a ballroom, solarium, bowling greens, an outdoor swimming pool and much more, eagerly importing ideas from elsewhere, such as the 'ruined castle' and ferro-concrete 'rustic' constructions intended to give this flattest of flat places a flavour of the Alps. A South Africa-born showman called Billy Butlin set up a hoopla stall on the North Parade in 1925, and swiftly diversified. The first Butlin's holiday camp was opened in Skegness in 1936, by the aviatrix Amy Johnson, and attracted some surprising visitors.

During the war, it became the Royal Navy training base HMS *Royal Arthur*, and among the personnel who served there was the jazz trumpeter George Melly, who recalled 'a certain architectural frivolity inappropriate to a Royal Navy Shore Establishment,' with a sky painted on the ceiling and an artificial tree in the base's reception, and a mock-Tudor-style canteen called 'Ye Olde Pigge and Whistle.' The *Luftwaffe* came calling often in the early years of the war, although no lasting damage was done. The pro-German propagandist 'Lord Haw-Haw' (William Joyce) elicited local hilarity when during one of his 'Germany Calling' broadcasts he announced that the *Royal Arthur* had been sunk.

In June 1947, Laurel & Hardy headed the bill at the demilitarised Butlin's for a week, cheerfully judging the 'Holiday Lovelies' competition and enduring a display of 'Knobbly Knees.'[23] An unlikely Redcoat of the late 1950s was the Irish observational comedian Dave Allen. In 1962, Paul McCartney and John Lennon came cross-country to recruit Ringo Starr (then playing with Rory Storm and the Hurricanes, who had a summer residency at Skegness) for a certain new band. Butlin's fell into unpopularity with the rise of foreign holidays, but following revamps in the 1980s and 1990s, remains a major part of the local landscape.

Lincolnshire's resorts are not for everyone. Tennyson enjoyed his holidays in Mablethorpe, but his vicar father was less sure, as early as 1815 complaining about the town's 'pot-bellied grocers' and 'dirty linen drapers.' The towns also increasingly attracted manual workers and their families desperate for some respite from laborious lives, including D.H. Lawrence's miner father, who came with the watchful young D.H.—an experience remembered fondly by the novelist, who gave his unhappy Morels a Mablethorpe holiday in *Sons and Lovers*. Mablethorpe made an attempt to move upmarket in the late 1800s, and there was even a small artist colony in the early 1900s, before it faded away, possibly negating a Newlyn School of the east.

Skegness, winced one 1930s visitor, 'is capable not only of absorbing the tripper but of making him picturesque.'[24] In 1964, Nikolaus Pevsner shuddered at the 'meretricious modes' of much of the town's architecture, and the 'frankly utilitarian, partly frankly show-business' appearance of Butlin's; 'the paraphernalia can only be described as in the Las Vegas style.' Nearby, he added, more in anger than sadness, 'there is a sea of caravans which makes the real sea twice a day retreat far out in shame.'[25] Simon Jenkins dismissed the whole area as 'some of the saddest country in England' and Skegness's environs in particular as 'a spreading stain of bungalows and mobile homes.'[26] Skegness is not my idea of a holiday either. But the town exerts a durable charm for many; Arthur Mee hymned its 'firm, clean sands, the safe bathing, the gardens with their thousands of rose bushes ... everything that young and old in search of recreation on holiday can desire.'[27] It is common to meet people who have holidayed there all their lives. Local media carry stories of lottery winners who say their large wins won't make them give up their caravans in 'Skeggie'. I met a woman in her seventies who had been going to Skegness every summer for fifty-one years, mostly in the same B&B, during the same two weeks of August. Her parents had brought her, she had brought her children, they were bringing their children, and one of these was bringing *her* children. This was force of nostalgia. 'It's friendly here,' she said. 'It's *English* England! Do you know what I mean?' She added, rather sadly, 'Besides, *anywhere's* better than Rotherham!'

Local people, too, sometimes say things like 'I couldn't live in *London*!' They simply don't feel London's or Manchester's psychosocial dilemmas apply to them, or should. Lincolnshire is one of the least diverse counties in England. The 2011 census showed that of 713,653 'usual residents' in the county, 663,741 were classified as White British, with a further 32,743 White Irish, White: Gypsy or Irish Traveller or Other White, making the non-white population of Lincolnshire 17,169, or about 2.4%.[28] These are small numbers, but as elsewhere diversity is highly concentrated, in Lincolnshire's case in Boston.

When we first knew Boston it was rare to hear any language other than English spoken. This is no longer true. The arrival of thousands of eastern Europeans from 2004 onwards injected energy into the local economy and facilitated Fenland food production, but also allegedly raised social tensions. Lincolnshire as a rule has low crime, and even lower levels of violent crime, but between September 2014 and September 2015, Boston briefly had the highest murder and attempted murder rate in England.[29] As one local official admitted, there had been 'significant negativity between our residents'.[30] Such sentiments may have affected Lincolnshire's pro-Brexit vote, overriding well-founded concerns about the likely economic impact, especially on the supply of farm labourers and healthcare staff (and Butlin's cleaners).

Sometimes, even in Skegness, all the noise fades out. Amusements stop amusing, brilliant lights blur, and sand strikes suddenly cold. The rides with their screaming riders still swirl but are meaningless, muted. People may be talking to you—and far-off people come briefly boomingly close—but although you can hear them you don't necessarily register what they are saying.

In Laura Cumming's 2019 family memoir, *On Chapel Sands— My Mother and Other Missing Persons*, an 'innocent' day trip turns increasingly creepy when a child disappears, in the middle of the day, on a level and mostly empty beach. The wide world narrows to a little missing girl; land slips, time slips, grains fly with growing rapidity into the bottom of the hourglass. Old secrets loom into sharp focus, and the shabby illusions of 1920s society. All relations are reimagined, and certain things beam brilliantly clear—the Vermeer-like light falling into a photograph where a woman stands by a kitchen sink, the sharp-edged peasant in the sharp-furrowed foreground of Bruegel The Younger's *Landscape with the Fall of Icarus*, while in the far distance the aeronaut crashes almost comically into the sea.

Cumming's account of a haunting incident in her mother's youth resolves itself upliftingly, but there can be vague horrors on the sea's horizon, looming up out of the alien element. In the 1930s and again in the 1960s, there were sea serpent 'sightings' off Skegness, cryptozoological cousins to the whales which occasionally beach themselves along here, to the fascination of the public and the annoyance of the council. The sea serpents recall older marsh monsters, like the strange fish on a Tudor brass in Grainthorpe, the dragon of the Spanish Armada that stretches scarlet between England, France, Ireland and Scotland in a naïvely bombastic sixteenth-century painting in Bratoft, and even farther back in demonology the dragon of Castle Carlton, slain by Sir Hugh Bardolph, which still coils in legend around the mound of his sycamore-sprouting motte.

I prefer Skegness in its winter forlornness, if only as somewhere to catch the train for London. Some winter days, I am the only passenger on this service, admiring vistas of frost-stopped fields, dead-reeded dykes with bobbing grebes, church towers, and little level crossings; the long route to change at Grantham, through infinitesimally rising country, feels like travelling through a geological cross-section. But even on summer days, when the train is busy, the atmosphere is usually agreeable, and the passengers often interesting.

One July journey, the whole carriage was transfixed by two criminals who proudly announced that they were on day release from North Sea Camp, a pioneering open prison founded at Freiston in 1935. The Camp has an unexpectedly good reputation (for a prison), because its first inmates helped build much-needed sea defences, and later prisoners long operated a large farm. It houses only non-violent offenders, the most famous of whom was Jeffrey Archer (2001-02), and has a strong emphasis on rehabilitation.

Those two local-born men, in their twenties, made even the frostiest passengers relent eventually, with their puppyish personalities, apologies for occasional swearing, and even their rough morality. They were both in for burglary; both swore they would never do it again. One passenger mentioned a recent stabbing in Boston, and one prisoner shook his head and actually said, 'I can't understand that kind of thing! I mean, we're scum—but we'd never do anything like *that*!' Everyone laughed. It was the kind of conversation you would never have heard on a London train. 'If only they were *all* like that!' the elderly lady near me exclaimed, as we fondly watched them alight. I sometimes wonder, were they really 'like that,' and what they're doing now.

*   *   *

Absolutions of a different sort were once available at Monksthorpe—an outdoor total submersion font, one of only two in England. The font, the size of a small swimming pool, belongs to an early (1701) Baptist chapel, now redundant. Total immersion feels a suitable ritual in this place where hamlets have names like Great Steeping, Irby in the Marsh, and Thorpe Fendykes. But it was once deeply controversial, dividing even Baptists, and associated with dangerous politics and dreaded Dutchmen. It also often attracted crowds to witness the amusing and maybe vaguely erotic spectacle—as it might today, if any modern masochist were willing to launch themselves into those cold and duck-weedy few inches, wearing only a thin shift.

Wainfleet All Saints, at the River Steeping's mouth, is also sometimes subject to immersion. It flooded as recently as June 2019, when 600 houses had to be evacuated after two months' worth of rain fell in two days, and the river broke its banks. But historically it has also had the opposite problem. It was a port once, if always a small one, subsisting in the shadow of King's Lynn, Boston and maybe even Wilegrip, but the entrance to its Haven long ago lost itself in the ever-swirling sediments of Gibraltar Point.

The most important river-borne visitors now are probably fish—European river lampreys (*Lampetra fluvialitis*) swimming up to spawn, the primitive, vampiric fish with a circular sucking disc instead of jaws, once so in demand as a royal delicacy that they were blamed for the death of Henry I. (A lamprey pie was incidentally made for Elizabeth II's coronation.) These not conventionally attractive creatures have become scarce thanks to pollution, and because sea walls and sluice gates bar access to many breeding grounds. During the drainage of Hatfield Chase, adjoining the Isle of Axholme, lampreys were even conscripted as protestors, 'narrators' of a ballad called 'The Powte's Complaint' (*powte* is a North Country word for lamprey):

> *Behold the great Design, which they do now determine, /*
> *Will make our Bodies pine, a prey to Crows and Vermine; /*
> *For they do mean all Fens to drain, and waters overmaster, /*
> *All will be dry, and we must die—'cause Essex calves want pasture.*

The lampreys are coming back, thanks to legal protection, a cleaning-up of the catchment, and today's subtler approach to flood defences. Every time I pass over the bridge near Partney I think some of these strange creatures might be passing below at that precise moment, on their never-ending journey from the days before dinosaurs.

But Wainfleet's greatest claim to notice is William of Waynflete, born William Patten (1395?–1486), another eminent county-born educator, as founder of Magdalen College, Oxford and Provost of Eton, Henry VI's innovative new school for the deserving poor. Eton has altered, but alumni of Magdalen are still called 'Old Waynfletes.' The free school he founded in 1484 as a feeder for Magdalen is now a museum—a red-brick piece of Plantagenet-turning-Tudoriana with polygonal, pepper-pot towers which, Pevsner says admiringly, 'lies like a ship at anchor in the fens.'

Waynflete was a conservative; his schools were set up partly to extirpate heresies, and he helped to suppress the Jack Cade peasants' revolt of 1450. He was also a Lancastrian, playing a pivotal role as Henry VI's Lord Chancellor in the 'Parliament of Devils' of 1459, which attainted Yorkist nobles after the battle of Ludlow Bridge. Awkwardly, these included the future Edward IV, and Edward's accession in 1461 had to be smoothed over by a substantial 'loan'. The wily Waynflete received an impressive three royal pardons from Edward IV during his career, in 1466, 1469 and again in 1471, despite having been instrumental in 1470's ill-fated Readeption of Henry VI. His diplomacy paid off politically: 'Thereafter he was frequently at court.'[31]

As well as Waynflete's tergiversation Edward IV had other reasons to be prejudiced against Lincolnshire in 1470. That was the year of the Welles Uprising, led by Sir Richard Welles, the eighth Baron Welles (and Baron Willoughby de Eresby), who styled himself 'grete capteigne of Linccolneshire,' and was furthermore assisted by other county grandees. Worryingly for Edward, at least symbolically, Welles also had the support of Sir Thomas Dymoke, the hereditary King's Champion. Welles seems to have been manipulated by his second cousin, the Earl of Warwick ('Warwick the Kingmaker'), who sought to supplant Edward in favour of Edward's brother, George. Lincolnshire's Lancastrian sympathies reflected great family alliances, but it is tempting to think there was also a trace element of older feelings—Lindsey/Mercian/Midlandian resentments against Northumbria/Yorkshire.

In February 1470, Welles' forces arrived at Gainsborough and

> ...droff oute of Lyncolneschyre Sere Thomas à Burghe, a knyght of the Kynges howse, and pulled downe his place, and toke alle his goods and cataylle that thei myghte finde.[32]

But the following month, Welles and his allies were defeated within forty minutes at Empingham, just across the Rutland border from Stamford; 'ther was many manne slayne of

Lyncolnschyre.'[33] The field became known locally as 'Bloody Oaks,' and later 'Losecoat Field,' because of the alacrity with which the fleeing army supposedly shed their Warwick and Clarence liveries, although the name is a false etymology. Welles, his father, and some of his senior officers were detained and executed, and the baronies of Willoughby and Welles taken away. Almost two centuries later, Lord Willoughby of Parham would be one of the staunchest of Lincolnshire's Parliamentary supporters. Had familial folk memory taught him never to put his trust in princes?

* * *

Soon after moving to Lincolnshire, we attended an auction in Louth, and were the only bidders on a substantial piece of folk art—a 9-feet-long oak beam carved crudely with fruit and foliage and the verse,

> *And one, an English home—gray twilight pour'd*
> *On dewy pastures, dewy trees,*
> *Softer than sleep—all things in order stored,*
> *A haunt of ancient Peace.*

There was contempt on the face of other auction-goers, who were probably thinking, 'Who'd want *that*?' But that piece of oak appealed both 'objectively' as object, and emotionally, a symbol of growing feeling for the county.

The verse was by Tennyson, from 'The Palace of Art.'[34] It transpired that the image was conjured by Tennyson's memories of Gunby Hall—a small William and Mary house surprisingly close to Skegness, mini-stately home to the Massingberds. The house resembles a prosperous estate in Holland, appropriate for a family with a proclivity for Puritanism. The interior is Golden Age-like, with its clicking clocks, portraits, dark cupboards, twist-stemmed wine glasses, and bowls of flowers in floods of sunlight. Even old wars have become part of Gunby's 'ancient Peace'; Reynolds' portrait of Dr Johnson's friend Bennet Langton shows the languid sitter with his elbow on Clarendon's *History of the Rebellion*, while the Old and Young Pretenders have been downgraded to decorative miniatures.

The makers of this place of peace were not notably pacific. The first Massingberd (the name comes from the Latin *ahenobarbus*, or 'bronze beard') to make it into county archives was Lambert Massingberd of Sutterton south of Boston, convicted of grievous bodily harm in 1288. Sir Oswald Massingberd was a senior member of the Sovereign Order of Malta during the sixteenth century, who killed four slaves and plotted to murder the Order's Grand Master. 'I did well to kill the slaves' he reflected in later life, 'but in not having at the same time killed the old and imbecile Grand Master, I did not do well.'[35]

Two Massingberd brothers, Henry and the well-named Drayner, fought for Parliament in the Civil Wars, and Henry became the county's High Sheriff under the Commonwealth. Two centuries later, Algernon Langton-Massingberd joined the Navy, then the Dragoons, and became a noted gambler and a friend of the Hungarian nationalist revolutionary Louis Kossuth—before eventually disappearing in 1854, somewhere in Peru. His memorial in Gunby's parish church reads tantalisingly '...who is supposed to have been shot at Fort Tabatinga on the Amazon River.'

Sir Archibald Montgomery-Massingberd, whose friends included Kipling, was made Chief of the Imperial General Staff in 1933, and Field Marshal in 1935. It was Sir Archibald who saved the house from demolition by the Air Ministry in 1943— the RAF had claimed it was a danger to bombers using nearby bases—telling everyone up to and including the King that Hitler was destroying quite enough beautiful buildings already.

Between these exciting episodes, the Massingberds were a mirror of squirearchical England—making good or less good marriages, begetting inheritors, adding extensions, planting trees, breeding dogs, getting religion, campaigning against alcohol and for women's rights. Emily Langton-Massingberd ran for election in 1889, one of the first women to stand for public office; she lost by just twenty votes. Her attempt to turn the Massingberd Arms into a temperance house succeeded better, although it probably did not endear the family to their tenants; it is now a farmhouse.

The last chatelaine, Diana Montgomery-Massingberd, who died in 1963, exemplified the briskly cheerful, slightly sadomasochistic, English country-house ethos, every morning into advanced old age polishing the Hall's striking early eighteenth-century staircase from top to bottom, recommending it as exercise to guests grumbling about her cold house.

*   *   *

The Holland part of Lincolnshire is a refraction of the wider Netherlands. The Belgae were early incomers from the east, and ever since there has been much intermingling around the North Sea's shallow basin. The relationship has frequently been fraught; the Flemings were often commercial rivals, or enlisted under the Dukes of Burgundy. But John of Gaunt was originally John of Ghent, Katherine Swynford's father was a knight of Hainaut, and Richard Fleming was a notable fifteenth-century Bishop of Lincoln. The eighteenth-century antiquary George Vertue claimed tantalisingly that Rembrandt moved to Lincolnshire for a while to avoid difficulties at home, and worked as a jobbing artist, painting 'sea-faring men's pictures.'[36]

In Boston, some older buildings are made from imported Dutch bricks, built in Flemish bond, presumably by Dutch builders—headers and stretchers in the same course, as opposed to English bond, which has alternate courses of headers and stretchers. There are certain vistas that could easily be in Gouda. In 1942, the town was a convincing stand-in for the Netherlands for the Powell & Pressburger film *One of Our Aircraft is Missing*. Every day can be seen evidence of old links, in the fields of tulips around Spalding and trundling Dutch lorries—heirs to the large, thin-wheeled Dutch-style wagons of the seventeenth century that agricultural historians call the 'Lincolnshire wagon'—that ply the region's roads, bearing company names like Mammoet and stylised logos of the mammoths that once plodded between the sundered Hollands.

England's Holland is not so low-lying as the other, is much less densely populated and less agriculturally efficient. Yet here, if anywhere in England, may be found evidence of the unifying, and world-altering 'North Sea Culture' posited by writers like Michael Pye. He claims North Sea comings and goings introduced the 'reinvention' of coinage following the post-Roman hiatus, commodity capitalism, joint-stock companies, market towns, the middle classes, abstract ideas of law, notions of freedom and rights, modern science and mathematics, landscaping, fashion and even the notion of romantic love.[37]

This is at best overstated, but it may also be inescapable when considering the Sea-rim's similarities not just of landscape and phenotype, but also of culture, from agriculture to Reformed religion. A first-time visitor to Boston from Amsterdam or Antwerp would feel a stab of familiarity on seeing its 'Stump,' the early sixteenth-century lantern tower of St Botolph's church. It is a stupendous structure, just under 272 feet high, and extraordinarily resilient given its location, immediately beside the tidal Witham, its foundations well below the water table, surrounded by claylands that have often been inundated by river or sea, or both at once.

The site of the town seems to have been too wet to build on when the Romans arrived, and it was only really established after the Norman Conquest. Thomas à Becket passed through furtively in 1164, fleeing the wrath of Henry II, part of a long journey in terrible weather from Northampton to France. The town caught up quickly, and in 1204 was given a market charter. By the late 1200s, three million sheep fleeces were being exported from here, and it became a major *entrepôt* and marketplace for foreign silk, pelts and wine, carried onwards up the Witham to Lincoln, and thence the Trent, and the markets of the west. Between 1279 and 1289, customs records show that Boston was the greatest port in England, levying almost half of England's customs duties. In 1314, Bostonians died at Bannockburn. The borough sent seven ships to help defeat the French at the Battle of Sluys (1340).

The Black Death wiped out half the town's population, but it recovered to become the second-largest port in England by the early 1400s—a member of the Hanse, with a major annual fair, and fifteen wealthy trade guilds. The strength of the town's links with the Hanse may account for the three crowns of the town's crest, because so much trade was done with Cologne, legendary burial place of the Three Wise Men. The grand 1340 tombstone of Wisselus de Smalenburgh (now Schmallenberg) in St Botolph's suggests strong sentimental ties with the Rhineland.

After the Battle of Poitiers (1356), the Black Prince entrusted care of his prize captive, the King of France, to the Rochfords of Boston. The Prince had other links to Lincolnshire, marrying Joan, the widow of Sir Thomas Holland of Swineshead, in 1362.[38] In 1390, John of Gaunt's son Henry, Earl of Derby, led a crusade from Boston to Prussia, to aid the Teutonic Knights fighting the still Christianising Livonians. This was a modest venture—just twelve knights, perhaps 300 men in all, including attendants and even musicians—but a high-status one, involving leading Lincolnshire families like the Tilneys, and showing the town's economic and logistical muscle, as well as Christian commitment. It was also militarily successful: English bowmen were vital to the capture of Vilnius in September 1390, and an English banner was the first to be planted on the city's walls.[39] Thanks largely to his crusading credibility, he would later become King Henry IV, while descendants of the sturdy Tilneys became ancestors to Anne Boleyn.

Richard Fleming (1360?-1431), rector of Boston, became a Papal envoy, despite having once admired Wycliffe, and founded Lincoln College, Oxford as a scholarly shield against heresy. He eventually became Bishop of Lincoln, and expiated old 'errors' by ordering Wycliffe's disinterment in 1428 and dumping of his remains into the Swift. Fleming's *transi* tomb in the cathedral's Chantry, an early example of a style more common on the continent, has his effigy lying in state, above a representation of his own skeleton.

Boston was a locus of magical interest—the town's Guild of St Mary was given special privileges by Rome, and a pilgrimage to the altar in St Botolph's Lady Chapel acquired the same merit as one to Rome. The celebrated alchemist George Ripley died in the Carmelite friary in 1490, presumably reflecting to the end on great mysteries, perhaps seeing in east coast sunrises an English 'Oriens,' his eagerly sought 'beginning of clarity.'[40]

Boston would not remain so brilliantly connected. The river silted up, there were riots against Hanseatic merchants, and wool and weaving switched to the West Country. As the town declined, economic hardship helped fuel a growing national feeling against undoubted ecclesiastical abuses. There was, however, still much residual faith, and Henry VIII's amorous-dynastic-religious intrigues caused enormous unease. In 1533, a hoaxer named Mary Bainton arrived in Boston by boat, claiming to be Mary Tudor, Henry's daughter by Catherine of Aragon, who had just been declared illegitimate. Bainton was greeted with enthusiasm by Bostonians who felt religious change was going too far and too fast. The real Princess Mary was then in the care of Lord Hussey of Sleaford and Boston, a delicate charge for a man who a few years later would be executed for his part in the Lincolnshire Rising. The tower of his house still stands in a dank field by the docks, and his face looms from a portrait at Doddington Hall near Lincoln—'the craven Hussey,' one historian calls him, with a 'shifty look and beady eyes,' arguably an uncharitable way of viewing a man placed in an impossible situation.[41]

The Tudor antiquary John Leland admired St Botolph's vastly, saying it was:

> ...for a paroche chirche the beste and fayrest of al Lincolnshire, and servid so with singging, and that of cunning men, as no paroche is in al England ... the stepil is both very hy and faire, and a marke bothe by se and lande for all the quarters thereaboute.[42]

That 'cunning' singing must have been excellent, given Boston was the birthplace of John Taverner (1495?-1545), who would have worshipped at St Botolph's, and been influenced by, or influenced, the music. Taverner was the last great pre-Reformation English composer, but was also a harbinger of a new and sophisticated English style, albeit influenced by Burgundian-Flemish contemporaries. This new style was called contrapuntal or polyphonic—music arranged or composed for several parts or voices at once, each with its own melody. The best remembered of Taverner's works are the *Missa Corona Spinea*, the *Missa Gloria tibi Trinitas*, and the *Western Wynde Mass*, in which

> ...the polished technique of motivic work and of systematic-continuous imitation appear in a remarkably advanced stage,

henceforth influencing English choral style by adding to its state-liness and clear sonority the advantage of close-knit construction.[43]

Cardinal Wolsey appointed Taverner master of the choristers at his Cardinal College in Oxford (now Christ Church) around 1525, but later had him charged with heresy. The refined composer languished with others in 'a deep cave under the ground of the same Colledge, where their salt fyshe was layde, so that through the fylthe stincke therof, they were all infected.' Later still, Wolsey relented, on the grounds of Taverner 'being but a Musitian.'[44] Doubtless strengthened in his principles by this experience, Taverner returned to Boston and became an eager agent of Thomas Cromwell, assisting materially in his work of Dissolution and persecution. In 1538, his labours reached an apogee when the famous Rood of St Botolph's—a great crucifix which had long depended from the chancel arch—was burned in the market place. 'The musical poet in him was silenced, and he became possessed by a fanatical obsession that drove him to acts of violence.'[45]

The 'fanatic' had his standards, though. Thomas Morley, songwriter for Shakespeare, whose writings on music would remain in print for at least two centuries, held up Taverner as a pattern of stylistic excellence, who would not stoop to such solecisms as using consecutive fifths:

> ...who never thought it greater sacrilidge to spurne against the image of a Saint, than to take two perfect cordes of one kinde together.[46]

Destroyer though Taverner was, he was hugely important in the development of English church music, his masses, motets and songs admired and copied even now, ironically evoking a sense of spiritual harmony. The angry young 'Musitian' became a prosperous alderman—partly on the proceeds of the sale of looted church furnishings—the great innovator a conservative cultural influence, as innovators so often do in England—as of course Christianity itself had long before. Whatever Taverner's views on 'idols,' he would have disapproved of his emotional-theological successors' distaste for, and even prohibitions against, sacred music.[47]

Boston was always full of clamouring religious voices, and few have been historically louder than that of John Foxe (1516-87). Foxe became a fellow of Magdalen College, Oxford, befriended Latimer and Tyndale, then resigned from Magdalen in protest at the statutes against Dissenters. Thereafter he published and sermonised incessantly. His most notable effusion was 1563's *Actes and Monuments of these latter and perillous dayes, touching matters of the Church, wherein ar comprehended and described the great persecutions and horrible troubles, that have bene wrought and practised by the Romishe prelates, speciallye in this Realme of England and Scotlande, from the yeare of our Lord a thousand, unto the tyme nowe present*, which later, lazier generations came to know as Foxe's *Book of Martyrs*.

Four editions of his unhealthily detailed and sometimes wildly exaggerated accounts[48] of trials and tortures, with its vivid woodcuts, came out during his lifetime, deeply influential on the burgeoning Puritan movement and poisoning English views of Catholicism well into the nineteenth century. After 1571, copies of Foxe's book were chained alongside the Bible in Anglican churches, and it was one of the very few books many English people between the sixteenth and nineteenth centuries would ever have owned.

St Botolph's interior has the tallest and widest nave of any English parish church. But whatever 'idols' or precious metals Taverner and other Dissolvers missed were fair game for Edward VI's representatives and the more systematic Puritans (with a brief pause during Mary Tudor's time). At St Botolph's, there was a huge sale of furnishings, altar frontals, jewels, plate, statues, vestments, and the costumes used in processions, and the painted walls were whitewashed. Stained glass was poked out and replaced with clear to let in the 'cleanly' light of the Gospel. Fourteenth-century misericords survived the smashers, so we can at least still see a medieval array of men tangled in vegetation, flowers sprouting human heads, wodewoses, hunters and harts, cats playing drums, 'pelicans' piercing their breasts to feed their chicks, and censer-swingers. The guilds were also broken up, their buildings often demolished to build other houses or repair sea walls.

The often irreligious newly rich were given old monastic advowsons, and the consequence was that their chosen incumbents were often intellectually underqualified, frequently family members or friends. 'Between 1560 and 1580, half the parish parsons are entered in the Lincoln episcopal note-books as uneducated and ignorant.'[49] The poor quality of these parsons sharpened Puritan critiques of the Elizabethan Church. Elizabeth was aware of the necessity of intellectual underpinnings to secure her throne, and this partly explains the great expansion of grammar schools during her era. Boston Grammar School was founded in 1555, one of fourteen grammar schools that survive in the county. Attempts to arm the Church intellectually gathered pace during the reigns of James I and Charles I; in 1634, Archbishop Laud established a library at St Botolph's, which survived the Protectorate, and now contains 1,200 books, including a 1549 *Prayer Book*, and works by the early Dutch printers Elzevir.

'Troublesome' presences could easily be extruded to Protestant parts of Europe, often as a stepping stone to the colonies. In 1607, around 100 Puritans from the Gainsborough area arrived in Boston to try to sail to Holland. They made their way down the Haven to board a ship, whose captain promptly handed them over to the magistrate—but only after they had been robbed. Following a brief incarceration in the Guildhall, they were freed, and made their way to the Humber, then Holland and ultimately America.

In 1612, a young and brilliant Cambridge man named John Cotton took on the vicarship of Boston—against the instincts of William Barlow, Bishop of Lincoln, who worried about his being 'unfit to be over such a factious people who were imbued with the Puritan spirit.'[50] Cotton cut a dash—vigorous, fastidious in his dress, the first vicar to wear a wig. He developed a reputation for erudite preaching, his sermons two hours long. His teachings diverged more and more from the Church's, yet he was allowed to continue in post thanks to the indulgence of James I and Cotton's canny adherence to prescribed outward forms of worship—the pulpit, the register chest and poor box, a chalice and paten. But by 1633, his luck had run out and he was cited for nonconformity. He resigned his living and sailed to the American outpost of Trimountain, whose name became Boston.

Other Bostonians played only slightly less pivotal roles in American history. Around 250 of Boston's 3,000 or so inhabitants would end up in Massachusetts. The Earl of Lincoln's sister Arbella, who lived much of her early life in Boston, married one of the Massachusetts Bay Company's chief investors, and sailed with him to America in 1630, aboard the flagship named in her honour. Her two sisters likewise married prominent Puritans who would become Founding Fathers. Also on the *Arbella* was Thomas Dudley, the Earl of Lincoln's steward, and his family. Dudley founded Newtowne (now Cambridge) and became Governor of Massachusetts, during which time he signed Harvard College's first charter.

His daughter Anne married Simon Bradstreet and became the first Englishwoman to publish poetry in America (*The Tenth Muse Lately Sprung up in America*, 1650). Bradstreet's works are still very readable, the polished products of her long study of the classics and the moderns in the Earl of Lincoln's library. 'A

Dialogue between Old England and New' shows complexity of feelings about the joined but diverging fates of Old and New England. Old England repines,

Oh, pity me in this sad perturbation, / My plundered Towns, my houses' devastation, / My ravisht virgins, and my young men slain, / My wealthy trading fallen, my dearth of grain. / The seedtime's come, but Ploughman hath no hope/ Because he knows not who shall inn his crop. / The poor they want their pay but also, their children bread, / Their woful mothers' tears unpitied.

New England replies, with sympathy—but also fanatic obduracy:

Your griefs I pity much but should do wrong, / To weep for that we both have pray'd for long, / To see these latter days of hop'd-for good, / That Right may have its right, though 't be with blood...[51]

The poem is an articulate summation of Pilgrim Father/ Mother attitudes, and a prefiguring of the coming America's combination of 'Manifest Destiny' and sugary sentiment, necessary militancy leading to a peaceable kingdom.

Another dauntless Pilgrim Mother was Anne Hutchinson from Alford (1590?–1643), whose town already had strong links with America. Farmer's son John Smith (1580-1631), born in nearby Willoughby, first went to America in 1606, following a colourful career of piracy and shipwreck, and war in the Low Countries and along the Holy Roman Empire's frontiers. He had been awarded a crest of three Turks' heads after killing three in single combat, been enslaved, escaped by beating out his master's brains, and travelled extensively in Europe's farthest east and the Mediterranean. He returned to Alford and retired to 'a little woody pasture' to study martial arts old and new—horsemanship, explosives, signalling, military history, and theorists from Marcus Aurelius to Machiavelli. This would prove excellent preparation for his transatlantic career.

Outspoken by instinct, Smith spent most of his 1606 voyage to America in the ship's brig for 'intending to usurp the government.' He was released on reaching Virginia, and proved instrumental in the founding of Jamestown, and adept at trading with the Algonquians. Even when relations with the Algonquians turned deadly and he was captured, he managed to save his scalp, thanks famously to Pocahontas, daughter of the tribe's overlord, Powhatan. He was made an honorary chieftain and allowed to return to Jamestown. In 1608, he was made President of Virginia, and drove the development of Jamestown, encouraging agriculture, building, and nascent industry—famously ordaining that 'he who will not work shall not eat.' But he would be defeated by famine, after a rat infestation destroyed stored food. His enemies intrigued, he was badly burned in an accident, and he returned to England for a rest.

But by 1614, he was back, mapping and sketching the Chesapeake coastline, and inking in new nostalgic names—Plymouth and New England. In 1620, he offered to lead the Pilgrim Fathers there; an essential incompatibility ruled this out, although they did use his map—as did other travellers, as late as 1873. His lucid recollections, writings on America, sailing and war at sea, with their strong emphases on individual liberty and social mobility, were widely read on both sides of the Atlantic. It is poignant to recall that when he died in 1631, this paragon of Old and New England virility could not muster the strength to sign his own will, failing even to complete the first letter, his last writing a splodge of ink followed by a scribe's words, 'the marke of the sayd John Smith.'[52]

Three years after John Smith died, Anne Hutchinson too went to America. She had been married to William, a successful clothier, and Governor of Alford Grammar School for twenty-two years, and was locally respected and admired, rumoured to have royal descent. But after 1615 she became increasingly unsettled by Cotton, whose sermons she would ride twenty-five miles to hear. When he decamped to America, she followed with her family. William became a Boston Selectman and prosperous farmer. But his wife's spiritual streak waxed ever stronger, and soon she found herself disagreeing vituperatively with John Wilson, Boston's pastor, over such matters as the importance of faith alone and the existence of original sin—and she carried many members of the congregation with her.

Soon, orthodox Puritans were clashing openly with Anne and her allies, who included Governor Henry Vane, while Cotton tried vainly to mediate. Mainstream Puritans disbelieved her claims of receiving personal messages from God, while Governor John Winthrop described her meetings as being a 'thing not tolerable nor comely in the sight of God, nor fitting for your sex.' Anne was imprisoned, then banished from the colony, her followers banished, disarmed, disenfranchised and fined. Anne was eventually excommunicated, and moved to Rhode Island, where she promptly ignited other arguments—only being quieted finally in 1643, when she and five of her children were tomahawked by Siwanoys. Other descendants survived, nine generations later producing Franklin D. Roosevelt, and another branch giving birth to the two Presidents Bush. In 1987, Massachusetts Governor Mike Dukakis officially revoked her order of banishment.

In November 1640, Lincolnshire MP Sir John Wray entreated the Long Parliament to:

> ...lay the Axe to the root, to unloose the long and deep Fangs of Superstition and Popery ... I shall humbly move that that the groves and high place of Idolatry may bee removed, and pulled down, and then God's wrath against England will be appeased

The following month, he returned to the attack, this time using a gun metaphor,

[Religion] will never bee safe, nor well at quiet, until these heavy drossy Cannons with all their base mettle, be melted, and dissolved: let us then dismount them, and destroy them, which is my humble motion.[53]

Wray's 'humble' suggestions were greeted with enthusiasm across the county, although Lincolnshire's churches were never systematically targeted, unlike those of Cambridgeshire and Suffolk. Even the most rigorous Puritans sometimes faced local obstruction or outright opposition, and their control would never be total. St Botolph's was not especially roughly treated, perhaps because the town's Parliamentary sympathies were never doubted. One Bostonian, Anthony Ascham, was even given the prestigious post of Parliament's Ambassador first to Hamburg, then Spain, although the latter posting brought him little benefit; he was murdered by Royalist émigrés.

The war sometimes came close to Boston, but the town was never really threatened, and was regarded as safe enough to keep prisoners of war. The main fighting in the town was verbal, between 'free-thinking' factions. Edward King, Boston's Military Governor, a devout Presbyterian, spent much of his time aggravating non-Presbyterian Puritans—most famously the Leveller John Lilburne, whom Cromwell had placed in King's regiment as a spy.

The Boston garrison was sent with others to besiege Newark in the spring of 1644, but the attack failed and the always fraught town became poisonously recriminatory. Lilburne accused King of neglecting Boston's defences. King accused Willoughby of responsibility for the Newark debacle, but lost the case and was ordered to make a public recantation in the market-place. He refused, was imprisoned, released but relieved of his command. Unquiet to his end, King was destined to spend much time in courts or prison after 1660, by which time St Botolph's somehow surviving Charles I coat of arms had been shamefacedly rehung in the nave.

Even the strongly Puritanical Theophilus Clinton, Earl of Lincoln, a Boston resident and friend of John Cotton, was impeached in 1647 for not having subscribed to the Solemn League and Covenant. The three cannon that bulk in Boston's Guildhall were rarely required to speak, but on the other hand they had a lot to listen to. Nonconformist 'reasoning' may have continued to colour Bostonian consciousness into much more recent times. In 1860, a cormorant that had settled on the Stump was shot, seemingly for no reason other than that it was sinisterly black, and had arrived the day before the town's MP and native son, *Illustrated London News* founder Herbert Ingram, drowned in America.[54] Perhaps in the back of churchwardens' minds were dim Puritan remembrances of Milton's use of the bird in *Paradise Lost* as a symbol of Satan, and Ironside use of 'cormorant' as synonym for Royalist officer.

*   *   *

Boston has always stared seawards, and the docks still carry on coasting trade with the continent, mostly in fertiliser, grain, steel and waste. But like most small ports, it had been in long-term decline even before Brexit complicated matters. Great steel canopies bear the brave words 'Port of Boston—Into Europe,' or simply 'Port of Boston' with the town's crowns, but they have not been painted in years, and the working areas underneath often yawn empty.

Along the riverside, seized-up hoists flake ferrous, warehouses with blanked-out windows moulder damply, and enormous buddleia bushes springing from quay-wall crevices trail branches into the brown Witham. A few small trawlers still tie up alongside, but in the sticky mud between can be seen the bones of others. Even the gulls struggle with the sticky mud and sometimes inch-thick layers of Azolla weed, an invasive American plant fed by fertiliser run-off, that floats in rafts downriver to get trapped behind Boston's rarely opened Grand Sluice, blocking out air and light for wildlife, and confining pleasure boats to berths. The weed can only be controlled by constant raking out or an imported species of weevil. The waterway's chief significance now is as potential source of danger.

A vague fear of flooding floats above all this coast. A constant faint sense of danger is in the ozone, fed by historical experience. Maps are liberally sprinkled with everyday reminders—Sea Lanes, Sea Roads, Sea Views, Marsh Lanes, Coalshore Lanes, Banks, Bank Ends, Sluices, Locks, Brookes, Fitties, Cotes, Gowts, Ings, Eaus, Bridges, Creeks, Pullovers, Gaps, Havens and Outfalls, and suffixes le-Marsh, in-the-Marsh, and on-Sea.

Sometimes, after days of rain, all the waterways bulge brownly, funnelling waters from the Wolds to within inches of the top of embankments. Mats of weed and detritus are pushed up against bridges, and the Environment Agency issue alerts, then warnings. Our farmer neighbours peer over bridge parapets and make worried faces, and non-farmers' attentions are increasingly drawn to such technical details as the precise elevation of roadways, the condition of banks and sluice gates, the capacities of pumping stations, and the red road signs bearing an arrow and the simple messages 'Out' and 'ER,' showing the Evacuation Route just in case. 'We're prepared for flooding. Are you?' challenge East Lindsey District Council posters—but *are* they? Can anyone ever be?

Waters have risen and receded all through the county's story. Lincolnshire's peat deposits are at least as old as the Bronze Age (and probably much older), evidence of frequent wettings, as are Iron Age deposits of clays and silts. There were sea-level rises during the Romano-British trangression of 300–530, which probably caused the loss of Roman settlements at Old Clee, Skegness and Wainfleet, but also swallowed offshore islands, whose material drifted onto the beaches, accretion to offset some of the erosion.

Storms could add as well as take away. During Saxon times, large dunes were raised along much of the Lincolnshire coast, from Cleethorpes down to Theddlethorpe, and they still play a role as flood defenders. Thereafter there were falls in sea level, which allowed land reclamation and the establishment of new settlements like Conisholme, Marshchapel and North Somercotes. The Medieval Warm Period of 950-1250 facilitated a Norman economic boom, and grapes famously to be grown at Lincoln[55]—but it also started the sea creeping up again, with another almost immoral-sounding trangression. As muds and sands swirled endlessly around, little ports like North Cotes became unviable, and even larger ones like Saltfleet, once one of the great ports of England, became simultaneously eaten up by seas and stuffed up with silts. Some of the mud and sand deposits of the north Lincolnshire coast are 50 feet thick.

On 29 September 1014—an eventful year during which Sweyn Forkbeard died at Gainsborough, and King Æthelred's army was defeated by Sweyn's son, Cnut—

> ...came the great sea-flood, which spread wide over this land, and ran so far up it as it never did before, overwhelming many towns, and an innumerable multitude of people.[56]

Storms in the 1280s are thought to have altered the coastline radically, sweeping away barrier islands and large parts of Mablethorpe. Monks at Louth Park Abbey recorded that Mablethorpe's St Peter's church was 'rent asunder by the waves of the sea.' Another contemporary record adds the piquant detail, 'the chalice and pyx, in which the body of Christ was served, being found crushed under a heap of stones.'[57] The ruins could still be seen at the lowest tides into the 1870s. Mablethorpe's remaining church, St Mary's, was moved about a mile inland as a precaution—and now is half that distance, its squat little tower giving the building a suitably ship-like shape.

Equally severe visitations were seen in 1335, 1430, 1443, 1529, and 1540-60.[58] In 1570, the little town of Mumby Chapel was taken, in a storm so strong a ship was dumped on top of a house.[59] Another chapel, that gave its name to Chapel St Leonard's, is now a drowned dream of devotions, lost out there somewhere where the North Sea meets another shifting sea, this one of caravans. The highest historical tides are marked on the walls of Boston's St Botolph's, and every few years spring tides propelled by northeasterlies wet the feet of the lowest streets. At least, they used to—a huge new flood barrier was completed in 2020.

There is an 1863 poem about the flood of 1571—Boston poet Jean Ingelow's 'The High Tide on the Coast of Lincolnshire,' admired by Rosetti and Tennyson. The poem is written from the point of view of an elderly woman, who remembers the terrible swiftness with which the sea came rolling over the fields, and tells a tragic tale in sixteenth-century style language.

It starts with the flood's first presentiments just as an otherwise unremarkable day is drawing to its 'golden death.' Warning bells blare out shockingly from the Stump, and there is a sudden flight 'of mews and peewits pied / By millions crouch'd on the old sea wall.' The narrator's daughter-in-law Elizabeth is far out in the fields, with her grandchildren, calling in the cattle unawares, her immemorial milking song suddenly startlingly loud:

Cusha! Cusha! Cusha! calling, / For the dews will soon be falling; / Leave your meadow grasses mellow, / Mellow, mellow.

Then the narrator's son comes charging home on horseback, shouting in panic.

The olde sea wall (he cried) is downe, / The rising tide comes on apace, / And boats adrift in yonder towne / Go sailing uppe the marketplace.

He and his mother watch helplessly as a 'mighty eygre' goes roaring upriver, and 'bankes came downe with ruin and rout'. In just a few minutes, 'all the world was in the sea.' Mother and son spend all night trapped on the roof of their house, frantic about Elizabeth and the children, listening shiveringly to Boston's bells, and watching the Stump's 'lofty beacon light, / Stream from the church tower, red and high.' In the first light, her son will find his wife and children dead but deposited gently at the cottage door, the 'pretty bairns in fast embrace,' the sun shining on Elizabeth's unfeeling face.[60] Similar things must really have been seen over centuries of inundations.

Monkish chroniclers often exaggerate, often seeing storms as not just terrifying events in themselves, but also moral lessons. But even secularised reporters can be awed by extreme weather. An 1810 edition of the *Lincoln, Rutland & Stamford Mercury*—Britain's oldest newspaper, still published weekly—exaggeratedly described that November's storm as '…the most awful visitation with which the County of Lincoln has been afflicted in the annals of time.' But they add more details than medieval writers—more interested in people as individuals, but also in economics. That same report told of the death of a serving maid drowned 'whilst milking the cows in a pasture' (like Elizabeth in Jean Ingelow's poem), and how one farmer mistook the oncoming waters for a sudden fall of snow, and sent his son out to check on the sheep, unwittingly sending him to his death. Those sheep probably perished anyway—according to the report, 15,000 were lost between Wainfleet and Sutterton—and at least 20,000 acres of farmland flooded, with water 5 feet deep on the London Road:

Almost all the land to the right of that line and some on the left is flooded; and the wind gives that vast expanse of water an undulating motion, which makes it in everything resemble a sea. The roads towards the sea and Fosdyke Wash continue to be horse-belly deep in water and are passable only with great danger and difficulty. All sorts of implements are encountered floating in the way and the tops of gateposts and a few tall objects are the only indices to the real road.

Barges were driven up into fields, a large haystack was moved intact four hundred yards by the tide, and 'Two casks of spirits, cast ashore at Gedney were found by two labouring men who helped themselves so plentifully that one of them died in consequence.'

Others died less convivially. Reports from Saltfleet, north of Mablethorpe, mentioned the loss of ships from Bridgewater, Cromer, Hull, King's Lynn, Newcastle, North Shields, South Shields, Stettin, Stockport, Sunderland, Whitby and Wisbech. The account attests not just to a disastrous night, but the interconnectedness of the east coast. The following week, storm stories were still coming in, but now journalistic attentions have moved inland, and to the dreadful sufferings of the gentry:

> The tremendous gales have done very extensive damage amongst the timber in the parks in the neighbourhood of Stamford. In the marquis of Exters [sic] beautiful domain [Burghley House, home of the Cecils] more than 100 large trees have been blown down many of them in avenues, the regularity of which is of course destroyed by the chasms.

As if this were not punishment enough, 'Two post-chaises were blown over between Stanford and Bourn.'[61]

I have met people who remember the night of 31 January 1953, when Mablethorpe's cobbled-together sea walls were breached by a storm surge. Concrete crumbled, dunes melted, and the Marsh was flooded for miles, with people and animals needing to be rescued by army amphibious vehicles.

The *Grimsby Telegraph* of 2 February 1953 is headlined '1,000 still untraced in Lincs.—100 bodies on the "Isle of Horror"— Army takes over the "Lincolnshire Dunkirk".' There is a picture of flooded, genteel Sandilands and a picture of 87-year-old Mrs Sarah Brecknell of Sutton, shocked-looking, but wrapped in blankets and eiderdown, awaiting evacuation with her canary. Other evacuees in flat caps, demob suits and long coats are being ferried away on the back of a truck, with one woman in a headscarf waving cheerily. 'They took it with a smile,' marvels the reporter, watching Mablethorpe housewives board the lorries taking them to emergency billets in Alford and Louth, while saying things like 'Wet outlook, isn't it?' and 'This sea-water has spoiled my make-up!' Not only that, but a black dog was rescued and 'Polly, the parrot, came to further liven the gathering with her baby-voiced phrases and jeers.' He concludes, 'Mablethorpe looked broken and forlorn. But its people showed the spirit of the wartime British. They were down. But they were not out.'

In another photo, two men in suits and ties stand up to their thighs in the sea inside the Sun Castle in Skegness, having a nice cup of tea. The style and tone of the coverage was perfectly Pathé—clipped sentences, constant references to the war, and of course the weather, people 'keeping calm and carrying on,' sentimental stories about animals and tea—while in the background the army and air force cope with brisk efficiency. It is the way the English like to think of themselves in the 1950s, and often really are—muddlers-through, but resilient and capable of greatness. The headlines exaggerated, although the eventual attrition was shocking enough—seventeen drowned at Ingoldmells, eleven at Sutton-on-Sea, eight at Mablethorpe, four at Saltfleet, and one at Trusthorpe. Huge walls at Mablethorpe were thrown up hurriedly thereafter, and to date nothing like 1953 has been repeated.

To date. In 2019, a sculpture by the sculptor Marcus Vergette, the *Time and Tide Bell*, was erected on the beach at Mablethorpe's North End, one of sixteen envisaged around the country, intended to make people think about global warming. At high tide, a bell rings to remind walkers and ward off evil modern spirits—parallels with classic coast-tales of drowned churches and immoral humans punished. It is a timely sculpture indeed, because the most recent sea level rise predictions are more than usually pessimistic. They even evoke Ben Smith's 2019 fantastical dystopia *Doggerland*, which envisions people living precariously on rusting wind turbines a hundred miles out from what remains of England's east coast, a marooned tribe for whom 'The Company' is king, floating plastics are precious, and land is almost legend.

These predictions suggest the loss of almost the whole coastal area by 2050, including Holbeach, Boston, Wainfleet, Skegness, and Mablethorpe, and large tracts of the Fens by flooding up river valleys. Gainsborough would be under the Trent, the lowest parts of Lincoln in the Witham, and large settlements like Coningsby, Spalding and Woodhall Spa at best islands.[62] And our house, standing as it does 6 feet above high-water mark, just under a mile from the water's usual edge.

I may have seen a glimpse of the future. One September night in 2006, after a warning of potential tidal overtopping, with the village noticeboard newly bearing RSPCA posters advising farmers to move their livestock, I went to 'our' beach to see an astonishing scene—something straight from a Dutch genre painting.

The wind was raging all the way from Jutland, snatching away the words of a few worried watchers with lights, huddled together at the sea-end of the sand path. Their tiny figures—

farmers, the wildlife warden, a couple of local residents, some of whom I knew slightly—were framed by thrashing vegetation, and the halyard of the army flagpole was whacking viciously against the post. Theirs were the only lights anywhere—ineffably brave, even touching—except for the serenely untroubled full moon, coasting above a *Grand Guignol* diorama as if it had nothing to do with the turmoil below.

The army flagpole is normally about 9 feet above sea level, but now the water was less than half that distance away, and coming on fast. Huge planks, torn-away tarpaulins and assorted rubbish had already been cast up into the lower branches of the buckthorn that a few hours before had been feeding foraging redwing from Scandinavia. Other drifting detritus was being driven towards the land on the heaving breasts of waves completely covering the usual placid plain. It was like a Doré engraving for Dante, or the last days of Doggerland; suddenly, the land seemed really to be 'a sea in waiting,'[63] the great floods of Genesis and Gilgamesh no longer just stories. This was less a bracing coast than a coast bracing.

The watchers looked up as I joined them, and we exchanged the usual laconic words usual to men who don't know each other well, but have unexpectedly been thrown together against some powerful common enemy. 'All we can do is wait!' one shouted at me, with an attempt at a smile, and really there was nothing else to be said.

Just behind the dunes, the cattle that are released onto the nature reserve in autumn to browse pest plants that would otherwise overtake the rare species were moving uneasily, lifting their muzzles and shifting their hooves as if they sensed danger, lowing louder than usual. Their owner had just arrived, reversing his huge trailer into the tiny car park, just in case it was needed— and now he stood beside me, chewing his lip as he watched and waited, helpless, keeping calm and carrying on. There were passing comments and tiny jokes as we watched and waited, as the moon tracked across—watched and waited, as large pieces of wood travelled effortlessly from north to south and were tossed into trees—watched and waited, as the water inched up...

And then, finally, thankfully, turned—peaking 3 feet from our feet, falling away at last as if suddenly exhausted. Drools of salt died disappointedly, and sank into the sand. We watchers and waiters exhaled, smiled at each other as if almost embarrassed ever to have worried. The cattle owner grunted 'That's that, then!' and spat, before nodding to us all and returning to his trailer, to drive back through the tempest to normality. The moon tracked on oblivious, off to move waters on the opposite side of the world.

Early the next morning, several of us were back at the beach, now startlingly still and sunny, as if nothing remarkable had ever happened there. We nodded to each other as we sploshed through the sodden scene. Seaweed, landweed, Estonian milk cartons, German fruit juice containers, a Romanian cigarette packet, an Italian olive oil barrel, a small piece of wood with Cyrillic script and a larger one with 'A. A.' burned into it, lobster pots, a yacht varnish tin, plastic bags, rope, gummed-up Turk's head paintbrushes, pine logs, doorframes, scaffolding planks, and an intact set of caravan steps. Dead things too—a gull, a guillemot, a seal with teeth bared in rictus. Early though we had been, the crows had been earlier still, their cruciform footprints thick on the sand around the corpses, red stripes already opened along the seal's flanks, her gentle eyes already gouged out and gorged. Beside her lay a yacht buoy, with the ironic name 'Onward Star.'

The circle of life, the eater eaten, the ill wind that blew some good, we humans similarly profiting by windfall, combing for coal, dragging firewood out of bedraggled trees—old rhythms and routines resumed with scarcely a backwards glance, all of us forgetting the night's grandness in the grind of reality. As I tugged a piece of lock gate along the shore, I smiled as I thought of Joseph Banks' Portuguese philosopher friend at Sutton on Sea's drowned forest, lugubriously remarking on the practicality of those who live surrounded by memorials of immersions:

> The people of the country have often found among them very sound pieces of timber, fit to be employed for several œconomical purposes.[64]

4

LITTLE KINGDOMS

'*The centuries that one low roof has seen*'
—Helen Waddell, *Songs of the Wandering Scholars*

The cottage—The garden—Churches of the Marsh—
The lost Kingdom of Lindsey—Lincolnshire dialect—
The RAF and Lincolnshire

It is strange to think of that 2006 night, let alone much worse ones, when standing at the cottage door in late August, looking out onto great fields and the cathedral-like church beyond, inhaling the hot breath of harvest, listening to the tuning-up orchestra of owls. In high summer, the Marsh is a heavy, dust-filled land, that feels and smells like the solidest place on the planet.

This is a modest house in a modest place, 'an insignificant foothold on the earth ... ignored between the hills and the sea.'[1] The building is of no architectural or historical interest. The thirteen acres originally attached to it were sold off decades ago, its old well is buried beneath next door's barn, and most of its (always modest) original features discarded by dourly practical or furnishing-fashion-following owners. It is absent foundations, but stands slightly slumpingly on the same material from which it was fashioned, circa 1840—the Outer Marsh's silt, laid down by old deluges and hand-fashioned into rough lozenges by local labour, probably in nearby Brickyard Lane, in kilns fired by seaborne coal.

It was—still is—small, a bit damp, dilapidated and draughty, with a redundant chimney. It had been on the market a year and a half when we bought it, and was full of the design mistakes of decades—asbestos, chipboard, linoleum, melamine, plywood, and PVC—much of it eye-wateringly painted in 1980s hues. Plug sockets were scorched or missing their front plates, pipes were held together with sticky tape, and the kitchen sink was propped up on an upturned basin. There was decade-old pastry in the rusty freezer, behind which a mouse lived, cousin to those that raced up and down in the attic—and we filled three skips with refuse, including a whole carpet found buried in the garden. Could such a place ever really matter to anyone?

Yet some of its old owners must have loved this place, thought it important, seen it as more than just a means of keeping out the rain. Its builders, the Atkinsons, rest from their labours under a nettle-beset table tomb in the churchyard, upon whose lichen-splodged surface I have traced the eroding letters of their names, and wondered what they were like. Sometimes at least, Atkinsons must have stood at this door like I do—eyeing the weather, aimlessly wrapped in some reverie, looking out over an old-new country of church and circling rooks, ripened crops, statuesque ash and sibilant sycamore spread out against the sky, a patiently waiting England etherised.

On a summer's day—or a spring's, autumn's or winter's—the house takes on unsuspected consequence. Its every inch is haunted by memories of all its owners, their good and bad decisions, their faults and qualities, their profligacy or prudence, their scepticism or faith. Art historian Mario Praz believed a house's interior is almost sentient:

> ...a museum of the soul, an archive of its experiences; it reads in them its own history, and becomes perennially conscious of itself; the surroundings are the resonance chamber where its strings render their authentic vibration.[2]

This little oblong of weathered red bricks and roof tiles, its small-paned windows and spider-strung corners, its inconvenient angles and evidence of historical movements is a tiny world all to itself, encompassing multiple sub-worlds shaped by a lifetime of accumulated objects, glimpsed in convex mirrors that bend and cast the clear Marsh light round. It is a world that has already passed, palsied with age—a world that is always passing, while I waste time standing at the door—a world that looks obsessively in on itself but is also always looking out, as if expecting new 'owners' imminently.

Every inch of the house shows evidence of some work done for good or ill, often wasted expense of money or thought—thousands of ergs, hours, pounds. Iron guttering, new wooden windows, careful opening up of old fireplaces, attempted restitution for past owners' architectural insults, our paint jobs overlying theirs, our pictures hanging where once theirs hung—surely all this was worth doing.

The house on dog-day evenings is an intimately-known and quietly breathing thing, respiring in gentle time with us, a-scuttle with insects, bats shifting feet in the attic, and occasional spectacular visitors, like the swallow who flew into the kitchen by mistake to dash itself in fright against a non-opening window, requiring swift but careful capture and release—flitting away a few seconds later across the farmyard like a firework, leaving a vision of frantic eyes, coiled cobalt, and a ghost-itch always in my hand of tiny talons, scratches from the spirit of flight. In the west-facing front garden, dogs pant in the shade of the walnut, and pollen-strewn cats prostrate themselves among parsley—but out in the east-facing back, the air strikes suddenly cool, and the world seems to be slowly going to seed, the last luxuriant outbursts of plants faintly sad, like the long hairs that sprout from the ears and noses of the old.

Those flower-beds were once worked over by our chickens and turkeys—kept because suddenly we could, and it felt 'country' to have free-range fowl, although real country people buy their eggs from supermarkets, and normally see nothing wrong with intensive chicken farming. Domestic fowl are incompatible with neat gardens—even the smallest making long raking scratches and turning over soil with their beaks, in search of food or somewhere to lay. We found less useful things—broken churchwarden pipes, crazed fragments of early Victorian blue-and-white pottery (Willow Pattern for romance, English rural scenes for reassurance), old medicine bottles, a little silver spoon and a tiny model of a mouse playing a cello. The birds gave eggs and sometimes meat, but they were mostly for ornament or entertainment. The last were taken by foxes years ago, and the houses I made have long ago been unmade. Still sometimes I think of our psychopathic Old English Game cock calling angrily out of the predawn, 'see' him chasing us up the garden while his comfortable bantams bickered in the borage, or the stag turkey halting hikers unnerved by having outraged 20lb black birds with engorged empurpled faces hissing and pecking at their knees.

The cottage feels *alive*, in a way the flat in London never did. The quiet that prevails at night, and often for whole afternoons, somehow feels fuller, and more personal, than the noisiest days in Deptford. Just as flowers have colours within colours, there are sounds within this silence, although we cannot hear all of them.

This 'silence' is an increasingly rare and expensive commodity, non-existent in London and even here often interrupted by cars, or power-tools being wielded to admittedly necessary effect in some distant barn. Modern farming is noisy, and some farms make as much noise as industrial estates—at least during harvest, when combines come and go until late, and the smallest hours hum with the noise of the grain-drier. From time to time, the Marsh dark is broken by gunfire—the RAF on night exercise, dive-bombing black sands and black water, white targets and wave-tops—a simulacrum of how the coast might have resounded had Germans really come.

Quietness is a sound in itself. Some find it too loud. One guest, waking at 3am, swore he could hear long whispered conversations in his otherwise empty room, still going on as he fell back uneasily into sleep. We fill voids with voices, products of our imaginations and nervous systems, making the most vacant places swell with possibilities—random thoughts, remembrances, reproaches. The moon-phased long-case clock in our main room stands like a nightwatchman, tolling the knell of the smallest hours, telling of its own longevity and the sheer improbability of getting here intact, all the miles from Revolutionary Paris to complacent *l'Angleterre profonde*.

Outside, there is no real silence, just as there is no complete darkness. Wind, the sea, running water, birds, and animals make the least peopled places thrum and sometimes sing, and when you really know a place you learn its surround sounds, in different weathers, different seasons—the way poplar leaves sound different from willows, how hawthorns squeak, the noise rain makes as it batters a leaf canopy or splatters back up from the ground, how summer storms sound different from winter ones, the splosh of a water vole as it plops-slips across the dyke in fright. And these are only the sounds we can hear. Bats bounce radars across dimensions off-limits to us, and smaller animals are even less audible without special equipment. One species of water-boatmen—the little insects that 'row' across the surfaces of ponds—has the highest amplitude relative to its body length of *any* organism.[3]

The quietest times are often on full moon nights, when the silver ball could be standing still and everyone but you is asleep. Moonlight falls onto the carpet, ossifying and whitening while also making new shadows. The house takes on new meanings, like in those nocturnal interiors by Xavier Mellery, where statues could almost be alive and empty stairs could be creaking, and something seems always about to happen. Outside, the road becomes a silvered stream, antithesis of the black and hopeless dyke, and you could read if you wanted, although who would when an argent universe awaits attention? There is an extraordinary stillness, like the moment in the Protevangelium of St James when all Creation stands still—shepherds stooping over lambs, birds in mid-flight— while Joseph yearns desperately for a midwife. The world inhales and holds it for long, long moments, before releasing its breath again so gently you don't notice.

Down on the beach, the moon wobbles in broken puddles, follows you along among the high wisps, while somewhere plovers pipe, and roosting gulls shuffle watchfully. Other animals also respond to lunar power—a woodcock in the top of a tree is silhouetted dumpily against the sphere, badger cubs snuffle for worms beside my frozen feet, young weasels roll in play, and a muntjac barks over by the church, maybe making the Atkinsons jump. When the moon goes briefly behind a cloud, there are occasional other illuminations—the greenish fairy-lights of glow-worms waiting for a mate on a five-bar gate. This is light of a kind never seen in any city, light as seen by preindustrial progenitors, light' as evidence of universal order and reasonableness—light of the kind that captivated Robert Grosseteste and Isaac Newton.

On bright winter afternoons, when birds flit off frost and the bats in the attic are hanging between life and death, we listen as well as watch as the sun beams in simulacra of summer—playing with perceptions, flickering shadows of leaves endlessly across the panes and when the leaves are gone, the skeleton branches. Winds wind their ways through the solidest bafflements, rattling shutters, stirring heavy curtains, sending scouts down the chimney to fan the fire that bulges in the grate and is replicated in miniature in the room's multiple mirrors. The cow bell beside the door *clonks* and *clonks* when the wind is on the front, as if some monomaniac badly wants to come in. Other days, rain taps on glass, runs rivulets down the doors and makes them swell, and hail beats tattoos on the door canopy. Ice traces deltas on window panes. Snow mounds against the front door, flops in as you walk out, and holds the plain in thrall.

Then there is autumn, when crane-flies hang in the soaking grass, mumblingly lapping last night's liquidised fog. Fruit trees fill with wasps, fighting over the last sweetness of summer; deferring the dreadful day when there is no more fruit, or warmth. The small sun-traps that can still be found are thronged with life, and ivy, the last thing in flower, is forested with flies. Ladybirds are strewn on thorns, brilliantly crimson against the brown, like the scattered drops of a wounded hart, or drops of a martyr's blood. Dragonflies flap weakly where they have fallen out of the summer, and clamber gratefully onto your hand, where they sit wonderfully large and shining, each leg with its own weight and pressure as it shifts on your finger tips and turns its amazing alien face to look at yours. When you place them carefully on bushes, they hang there for a while, brittle and gaudy as Christmas decorations, before they flick away for one last hawk.

The house is haunted by large house spiders (*Tegenaria domestica*) that have issued in under the kitchen door seeking refuge from suddenly drenching dews and plummeting temperatures, or that you have carried in unnoticing on firewood—stalking along the white-painted beams of the ceiling, clambering up curtains, stalking across the hearth, rushing across perilous plains of carpet. Some of these are very large by British standards, almost as large as the cardinal spider (*Tegenaria parietina*) that frightened Thomas Wolsey by clambering out of his slipper at Hampton Court. I save these from cats, and feel sad to find their exoskeletons in the kitchen sink into which they have fallen during the night, unable to climb back out, while the porcelain strikes a deathly chill up through insufficiently hairy legs into their desperately lifted abdomens.

Autumn and winter afternoons are for cutting up driftwood with a handsaw—to the bemusement of your kind neighbour, who offered use of a chainsaw, and was puzzled when you declined. Lights inside the house click on one by one. You keep sawing in gathering darkness, relishing the cold, the fingernail moon and the distant bark of a fox. That elicits a gentle *ruff* from the Jack Russells inside by the fire, now lifting their heads in enquiry, their brown eyes filled with the shadows of the season.

*   *   *

Zooming out from parochial concerns, panning along horizons, the Marsh's bounds become wider still and wider. The village names could be the libretto of a so-far unwritten North Midlands Symphony—Aby, Addlethorpe, Austen Fen, Gayton-le-Marsh, Grainthorpe, Great Carlton, Grimoldby, Humberston, Marshchapel, Orby, Saltfleetby St Clements, Theddlethorpe All Saints. That is before you add in the Gothic-lettered Ordnance Survey details that give those maps such suggestiveness—sites of castles, deserted villages, earthworks, moats, monastic foundations, salterns, and cultivation terraces. Other traces of old occupancy are still to be added; in 2015, part of a Bronze Age causeway was found on Cleethorpes beach.

I have flown above the Marsh in a glider from the old RAF Strubby—incidentally birthplace of Thomas Wilson, whose 1553 book *The Arte of Rhetorique* was much resorted to by Shakespeare. From above, this great space suddenly makes sense, impressive not just because of its extent, but also because geography hard to comprehend at ground level is seen all at once and interrelated. Centuries of combined effort can be seen at a glance—the endlessly repeated actions that over mostly unnamed generations have restrained those waters, fashioned and tended those fields, surfaced those roads, pushed up those houses, barns, pubs and pumping stations. This peregrine's eye perspective is a perfect complement to the view at water level, when often all you can see is your prow pushing through weed, scudding duck, raised embankments and sky.

Some Marsh buildings harbour redolent curios—ships' timbers reused as barn beams or drawing-room panelling, masts rotting forgotten in fields, bits of dinghies in back gardens, cannon used as gateposts and cannonballs as finials, seventeenth-century sundials, eighteenth-century follies, World War Two military surplus, and 1970s cars so covered with green scum they could be a hundred years older. In the Manor House at Saltfleet are resilient evanescences—some of England's oldest wallpaper and a 1673 message incised on a window with the names Robert Fox and Jan Hardy, with a lover's knot. Cromwell is supposed to have stayed here as a guest of Lord Willoughby, the night after almost being killed at Winceby. Years later, Charles II is reputed to have stayed in the New Inn over the road, an early and unusually upmarket example of a Lincolnshire seaside holiday. The Gayton Engine, a utilitarian 1850 pumping station lit by a Venetian window, holds a chugging 1945 mechanism which attracts diesel devotees, and a small array of redundant dyking tools and eel-spears, whose shapes hadn't changed for centuries until overnight they became outmoded.

We have bits of ships in our garden, salt-stained and barnacled, enigmatic lumps that once fulfilled some vital function. I like to think the teak door I salvaged at Mablethorpe came from Colonial Secretary Joseph Chamberlain's beautiful yacht, broken up on the beach about 1910, just one of many ships dismantled there in the early twentieth century, from sturdy ice barques to elegant three-masted schooners. Occasionally, at the lowest tides, the outlines of a few of these can be seen and touched, slimy protruding timbers, craft reverting to concept. Beams, bulkheads, ribs, spars and trenails resound beneath the sands, summoning old creakings of halyard and hull, cabins lit by swaying oil lamps, once-important journeys, the wraiths of wrights.

Even the romantic accidental wrecks are barely remembered. The Donna part of Donna Nook, north of Mablethorpe, *may* derive from an Armada ship of that name allegedly wrecked there in 1588 by the mythologised 'Protestant winds.' One clipper, the *Rimac*, whose graceful lines belied her trade of Peruvian guano-carrier (thus the name, after the river that flows through Lima), has left her name attached to the stretch of coast where she foundered, possibly fœtidly, in 1874. Her salvaged windlass was used for years afterwards to haul boats up the ramp at Saltfleet. The much-tried *Try* was wrecked twice at Saltfleet Haven, first in 1892, when the captain's wife and children drowned, before finally succumbing eight years afterwards to the same sandbank. We have salvaged name plates of more modern vessels—a trawler called the *Nimrod*, and a vessel *Specksioneer* (a Dutch whaling word, meaning chief harpoonist), a lifebelt from *Three Sisters R*—identifiers from old odysseys, jettisoned into the seas of time.

But it is the churches that stand out most. Their endless variegations of form, materials and decoration captivated John

Piper, who delighted in their benign ageing, predictable from a war artist who had seen air-raid destruction at first hand. John Betjeman, too, was a frequent visitor, the Marsh's churches occasionally the objects of his verses. In 1948, visiting the over-restored church at Huttoft, he worried about an England 'seemingly so indifferent / And with so little soul to win,' but found himself reassured by the sound of skylarks and the 'white light' of the Marsh, and inside the unusual sight of an Indian priest officiating—evidence for the poet of Anglicanism's outward reach, and suggesting hope for the history-gentled creed's survival.[4] Even Simon Jenkins, no devotee of eastern Lincolnshire, has to confess the Marsh is 'blessed' with its churches.

Spilsby greenstone (a kind of sandstone seemingly especially prone to having fist-sized holes punched into it by weather), ashlar for finer work, Plantagenet and Tudor brick, cement, re-used earlier masonry inserted halfway up walls by thrifty medieval builders, and roof lead somehow merge harmoniously, any original rawness long ago rendered inoffensive by interplay of elements, and mats of moss. Many Marsh churches are raised on artificial eminences—salt hills, formed over centuries from leached sand discarded in salt-making. But they are now mostly driven past, obscured by trees, made to look small by wind turbines, rendered redundant by rationalism. They look like they've always been there, more and more weather-worn, pitted and stained, their different materials merging until their walls are like sea beds upheaved. Sea beds set with ugly angels gaping onto graveyards, grotesques vomiting water, medieval peasants picking their noses and playing instruments, coats of arms of the extinguished distinguished flaking into dust and flowering with lichen.

The tenth-century crucifixion/sunstone in the tiny medieval church at Conisholme recalls a lost realm—the Kingdom of Lindsey, most mysterious of the Anglo-Saxon realms, ages upon Dark Ages ago annexed by more powerful neighbours, but whose name persisted for centuries as a bishopric and still lingers in local government.

Much in Anglo-Saxon history is conjectural, but even by these standards Lindsey is lost in sea-fret. The major Anglo-Saxon Lincolnshire landmarks—the church towers of the county's north and west, the moot-marking Elloe Stone at Moulton—are from much later. What we can glean about the Kingdom comes largely from examination of Anglo-Saxon cemeteries, and even these finds raise questions about how the dead lived and regarded the world. Some are pagan, some Christian, some mixed. Brooch, buckle, coin, loom weight, pin, pottery, tool and weapon mount styles bear a range of motifs—Celtic, classical, Christian, Frankish, Norse. Why did Anglo-Saxons so often fill their graves with Roman stones? How did tropical cowrie shells get here? There are a few crop marks and street patterns, and many Anglo-Saxon place-names—Barlings, Beckering, Billingborough, Billinghay, Hagworthingham, Horbling, Minting, Threekingham and Winteringham, to name just some.

These are shadowy nation-founders—for most people little more than legend, and for some not even an interesting one. A nineteenth-century dialect dictionary records the disappointment of a man from Bottesford, who came across a precious piece of history by chance, an Anglo-Saxon cinerary urn containing a bone comb:

> I once fun upo' th' top o' th' Holme Lordship a big broon pot, as I was digging for rabbits, bud when I opened it ther' was noht at all i'side but white ashes an' a peäsce o' an awd reightlin coämb.[5]

Other clues to life in Lindsey have been lost, like the Latin/runic inscription found in Caistor in 1770, and the Witham Bowl found in 1816, known only through a contemporary description and drawings—a silver-gilt bowl with four mounts in the form of toothed cats, and in the middle a creature like a long-necked dinosaur, whose blue-glass eyes would have stared challengingly above the level of the rim.

We know almost nothing even about Lindsey's kings, except possibly some names, courtesy of the Anglian collection, four manuscripts of Anglo-Saxon regnal lists held between the British Museum, Corpus Christi College, and the Medway Archives—Godwulf Geating, Finn, Frithulf, Frealaf, Woden, Winta, Cretta, Cuedgils, Caedbaed (whose name is British rather than Anglo-Saxon), Bubba, Beda, Biscop (revealing Christian influence), Eanferth, Eata, and Aldfrið. *Possibly* their names, because the inclusion of Woden (Odin) shows this pedigree is at least partly phantasmagorical, like those of Christian monarchs who claimed descent from the kings of Israel—but then all the Saxon genealogies, except Wessex, include Woden. Lindsey was occupied first by Bernicia, then Mercia, then Northumbria, and finally Mercia again; many of its named native rulers may not have been kings at all, but ealdormen with allegiances elsewhere. The kingdom encompassed most of modern Lincolnshire, except in the south, where it abutted the territories of the Spaldas (the 'dwellers by the gulf,' after whom Spalding is named).

In the early seventh century, the recently consecrated bishop Paulinus left Canterbury on a northern mission. His first Lincolnshire convert was one Blæcca, *praefectus* (the king's reeve) of Lincoln, and by 627 there was a church in the town. Soon he was carrying out mass baptisms in the Trent—a tall figure, according to a rarely descriptive early medieval report, slightly bent, with black hair, a thin hooked nose, and an emaciated face. Paulinus was followed by Etheldreda, Guthlac, and others, as Lindsey passed under Mercian control, Christianising so quickly it was made a separate see in 677. The list of its bishops is more trustworthy than the list of its kings, unbroken from Eadhæd around 678 until Burgheard *circa* 875. In the ninth century the Danes conquered all of Lincolnshire and swept away the see.

When episcopal authority was eventually resumed, the revived see did not last long before being merged into the diocese of Dorchester. It would be two centuries before other Northmen set that right. Remigius de Fécamp, camp-follower to the Conqueror, created the Diocese of Lincoln in 1072, and ceremoniously consolidated by laying the first stones of the cathedral.

Lesser churches offer insights into county arts and attitudes. The 1405 doorway at Yarburgh shows Adam and Eve, a nesting bird and pomegranates, and the inscription 'Wo so looks thys work opon / Pray for all yat yt be gun.' A 1424 brass to Sir Robert Hayton at Theddlethorpe is the latest known depiction of a bascinet, a helmet with chain mail falling to the shoulders, an even then-outdated example of armouring. A sixteenth-century village resident once idly outlined his shoe on a sheet of lead, and scratched a ship he probably saw from the tower. The massive Bertie monument in grey, white and black marble in the chancel looks cold-eyed out through clear uneven glass across the windswept marshes, through the constant sweeping of ash trees and calling of rooks towards the sea—across which similar monuments to similarly stern families stare back in hyperborean communion, from a thousand Flemish, Dutch, Danish, German, Polish, Swedish, Lithuanian, Latvian, Estonian and Russian churches.

At Saltfleetby All Saints, the tower leans strongly towards the setting sun, the lead looks like it's about to slide off the roof, and a horrible, toothed man leers up like Frankenstein's creature from the base of the font. At the back of the nave stands a sophisticated, superfluous pulpit, which somehow came here from Oriel College, Oxford—an elegant example of the carver's art, wonderfully out of place in this most rustic of spaces. At Saltfleetby St Peter's, the stump of the old church is forsaken (except by jackdaws and pheasants) in a field, left behind when the rest of the building was moved half a mile west by muscular

Christian Victorians. Sometimes the curiosities are not easily seen, like the fifteenth century bells of South Somercotes with their beautiful lettering, one inscribed 'I am of sweet sound; I am called the bell of Gabriel.' In Ingoldmells, Mrs Dawson, housekeeper to the Rev Joseph Edwards, is memorialised in a strikingly long inscription, starting with her highly respectable parentage, finishing with the 1866 day the 'King of Terrors' came to take her, just before Edwards was to give a talk (which she insisted must go ahead). Her respected Reverend was noted as preacher and educator—and bankrupt, sent to prison after a spirited court performance in which he called his creditors 'buffoons,' and said he was being greatly condescending even speaking to them. When he got out, he went back to his pulpit and resumed his old activities. When he died in 1896, the *Daily Telegraph* felt able to give him the accolade of 'the most notorious begging letter writer in the Church of England.'

At Burgh le Marsh is a story that could have come from Daphne du Maurier—the sexton who defied wreckers, locking them out of the church whilst tolling the bell to warn a ship to stand out from the land, tolling so manfully he died of sheer effort. The lectern was carved by Jabez Good, a Jabez-of-all-Trades as craftsman, barber, historian, poet, 'general dealer, and curioso,' whose 1900 book *A Glossary or Collection of Words, Phrases Place-Names, Superstitions, etc., current in East Lincolnshire* was one of the first serious studies of Lincolnshire dialect. Outside, a gravestone of 1610 has a Latin Q&A inscription, ending 'Do you inquire where the soul of the deceased is? Doubtless it has sought the stars.'

At Croft, an unknown knight seems to float, despite being a brass on the floor—one of the oldest in England, a rounded half-figure, his armoured gauntlets joined together in prayer, mail covering his not-so-humble head. A medieval eagle lectern used for resting the Bible tells a story of its own—found dumped in a ditch, complete except for talons, two of the little lions guarding its base years later returned, after someone spotted them at a Leicester car boot sale. Crude ship graffiti scud across wooden panels, and 'H. E.' has democratically initialled the face of Elizabethan-Jacobean worthy Sir John Browne. A door bears the inscription 'God Save the King 1633,' and the names of the proudly patriotic carvers, one called Harbar Newsteade. Someone less patriotic tried to scratch out the word 'King.' A tithe map of 1848 stored in a tube covers the tower floor when unrolled—a masterpiece of the surveyor's craft, a punctilious plan of the parish, showing who owned which field, and their sizes and shapes. Property rights properly set out, Church rights, soil security, tenure—Lincolnshire's preoccupations while the rest of Europe was embroiled in violent revolutions.

The nonagenarian who proudly showed me all these things is a historian in his quiet way, a servant of both past and future, who several years ago examined every surviving gravestone and deciphered their names, dates and inscriptions—an act almost as laborious and more pious that that of the Presbyterian mason in Scott's *Old Mortality*, who recut eroding inscriptions, but only on the tombstones of his sect. We stood a long time under the restlessly rushing beech in the churchyard on a day when trees were falling across the county, talking of the dead in the present tense.

Hannah-cum-Hagnaby is a prim Augustan vision of 'decent' box pews, integral font and altar rails, with a fashionable Venetian window looking out onto the east. St Peter's at Markby preserves musty sanctity—built from the stones of a priory, one angle of a sacred trigonometry with a nunnery and an abbey, and now a scanted wayside church with a mossy thatch instead of lead, where trapped butterflies beat themselves desperately to death. At South Cockerington, the effigy of Sir Adrian Scrope (1616– 66), a gallant Royalist related to a regicide, is always arising from his couch in full armour and frilled ruff, and as I ponder this sartorial improbability, three ladies come up to ask, 'Excuse me, are you the new vicar?'

Then there is Skidbrooke, once mother to the major port of Saltfleet. Saltfleet has diminished greatly, Skidbrooke much more so, the always too big St Botolph's left hulking at the end of a long track, surrounded by trees. On a dramatically lit late winter day, we came armed with a copy of Pevsner, primed to see his selected features, tick them off as historical duty done. But as we neared, we could see there was something awry.

This wasn't the church Pevsner had seen, but a set from a Hammer horror—the huge imposing edifice windowless and doorless, with pigeons flapping out of openings as we approached. Through the doorway, more signs of pigeon— feathers, guano, sticks, vermiculated corpses, and live birds flying up from ledges and out between columns, their wings whistling their consternation. Bats too, of course—dry drifts of their scat, and a dead one in a cistern that once held holy water. Leaves of yore rustled dispiritedly across the red-tiled floor, or gathered in corners to hold dry converse.

The church gaped freezingly empty—no glass, no early Stuart pulpit, no altar table, old chest, or font cover. Merciless sun striped millennium-old masonry, casting clarity on Skidbrooke's state—animal effluvia, human neglect and worse—love hearts and swear words on walls, painted pentacles, smashed bottles, cigarette ends, chocolate wrappers, a condom, stains against walls the same shape as the stains in urinals. Grotesque heads of long-haired sea monkeys and the still *in situ* tablet to a respected rector had obviously been backdrop to who knew how many shabby Saturday night Saturnalias for the misspending youth of the Marsh, childishly defiant 'spook'-defying beer bouts, and 'Satanic' ceremonies.

111

It felt like a strange testament to St Botolph's relict dignity that some had taken such trouble to slight this place in its coldly eerie setting of dirty streams, mile-long fields, and bumpy little roads plied by too-big tractors, the last farmers heading home before dark. We walked quietly back down the long track, listening to curlews, realising how far we'd come from London.

*　　*　　*

On New Year's Eve 2000, we went to the beach for midnight, to welcome in the New Year in the uttermost east. A million mental miles away, people were hyperventilating about the 'Millennium Bug,' when all the world's computers were going to stop working, ushering in an apocalypse of inconvenience. At that moment, in Greenwich, Tony Blair was at the Dome, hosting the world's worst party, yanking the Queen's hands during an especially bad rendition of *Auld Lang Syne*, after which highpoint hundreds of tired and emotional guests had to wait hours for broken-down trains. But on the beach, under cold and mizzling rain, there was nothing at all beyond the subdued susurration and swash of the waves, except for a single purple firework that arced into the air, miles to the south near Mablethorpe. That single squib held more promise than all the goings-on by the Thames.

The Marsh felt especially sequestered in the first years. The summer of 2000 was unusually wet, and then there was that year's fuel strike, which almost brought down the government. 2001 saw the foot-and-mouth epidemic, and farmers barricaded their tracks with buckets of disinfectant and giant signs warning of disease. 'The countryside is closed,' shouted the *Daily Mail*, and the Marsh seemed double-locked. Even the skies were almost empty of airliners, and remained so, until Doncaster Airport opened in 2005, with a consequent reordering of flight paths. It was possible to walk all day and meet no one—to swim in a sea of your own. Everything seemed both clear and mysterious, new as well as evergreen, down to the grasses that swayed and swished in the wind like a luxuriant pelt, ultimate symbol of eternal return. Something of that flavour returned briefly during the first year of Covid, when the skies were empty of airliners and the roads reverted to almost deserted.

The few people you did meet were not brittle like those of London. Many would stop and talk quite naturally, often surprisingly confidingly—starting off with dogs or the weather, but quickly going on to the most intimate details of their health, or family problems. Even BBC Lincolnshire journalists lacked the frigid 'professionalism' of BBC London, carrying on pre-on-air conversations and scoring points off each other on screen, often unconsciously revealing attitudes that in London would have earned them a reprimand or 'sensitivity' course.

Shop assistants referred to customers as 'ladies' and 'gentlemen,' called you 'duck,' cracked dry jokes, or moaned about the length of their shift. They were helpful if you couldn't find something, smilingly patient with children, and made much of dogs, and would round prices down instead of up. And everything was much cheaper anyway; shops here were often family-run, a means of making a living rather than of making a fortune.

They used informal grammar—'I was sat there,' 'he was stood,' 'he was guilty to an offence,' 'do you want your coffee pouring?' and double negatives—and dialect words deriving mostly from Norse, and Old and Middle English. The Burgh-le-Marsh glossarian Jabez Good remarked of the local vernacular,

> ...it contains more pure Saxon than most other dialects in England; for the requirements of the Lincolnshire peasant have rarely been such as to need the help of more expressive words derived from Latin or other sources. He can express his thoughts

and carry on his conversation, without bringing into play, words of a stock other than English.[6]

Lincolnshire dialect traditions are as rich as those of Yorkshire, but much less well known. You come across them unexpectedly; 'Oh, it's *snided* with geese down there,' one of my neighbours was assuring me, before catching himself and smiling, realising I was one of the 'frim foäk' (outsiders) who might not understand such terminology (it means 'crammed'). He also referred to fluffy clouds as 'hen-scrattins' (scratchings), the nearby bridge as the 'brig,' and to driftwood 'rudged' by the tide.

Other overheard terms include 'dunt it' (doesn't it), 'forruds' (forwards), 'gleg' (a glance), 'mizzling' (raining finely), 'pack-up' (packed lunch), 'puthering' (raining heavily), 'sich' (such) and 'arsy-versy' (topsy-turvy) while in the season, you can buy large bags of 'tates' from potato-growers' gates. The most striking new sound to an outsider is the combined vowel diphthong, where two vowels are sounded separately but almost run together, so 'don't' becomes 'do-än't,' 'no' 'no-ä,' and 'road' 'ro-äd.' Place names of course have their own conventions—Coningsby is 'Cunningby,' Saltfleetby 'Soloby,' Grainthorpe 'Grantrup,' Bolingbroke 'Bullinbruck,' and Burgh le Marsh 'Borough' (although Burgh on Bain is 'Bruff').

Tennyson honoured his natal county's accents, dialects and cautious instincts in poems like 'Northern Farmer, Old Style':

> *Wheer 'asta beän saw long and meä liggin' 'ere aloän?*
> *Noorse? thoort nowt o' a noorse: whoy, Doctor's abeän an' agoän;*
> *Says that I moänt 'a naw moor aäle; but I beänt a fool;*
> *Git ma my aäle, fur I beänt a-gawin' to breäk my rule.*
> *(Where have you been so long, and me living here alone?*
> *News? There's no news; why, Doctor's been and gone;*
> *Says I mustn't have any more ale; but I'm no fool*
> *Give me my ale, for I'm going to break my rule)*

The Northern Farmer goes on to recount the tale of his life, from 'allus' voting for 'Squoire an' choorch and state,' the death of 'moy Sally,' being accused of fathering 'Bessy Marris's barn,' and how he had tamed 'Thornaby waäste,' amid a traditionary haze of 'bogles,' ominous insects and marsh birds. He ends with the farmer's (and patriot's) final question—'who's to howd the lond ater meä?' ('who will hold the land after me?'), hoping whoever it is will not use the new-fangled steam plough:

...summun'll come ater meä mayhap wi' 'is kittle o' steam / Huzzin' an' maäzing the blessed feälds wi' the Divil's oän team.[7]

Edward Campion, born in the Marsh in 1908 and brought up by dialect-speaking grandparents, wrote a glossary of Tennyson's dialect terms.[8] He noted that Lincolnshire dialects are not easily separable from the south Midlands dialects of Chaucerian English, and that many dialect words from Lincolnshire can also be found elsewhere. A Lincolnshire system of counting sheep recorded in 1890—one to ten is *yan, tan, tethera, pethera, pimp, sethera, lethera, hovera, covera, dik*—has an almost universal ring, the sort of words shepherds anywhere could have used. One writer on linguistics even likens it to Native American counting recorded at about the same time, although it is possible that the American recorder had observer (or auditor) bias, filtering what he or she heard through English dialect-attuned ears.[9] But the dialects here do have special qualities, borne of relative isolation from Latinising scholars or Frenchifiers—who for example turned the Old English Eä (drain) into *Eau*—and an agricultural economy which did not encourage industrial-era influxes of outsiders with vocabularies of their own.

Campion distinguishes carefully between four word ways, which diverge in particulars—northern, mid-Lincolnshire, Boston and the Fens, and Axholme—the last more Yorkshire like the others, because of the Isle's position on the far side of the

Trent. He specifies a word once commonly used across the Marsh, 'farweltered,' to signify a sheep that has fallen over and is unable to get back up again—which becomes 'farwelted' in the north of Lincolnshire, but 'cast' in the south. Far Welter'd is also the name of a present-day society that celebrates the dialects of the county's east.[10]

The study of dialects can never be a precise science—the word 'snided' my neighbour used to signify crammed, Campion uses to mean cold—but the similarities between medieval English and today's still lingering words are often striking. Some usages really do span centuries, from the fourteenth-century text 'The Dancers of Colbek' by Bourne monk Robert Mannyng—'They oute of that stede were went' ('They out of that place were gone')—to the old people Campion knew in Long Sutton who would say things like 'you never ought to have went.' 'Gress' is grass in dialect, and in *Sir Gawain and the Green Knight*; 'nobbut' too is 'nothing but' in both. Herons were 'heronsews' to wildfowlers and to Chaucer. As Campion concludes, 'The dialects of today are attenuated, but they are well worthy of study.'[11]

There were few social events in the Marsh, and they were rarely enticing—vegetable shows, gardening clubs, cookery lessons—so it was not always easy to meet people. But when you did, they could not have been kinder or more practical. They would go out of their way to help with your car, or lend you a cement mixer—even if privately they thought you a useless townie, or eccentric for making your garden into a wildlife reserve, or wanting wooden rather than plastic window frames in your house. If there were no dinner parties, there were recently shot rabbits or braces of pheasant, left hanging at your back door, or invitations to help yourself to unwanted fruit.

This was not the 'close-knit community' of cliché; probably all villages have long-running resentments, and doubtful families who live in scruffier houses lurch from casual job to casual job, spend too much time in the pub, take rather too much interest in the contents of your shed, and perhaps not entirely coincidentally know where to get things oddly cheap. But even these can be helpful, and others who don't know your name probably know your face and where you live. They nod when you meet them, lift a hand when you pull in to let their vehicle go first, and gratuitously share useful information from fallen trees to power cuts, roadworks to haystack fires, thefts to tidal surges. They notice you, look out for your property, and when you do get to talk to them, accord you the ultimate sign of acceptance— telling you about the idiocy of London.

* * *

If we took wild things by surprise, they more often took us the same way. The first time we turned into our road, an auspicious heron hoisted himself out of reeds along the roadside ditch and ever since we have shared our bucolic breathing space with extraordinary animals.

The sea offers bass, blennies, cockles, dabs, flounders, jellyfish, mackerel, oysters, pipefish, plaice, sand eels fleas, shrimp, urchins and whelk. Other denizens are more formidable. I came across a pomarine skua on the beach unable to fly because he had tried to swallow a gull whole, and it had become stuck halfway down. Skuas are kleptoparasites—animals which steal the meals of other animals—so maybe he had stolen this gull from another bird. He had need to regret his greed, because his meal was nearly the same size as him. But if he could not fly, he could still run, and it took me several minutes to catch him. He squirmed madly and scratched my hands badly as I wrestled with him, trying to hold onto his meal while I tried to take it from his crop without damaging him. Skuas are determined birds, and only the very largest gulls or eagles dare take them on. Succeeding at last,

117

I let him go with some relief so he could get away, glaring back over his right wing in disgust as I stood there scratched and panting, still eyeing up the mangled gull dangling from my hand. 'Skua' comes from the name of a Faroese island, and you can easily imagine these formidable birds flying expertly abeam of Vikings or in the wake of Saxons adventuring the whale road.

I once found a ten-inch crab hundreds of yards from the water's edge, with the tide still falling, and picked it up as I thought carefully to carry it to the water. The unimpressed crustacean reached casually round behind and fastened his largest claw onto my thumb. The blood supply was cut off, making my thumb instantly numb and white, and the marks could still be seen three days later. I raced to the water and put him under the surface; I can't help thinking he maintained his hold longer than he strictly needed to. When snorkelling, similar crabs can sometimes be seen scudding indignantly sideways into the flying grit, although so far, I have avoided having my toes treated like my thumb.

A greater danger is the lesser weever fish, unobtrusive silvery-brown creatures which lie just under the sand in shallows, waiting to charge out on prey. Their scientific name, *Echiichthys vipera*, suggests their most distinctive characteristic—venomous dorsal and gill-cover spines, which can cause severe pain and temporary local paralysis. More impressive-looking, although not dangerous, is the wolffish, one of which I found at Mablethorpe, a 3-feet-long torpedo with a warhead of teeth. I found a juvenile porpoise at Cleethorpes, so recently dead there were still bubbles around its blowhole—a sad find for a fine afternoon, with the black-and-white Spurn Point lighthouse seemingly just a short splash away, and ships like Humbrol-painted Airfix toys beating bravely up the channel. Porpoises go far up the river sometimes following fish; one cold and rainy Grimsby walk was redeemed by the sight of three black backs breaking surface 10 feet offshore, shucking silver droplets into the matt-grey universe.

Swans pass over in little squadrons, their wing downbeats whistlingly audible, and crash ungracefully on crops. Barn owls ghost along dykes, long-eared owls quarter salt marsh creeks, and little ones give you glares above crunchy beakfuls of beetles. I rescued a wood ash-soft barn owl once from the side of the road, where he lay stunned but otherwise unhurt, and took him home. I needed to go out, so put him in a dark and quiet room, in a cat carrier with the front open, with some raw meat and water. When I got back later, he was looking at me severely from the top of the stairs, above the headless body of our free-flying zebra finch (which I had quite forgotten about in my earlier haste). He flapped from there onto a bookshelf, defecated down some books, then flew out the still open door, without even a *too-woo* for the *tuwit*.

More grateful partridge bob in and out of the garden looking for seeds, below the sycamore in which a turtle dove once rested on an afternoon full of promise:

> *For, lo, the winter is past, and the rain is over and gone; /*
> *The flowers appear on the earth; the time of the singing of birds is come,*
> *and the voice of the turtle is heard in our land.*[12]

Another day, a pair of cuckoos courted in the back garden, a long drawn-out affair which underlined the limited scope of their repertoire. But all was forgiven when one passed close as I stood on Zion Hill at dawn, calling as he flew, the air so clean and first-time seen I saw the muscles working in his throat. Curlews whistle in the morning's thinness, lapwing hop with risen crests, and paper-chains of gulls trail September's tractors. Moorhens scuttle in dykes, kingfishers zip away, and redshank launch up and out, *pheeping* alarum to all. Buzzards pass low across the road carrying still-wriggling rats, while blackbirds bookend seasons—

blacker than black in the greener than green of March, or spinking in greying-out gardens on the bitter edges of December nights. Their song-thrush cousins smash snails on regularly used rocks surrounded by shattered calcium carbonate, and so sweetened sing even better. Starling murmurations billow and bulge in wintry airs, sparrows bicker and spik under eaves. Crows *crex, crex* and scrape cruciform claws, eye you interrogatively, and wood pigeons swoop and flap and stipple their shadows on furrows. Pheasants crouch in newly-tilled fields, comically wings down, believing I can't see them—resplendent birds in acres of brown—or cocket away alarmed by distant thunderclaps, a frenetic flight through fatly ominous air. In the summer, merlin, swallows, warblers and wheatears make landfall here. In the winter, there are redwing, snow buntings and above all geese— bearing down heavily from the north like Lancasters returning from a raid, their carelessly dropped trumpetings inducing wanderlust far below.

I remember my first bittern, rising out of icy reedmace just feet away—a speckled arrow in a sparkling brown-white world, lifting leggily away to flop leggily into another iced reed bed, and vanishing instantly, a swaying stalk among swaying stalks.

I once saw three cranes flying over a football field—striking silhouettes to see above suburbia. They looked like the crest of Thomas Cranmer, whose ancestors came out of The Wash carrying three cranes as arms (birds they would have seen on their Sutterton estate), but which the always insecure Archbishop Christianised—and gentrified—into pelicans. Other rarities have been helped here, like the emu that astonished me in Alford, peering over a garden hedge.

* * *

These avifauna share national airspace. RAF Chinooks, Eurofighters, Typhoons and Tornadoes fly and conduct target practice at Donna Nook, while RAF Scampton's Red Arrows deal their impressive diamond nines across the firmament. A couple of times a year, you can see the planes of the Battle of Britain Memorial Flight, which bring out people to stare in fascinated nostalgia, 'lest we forget'. The Lancaster symbolises Britain as flying fortress, the Hurricanes and Spitfires Britain as chivalric realm, and all three in combination Britain as both bare-knuckle boxer and example to the nations. Even a hovering kestrel can haze into patriotic mirage seen through such misted lenses, like the one being watched by a medieval falconer at the opening of the 1944 Powell & Pressburger film *A Canterbury Tale*, which segues into a Spitfire watched by the same man, who is now wearing a 1939–1945 issue tin helmet.

The RAF has a strong hold on Lincolnshire affections. This is a legacy of the '39–'45, when much of the county was given over to airfields—around 100 all told, including dummy runways and emergency landing strips. There are still six operational stations today, essential to the defence of the Eastern Approaches, and NATO aerospace. During World War Two, Lincolnshire was nicknamed 'Bomber County,' and the term is still used, although some now regard this as being in poor taste. Since 2015, there has been a new landmark on Lincoln's skyline: the Spire of the International Bomber Command Centre on Bracebridge Heath, at 102 feet high the same length as a Lancaster, walls of names of almost 58,000 personnel killed during World War Two round its base.[13]

Across the county there are air heritage attractions, old control towers, observation posts, vintage Nissen huts, tank traps used in gardens, roads named after famous planes or fliers. In the Marsh village of Manby, there are roads named Vampire and Venom, and the village sign is a Jet Provost. East Lindsey

District Council's office is called Tedder Hall, after the former Air Chief of Staff and weaver of the 'Tedder Carpet,' a method of saturation bombing. There are also scattered plaques marking crash sites. One plane crashed at Ruskington on 11 December 1941, killing a Royal Canadian Air Force pilot on secondment to the RAF—John Gillespie Magee, buried at Scopwick, remembered for his sonnet 'High Flight,' with its exultant opening, 'Oh, I have slipped the surly bonds of Earth...' and transcending ending, 'Put out my hand, and touched the face of God.'[14] But the most famous bombers must be 617 Squadron, Guy Gibson's 'Dam Busters,' who were stationed at Coningsby, trained on The Wash, and drank copiously in the half-timbered, monkey-puzzled, adder-slithered, Surrey-reminiscent ambience of Woodhall Spa.

There are less ethereal military memorials—the firing targets, a turretless Churchill tank on a beach, and the occasional visitations of the Army Ordnance Corps, who close off the beaches with red flags, dig a pit and fill it with time-expired explosives, then detonate the lot by electrical charge. There are also pillboxes from both World Wars, grim concrete protrusions disguised against the dunes or sometimes set dangerously on top, in their stripped-down solidity and narrow gun slits reminiscent of thirteenth-century knights' helmets. This was a front line against more than the sea. This was the *German* Ocean, after all—where Cockneys poked Lee Enfields out over the flats, in case of Wilhelmine shock-troopers or *Kommandos*, and doubtless grumbled and shivered in disgust at their bitter, boring lot. These must have been dismal postings in winter, with easterlies whistling through all apertures, curtains of rain trailing over the dank salt marsh with its cold black ooze and coppery waters, its corpse-reek of disturbed gas.

Never required as fighting stations, and ages ago abandoned, the emplacements still await their country's call, clouded with green, grey and orange lichen, trees sprouting and dying where once heavy machine guns rested in readiness for commands that never came. Some slump, others get yearly more lost in brambles and the sprawling clematis called 'old man's beard,' but they give a chamber-tomb quality to their fields of fire, and frame brilliant vistas as lozenges of light.

* * *

Spring blossom makes the hawthorns brave, and walkers on gusty days are showered with tiny flakes of heroic white, like John Boorman's burnished Arthurian knights riding out in *Excalibur*. The summer sand sprouts samphire, the salt marsh flushes purple with sea lavender, and June's dunes come alive with Aaron's Rod, birds-foot trefoil, cowslips, field scabious, great mullein, ladies' bedstraw, rosebay willowherb, southern marsh orchids, thistle, viper's bugloss and woody nightshade. Rushes bristle and swish in pools, buckthorn, rowans and willows flash silver, and elder trees blanch deathly white.

Ivy insinuates up old buildings, dog roses strive to out-perfume honeysuckle, and delicate flowers of bindweed glow white amongst dark green, luminous as Limoges porcelain. Puffballs swell grotesque in the autumn, and sometimes explode with a *poff* as you watch. In the dunes, and the fields just behind, there is a smell I have never smelt anywhere else—a delightful, peppery aroma, un-analysable, but probably a combination of old, clean waters, new warmth and a bouquet of wild grass and herbs, wafted by the breeze like essence of post-Ice Age meadow, the natural world before we ruined it (or were here to appreciate it).

Inland, you can find chamomile, cuckoo pint, fat hen, groundsel, hemlock, lords and ladies, marsh marigold, scarlet pimpernel, tansy, teasel, watercress, wild barley and wild garlic. Even the commonest plants impress in large quantities, like the knee-deep drifts of buttercup and dandelions that gold the old fields, among which Lincoln Red shorthorns munch dreamily. Rioting ragwort in the dunes hosts thousands of the burnet moth's orange and black caterpillars, an odd colour clash with the red and dark brown adult form. Mare's tails and plantains nod in ditches or along the hard tar-tainted edge of roads, like pictures from children's books about prehistory. Here and there, leviathans stand—alder, ash, lime, sycamore, willow, and even some elms, for some reason escaping the Dutch Elm desolation. In July, when the trees weep nectar, windscreens become tacky, jackets and shoes stain with dust of flowers, and our local lime tree is audible from 20 feet, swarming with thousands of insects.

No-one could ignore the insects, from the showiest butterflies to the smallest moths, the superbly aeronautical dragonflies to the gangling St Mark's Flies that bump into your face trailing their legs, neat mosquitoes to fuzzy, heavy bumble bees, overturned ladybirds awaiting righting, and ticks awaiting the unwitting. Painted Ladies from the continent come here, sometimes passing overhead inland in large groups, to join the Common Blues, fritillaries, Peacocks, Red Admirals, skippers and small tortoiseshells. Butterflies mate in mid-air, and sometimes die in fluttering *flagrante*, in sheer insectasy, spinning out of control to die among tangled vegetation. Dragonflies— normally glistering past so fast you can hear the dryness of their passing—can also occasionally be seen in aerial acts of eroticism, members of the insect Mile High Club, briefly heart-shaped in abdominal conjoinment, before the female peels away to place ova in ponds, her mate soon to expire, switching off like a light in mid-flight. Their hideous young, humorously called nymphs, terrorise the shallow ponds, snatching even minnows with telescopic jaws.

Hummingbird hawkmoths whirr business-like by, headed for our horseradish, more purposeful-seeming than the tiny white moths that flutter feebly about my boots, disturbed from dewy dreams in the dunes—and solider by far than the fairy-like moths that meander around each other in sunbeams slanting through trees, their movements so vague, their antennae so long and fine, that at first you think you're seeing things. The summer garden is busy with yellow-and-brown hoverflies, and cold autumn evenings with gnats the size of full stops. Millipedes labour across paths, mason bees bore in dry sand, grasshoppers *boing* away out of sheer showing-off, and bluebottles clean their eyes on your arm. The undergrowth is sometimes as manically alive as a painting by Richard Dadd, as full of minutely observed, ultimately incomprehensible forms. Out of sight, worms work through layers upon layers of litter, aerating, ingesting and excreting interminably, turning dead larvae and leaves into life, vermiculating vitamins out of trash.

Spiders await, or race out to chase—water spiders in bathyspheres, wolf spiders daring the awful open, jumping spiders pouncing from the shadows, crab spiders pretending they're petals, house spiders weaving shrouds in sheds. In the bathroom, *Pholcid* spiders—the famous 'Daddy long-legs'— shake fascinatedly in the warm droplets from showers, and offer delicate death to coarser arachnids. In the autumn, millions upon millions of minute spiderlings anchor gossamer to grass and cast themselves into space, a Brownian instinct obviously, but maybe also in some miniscule way an elemental sensation akin to Magee's slipping of the surly bonds. In early or late lights, their countless intertwined landlines give a gauzy gleam to grass, and the dullest field looks briefly like the Edwardian idea of Faery.

The multi-legged or belly-crawling banquet is irresistible to embarrassed-looking frogs, jerkily nervous lizards, newts like salamanders from medieval bestiaries, beaded unblinking snakes, and toads which, when we place them back down again, look at us for a long pitying moment before walking away slowly in search of slugs and cleverer company. On warm wet nights they creep across back roads, gulping lumpily in headlights, necessitating frequent stops to lift them out of the way.

Aquatic invertebrates are nourishment for larger invertebrates and little fish, and little fish for large—the Great Chain of Eating from fry to minnow and stickleback, stickleback to bream, golden orfe and perch. At the top of the Piscean pile is the pike, sometimes seen if you stand quietly on a bridge—small sharks of the sweet waters, for the Tory thinker Sir Roger L'Estrange (1616-1704) Hobbesian metaphors for the Great Chain of Being, and the necessity of kingship:

> Now the *Pike* has not only Reason on his side, but Prescription also, and Authority, against the Clamorous Envy of an Impetuous Rabble. And at worst, where arguments cannot prevail, he does himself right by Force, which is a remedy that holds among Men, as well as among Fishes.[15]

Lincolnshire Piscators honour tyrants too. I watched a man pull a pike out of the River Lud, 12 inches of snapping, twisting British racing green and black, who took a gleeful selfie then grinned at me in pride, before carefully cutting away the line, and putting the fish back rather hastily. 'You've got to watch your fingers with those bastards!' he observed. 'But it's always a thrill!' He heaved a sigh of satisfaction and cast his line back out over the waters, an Izaak Walton for the 2020s.

If pikes dream while they hover open-eyed among the other stripes of reed stems, they probably dream of otters—in Lincolnshire still rare, albeit recovering. I have only ever once seen one, a sleek brown side glimpsed for a second slipping under a bank on the Foss Dyke. I live in hope and in the meantime make do with other mammals. Not that these are in any way inadequate. Water voles criss-cross duckweed dykes, their mouths filled with foliage, swimming out of *The Wind in the Willows*, swimming back slowly from almost-extinction. The cat brings in half-masticated mice, shrews and voles, and lays young rats reverently on the back path—kin to those pursued by the white ferret that once darted across the farmyard next door as I glanced out the kitchen window (or was that a cryptid?). The black rabbits I often see in the dunes are definitely not cryptids, but somebody's un-hutched pets passing on recessive genes among the wild warrens. Hares lope or box out in the amphitheatre of air, ear-lifting with meltingly intelligent eyes, one of whom I once encountered right down on the early morning tideline, I don't know to whose greater surprise.

Moles snatch worms unchivalrously from behind, sifters of history which have been known to throw up old coins from 'the long unlooked-for mansions of our tribe.'[16] One once uplifted itself out of the ground right beside me in a field near Alford. Moles are likeable animals, their old English name of 'mouldiwarp' charming even by the standards of old English animal names. William III's horse once stumbled over a molehill in 1702, throwing the king with fatal results, and Jacobites raised glasses to 'The little gentleman in black velvet.' In Robert Burton's *The Anatomy of Melancholy*, the mole is an exemplar of fortitude:

> Comfort thyself with other men's misfortunes, as the mouldi-warpe in Æsope told the fox for complaining of want of a tail. You complain of toies, but I am blind, be quiet.[17]

Bats of two species inhabit our house—pipistrelles (the commonest, smallest kind) above the library, and some larger kind, unidentifiable because of where they dwell in the inaccessible crawl space above the bathroom. As the light thins, they peel out from behind fascia boards and zip away zigzaggedly, at times passing so close you can feel the wind of their wings. There are occasional even closer encounters, when they come in the bedroom window by mistake, on one occasion falling to the floor and clambering up the back of the armchair, a pocket-size pterosaur furry and scratchy to the touch, with warm leather wings, twisting its ugly head in its terrified desire to be away.

Badgers shuffle and snuffle along verges, or trot recklessly across roadways, their humped carcasses sadly familiar sights (and smells)—sad, except perhaps to cattle farmers, crows, and hedgehogs, whose spines avail little against a badger's jaws and paws. Our hedgehog house is always empty—empty, that is, except for walnuts stashed by grey squirrels.

Grey squirrels don't have the twitching delicacy of the reds I knew in Ireland, or once fed by hand in Poland. Thanks partly to Beatrix Potter, the reds are frequently seen as symbols of unspoiled English nature, so much so some conservationists bemoan campaigns to control the numbers of greys.[18] 'Englishmen,' emoted one 1970s expert, 'have been menaced for half a century and more by the American grey squirrel.'[19] The grey squirrel is clearly naturalised, but it is not yet 'nationalised'– regarded as just another part of the national natural environment.

Useful animals like the common carp, fallow deer, pheasants and rabbits—all apparently brought by the Romans—were early embraced into the animal national family. Less useful ones have also been accepted, if long enough present—the house mouse (Iron Age), the black rat (probably twelfth century) and the brown rat (eighteenth century). Other animals may be liked, but never seen as fully 'belonging'—Canada geese (1660s), the little owl (1840s), sika deer and red-necked wallaby (1860s) and ring-necked parakeets (1960s). Animals once present which went extinct are vaguely seen as absent 'family' in national natural consciousness, and arouse powerful emotions when they reappear, are reintroduced, or are being considered for 'rewilding'—beaver, bison, crane, great bustard, lynx, pelican, sea eagle, white stork, wild boar, wildcat, and wolf—when the practical reservations of people like my farmer neighbours war with a widespread public belief that such animals 'belong' by some eco-moral right. Unattractive species whose impact is wholly negative are never likely to be seen as anything other than invasive 'foreigners,' meriting ruthless controls, maybe even extermination—mink (1930s), the coypu (1930s, eradicated by 1989), and signal crayfish (1980s).

No one would however question the 'indigenous' status of some animals—like the dog-fox sitting with his back to me whose ancestors snatch geese on medieval misericords, or the stoat that stared at me for a long moment along the old railway line, before running away to avoid being turned into ermine. The roebuck I saw down a long wood ride, standing on his back legs to crane into a tree's new leaves, could have been copying a manuscript marginale. And the roe hind and two fawns I watched in a barley field one impossibly velvet evening, as she licked her young ones long and lovingly in the full strength of summer while insects rose all round, could have been a monkish parable, a premonition of the peaceable kingdom to come.

All this drowsy, hot and heavy substance—all this beauty and profligacy of life. Could *all* this really just *go*, lost perhaps in a single winter, or even one terrible night of storm? A few hundred yards away from that barley field, the waves that wash across Doggerland whisper a possible answer.

5

TALES FROM THE RIVERBANK

'Swamps of wild rush beds, and slough's squashy traces'
—John Clare, *Song*

<small>CROWLAND—HEREWARD THE WAKE—GILBERT OF
SEMPRINGHAM—TATTERSHALL—FENLAND POETS—SPALDING</small>

North and east of Peterborough, you are in Fenland—lonely,
level, topographically evocative. Once over the Welland, you are
in Lincolnshire, and the 'Slodgers' of the Cambridgeshire and
Norfolk fens have metamorphosed into Yellowbellies.

The larger towns of Lincolnshire's section of the Fens—
Crowland, Market Deeping and Spalding—are interspersed with
names that smell equally of magic and mud. Bicker Haven,
Brotherhouse Bar, Cowbit, Gosberton Cheal, Guthram Gowt,
Hangman's Corner, King John's Farm, Leaden Hall, Lutton
Leam, Moulton Eaugate, New York, Old Guide House, Pode
Hole, Poet's Corner, Potterhanworth Booths, Shepeau Stow,

Snake Hall Fen, Sot's Hole, Tanvats, Timberland Delph, Tydd Gote, Tydd St Mary, Wasp's Nest, Whaplode St Catherine, Whipchicken Farm—the names are almost as fertile as these fields which produce so much of England's food.

The East Midlands agricultural area, which includes all of Lincolnshire except the non-Fenland north and north-east, produces 26% of England's field vegetables, 25% of its oilseed rape, 23% of its sugar beet, 21% of its hardy nursery stock, 20% of its wheat and 20% of its poultry.[1] Lincolnshire by itself is estimated to produce 12% of England's home-grown food, with a total agricultural output of over £2bn in 2019. Food chains provide 24% of jobs in the Greater Lincolnshire area, and 21% of the county's economic output.[2] The Fens are at the heart of this huge agri-endeavour, vital in war and peace.

There is always something going on in these fields—people growing flowers and pick-your-own strawberries, enigmatic 'experimental' or 'innovative' crops (most recently, an onion that apparently doesn't make you cry), gangs of vegetable pickers bending and straightening, sheep on the slightly higher ground where they are less likely to get liver fluke. Cows are rarely seen in the Fens, both beef-rearing and milk production mostly confined to the Marsh, or leaving Lincolnshire altogether, often for huge, intensive facilities in the north-west, where the main markets are closer, and the climate more congenial. Increasingly, Lincolnshire's contribution to the cattle industry is as provider of winter feed, carried cross-Pennines by ponderous trucks bearing Cheshire and Cumbria phone numbers.

From August to early October, the Fens' huge perspectives are pounded by even more impressive machines—hugely costly combines, sometimes co-owned by farms, threading dangerously along often narrow roads on their way to the largest of these larger than usual fields. Some combines can harvest up to 100 tonnes per hour, with under 1% loss, all this mighty efficiency controlled by a tiny man in a padded seat in a lofty cab, monitoring an array of screens. In the slanting lights of the season, the slow-moving combines look like leviathans that have clambered laboriously up onto the land, with their wide churning mouths and plumes of dust behind, accompanied by tractors towing trailers, to catch the grain that courses up from the cutting head and out sideways through a chute. With eyes always on the weather, the combines can be worked into the small hours, gleaning gigantically by powerful lights. Some nights, they could almost work by the dust-stained huge moon that drags tiredly close to the Earth.

Other types of harvesters swim solitarily in the English Saskatchewan, not even stopping as they excrete oblongs of hay, to be picked up later by tractors with prongs, and piled in sweet-smelling, temporary Cubist installations. When these installations are uninstalled for transportation on trailers, horizons look even emptier than they did before, and drivers drop wisps all the way to the yard, and festoon overhanging trees with crisp golden stalks. Yet other harvesters simply cut, and leave crops toppled in lines in fields, like soldiers mown down by Maxims. These fallen are then 'tedded' by small tractors with revolving tines which shake out damp, dirt or insects, and spin them into bales, before taking them away to be wrapped in plastic.

For a few days after the harvesters have gone, the stubbled fields look raw, feel slightly shocked—the only movements crows, pheasants or wood pigeon, prospecting, presumably often vainly, for largesse left behind. But then the old story restarts, and the recurring rhythm is heard again, as other machines move in, to make deep cuts or tyre-chevron marks across the fields, spread manure, pulverise lumpy clay into wonderfully uniform tilth for seeds and a smorgasbord of chemicals. The soil afterwards can seem to sparkle, as if this artscape has been sprinkled with glitter paint, and a chemical smell hangs unpleasantly in the air. This is the antithesis of the Arcadian idea of agriculture, or that of BBC's *Countryfile*—a programme regarded with derision by many farmers, who probably prefer *Clarkson's Farm*. But *Countryfile*'s messages about animal welfare, conservation, local breeds and sustainability do, and must have relevance; agriculture cannot be just a question of maximising yield year on year while the wider environment worsens.

Farming is infinitely easier in many ways than it has ever been, but it is still statistically one of the most dangerous jobs in the UK, in 2021 second only to construction.[3] Farmers need all the padded cab seats and technological aids they can get. The pre-mechanisation injuries of animal bites or trampling, arthritis, backache, bruises, cuts, fever, repetitive strain and rheumatism have been augmented by new ones—joint pains and obesity from sitting for hours in the same position, chemical poisoning, loss of hearing from the constant thrumming of engines, falling from heights and crushing by machinery. Farmers too are often bored and lonely, corollaries of whole afternoons spent alone in cabs, performing the same tasks over and over and over, with just the radio or mobile phone for company. Then when they get home late, there are forms to be filled in, much-needed subsidies to be applied for—and at the end of each year, usually not very much to show for it. All this to feed an often ungrateful, or at least unheeding, nation.

The busyness of the A-routes with their lorries and Skegness- or Hunstanton-bound tourist traffic accentuates the quietude of the smaller roads, which are frequently potholed, narrow and undulating, with difficult to overtake tractors. Some roads are below dyke water level, little Edwardian farm-labourers' cottages overshadowed by menacing embankments. Sometimes you can see the mastheads of yachts above rooflines. Other dykes line up at glittering right angles to the sun, or make mirrored parallelograms in onion fields. Cabbages sit obediently in rows, while huge water sprays play upon their uniform heads. Caravans stand in plastic uniformity in out-of-season parks, their slug-shoulders rounded against the wind, little signs in their windows giving the arguably superfluous information that they contain 'No valuables.'

The spread-out farms look shuttered, suspicious, with signs about CCTV and a security scheme called Farmwatch. One hand-painted sign I saw read 'Privata propertie'—a medieval sentiment expressed in near-medieval orthography. This is wary country, with a high water table of old grudges and resentments, that could lend itself to criminality, real or imagined. Fenland farmers have frustrating and long experience of frequently unpunished crime, from theft to fly-tipping, badger baiting to vandalism.

Badger baiting has been illegal since 1835, and protections were beefed up in 1992 and 2004, but still every year thousands are killed, and very few baiters are caught. Baiting often takes place at night, when huge tranches of the countryside are black, except where lines of lights reveal the presence of some safely distant linear settlement—a place, perhaps, like Deeping St Nicholas, at six miles long England's longest village. The emptiness makes it easy for the 'sportsmen' to see approaching lights, whether a rare police car or, more likely, an irate farmer, wanting to see who's doing what on his land.

The baiters locate the sett, and send a small dog wearing a radio collar down to find the badger, and hold it at bay while they dig down. The dogs often get bitten severely, and this can lead to extra cruelty as their owners don't dare to bring them to vets who might ask awkward questions. Sometimes setts collapse as they are being dug, burying both badger and terrier. The badgers once unearthed are set in a circle so dogs can be set on them—sometimes with large sums gambled on the outcome. Afterwards, all there is usually to see are tyre-tracks and boot-marks, flattened earth, and in the middle the mangled corpse of the unlucky animal, and gobbets of badger (and often dog) blood and soft tissue. Sometimes, the badgers are taken away alive to be sold for hundreds of pounds, for baiting elsewhere.

Hare coursing was only made illegal in 2005, and when legal was long fashionable; it is mentioned in the oldest English book on hunting, *The Boke of St Albans*, written by Juliana Berners in 1486, part of the family after whom London's Berners Street is named. Coursing is carried out in daylight, and some hares do escape. The quarry is easily visible from the long straight roads, and greyhounds or lurchers can be quickly slipped from their leash in a lay-by, while men in baseball hats or flat caps watch the hare's increasingly desperate jinking through binoculars, before the vicious 'ragging' and disembowelling. Some farmers try to trap coursers' vehicles while they call the police, but sometimes this just means opening themselves to physical violence and revenge attacks on their property. Over 1,000 suspected coursing incidents were reported in Lincolnshire between December 2020 and February 2021.[4] It is but fair to note that Lincolnshire Police has a huge area to cover, with limited resources, and most wildlife crimes do not carry sufficiently strong legal deterrents. Now, as often, the writ of law is not always easy to exercise in the edgelands.

* * *

The Fens in the Bronze Ages were a hubbub of activity greatly contrasting with today's unpeopled vistas—densely populated in places, cunningly cultivated and exploited. Excavated middens show they had an unexpectedly exotic diet, including cormorant, goshawk, merganser, pelican and sea eagle. Up-close examinations of unpromising-looking Fen materials reveal stains of significance—the spoor of banks, boats, boundaries, burials, causeways, drove-ways, fish traps, fords, middens and sluices, and even concentrations of phosphates, where 3,000 years ago cows almost as savage as aurochs bespattered manure. Metallic-smelling drainage ditch upcast conveys essence of England-before-England, Britain-before-Britain, Bronze smelting into Iron. The Welland became, or continued as, a tribal boundary, between the Catuvellani of the south bank and the Corieltauvi to the north.

The Romans came, saw and conquered this area easily, but they tended fastidiously to skirt the Fens, their roads to the coast going round a long way to avoid the unclassical and sometimes dangerous topography. No villa sites have been found in the Fens, although in 1965, parts of an impressive Roman bronze ritual diadem were found in Deeping St James, and there are late Roman cemeteries, mostly strongly Christian.

The succeeding 'barbarians' saw it more favourably, already accustomed to such topography in their Netherlandish and North German Plain homelands. They didn't much like towns, so the relative lack of suitable building sites for permanent settlement did not trouble them as much as it probably did the Romans. They did, however, make little villages on what are now called townlands—naturally occurring raised silt banks that protruded sufficiently above the surrounding area to make it worthwhile to erect buildings. Economic life seems to have been more equal than in many other places, with more small farms and fewer large ones, and an emphasis on freeholding.

Their rare roads also followed the natural line of the silts; *sticca*, their name for the slight ridge that linked the site of present-day Boston to the Wolds, survives in the village names Stickford and Stickney. Just east of those lies the lowest land in the East Midlands, a cluster of farms just below sea level, one named Engine Farm, hinting at the endless effort of controlling water.[5] Between the middle of the fifth century and the coming of the Normans, Anglo-Saxons carpentered, drained, dyked, fished, fowled, grew, pastured, reeded, sailed, smithed and turned out rare precious objects, like the Fiskerton pins now in the British Museum,[6] self-reliant but also trading, jealous of their rights.

These practical people also had a strongly mystical side. To some at least, the Fens were not just an everyday landscape, but also a haunted margin territory, a Nightland, an abode of demons—but also a possible refuge. The Fens were a place apart—a suitable place to escape from a world of war, study the strange new Scriptures from the east, find this odd new God peering back at them from the wind-whipped surfaces of pools. The old gods persisted here and there, long co-existing with inconsistent Christianity, bound up with the territory and these ever-more 'English' people's perceptions of their ethnicity— muscle-bound deities for blood and mud, like Weland the Smith, conjured by Paul Kingsnorth in his 2015 Fens-set visionary novel *The Wake*, in which the narrator, Buccmaster of Holland, speaks passionately of a deity who

> ...is in our blud and our land, eald he is ealdor efen that the lost gods under the mere eald he is licc the fenn and the seas.[7]

But Weland's folk-forge was cooling, as Western Europe looked increasingly east. At the forefront of Christianisation were other musclemen, or former musclemen, who had taken the knee to the New Testament, and accepted a personal saviour instead of a tribal protector, and linear rather than cyclical history.

In 697, the monastery of Beardeneu (Bardney), in the Witham valley, was given the relics of one of the doughtiest Christians of the age, Northumbria's King Oswald, who had been killed in 642 at the Battle of Maserfield. The monks of Bardney at first refused to accept the relics, 'because, though they knew him to be a holy man, yet, as he was originally of another province, and had reigned over them as a foreign king, they retained their

1. St James's at Louth

2. Pillbox from the saltmarsh

3. The Alkborough maze

4. The Fens from the churchyard at West Keal

5. Tattershall Castle and church, seen from the banks of the Bain

6. Harlaxton in the rain

7. Crowland Abbey

8. Thornton Abbey gatehouse

9. The Humber Bridge

10. Inner Marsh near Manby

11. Cows in the Marsh

12. Crowland statues

13. A field in the Outer Marsh

14. The *Ross Tiger*—a preserved trawler at Grimsby

15. The Boston Stump, or St Botolph's church, and the River Witham

16. Tattershall Castle and Holy Trinity Church, Tattershall

ancient aversion to him, even after death.' They left the wagon carrying the relics outside the monastery all night, under a tent, only to be chastened when 'a pillar of light, reaching from the wagon up to heaven, was seen by almost all the inhabitants of the province of Lindsey.'[8] They duly changed their minds, washed the bones reverently, and set up a special shrine, surmounted with his banner. The remorseful Abbot decreed that thereafter no traveller should be refused admission, and all locks should be removed—leading to a local saying 'Are you from Bardney?' directed at those who have left a door open.

The shrine speedily became a pilgrimage site—its bones, dust and mere proximity equally efficacious in curing ague and casting out demons. The Mercian King Æthelred abdicated in 704 to become Bardney's Abbot, swapping his temporal crown for one incorruptible.[9] Vikings rowing up the Witham were less awed, destroying the monastery in 870, and killing nearly 300 monks. In 909, King Alfred's son-in-law Edward ordered a cutting out expedition to the abbey's remains, to salvage what remained of the relics, and translate them to their new minster at Gloucester. Bardney was rebuilt by the Normans, and became the centre of a huge 20,000-acre estate, its abbots sitting in Parliament as Lords of Lindsey. A whiff of old reverential habit continued to cling until the Reformation, and six of its monks were condemned to death for their parts in the Lincolnshire Rising. Today's parish church is littered with abbey stones dug up between 1909 and 1912, fragments of a shattered belief system, while the chief whiff over today's village is the smell from the sugar-beet factory.

Another sainted member of the early English Church Militant set his sights further south. Guthlac (c. 674-715), a former soldier from an aristocratic Mercian background, who had spent nine years fighting on the western marches of Mercia, somehow found his way to Crowland in 699, nosing his way through the vast expanses of reeds in a little boat, in search of... who can say?

Perhaps he felt himself moved by forces beyond control; 'The secret spot, empty and desert, uninhabited, stood in God's mind.'[10] According to his biographer Felix, Guthlac had already spent two years in the abbey at Repton, but made himself unpopular because of his abstinence from alcohol. At Crowland, he found himself an ancient burial mound, which had been partly rifled—this sounds too metaphorical to be true—and built himself a cell for contemplation.

But he was not destined to be left alone. The first to come were demons:

> ...ferocious in appearance, terrible in shape with great heads, long necks, thin faces, yellow complexions, filthy beards, shaggy ears, wild foreheads, fierce eyes, foul mouths, horses' teeth, throats vomiting flames, twisted jaws, thick lips, strident voices, singed hair, fat cheeks, pigeon breasts, scabby thighs, knotty knees, crooked legs, swollen ankles, splay feet, spreading mouths, raucous cries.[11]

They 'brought him to the black fen, and threw and sunk him in the muddy waters.' They dragged him through brambles, 'tormented him in darkness,' beat him with iron whips, and 'brought him on creaking wings amidst the cold regions of the air' to show him 'all the north part of heaven as it were surrounded by the blackest clouds of intense darkness.'[12]

On another occasion:

> Suddenly he heard a noise as of a herd of beasts rushing together and approaching his dwelling with a mighty shaking of the earth. Straightway he saw manifold shapes of various monsters bursting into his house from all sides. Thus a roaring lion fiercely threatened to tear him with its bloody teeth: then a bellowing bull dug up the earth with its hoofs and drove its gory horn into the ground; or a bear, gnashing its teeth and striking violently with either paw alternately, threatened him with blows ... the hissing

of the serpent, the lowing of the ox, the croaking of the raven, made harsh and horrible noises to trouble the true soldier of the true God.[13]

Guthlac was 'comforted' by St Bartholomew, who gave him a scourge to help him forget his troubles. The demons were British-speaking, and some have speculated that the demons may merely have been local people trying to drive him out, seen through feverish malarial eyes. Maybe malaria was part of his mystagogy, but Guthlac became venerated for seeing such things: 'Far and wide his wondrous works grew renowned, famed throughout the cities in Britain.'[14] He was also famous for accurate predictions, and swallows would sit on his shoulders and sing. The Mercian prince Æthelbald was just one of many eminent people who wended the watery ways to Guthlac's cell, to consult him on geopolitical and metaphysical matters.

Guthlac died in 715, his last days spent mostly talking to angels.

> Then having eaten the Eucharist, the glorious food, he humbly raised up his hands; likewise, he opened his eyes, the holy jewels of the head; looked then, glad in heart, towards the heavenly kingdom, towards the reward of grace; and then sent forth his spirit, beauteous by its acts, into the joy of heaven.[15]

His soul emerged from his mouth in a beam of light, and with a 'nectar-like odour.' The grieving servant who sailed to tell his equally saintly sister, Pega, who had a hermitage just across the Welland, had a very Fen-like, terraqueous journey:

> The ship sped under the sorrowful man. Hot shone the sky, radiant over the houses. The sea-wood hastened, nimble, quick on its course; the water-horse darted with its cargo to the haven, so that the sea-floater after tossing in the waves, trod on the land, ground on the sand.[16]

Arriving the following day, Pega 'found the island of Crowland filled with the scent of ambrosia.' Was this phantosmia (olfactory hallucination) hers, or Felix's, or everyone's, or is it a vestigial remembrance of a real eighth-century smell on a particularly sensation-filled day? Scent can be the strongest and longest-lasting of all the senses, and perhaps the least likely to be deceived.

Guthlac spoke to Æthelbald in a dream, prophesying that he would accede to the Mercian crown without bloodshed, and Æthelbald replied that he would found an abbey if the prophecy was fulfilled. When he did become king (bloodlessly) in 716, he raised the first of three abbeys that were to stand on the site. It became another hugely popular Fen pilgrimage site, whose reputation for special protection somehow survived an earthquake and three devastating fires.

The Abbey was also famous for its peal of seven bells, which may have been the first to ring out across England, and must have been a cheering as well as talismanic sound across the watery 'wastes'—a guide home, as well as a guardian against evil. Church bells were thought to drive away storms and thunder, demons and unquiet spirits, and peal-ringing is unique to England; one medieval nickname for England was 'the ringing island.' Crowland's bells even had names—Guthlac, Pega, Bartholomew, Bega, Beccelm, Tatwin and Turketyl.[17] There are six bells today, the tenor from 1430, and in 1925 their peal was the first to be broadcast live on the BBC.

The county's bells still feel filled with significance. 'Ring out the false, ring in the true ... Ring out the darkness of the land,' entreated Tennyson in 1833, desolated by the death of Arthur Hallam, desiring a religious rebirth.[18] Dorothy L. Sayers' classic Fens-set 1934 story *The Nine Tailors* was centred on the bells of the village of Fenchurch, opening with Lord Peter Wimsey's car breaking down in a snow storm near a huge chiming church, and culminating in a deadly flood, whose onset is warned of by the same bells, by way of stolen emeralds, murder, bigamy, and the aristocratic sleuth taking a hand at change-ringing. In October 2021, bells clanged across Lincolnshire to draw attention to climate change, the twenty-first century's way of driving away storms and thunder.

The church's most striking feature is the zig-zagged Norman arch of the vanished central tower, alone impressively in the air despite earthquake and fire, a legacy of the Abbey's third incarnation and testament to its architect's skill. The glassless window of the thirteenth century west front of the south aisle frames air, decapitated statues loll against walls, chapels have been demolished, and the light flooding from the west window into the surviving aisle (now the parish church) shows up awkward angles and broken proportions. It is difficult to imagine the Abbey at its thirteenth–fifteenth-century height, epicentre of some fifty estates stretching across Lincolnshire, Cambridgeshire, Huntingdonshire, Leicestershire and Northamptonshire.[19] Some of these manors may have been held fraudulently, because Abbey-loyal scribes forged at least fifteen charters of privileges and possession following the destruction of records in 1091, and incorporated them in histories as fact. Crowland has a reputation for creative writing; the celebrated *Croyland Chronicle*, long ascribed to the twelfth-century century Abbot Ingulf (also William the Conqueror's secretary), is a fifteenth-century forgery.

When the Abbey was dissolved in 1539, it was a massive interruption in an already ancient story, but not quite the end. A manuscript telling the story of Guthlac's life was owned and annotated by John Dee, the Elizabethan mathematician, astrologer and antiquary, and Guthlac is even still sometimes revered by Anglicans with an interest in the Lesser Saints, as well as some Catholics and Orthodox. The site of his cell is still indicated, and a field a mile away, where he first legendarily made landfall, is called Anchor Church Field.

The badly worn statue, usually assumed to be Christ holding the orb of the world, which probably once adorned the Abbey was re-erected on the apex of the Trinity Bridge—Crowland's other unique landmark, a steeply pitched, cobbled, triangular bridge that used to straddle two brooks—during the eighteenth century. By then it was no longer an object of reverence, but just a curio, matily English rather than majestically remote. Too familiar, perhaps; in 1925, the rector wrote irritably in the church guide:

> In spite of anything that may be said to the contrary, let it be said for once and for all that the statue does NOT represent Oliver Cromwell with a penny loaf.[20]

*　　*　　*

Another famous piece of Crowland writing is the twelfth-century *Gesta Herewardi*, purportedly written by Leofric of Bourne—the first to set out the deeds, or claimed deeds, of Hereward Leofricsson, the Mercian nobleman mythologised as 'Hereward the Wake.' The Wake was legendary leader of the gallant but doomed Anglo-Saxon resistance to the Normans, an English icon whose exploits may have helped inspire the stories about that other English outlaw, Robin Hood.

According to the *Gesta*, Hereward was a restive *thegn* with modest estates in southern Lincolnshire, a tenant of Peterborough Abbey. Outlawed by Edward the Confessor, he warred and had other adventures in Cornwall, Flanders, Ireland and the North, including rescuing a princess and killing a monstrous bear with a human head. Returning to Lincolnshire, he found the Normans had confiscated the family estates and murdered his brother. He killed fifteen of them in revenge while they were scorning English valour at a feast. He then waged a long and sometimes successful guerrilla war against the invaders—including unhorsing the Conqueror himself; the Normans' deadliest weapon, their cavalry, was always at a disadvantage in boggy terrain. He and allied Danes raided Peterborough Abbey, allegedly to save the foundation's treasures from the Normans. (The twelfth-century *Peterborough Chronicle* notes wryly that these treasures never came back from Denmark.)

The Normans were outraged by these insults to their prestige, and besieged his forces in Ely in 1071. They took the town eventually through treachery, after less successful strategies, including witchcraft; a witch bared her bottom repeatedly at the town from a wooden tower, until the shocked Hereward had her burnt down. But Hereward got away into the Fens, to carry on a hunted and wandering existence. The *Gesta* claims he negotiated with William and died in peace. Geffrei Gaimar's twelfth-century *Estoire des Engleis* ('The History of the English') maintains that he made peace with William, then entered his service as a warrior, before being murdered by jealous Norman knights. A modern historian, Peter Rex, suggests he may have gone into exile overseas.[21]

These are colourful stories, but they have a factual basis. There was a real 'Hereweard,' attested in the *Domesday Book* as having held the equivalent of 240 acres in and around Bourne, before absconding because 'he had not held to the agreement.' 'Agreement' in the context of the Conquest sounds not unlike 'extortion,' and whatever the true nature of this transaction, a legend grew of a native-born natural leader cheated out of his rights by cruel foreigners, forced into exile and rebellion.

The story has always been partly wish-fulfilment, a means of expiating English embarrassment at the apparent ease with which the country was overthrown by fewer than ten thousand invaders, in a single afternoon at Senlac. The Wake family who 'inherited' his estates claimed descent from his daughter, but it is also possible they simply gave Hereward their own surname as his soubriquet to legitimise their ownership and signify their metamorphosis from Norman to Early English. In his lifetime, and for at least a century afterwards, Hereward was never referred to as 'the Wake,' but rather 'the Outlaw,' 'the Exile' or simply a *vir strenuus* ('hard man'). The Wakes puffed up his pedigree to aggrandise their own, making him the son of Leofric, Earl of Mercia, and Lady Godiva, an icon in her own right. (Godiva's brother was the founder of Spalding Priory.) They were successful, the Wakes cascading down through subsequent high level history; Richard II's mother Joan was a Wake from Bourne, as well as the 'Fair Maid of Kent.'

Unreliable medieval accounts were eventually augmented by unreliable nineteenth-century accounts, when Hereward made it into Thomas Bulfinch's 1855 classic *The Age of Fable*, and a hugely popular novel, *Hereward the Wake, or Last of the English*, by Charles Kingsley. For Kingsley, The Wake—bluff, brave, determined—exemplified the 'Teuton' type, as opposed to the less English 'Roman,' and a symbol of 'ancient liberties.' Hereward acquired a sword named Brainbiter, a fabulously fast (if ugly) horse called Swallow, rivalrous love interests, and a vocabulary derived from Victorian drawing-room ideas of how a regrettably unpolished but naturally chivalrous eleventh-century national progenitor might have spoken:

> 'I know' said Hereward, 'that the French look on us English monk-made knights as spurious and adulterine, unworthy of the name of knight. But, I hold, and what churchman will gainsay me?—that it is nobler to receive sword and belt from a man of God, than from a man of blood like oneself'.[22]

The following century, Hereward would become a *Boy's Own* comic hero, a Pink Floyd song reference, a Peterborough radio station, and a storyline in *Doctor Who*. Paul Kingsnorth's 2015 novel *The Wake* gives a notably original twenty-first century reimagining of a home-grown hero, an assured autochthon amid a swirling sea of ecocide and ethnic cleansing.

Fen life seems often to have been mercifully monotonous, the region largely bypassed by big events, the endless slog of agriculture, drainage, fishing, fowling, salt-making and wool interspersed by flooding. In toilsome conditions—one road near Billinghay is wearily called Labour in Vain Drove—Fen farmers grew cereals, flax, hops and woad on clinging soils, and raised livestock which had a national reputation—geese, sheep, sturdy horses, pigs, fat beef cows and famously powerful draught oxen. There were disagreements and discontents, and agricultural prices fluctuated, as they always do, often bringing real hardships even to some knightly families, whose fees (incomes) were increasingly unequal to the military expenditure expected of them.

But by the fourteenth century, the wool trade was creating fortunes across Lincolnshire either directly, or indirectly through trade. By 1334, Holland was the wealthiest part of the East Midlands.[23] Even the Black Death (and other plague outbreaks) may not have made all that much difference to larger patterns, at least at Crowland:

> ...although the Black Death undoubtedly carried off a large proportion of the population, yet the number of holdings left on the lord's hands was remarkably small, and the majority of vacant plots was taken up immediately by new tenants [often with the same surnames] on the ancient conditions.[24]

The Hundred Years' War (1330s–1450s) was a longer-lasting problem, and the precipitous falling away of trade coincided with major floods and the silting up of east coast harbours. Bicker, a major port, saw its famous Haven dry up and shrink, and now the village is eight miles from open water—the outline of its former prosperity traceable only in the serpentine roads that follow the old waters.

There were reliefs to the monotony, in feuds, financial scandals like breaking usury laws, libels and scandals, often caused by women, for whom their husbands were legally responsible. 'The position of women in medieval law was favourable to the virago, if humiliating to her sex as a whole,' notes Frances Page wryly, noting the story of Margery Sarre versus Robert Stirmy, who was obliged to defend his wife Alice, who had allegedly wounded Sarre with 'a certain fork' and 'a certain stone.' But men could make trouble all by themselves: solemn inquests constantly being gathered to hear tales of petty thefts, rude names, fisticuffs and knife wounds, knocked-out teeth, and villeins rolling angrily together on the ground.[25] There were continual squabbles over animals, boundaries and drainage, with Crowland, Deeping St James and Spalding engaging in sporadic sabotage of each other's dykes and land markers, and rustling livestock.

There were also timeless festivities and games, which continued into the seventeenth century at least in the remoter parts of the Fens, despite the efforts of Puritans (who got maypoles banned in Lincoln as early as 1580) and the likely irritation of many landowners. In 1601, the now inconsiderable hamlet of South Kyme had a 'Summer Lord of August,' the son of a prosperous yeoman, who rode around local villages with a twelve-strong escort including flag-bearers, drummers, and guards carrying reeds with painted paper heads to look like spears. Celebrations of this kind could go on for days, with drinking, dancing, feasting, races, and plays on the village green—all part of an ancient ritual calendar, which although still semi-pagan, for centuries benefited from the shrewd indulgence of the Church.[26]

Such martial mock-ups must have been informed by the exploits of landlords like the Umfravilles, nationally famous as brutally effective Scots-fighters; Robert de Umfraville (d. 1436) was nicknamed 'Robin Mendmarket' by the Scots because of the thoroughness with which he once emptied and burnt the town of

Peebles. One of Anthony Powell's recurring characters in his novel-sequence *Dance to the Music of Time* is one Dicky Umfraville—horsy, witty and womanising, capable of enormous charm but with a suggestion of 'madness' about him, as if not under complete control. Medieval knights must have been a little like this—clever, restless, violent at the drop of a gauntlet. Powell always had an interest in Lincolnshire history, and was very proud that his mother was descended from the Dymoke family of Scrivelsby, the hereditary King's Champions of England. Was he thinking of Kyme's truculent knights when he christened this enigmatic person?

There were also more religious visionaries to lend subfusc significance to the scenery. Gilbert of Sempringham was born around 1083, unluckily with a 'repulsive physical deformity' which unfitted him for his (Norman knight) father's profession of arms, and made him a figure of fun even to the servants. As a child, he was so eager to become a priest that he would gather large numbers of children at the riverside and ask them whether they were christened. If not, he '...made his fellows, as if in a game, to make the child naked, and so dip him thrice in the water, he standing sadly and saying the very words of baptism.'[27] He studied in France, and when he came back his father had got over his disappointment sufficiently to present him with the livings of two new-built churches, one in his home village.

This was the genesis of the Gilbertine Order, founded around 1131, the only monastic order ever founded by an Englishman, which at the time of his death had thirteen houses, containing 700 canons and 1,300 nuns. Gilbertines were required to show charity, chastity, humility and obedience, and their daily diet was to consist of coarse bread, 'two messes of pottage, and a draught of water, and nothing more.' Their garments and bedding were required to be 'mean,' and they were furthermore promised 'much watching and labour, and very little rest.'[28] This was the kind of prospectus the age found irresistible.

Gilbert was a strong supporter of Thomas à Becket against Henry II, helping him get away to France in 1164. When the king's justices summoned Gilbert to account for this, Gilbert stoutly responded that it had been his duty as a churchman to help his Archbishop. Impressed by his courage, and mindful that the Englishness of his order meant that no revenues needed to be sent to Rome, both Henry and Queen Eleanor grew to honour Gilbert, and protected him when necessary. When he died in 1189, apparently aged 106, the Order was suddenly shockingly headless, although his passing was serene:

> The last day of his temporal life, when all were out of the house, he sat by the bedside, he that was successor in his office, taking heed at him what he would command. And after he had long been still in silence as man who should soon pass, he no man seeing, no man hearing, but with the Holy Ghost replete, thus spake in the ghost.[29]

In 1202, Gilbert was canonised by Pope Innocent III, at the request of King John and the English Church. The order, which at its height would have twenty-five houses, inevitably became compromised, even during Gilbert's lifetime, and had its share of scandals. In the 1280s, Gilbertine priories were co-opted into brutal state policy, used by Edward I as places to sequester Welsh princesses, to ensure they could never have children. Enforced 'tonsuring' of potential rivals for thrones was a tradition that went back at least to Charlemagne.

The most famous of three princesses taken was Gwenllian ferch Llywelyn (1282-1337), only child of the last native prince of Wales, Llywelyn ap Gruffudd, and Eleanor de Montfort. Edward I had been at Llywelyn's and Eleanor's wedding in 1278, but by 1282 they were no longer on visiting terms. Llywelyn was murdered on Edward's orders, and his daughter spirited away at just a few months old to Sempringham, never to emerge. Since 1996, there has been a monument to her near the church, the original cairn replaced with a Welsh granite boulder, bearing a tablet of Welsh slate.

Perhaps Gwenllian would have had an even worse time had she not been sent to Sempringham. It is nevertheless poignant to think of the exile whiling away fifty-four years in such conditions and always subject to special watchfulness, in this utterly un-Welsh setting, never knowing her parents or how to spell her own name, or even who she was until late in life (perhaps that was a mercy?). But the Order's chief problems were always financial, indulgence by several kings, a consequence of both poor management and geopolitical-theological isolation, a prime example to Reformers of the impossibility of monastic life. All Gilbert's great efforts proved ultimately to have been 'spake in the ghost.'

* * *

Ralph Cromwell built not just a castle at Tattershall, but also a church and almshouses that give the 2020s churchyard a hint of real 'ancient Peace.' Cromwell, a veteran of Agincourt and now Lord Treasurer to Henry VI, refurbished a 1230s castle in monumental 1430s style—one of the 'happy few,' making a flamboyant seigneurial flourish for an age besotted with chivalry and heraldry. The plum-red gatehouse and 110-feet keep loom improbably out of the River Bain's flatlands like a point on a ley line linking Boston with Lincoln. From the Bain's bank, the castle and church can look like an intact late medieval landscape, towers rising out of rustling reeds—an effect marred by the busy A153, and the whine of jet skis from a holiday park. By the twentieth century, the castle was being used as a cattle byre. The fireplaces almost ended up in America—there was talk of taking the entire building—until Lord Curzon of Kedleston stepped in in 1912, to buy it for the National Trust. Tattershall's graceful church feels more alive, thanks to the ladies who keep the church open for today's pilgrim-tourists, selling teas and cakes, and plants from their gardens. The church's sixty-plus windows, once famously ornate, are now almost completely colourless, giving a conservatory effect on sunny days. Sun would sparkle on splendid fifteenth and sixteenth brasses, except these need to be covered over, because of the acidic effects of bat droppings. But the sun *can* reach another monument, with a strange and tiny claim on English literature.

In the middle of the nave is a small rectangular stone, incised 'T. Thumb Aged 101 Died 1620.' The story of Tom Thumb, thumb-sized son of a labourer in the days of King Arthur, who is swallowed by a cow, carried off by a raven, vomited by a giant, hangs things on sunbeams, and eventually dies of a spider bite, is alluded to in Tudor times, although his first surviving print appearance, written by 'R.I.,' dates from 1621.[30] 'R.I.' could have been Richard Johnson (1573-1659?), author of other once-widely read romances like *The Most Pleasant History of Tom a Lincolne* and *The Seaven Champions of Christendom*. The diminutive folk-hero, who links British, Christian and Norse miracle-stories to writers like Ben Jonson, Michael Drayton and Henry Fielding,[31] has long been associated with Lincolnshire, with a tradition he had been buried at Lincoln.[32] His Lincoln tombstone has disappeared, unless this is the same stone, transported here by some humourist. The script on the stone looks right for the 1620s, and perhaps it is—the striking name and size just happening to stick in the mind of 'R.I.'—a case of euhemerism, when myths become attached to real people.

Fen literature frequently surprises. Robert Mannyng (*c.* 1288-1338), from Bourne, was probably the first poet to write in

English as we know it. His *Handling Synne* of 1303 was a translation from a French original, like his other major work, *Chronicle of England*—but what he lacked in originality he made up in poetic freedom and lack of affectation. *Handlyng Synne* deals with conventional morality, but he improves enormously on the colourless originals. What is more important is that he wrote for *English* readers, of no or little education, using vivid stories to drive home morals:

> Haf I alle in myn Inglis layd, / In symple speche as I couthe, / Þat is lightest in mannes mouthe.

Kenneth Sisam, the historian of the fourteenth century, calls *Handlyng Synne* 'the best picture of English life before Langland and Chaucer.'[33]

The most famous of Mannyng's stories is that of the Dancers of Colbek, about twelve 'fools' who danced and sang in a churchyard, and enticed the priest's daughter, Aue, to dance with them. The priest orders them to stop—'Karolleþ no more, for Crystys awe!'—but they ignore him, so he curses them to dance for a year. In obedience they do, but Aue dances away with them. The priest sends his son after them to rescue her, but when he takes her by the arm, 'Þe arme for Þe body wente,' while her body dances on. The grieving son brings the detached arm back to the priest, and the priest realises he has cursed himself. 'He toke hys doghtyr arme forlorn / And byryed hyt on Þe morn,' but every morning the arm is found lying on top of the grave. The daughter and her father both die, and the Emperor sets the arm in a vessel in the church 'Þat alle men myȝt se hyt and knawe.'

At another end of the poetic spectrum are two rectors of Coningsby, Tattershall's contiguous neighbour. Laurence Eusden was rector here between 1725 and 1730, a rare distinction for a little Fen town, as he was also Poet Laureate. But Eusden was also a figure of fun, featuring in Pope's *Dunciad* as a drunken parson and in Swift as the personification of bathos, the awfulness of his oeuvre perhaps only tolerable at the famously uncultured courts of Georges I and II. Today, he features occasionally in satirical books, remembered affectionately for two lines of his 'Coronation Ode' for George II—

Thy virtues shine peculiarly nice / Ungloomed by confinity to vice.

The other poetical parson connected to Coningsby is John Dyer, installed here in 1755, but who died just two years later, his tuberculosis probably worsened by the air. He had just published 'The Fleece,' an ambitious poem about sheep husbandry, one of many instructive poems that convulsed eighteenth-century London literary circles. Samuel Johnson scoffed about 'The Fleece,' 'The subject, Sir, cannot be made poetical. How can a man write poetically about serges and druggets?'

Dyer could be a good poet, admired by Wordsworth, and was besides following the example of eminent authors, including Virgil, who had written about sheep diseases and manure. But 'The Fleece' *does* have a comic quality:

> *In cold stiff soils the bleaters oft complain*
> *Of gouty ails, by shepherds termed the halt:*
> *Those let the neighbouring fold or ready crook*
> *Detain: and pour into their cloven feet*
> *Corrosive drugs, deep-searching arsenic*
> *Dry alum, verdigris, or vitriol keen.*[34]

Happily, the animals are grateful to share their wool with us:

> *As the sleek ram from green to green removes, On aiding wheels his heavy pride he draws, And glad resigns it to the hatter's use.*[35]

They seem suitable residents for this quirky combined town, with its overflying jets, one-handed church clock (the largest in the world, with a face of 16½ feet) and the crude plaster head over the archway of the Fortescue Arms, supposedly a representation of 'Tiger Tom,' an unusually violent early nineteenth-century robber. Outside the town is the Leagate Inn, the last standing Fen watch house, part sixteenth century, still with the iron bracket where a lantern was hung to guide night travellers across the uncertain terrain. Tiger Tom would have known the Leagate light; perhaps sometimes he drank in that pub, sizing up prospects.

Another poet didn't care for the Fen air either—Paul Verlaine, who spent some of 1875 teaching French and drawing at a highly respectable Protestant school in Stickney. This was an unlikely billet for a flamboyant, mercurial bisexual, who had been sympathetic to the Paris Commune, had just spent two years in prison for shooting his lover Arthur Rimbaud, and was now showily Catholic. But the poet liked the people of Stickney, and even their food. He lived quietly, reading deeply, and walking across the Fens with his pupils. He drew a caricature of himself in Lincolnshire mode, a figure in a tall hat and a pipe in his mouth, clambering over a fence. 'My life is madly calm,' he wrote to a friend, 'and I am so happy in it! I am horribly in need of calm.' His hostess, the schoolmaster's wife Mrs Andrews, remarked later 'While Mr Verlaine was living with us, I did not know he was such a great poet.'[36]

But he was working on poems at Stickney, and while still in England published his famous collection *Sagesse*, which included Catholic poems, but was also influenced by local music:

À Stickney, Verlaine écrira plusieurs poèmes de Sagesse et d'Amour, et sera sensible à la beauté des hymnes anglicanes.[37]

He was also desperately pining for Rimbaud. The last letter he ever sent Rimbaud was sent from Stickney that December, to which he never received a reply. In need of money, he moved to Boston in the spring of 1876, in the hope of obtaining what he called 'lessons at people well off's.' He and his visiting mother lodged with an Italian photographer in the town, who had a sideline 'museum' of natural curiosities, including a whale's skeleton.

> At Verlaine's suggestion, they emulated Jonah by placing a table and chairs inside the whale's belly and spending their leisure hours there over a glass of beer and a pipe.[38]

Other Fen literature has a darker tone. M. R. James' 1895 story 'Lost Hearts,' set in Aswarby near Sleaford, tells the story of a nineteenth-century alchemist who murders and disembowels children to attain immortality. Robert Aickman and Elizabeth Jane Howard both wrote supernatural stories about eastern England's inland waterways, Aickman particularly committed to this environment as a co-founder of the Inland Waterways Association. Howard was probably introduced to the Fens by her husband, Peter Scott.

L. P. Hartley's 1964 novel *The Brickfield* is set in a town called Fosdyke (not to be confused with the village near The Wash), where a lonely boy embarks on a passionate affair that ends when his girl is found drowned in a brick-pit. Graham Swift's 1983 *Waterland* declares the Fens are 'a landscape, which of all landscapes, most approximates to Nothing.' That 'Nothing,' however, has room for abortion, incest, kidnap, mental illness, murder—and eels. Daisy Johnson's 2016 *Fen* combines drainage, folklore, female sexuality and animal-human hybrids. Even John Gordon's children's books, *The Giant Under the Snow* (1968), *The House on the Brink* (1970) and *The Fen-Runners* (2009), are profoundly unsettling—his characters separately realising that terrible forces lie just under the quiet and ordered earth, like waters always on the cusp of breaking through.

*   *   *

By the 1530s there were different winds howling across the Fens, new religious cloud-kingdoms. Economies were altering, old tiers were tired, and the universities were filled with intellectual ferments as urgent as Henry VIII's craving for a son. That eventual son, Edward VI, had a strong Fen-born ally, East Kirkby boy Thomas Goodrich, who as compiler of the *Book of Common Prayer* and Edward's Lord Chancellor was powerfully instrumental in bedding down the Reformation.

The Gilbertines were dissolved without protest in 1538–39, as Thomas Cromwell's commissioners made visitations throughout the Fens, carrying their conclusions with them. They left a trail of devastation at places like Sempringham, where the priory stones were taken by the carpetbagging Edward Fiennes de Clinton—later Elizabeth I's Lord High Admiral, then first Earl of Lincoln—to build himself a huge house (itself now gone). The ruin of Barlings Abbey is almost Ozymandian, where a section of west wall stands stolidly among milk thistles, longhorn cattle and the lumps of former fishponds, in outline like an Assyrian lion. High up on the wall and on its edge, a stone man seems stuck in eternal outrage, his mouth forever open as if howling at all this sacrilege and sky.

There were lucky survivals, like at Kirkstead's church of St Leonard, where there is some of the oldest woodwork in England, and one of its earliest military memorials, to the second Lord Tattershall, who died around 1212—a powerfully impersonal effigy wearing a cylindrical flat-topped helmet, a sinister long slit for his eyes. The effigy's robotic menace is augmented by the fact that the helmet has no breathing holes, which were only introduced in 1225.

The disappearance of the monasteries and the rise of new and often unscrupulous landowners heralded radical changes. The Crown became a major landowner in Lincolnshire, and common lands started to be enclosed. There was legislation in 1548 aimed at regulating livestock, fishing, the mowing of fodder, and the cutting of reeds. In 1601, Queen Elizabeth passed the General Drainage Act for 'the recovering of many hundred thousand Acres of marshes, and other Grounds...' But the 'Undertakers' who went into these areas to actualise her aims found Royal writ did not run far in the Fens. James I had no more luck. But his son Charles was more determined. Much of the anti-Royalist sentiment that suffused the Fens during the Civil War was a consequence of Charles I's large-scale drainage schemes.

The Fens' chief Civil War battlefield was Crowland, although there were frequent skirmishes along the Nene and Welland. In March 1643, there was a rumour that Royalists were about to declare Crowland for the king. A minister from Spalding wrote to the town to dissuade them, only for him and three elderly colleagues to be abducted and taken to Crowland as hostages. When the Parliamentarians besieged the hastily fortified town, the four captives were tied to stakes and placed up on the ramparts, where they were lucky not to be hit. When they realised the Godly identity of this human shield, the Parliamentarian forces withdrew—but returned the following month with artillery. The town fell in April, but had to be evacuated twice the following year. Royalists took the town once more, but were eventually starved into surrender.

After the war, talk about drainage resumed. The Fens were the last large and largely wild landscape in lowland England, and their people notoriously independent-minded. This was intolerable to the Augustan sensibility that started to emerge after the Civil War, which emphasised efficiency, progress and rationality. As the century went on there was increasing pressure to 'tame' this recalcitrant region. There was also a Calvinist notion that these Fenlanders with their irregular habits were idle and improvident, living in a morass of the soul as well as soil.

Newer forms of agriculture started to appear, interspersed with ancienter arts. When Daniel Defoe passed through in the 1720s, he looked upon the Fens with an appraisingly mercantile eye typical of that period. He enthused about drainage pumps, hemp planting, and the carriage of live fish by cart, but was really fascinated by duck decoying. The trained decoy ducks, he marvelled, '...fail not to let [foreign ducks] know ... that the English ducks live much better than they do.' This enticed them to migrate to England to be taken. That done, the 'traytor' decoy ducks go 'fearless' to the decoyman and are 'strok'd, made much of, and put into a little pond just by him, and fed and made much of for their services.'[39]

Aristocrats like the Monsons and the Earls of Stamford, who stood to benefit from enclosure and drainage, lobbied tirelessly until, finally, the Witham Act of 1762 decreed the construction of a new Grand Sluice at Boston. This blocked the incoming tide and allowed millions of gallons of standing water pumped from the fields to be pushed out at low water. Water control became increasingly coordinated, a matter for the state rather than individual landowners, and so it has remained. Modern Lincolnshire is covered by eleven independent internal drainage boards—Black Sluice, Isle of Axholme & North Nottinghamshire, Lindsey Marsh, North East Lindsey, North Level, South Holland, Upper Witham, Welland & The Deepings, Witham First, Witham Third, Witham Fourth—with the Environment Agency responsible for larger rivers and sea defences.

Locals resented not just their losses of income and traditional rights, and access to once-common land, but also customs like stilt walking or ice skating across washes that no longer flooded and froze in winter. The agronomist Arthur Young was sympathetic, but felt it would redound to their benefit:

So wild a country nurses up a race of people as wild as the fen; and thus the morals and the eternal welfare of numbers are hazarded or ruined for want of enclosure.[40]

By now, a dangerous wider war was going on, England at times alone against Napoleon, and there was a dire need for home-grown foodstuffs. In 1803, the first President of the Board of Agriculture set the bucolic-bellicose tone:

Let us not be satisfied with the liberation of Egypt or the subjugation of Malta. Let us subdue Finchley Common; let us conquer Hounslow Heath, let us compel Epping Forest to submit to the yoke of improvement.[41]

The Fens too found themselves under patriotic-economic-scientific, and then just economic-scientific, bombardment, and were increasingly subjugated, as William Cobbett discovered:

The whole country as *level* as the table on which I am now writing. The horizon like the sea in a dead calm: you see the morning sun come up just as at sea; and see it go down over the rim in just the same way as at sea in a calm. The land covered with beautiful grass, with sheep lying about upon it as fat as hogs stretched out sleeping in a stye. Everything grows well here: earth without a stone so big as a pin's head; grass as thick as it can grow on the ground; immense bowling-greens separated by ditches; and not the sign of a dock or thistle or other weed to be seen.[42]

Cobbett noted only one deficiency, 'the want of singing birds,' which he did not realise was intimately connected with the aforesaid lack of docks or thistles—a connection even now not fully realised in the Fens.

Cobbett had been appalled by the poverty he had witnessed at Holbeach, yet at Crowland his observations were gentled:

Everything taken together, here, in Lincolnshire, are more good things than man could have the conscience to ask of God.[43]

The American poet Robert Lowell later gave Cobbett's Crowland observations a more cutting, even ominous, inflection, in his 1946 poem 'The Fens', describing the 'rack renting system' and bailiffs belying these 'good things.' Another poet, John Clare saw suffering, suffered himself, as he endlessly tramped the country between Peterborough and Stamford in search of work and inspiration, and watched in sadness as the Fens became regimented:

> *…Gain mars the landscape every day—*
> *The meadow grass turned up and copt,*
> *The trees to stumpy dotterels lopt,*
> *The hearth with fuel to supply*
> *For rest to smoke and chatter bye;*
> *Giving the joy of home delights,*
> *The warmest mirth on coldest nights.*
> *And so for gain, that joy's repay,*
> *Change cheats the landscape every day…*[44]

Clare was a poet of both place and displacement, who took uncomplicated pleasure in places, and the little animals that lived in them—creatures as inoffensive as he was, as overshadowed by the future. On one occasion, he wandered over the Welland into Market Deeping, and unburdened himself to a stationer, J. B. Henson. Henson saw merit and commercial possibility in his poems, and in 1818 advertised for subscribers to crowd-fund his find. He portrayed Clare as an unspoiled son of the soil, a poetical poster-boy for an age in search of 'authenticity.' Clare's poems were, he said, to be seen in their class context, 'in the humble situation which distinguishes their author.'[45] As a result, Clare was taken up by a Stamford publisher, and launched onto the London literary scene and Parnassian perpetuity.

Ever-growing tameness may also have had the effect of driving away some ardent spirits, like Donington's Matthew Flinders, who with George Bass of Aswarby, surveyed the coasts of Australia and Tasmania in what Flinders called 'a fever of discovery.' Maybe the example of the Fens' 'colonisation' even fuelled their belief in imperialism as beneficent as well as necessary.

Flinders, the son of a surgeon, was induced to go to sea by reading *Robinson Crusoe*, and served on the *Bellerophon* and *Reliance*, and as a midshipman under the famous Captain Bligh. He saw naval action on the 'Glorious First of June' (1 June 1794), and tribal warfare in the Torres Strait. He and Bass together explored Botany Bay in Bass' little boat, the *Tom Thumb*, and established the existence of the strait between Australia and Tasmania that now bears Bass's name. Flinders went on to circumnavigate and make the first inshore survey of the whole Australian coast. He also popularised the name Australia, as a more convenient way of referring to New Holland, New South Wales and Van Diemen's Land (Tasmania).

Bass was the son of a farmer who qualified as a ship's surgeon at eighteen. As well as his coastal explorations with Flinders, he gathered natural history specimens and corresponded with Joseph Banks, and tried to be the first Englishman to cross the Blue Mountains, forty miles inland from the new city of Sydney. Tiring of the naval life, he dabbled in trade, and was one of the first to bring Merino sheep to Australia, simultaneously establishing one of Australia's most important industries and spelling long-term ecological disaster for much of the continent's interior. Bass was discharged from the Navy and returned to England by way of Canton. He got married, then soon after set sail again on a marathon trading trip from Brazil to Australia via Tahiti. He left Australia on 5 February 1803 on an even longer trip—fishing and sealing around New Zealand, then to Chile to fetch farm animals to be brought back to Australia—and was never seen again.

Both Bass' and Flinders' names are attached to numerous Australian landmarks and institutions, from hills and roads to administrative divisions and even an Anglican College. Flinders is also remembered with gratitude for the Flinders bar, an iron oblong inserted into a compass binnacle to counteract the ship's own magnetism, and so aid course-keeping. Although European settlement of Australia is now often decried, Bass and Flinders seem to have escaped censure thus far—possibly because Flinders at least was noted for liberal racial attitudes, on one occasion defusing a dangerous situation by whipping out some scissors and treating hostile Aborigines to a haircut.

He seems generally to have been likeable as well as highly capable. In April 1802, he met the French captain Nicolas Baudin in what is now called Encounter Bay in South Australia. Baudin was travelling in the opposite direction around the coast, surveying for Napoleon. So far as both commanders knew, England and France were still at war—the Treaty of Amiens had been signed the previous month, but news had not got through to their ships—and it speaks well of both captains that this rendezvous went off peacefully.

Flinders was even liked by cats, with an inseparable pet named Trim, with whom he travelled thousands of miles between England and Australia, and underwent shipwreck, capture by the French and six years' imprisonment on Mauritius. Trim was allowed to roam the island while his master was imprisoned, and when one day he did not come back, Flinders was so woebegone he wrote a little book, *Trim: Being the True Story of a Brave Seafaring Cat*.

Flinders got home, but his health had been compromised, and he died in London in 1814, aged just forty. His headstone vanished during the expansion of Euston Station in the 1840s, leading to a long-standing myth that he was buried under Platform 15. Then his remains were rediscovered sensationally in 2021 during the digging of the HS2 rail link, and there is an ongoing campaign to have these reinterred at Donington. He and his wife Ann, whom the eugenicist Sir Francis Galton described as having 'above average mental powers,' had a daughter called Anne, who married a civil engineer called William Petrie. Their son became the renowned Egyptologist Sir William Flinders Petrie, called the 'Father of Archaeology'—a satisfying conjunction of stars, and two complementary kinds of inquisitiveness.

*　*　*

Sir Joseph Banks (1743-1820) was yet another wanderer on wild shores, both literally and metaphorically, and one of the world's most important botanists.

Banks' father had been a Sheffield attorney, so successful that in 1714 he purchased a huge family house at Revesby, near Coningsby. Banks lived here from the age of two until he was sent up to Harrow, Eton and Oxford, and started to take an interest in botany. In 1761, he inherited the estate. Five years later, he went on a voyage to Newfoundland and Labrador to collect botanical and other specimens. Between 1768 and 1771, he travelled with Captain Cook aboard the *Endeavour*—which cost him £10,000 in expenses—to view the transit of Venus, and visit Java, Tahiti, New Zealand and New Holland. He liked Tahiti so much that when he returned he erected Tahitian hut-style follies at Revesby (sadly gone, like his house), although the house has been replaced by a fine nineteenth-century edifice designed by William Burn.'

He brought back with him over a thousand specimens of plants previously unknown in the West, including acacia and eucalyptus. In 1772, he was the first Englishman to make a scientific trip to Iceland. By now, his reputation as botanist had reached royal ears, and he became (unpaid) scientific adviser at the Royal Gardens at Kew, and provided many of its specimen trees. In 1778, he was elected President of the Royal Society, and remained so for forty-one years, shaping the course of British science for half a century.

Banks was omnivorous in his interests, voluminous in his correspondence, and generous with his money and time. He was just as much interested in the remains of Doggerland, fen drainage schemes, or wool-spinning at Louth as in the huts of Tahiti, the hot springs of Iceland, or the establishment of the New South Wales penal colony. He bred Merino sheep (then a rarity originating in Spain, whose export had been forbidden for centuries) to be sent to Australia, and advocated the cultivation of breadfruit in the West Indies—this latter scheme involving the financing of a ship called *Bounty* under a certain Captain Bligh.

He also financed Matthew Flinders' expedition to circumnavigate Australia, and William 'Strata' Smith's literally ground-breaking studies of British geology. He was a founding member of the Linnaean Society, and amongst much other activity documented the doomed Great Auk, and added the natterjack toad (*Epidalea calamita*) as a new British species, presumably after seeing them at the Saltfleetby-Theddlethorpe dunes, one of their rare English strongholds. He was also a founding member of the Royal Horticultural Society—and Vice-President of the Lincolnshire Agricultural Society. His collections are a cornerstone of the Natural History Museum, and his name a talisman in his home county—testaments to a life of insatiable curiosity.

*   *   *

The Spalding Gentlemen's Society, founded in 1710, is the oldest provincial learned society in England, and the country's second-oldest museum (after the Ashmolean)—a remarkable organisation to find anywhere, but especially in a small town in an unfashionable county.

Founded by lawyer Maurice Johnson, whose 1450s house is now the town's museum, the Society cultivated correspondence on literary and scientific subjects. William Stukeley was an enthusiastic ally as well as friend, and the Society soon attracted a stellar roster of correspondents, members and visitors—Joseph Addison, Joseph Banks, John Gay, Isaac Newton, Alexander Pope, and Hans Sloane just some of many. Spalding's connoisseurs and dilettanti were part of a quivering intellectual web that stretched across Europe. Linneaus corresponded with Maurice Johnson, as well as a Deeping St James-born clergyman-botanist called Adam Buddle, after whom Linnaeus named the buddleia that magnetise so many lepidoptera to Lincolnshire gardens.

The Society still has programmes of lectures, and many of its members are actively involved in literary and scientific spheres. Their headquarters on Broad Street is one of the few places an eighteenth-century style museum can still be seen. The local exhibits exude authentic fen-smell—an opium pipe from Bicker (opium was widely grown as a curative against fever), guns made by Geest of Spalding, early photographs of wildfowlers, animal traps, the jaw of a pike, naive oils of old Spalding, outsize horseshoes for use on boggy ground, customs seals from Boston, Delft tiles showing subjects as diverse as the Expulsion from Eden, and a seated man chatting to a bipedal cow that happens to be wearing a coat.

But Deep Time and the wide world are also present—mammoth teeth, bits of an elephant bird, a poignant Great Auk egg, Roman antiquities, medieval charters, porcelain from Bow and Bristol, eighteenth-century gallstones from St Thomas' Hospital, George IV playing cards, bone watch stands made by Napoleonic POWs, a Welsh harp stand, fly whisks from West Africa. Upstairs is a library in which to lose oneself, shelves of substantial editions with subtly enticing plain covers stamped in gilt lettering, including a 1574 edition of Ptolemy's *Geography*, whose frontispiece shows the sage in medieval Ottoman dress.

While the Gentlemen conversed agreeably as well as usefully into the nineteenth century and beyond, many in the town outside preferred to listen to charismatic preachers. One was a fiery young 23-year-old recruited in 1852 by Spalding's Free Methodists after he had fallen out of favour in staider Methodist circles in Nottingham and London. William Booth (1829-1912) had been apprenticed to a Nottingham pawnbroker, but at fifteen had a different kind of conversion. He became an itinerant preacher, focusing on the worst parts of whatever town he was in, and was predictably almost penniless when he was contacted by a Spalding chemist active in the Free Methodists.

During two high-octane years in Lincolnshire, Booth had electric effects, preaching almost every day all over the county, with crushed-in congregants frequently collapsing in tears, and at the end of meetings queuing up to convert to his kind of Methodism (thirty-six, after one meeting at Caistor). After successful meetings, he would come home and 'leap up the steps like a school-boy, humming snatches of some favourite hymn-tune.' His circuit was enormous, and he got around mostly on foot, in all weathers. He recollected,

> I have tramped many a mile in these Fens, up to the ankles in mud, not knowing sometimes how to get my feet out again without leaving my boots behind me ... I was a weak and puny fellow when I went to the Fens ... [but] those long journeys on foot and the splendid hospitality of the Lincolnshire people simply made me.[46]

Fortified, he left for London, a narrow-minded and rigid person who yet did great good through his book, *In Darkest England and the Way Out*, and his Whitechapel Christian Mission which became the Salvation Army. Back in Spalding, the sect he had done so much to entrench continued to grow, and expanding into politics, especially agricultural labour organisation. The chapel he had inspired was replaced by an enormous one in 1879, capable of holding 1,100. But this was demolished as early as the 1950s. The greying bandsmen of his Army whose silvery sounds sweeten the Christmas streets of Lincoln and Mablethorpe recall the gallant orchestra of the *Titanic*.

Spalding can sometimes feel slightly purposeless, a little depressed, stripped of its agricultural bustle and some of its economic rationale. Even the tulip industry has wilted, the once spectacular Flower Parades finally discontinued in 2013. But on 29 May 1967, the Tulip Bulb Auction Hall played unlikely host to a secular kind of ecstatic experience, a now near-mythical concert.

'Barbeque 67', when Jimi Hendrix shared the bill with The Move, Syd Barrett's Pink Floyd and Eric Clapton's Cream, has been called the UK's first rock festival, and was utterly shambolic. The town council innocently underestimated the numbers who might want to attend, and the town was swamped by 30,000 fans, who broke through perimeter fences, made makeshift camp on a football pitch or slept in doorways. The concert was also a technical disaster, with appalling sound. Pink Floyd 'conjured up a mixture of mirth and bafflement' from locals, Eric Clapton was pelted with toilet rolls, and Hendrix was jeered and sworn at as he tried to tune his guitar.[47] Such attempts at cultivating youth have not yet been repeated.

The town of the 'dwellers by the gulf' stands still on its soil, locked into a non-cancellable contract with excellent earth. Just outside the town's limits, but always in plain view, the Fens roll to each horizon, brooding as they have always done, indifferently awaiting the turn of each highly fertile year, or the ultimate return of water.

6

LIGHT ON THE HUMBER

'Know ye all that I am King of all the Floods, that North of Trent doe flow'—Michael Drayton, *Poly-Olbion*

Grimsby—Immingham—Barton-on-Humber—
Scunthorpe—Brigg—Alkborough

The Wolds slump into the Humber on Lincolnshire's northern frontier, fringed by sand and slime, reeds standing to attention, beaches of broken brick and flint, lumps of concrete and solidified tarmacadam, sometime islands, the stakes and stumps of structures of doubtful date and long-forgotten purpose. This is an ancient dividing line—starker by far than the county's fenny edges, second only to the coast in its clarity.

The 30-mile-long Humber estuary is a wide and bending valley whose sides are too low to afford real shelter from any direction of wind, with a great sweep of mostly shallow water lining its shifting bed. Winter easterlies blast up the estuary with hyperborean hints of Sunk Island and Spurn Point, the drowned town of Ravenspur, brimming Frisian *halligs*, Jutland, the North German plain, the Baltic, Karelia and Siberia. White and glaucous gulls roll and shriek with the gale, and the tense wires of the Humber Bridge thrum of turbulent tides, threatened embankments and perishing supports. Such winds recall redolent sea areas—Dogger, Fisher, Forties, German Bight, Viking—night watches in illimitable ocean, small ships far out from anywhere, phosphorescent porpoises at the bows, stars spread extravagantly overhead, and coffee cups sliding across the chart table as the calm cadences of BBC announcers relativise the world's massive meteorology, breaking down vast forces into vectors of veering winds and moderate-to-poor visibility.

Even when the wind comes instead from the south, it is often cool and stiff, and trails sullen dampness from Atlantic weather fronts. On such days, sheep seek shelter below the massive supports of the Bridge, their wool the colour of the concrete, quietly sipping green waters weeping from the far-above roadway, masticating and staring blankly back, to the rattle, rush and swish of traffic passing endlessly between Yorkshire and Lincolnshire. The world is a watercolourist's 'North Country' palette—greys beyond number, washing into or highlighting gradating greens, and browns from fawn to chocolate. Rain pools the paths of the Viking Way, spots clay-pit ponds, and runs down the red roofs of the still-working early nineteenth-century brick and tile works. The great river is battleship-grey on days like this, except where it is brown with moveable sandbanks that make the Humber one of England's most dangerous and dynamic highways—where the outfalls of north-central England come together and contend with the menacing *Mare Germanicum* for mastery.

Asgard had four rivers of milk, Eden its four rivers corresponding cabbalistically with cardinal directions, elements and gospels, but this watershed outdoes both in quantity, and rivals them in romance. The Ouse descends from York, bringing the Aire, Derwent and Wharfe by the way—not to mention the Don, incorporating Idle, Torne and others, and trace-elements of Celtic mythology (Dôn was a Welsh river goddess). The Trent brings tribute all the way from Burton, Derby, Leicester, Nottingham, Newark, Stoke, and Stone. Then there is the Ancholme, the Foulness, the Freshney, the Hull, smaller becks, cuts and drains, and all the capillaries that bleed into these, or directly into this short but puissant waterway, gateway to the guts of England, lined with economically important, emotionally resonant ports—Goole, Grimsby, Hull, Immingham—names from the ages ranged along an ever-altering river whose name is so old no one knows its etymology. The river and its huge hinterland hold English identity in its entirety, from ur-myth to rawly new, a continuum of change, a paradoxical kind of continuity.

The Humber Wetlands is a UNESCO-recognised environment, and an English Heritage area of archaeological interest—a great headwater holding billions of litres of moisture, and a myriad of memories. Much of Lincolnshire is affected by the river in some way, its environmental and historical presence felt as far south as Louth. Its massive twice-daily outpouring alternately thickens and scours the seabed for miles to the east, north and south, constantly altering topography, creating a huge churning habitat for wildlife, and a perilous highway for humanity. Mud and stones roll endlessly across old Doggerland, and human traces are deposited along the strands to the south—plastic barrels, telephone poles, fertiliser sacks, footballs, and a board advertising 'Supper Cruises to a Seventeenth Century Inn.'

The Humber Wetlands is made up of eleven regions—the Vale of York, Yorkshire Wolds, Hull Valley, Holderness, Southern Pennines, Humberhead Levels, Trent Levels, Lincoln Edge, Ancholme Valley, Lincolnshire Wolds, and Lincolnshire Marsh.[1]

These areas cover a large compass, and differ greatly from each other, but all are in some way beholden to the Humber, as shaper of geological, economic, political and religious fortunes. As William Lambarde (1536-1601) noted,

> Humber hath not as a ryver of itselfe anye begginninge ... but may wel enoughe be said to begynne withe the head of any of those ryvers which it receyvth.[2]

The river has always been a deliverer or dealer in disaster. High spring tides usher in the once auspicious tidal bore, the Aegir, which can bring a roaring 7-foot wall of water far up the Trent. Outgoing tides export high-seas hopes and merchant adventurers, incoming ones import ideas and wealth. Grimsby & Immingham combined was Britain's biggest port by tonnage until it lost the lead to London two years ago, but it nevertheless handled 51.2 million tonnes in 2020.[3] But sometimes the river brings too much sea, or dangerous strangers.

Like the Mediterranean, the Humber both divides and unites, marking the extremity of Lincolnshire while paradoxically uniting its northern districts with East and South Yorkshire, and with Nottinghamshire, and so all the areas they abut. However, as with Mediterranean unity, the Humber's ability to bring together should not be overstated. Even in prehistoric times,

> The Humber seems to have been a divisive force in early settlement patterns, unlike the Welland and the lower Trent, where settlements of the same people were made on both sides of the river.[4]

Later, the river was long the frontier between rival kingdoms, then dioceses in the centuries when bishops were taken seriously. In a more bathetic age, the Heath government's proudly announced 'Humberside' local authority of 1974, with its motto 'United We Flourish,' was hated on both banks, seen as what one mainstream writer called a 'chimerical mongrel' created by 'some nameless, faceless, soulless Whitehall mandarin bent on administrative rape.'[5] The boundaries of that local authority have an almost arbitrary appearance, encompassing places as different as Bridlington and Scunthorpe, Howden and Grimsby. Some cartographer seems to have found a satisfying sort of symmetry in the fact that both Yorkshire and Lincolnshire contain little villages called Wold Newton, and did loops specially to annex both.

Heath's, Callaghan's and Thatcher's administrations all lavished money to co-opt northern Lincolnshire into modernity, building the M180 motorway to link the M18 at Thorne in Yorkshire with Scunthorpe, and ultimately Immingham, although it never got further than Barnetby-le-Wold. This is still Lincolnshire's only motorway. There was once a proposal to extend the A1(M) into the southwestern corner of the county, but the long-serving local Conservative MP (and ecologist) Sir Richard Body, who was on the county council's planning committee, told me gleefully that he had vetoed this by a single vote.

County pride on both sides proved ultimately stronger than London, or even the unificatory symbol of the Bridge, opened to general admiration in 1981, and the entity only 'flourished' for twenty-two years. The Humberside official identity survives only in the organisation of local emergency services, a BBC station, and the pocket-sized Humberside Airport, near Kirmington, which flies to Aberdeen and Amsterdam, and seasonally to sunnier places, but is most used by helicopters engaged in search and rescue, or the oil and gas industries.

But there *are* commonalities of culture. Impressive artefacts have been freed from their sedimentary sepulchres and made their ways to little-visited museums at Doncaster, Hull and Scunthorpe— prehistoric boats from North Ferriby in the East Riding, found in the 1930s,[6] an angry-looking Celtic stone head recovered near Doncaster, and the Late Bronze Age Roos Carr figurines from

Holderness, discovered in 1836—haunting 14-inch men made crudely of yew, with challenging quartzite eyes and detachable penises, and their serpent-prowed boat. One of these effigies was given by a workman to his daughter as a doll, and it was not until 1902 that it escaped from toy status and rejoined the other four in the museum. For 150 years, the penises were assumed to be arms, and accordingly glued into the arm sockets—until some earthier researcher of the Eighties realised the error and restored them to their (im)proper places. The head and effigies were probably votive offerings to riverine deities, the anomalous sex of the figures perhaps an allusion to their androgynous nature, who could soar above both earthly and elemental barriers.

In their way, the boats were also an attempt to surmount materiality—nearly 50 feet long, 4-5 feet wide and 3-4 feet deep, capable of carrying fifty people or a massive cargo, like a tree's trunk for a Seahenge. Replicas made by enthusiasts show the boats were capable of travelling at six knots, and under sail, and could in good weather have crossed to the continent. The Roos Carr maker may have seen similar boats, or even sailed in one, and viewed them as semi-magical transports to new and unimaginable countries. A flat-bottomed 'raft' was found at Brigg on the Lincolnshire side in the mid-1880s, then a log boat in 1886; the latter went to Hull Museum, only to be destroyed by German bombs in 1943.

Other log boats have been found at Appleby, which like Brigg is on the River Ancholme (1943, now in North Lincolnshire Museum), at East Ferry on the Trent (1903, which also went to North Lincolnshire Museum then mysteriously went missing), and many smaller ones in the valley of the Witham between Lincoln and Boston. Probably more such craft await out under the estuarial ooze, melded blackly with 'bog oaks,' abandoned salterns, eel traps, fishermen's and shepherds' huts, channel and creek markers, haven straighteners and flood defences, and dropped detritus from pre-Roman times to today—the slimed stuff of Britain held forever in silty suspense.

Another boat type long used in and around the Humber is the flat-bottomed, high-bowed and clinker-built (overlapping planks) coble, ideal for launching from or landing on exposed beaches. This is one of the oldest of boat designs, which emerged in north-east England and probably stemmed from Norse originals. It is still seen today in inshore fishing craft, like the little crabbing boats that moor at Saltfleet.

But the river's most famous boat type is the Humber keel. Keel comes from an Old Norse word, *kjolr*—Hengist and Horsa landed in Kent in three 'ceolas'[7]—and signified a large, strong-bowed, carvel-built (flush-planked), flat-bottomed, short-masted, square-rigged boat, able to weather the worst conditions, and capable of carrying up to 100 tons quickly across shallow waters and up narrow channels. The hull below the waterline was dressed with tar, but the upper bodywork was often painted in bright colours and lightly varnished. They were able to sail close to the wind, and although they were often family boats, could be handled by a single man.

The Dutch introduction of leeboards (large pieces of wood suspended from the sides) gave more 'grip' on the water, allowing the use of increasingly taller masts, and so more sail. By the end of the nineteenth century, Humber keels could step a 55-foot mast, with a rectangular topsail as well as the mainsail—the extra sail increasing speed in open waters, and making it easier to catch wind when the keels were far inland. The handsome craft with their white sails were a common sight far up the Ouse and Trent until they became outmoded by road and rail, and a sail-operated one operated between Hull and Gainsborough until 1949.

The Romans' Ermine Street reached the river at Winteringham on the Lincolnshire side, and from AD 70 on there were ferries to Brough on the north. At the very lowest tides, it is even possible for the very daring (and tall) to walk across. In 1953, an eccentric Labour peer, the second Baron Noel-Buxton (1917–80), wearing rolled-up grey flannels and a lifejacket over his pullover, made the crossing to prove the Romans could have crossed on foot. The previous year, he had attempted to walk across the Thames at Westminster, but humiliatingly had been forced to swim part of the way. He was luckier with the Humber, making the one-and-three-quarter-mile journey from Brough to Whitton Ness in seventy minutes with the water never getting above his hips (although arguably he cheated, by getting a boat across the dredged shipping channel). He later wrote an engaging stream-of-consciousness book about his obsessions, *Westminster Wader*, a surreal and rather un-Labour like commingling of land-slip, time-slip and liberal reflections, rooting the Mother of Parliaments and England itself on soggily unstable ground:

> I have foreseen, without a wish to frighten, much falling of towers, and the return of the bittern, as Shelley foresaw it; when St Paul's and Westminster Abbey shall stand shapeless and nameless ruins, in the midst of an unpeopled marsh.[8]

Noel-Buxton was recently outdone by Hull man Graham Boanas (6 feet 9 inches in height), who struggled across the river for charity in 2005, swam it underwater in 2006, and in 2007 traversed the Liffey, Thames and Humber all on the same day.[9] The estuary has long had a European fame. Ptolemy wrote of a large British estuary which he called the Abus, and this is likely to mean the Humber. By the eighth century the estuary was well-established in European imaginative geography. Nennius, writing (or revising—his role is disputed) the *Historia Brittonum* sometime between 796 and 830, called the whole North Sea the 'Hunbrian'—a Welsh monk's acknowledgement of a phenomenon of Creation on the Saxon side of the island, a restless flux and reflux of Britannic aqua. Three centuries or so later, another

Welsh writer, Geoffrey of Monmouth, would bring the bourne into the 'Matter of Britain,' the origin-legend that linked Troy's Brutus to England's King Arthur, Arthur to the Plantagenets, and Britannic paganism to the Passion and the Holy Grail. Brutus' son Locrine chases Humber, 'kinge of the Hunnes,' into the water to drown—perhaps the first of the many 'Huns' that have dogged the coastal imagination.

A real Plantagenet, Edward II, granted a Royal Charter for the operation of a ferry between Hull and Barton-on-Humber in 1315, the Ermine Street crossing having long before fallen into almost literal desertion, the sections near to Winteringham prone to being blocked by great drifts of sand. While clearly more convenient than crossing on foot, or going upstream for miles, the ferry journey became notorious. John Taylor (1580-1653), self-proclaimed 'Water poet,' and accustomed to such undertakings as attempting to sail from London to the Isle of Sheppey in a boat made of brown paper, recalled one two-hour traversal of 'Humber's churlish streams' in the gratingly-titled 'A Very Merrie Wherrie Ferrey Voyage: or Yorke for My Money':

> ...*as against the wind we madly venter,* / *The waves like pirats board our boate and enter.*

Daniel Defoe, making the same journey in 1724, was even unluckier, spending four hours 'toss'd about on the Humber...' in an open boat with 15 horses, 10-12 cows and 17/18 passengers, 'call'd Christians.' He adds self-pityingly 'whether I was sea-sick or not, is not worth notice'—but he returned to London via York.[10] The Nottingham poet Henry Kirke White (1785-1806), who lived for a year at Winteringham, wrote a hymn entitled 'Oft in danger, oft in woe' after an overly exciting trip downstream to Hull.

The estuary's medieval consequence is shown by the fact that Hull's was the first of three Trinity House guilds to be chartered (in 1369, although there was no formal link to maritime activities until 1457)—bodies intended to improve navigation and make it safer, by establishing and maintaining channels, havens and lights, training pilots, and assisting indigent or elderly mariners. Newcastle founded a similar guild in 1505, and London only caught up in 1514. The complexity of estuarial navigation always needed explication, as suggested by this extract from an eighteenth-century Trinity House Humber Pilot's examination:

> Q. In turning down how near will you stand each way?
>
> A. I will stand to the Northd above and below the Spitt on the Sunk into 6fm to the Spitt is 12fm close by and to the southward say to Stanbro Flatt into eight faths and to the Burcom sand into 6 and 7 fm midd chanell 12 and 14 fm.[11]

Even the smallest craft need careful handling among movable anchorages and decrepit jetties:

> Entrance protected by high mud banks, so best follow sketch chart directions. Steer extremely close to collapsed piling and immediately curve to East side of haven until abreast of quay. Enter 1½ hours either side of H W S, 1 hour H W N.[12]

Entering the estuary from the east, the left bank shows as a long, low, brown-green-grey gradual fading-in of *firma*. A modern mariner will see the RAF's Donna Nook targets, churches at Grainthorpe, Marshchapel, Tetney and Humberston, Tetney's oil storage tanks, a huddle of immobile mobile homes at Humberston Fitties, the small cliff, seafront and stumpy pier at Cleethorpes, the sea-girt World War One Haile Sand Fort, and then Grimsby. Bronze Age, Iron Age, Roman, Anglo-Saxon and Viking explorers would have had to make do with shingle banks and trees as seamarks; later ones had the use of medieval churches and windmills and, after 1852, the Grimsby Dock Tower.

The Dock Tower is a startling piece of exotica to find along this very English estuary—an Italianate erection of 309 feet, made from one million red bricks, a Siena-inspired hydraulic dock gate-opener officially 'opened' by Queen Victoria and Prince Albert in 1854. Victoria allowed her precious Consort to ascend to the top in a lift, but now the way to the top involves rusting iron stairs of doubtful reliability rising through almost two centuries of grime and falling pigeon dust.

But the overview repays effort, giving giddying scenes of a country from a dream. To the left beats the full heart of England. To the right is the perennial promise of open sea. If the far-below flats are frequently prosaic, even unlovely, seen from here they can be figuratively transporting.

The view out to sea is almost indescribable. Just beyond the anchored-off ships, Spurn's piebald lighthouse, and the flailing forest of offshore wind turbines grounded in drowned towns, sea turns into sky somewhere beyond latitude and longitude. It is perilously easy for the eye to race away east, and 'see' azure utopia, some place from which *all* coasts could be in sight. The 'Independents' who embarked at Immingham in 1609, on their way to becoming Pilgrim Fathers, were seeking not just shelter from the storm (the storm they'd helped make), but a shining city on a hill. *Ex Oriente Lux*—but at times that light's almost too bright.

Gulls circle below as you face away from the comfortable south—the genteeler parts of Grimsby, Louth among its mounded green wolds—and gaze at the minimalist northern bank. North-eastwards, the perfect spire of St Patrick's, Patrington, stands like a chess queen on the shimmering Holderness plain. It would have been seen by both Henry IV (1399) and Edward IV (1471) as they rode past from the then-powerful port of Ravenspur on their way to claim kingdoms. North-westwards, a cluster of docks and high-rises, the raised flood gate, and the ocean-liner like silhouette of The Deep aquarium convey the hard charms of Hull.

Modern Grimsby presents mostly as subdued fish docks, and frying-food smelling industrial estates, a depressed town centre, and too much bad housing. Grimbarians have been fleeing for years, sometimes in unexpected directions—like Rod Templeton, a former fish-factory worker who ended up writing 'Thriller' for Michael Jackson. In 2016, *Shortlist* called it 'The worst place in Britain.'[13] In 2018, the Royal Society for Public Health said it had Britain's 'unhealthiest high street,' based on the number of payday lenders, betting shops, fast-food places, tanning salons and empty premises.[14] In 2019, Grimsby (and Gainsborough) were among the 'Ten most deprived towns in England.'[15] It has also featured on the Channel 4 programme *Skint*, and as ultra-gritty backdrop for the 2006 film *This is England*, which ends with an English flag being thrown into the sea. As Grimsby-born Davey Brett writes, 'Plenty of towns across England have suffered from the decline of industry ... but few others seem to attract the same kind of derision as Grimsby. It feels like the town is the punchline of a relentless national joke.'[16]

The near-disappearance of fishing has had effects like those of the near-disappearance of mining elsewhere—high unemployment, subpar social services, low educational attainment and a weakening sense of community. The decline of the industry is anecdotally associated with local crime, although perhaps today's drunken disorderliness is comparable with medieval nightlife:

> A weaver, zealous for the closed shop, said to his neighbour 'John Brown, if thou work in Grimsby I shall break thee head across', and the previous night a man broke the doors and windows of a house in St. Marykirk lane, crying out 'Without thou let me in to lie with thee, I will break an arm or a leg of thee'.[17]

Yet Great Grimsby really has *been* great, sending ships to fight in Scottish and French wars, a rival to Ravenspur and Hull, and between the end of the nineteenth century and the 1950s, the world's biggest fishing port (with daily catches of up to 500 tons), its sailors a byword for skill and bravery. There are remarkable accounts and photographs of fishing at its apex—the docks a forest of masts, the quays a sea of activity, and even for a brief period, big-game fishermen who hired Grimsby skippers to find them 700–800lb tunny. But the town also has legendary foundations, even a place in European epic.

There are twelfth-century versions of the saga of Havelok and Grim, but the early fourteenth century version, *The Lay of Havelok the Dane*, is the best known. It tells of Havelok, son of the Danish king Berkabayne, and Goldborough, daughter of the English king Æthelwold. They are both usurped of their rights, and Havelok is given by the Danish usurper, Godard, to the fisherman Grim, with orders to drown the boy. But Grim is awed by a mystical light that comes out of Havelok's mouth, and then finds the royal birthmark, a cross of gold on Havelok's shoulder.

He escapes with him instead to England, and is shipwrecked at the site of Grimsby. Grim builds a house from the remains of his ship, plies his old trade, and they sell fish as far away as Lincoln. Havelok takes service, unrecognised, as a scullion in the household of the English usurper Godric. Eventually, Godric, believing Havelok to be of low status, gives him in marriage to Goldborough, in order to humiliate her. But on the wedding night in Grim's hovel, the same mystic emanation shows Goldborough the true identity of her husband, and an angel tells her Havelok will be king of both England and Denmark.

Havelok, with Grim, returns to Denmark and reclaims his rights, before coming back with an army to England. Godard is hanged, Godrich burnt, and eventually Havelok founds a Benedictine abbey to give thanks (and expiate for his own

181

youthful church burnings). Havelok and Goldborough rule for sixty happy years, and all fifteen of their children become kings or queens. Wheel-of-fortune tales of this kind, about the absolute rights and moral necessity but also mutability of monarchy, have always been part of court culture, and must have been present in the self-justifying minds of both Henry IV and Edward IV as they spurred across Holderness.

George Oliver, vicar of Clee (part of Grimsby's neighbour Cleethorpes), preferred to believe in other legendary ancestors. In 1875, he published *The Monumental Antiquities of Grimsby*, which romanced about the town's ancient origins (like Rome, Oliver's town was built around seven hills). Unfortunately, he could provide little evidence that these hills had ever existed. It didn't help that his previous book about Grimsby had been 1866's *Ye Byrde of Gryme*, narrated by a raven.

Oliver was a very eighteenth/nineteenth-century English figure—the kindly, respected but abstracted cleric, often socially isolated, whose repetitive duties among the uneducated offered too little scope for his imagination. Clergy of this kind don't seem to exist much outside England—products, presumably, of long social peace and the shrewdly undemanding nature of Anglican belief. Some of these bored vicars wrote careful accounts of their church buildings or parishes, which are now invaluable sources of information, and a few literary classics (White's *Natural History of Selborne*, Sterne's *Tristram Shandy*, Kilvert's *Diary*). A more careful Lincolnshire scholar than Rev. Oliver is the Rev. Streatfeild, a former vicar of Louth and author of *Lincolnshire and the Danes*, who wrote disarmingly in his introduction:

> It is most unlikely that the greater part of this book, entering, as it necessarily does, into tedious details and technicalities, will find many readers.[18]

The *Lay*'s blending of bloodlines and dynasties makes it the perfect foundational story for a town which really was founded by Danes, possibly as early as 866. The twelfth-century writer Geffrei Gaimar, in his *Estoire des Engleis* (*History of the English*, the oldest known French-language history, probably written in Lincolnshire between 1136 and 1140) mentions Grimsby in connection with the Viking attack on York—'More than twenty thousand went on foot ... At Grimsby they passed the Humber ... All went to York.' Grimsby's Scandinavian connections grew clearer over several centuries, and the Humber became a Nordic port-of-call, until 'post-Conquest Lincolnshire appears as a kind of remoter suburb of Norway.'[19] At least one poet (and future earl of Orkney) noted the connection, albeit unflatteringly. Fifteen-year-old Rögnvaldr Kali Kolsson came to Grimsby around 1130, on his first trip abroad, spending five weeks with Bergen traders, their ship hauled up on the slime of the inlet:

We have waded the mud-flats / For five mightily grim weeks; / There was no lack there of muck / When we were in the middle of Grimsby...[20]

Henry II imposed tolls on the trade, and dispatched buyers to Scandinavia to buy gyrfalcons, large enough to allow him to hunt herons. Churchmen crossed the sea in both directions. When a house of Augustinian canons was founded at Grimsby in the twelfth century, it was dedicated both to St Augustine and St Olaf of Norway. The English Abbot of Grimsby travelled to Norway with Pope Alexander III's legate and told him on the way back about St Cuthbert's ability to calm North Sea storms. A Grimsby Abbey seal was found on the Norwegian coast in 1911.

Modern Grimsby can seem to be too busy (or sad) to have time for national or royal legends, but memories inhere in the thirteenth-century town seal, which shows 'Gryem' with sword and shield, and 'Habloc' and 'Goldenbvrgh' wearing crowns, while the Hand of God and a star light their way to destiny. The seal is reproduced boldly above the door to the Central Library, and there is a large Grim and Havelok copper relief on what is now Wilkos. In 1973, a larger-than-life nude statue by the well-known sculptor Wayne Hobson, showing Grim carrying Havelok on his shoulders, was unveiled outside Grimsby College, but suffered repeated vandalism (including the removal of Grim's penis and Havelok's head) and was eventually removed in 2006. Since then, the battered figure has languished in a storage depot in Cleethorpes. This seems a pity, even in an age when national symbols are increasingly objects of indifference or even execration.

Grimsby has other regal connections. Victoria and Albert were fêted when they opened the Royal Docks and Tower—but so too had been Richard I, who held a parliament here, King John, who gave the town its first charter, and even Henry VIII, notwithstanding his low opinion of Lincolnshire. John Whitgift, born in Grimsby around 1530, was a favourite of Queen Elizabeth, and as Archbishop of Canterbury (1583–1604) was instrumental in establishing uniformity on the Church, later endowing alms-houses that are one of Croydon's few redeeming features. During the Civil Wars, much of Lincolnshire was strongly Parliamentarian, but Grimsby's MP, Gervase Holles, was suspended from Parliament for his Royalist sympathies, went on to fight for Charles I at Edgehill, Banbury, Brentford and Newbury, was imprisoned, and later became an early antiquarian, writing memorials of his own family and notes on Lincolnshire churches.

Even Grimsby Town Football Club ('The Mariners'), an epitome of working-class recreation, was originally called Grimsby Pelham when founded in 1878, out of respect to the family of the Earls of Yarborough, powers in the borough between the sixteenth and nineteenth centuries. The Mariners' great days are over, but some among their weekend followers must talk half-humorously, half-proudly of matches none ever saw, such as the FA Cup semi-final appearances of the 1930s, the only Lincolnshire club ever to reach that stage. At the invitation of then Foreign Secretary (and Grimsby MP) Anthony Crosland, the unexpected figure of Henry Kissinger once watched Grimsby Town go down to defeat at the hands of Gillingham. It is rumoured that during the game Kissinger told Crosland the UK would have to give way to Iceland in the 'Cod Wars,' because Washington needed to hold onto its strategically vital airbase at Keflavik—with grievous results for the British fishing fleet.[21] Did the home fans yell, as they sometimes yell today, 'We. Piss. On. Your. Fish. (Yes We Do)'?

Tough pride is also suggested by the fierce black boars' heads sculptures set up on a roundabout, an allusion to the town coat of arms, which remembers a royal prerogative to hunt boars in Bradley Woods—something to think about when walking in those diminished woods today, whose most outré inhabitant now is the tearstained Black Lady, who has walked here since the Wars of the Roses searching for her children. The bristling boars are also a reminder that this seawards-staring burgh was also a market town for an extensive hinterland, so fond of blood sports that fifteenth-century town butchers were not allowed to kill bulls until they had been baited by dogs as a public entertainment, in the presence of the mayor.

But powerful memories of fishing pervade Grimbarian consciousness, poignantly on display in the town's National Fishing Heritage Centre (reportedly haunted by a smoking trawler skipper), and in the minds of the men who all their lives plied Grim's trade and now nurse the fading sea-longing in retirement—not to mention their wives and daughters, who had the even worse job of cleaning, gutting and selling the fish, and rearing new generations to risk their lives far beyond Spurn.

The EU's Common Fisheries Policy established species quotas for each EU member state, and clearly this was more advantageous to states with smaller territorial waters and fishing industries. The system, while intended to conserve endangered species, was also clumsy and wasteful, notoriously resulting in the dumping of unwanted by-catch, and open to abuse, such as in the 1990s when foreign vessels registered under British 'flags of convenience' in order to harvest UK quotas. Spanish vessels, in particular, were notorious for using illegal small-meshed nets, but were all too rarely penalised. British skippers complained bitterly about this—seeing themselves as 'playing by the rules' while less scrupulous foreigners got away with cheating. It is hard not to see in this some vestige of long-standing national resentments—'fair play' England against 'devious Dons,' the (moral, Protestant) Drake 'singeing the (immoral, Catholic) King of Spain's beard.'

The decline in the UK fishing industry long predated the EU, being caused by over-fishing and destructive bottom trawling—catches had been declining since 1938—but the EU's lack of responsiveness to legitimate concerns reinforced east coast disgruntlement. The local authority area of North-East Lincolnshire, which includes the parliamentary constituency of Great Grimsby, delivered the tenth highest Leave vote in the Brexit referendum, at 69.9% (three of the other highest Leave-voting areas were also in Lincolnshire).

Grimsby still has a Fish Dock and Fish Auction Market, open round the clock, selling huge amounts of fish daily,[22] but now most of the fish sold there is Icelandic or has come overland from Aberdeenshire. There are surviving ancillary services, even a boat-builder, and a few Grimsby-registered trawlers and crab boats, but twitches of life cannot disguise that the vigour has gone out of the formerly frantic, stinky docks, with their closed chandlers, icehouses, smokeries and warehouses, and quays where herring gulls pick delicate fish skeletons from black rubbish bags and screech into each other's beaks. There are odd little memorial areas to scrapped vessels and defunct companies, with ameplates, anchors, and decommissioned naval mines—the last a memory of both 1914-18 and 1939-45, when Grimsby boats played a vital role not just as food-gatherers for the Home Front, but also as coastal patrol boats, minesweepers, submarine spotters and, in the second war, as carriers of crucial ball bearings from Sweden.

We found the beached and burned-out remains of one small trawler, the *Nimrod*, at Donna Nook down the coast, and took her nameplates home. Her cast-iron funnel guard which once defied salt spray and storms now holds up honeysuckle. At the time of writing, the UK and EU governments are in dispute about post-Brexit fishing arrangements, but even if some deal beneficial to the UK industry can be struck, how many young people now would wish to work on a trawler?

This wistful town's now almost solely shore-based workplaces cede to fields of rapeseed bisected by the A180, a noisy, rattling road with its old concrete surface. In the distance looms Immingham's *Mad Max* skyline of factories, fuel tanks and flaring refineries, interspersed with yet more rapeseed, but before that there are endless diversions.

*   *   *

In the Middle Ages, the pleasant commuter village of Stallingborough was one of the largest towns in Lincolnshire. Before that, it is thought to have hosted a court of Mercia's King Offa—and to have been the birthplace of St Erkenwald (or Earconwald), Bishop of the East Saxons, Bishop of London between 675 and 693, and the subject of an eponymous fifteenth-century poem about the finding of a pagan tomb during building works at St Paul's. The miraculously preserved pagan awakes to tell Erkenwald that he had been an incorruptible judge in life, but is cursed to remain in limbo because he had never known the

Christian God. Moved, Erkenwald lets fall a tear, upon which the overjoyed pagan blesses him, and passes to heaven, his soul at last in the 'Upper Room,' his body allowed at last to decay.

Magical though it is, the poem also has shrewd advice for reformers, advising the rededication and reuse of pagan temples rather than their destruction, to make the new religion more palatable to the heathen. Such advice would have been anathema to Anne Askew, also born in Stallingborough, in 1521—one of Lincolnshire's many prominent Protestant agitators. Anne Askew married local landowner Thomas Kyme, but appears to have made home life swiftly intolerable thanks to her strong disbelief in the Real Presence in the Sacrament. She went to London, where she met Catherine Parr and Bishop Bonner, and was accused of heresy by her husband. Her brother Sir Francis, who supposedly gave her up to the authorities, seems to have felt a heavy burden of guilt, telling friends that from that day until her death he saw always in front of him a bright light, which he compared to that 'reflected from a great fire upon a glass window.'[23]

She went to the Tower of London where she had the distinction of being tortured personally by Lord Chancellor Wriothesley and Sir Richard Rich. She refused to retract, so in 1546 was carried to Smithfield in a chair, bound to the stake with chains, from which she continued to argue with the officiating priest even after the fire was lit.

It is difficult to connect fiery belief with the frigid red-brick church of 1780 that stands now in Stallingborough—the blind arcading of the exterior and dullness of the interior infinitely less alive than the trees which almost hide it. An eighteenth-century sundial on a medieval cross-shaft has lost its gnomon, and even its numbers are wearing away; an eroded figure of Britannia tops a gravestone from which someone has unpicked the metal letters of the inscription. A stained Union flag and tattered memorial poppy protrude below the monument of Captain H. S. Farebrother, MC, of the Norfolks, who died at Stallingborough from wounds sustained at the battle of Shaiba near Basra in April 1915.

Reminders of Catholic and pre-Christian practice linger at Healing, whose long-sacred (now dry) well attracted supplicants into the last century, to take the waters and tie rags to trees to show they'd been. Lincolnshire is famous among hydrologists for its chalk springs and blow wells, the latter almost unique to coastal north Lincolnshire—groundwater springs fed by rain percolating through the chalk of the Wolds, creating streams that get covered by clay as they approach the Humber or the sea. These hidden waters become pressurised, and bubble forth wherever they find an opening in the clay. It was widely believed that they never failed or froze. Old brass and glass in Great Coates church recalls 300 years of Barnardistons, whose ghost moat is outlined in Hall Close field. Another moat, at North Killingholme, still holds water, elemental counterpoint to the flaring refineries of South Killingholme and Immingham.

Immingham, through resolutely utilitarian and surreally modern, with its huge ships berthed alongside in 70 feet of water, possesses obsolescences of its own. In the west of the town is a large Ice Age erratic boulder called the Blue Stone, which has given its name to a pub and football team. Tradition avers the stone was once used to send a foghorn-like sound that could be heard ten miles away, and inevitably there are superstitions associated with moving it, but its chief power is as a reminder of the prehistoric Bluestone Heath Road, a trackway that runs thrillingly along the top of the Wolds from Candlesby to Caistor.

St Andrew's church's mortar contains seashells from the banks of the river. A medieval grotesque shows signs of melted tar on her head, showing how shipbuilding and caulking techniques were used by builders of land 'naves.' Early fifteenth-century bells bear naive mottos, like 'Seeke the Lord,' 'God saye his Chvrcr,' '*Hoc nomen Thesus est amor meus*' ('This name Jesus is my love').

A patriotic sign in the church speculates that the tenor bell 'rang out to celebrate the victory of the Battle of Agincourt.'

This was an important embarkation point for future *Mayflower* families from the Puritan-inclined country of eastern Nottinghamshire, southern Yorkshire and western Lincolnshire. The 'Separatists' had decided they could not be reconciled with James I's Church of England, and so determined to cut ties with England altogether.

On 12 May 1608, a Hull sailing barge called the *Francis* was lodged on Burcom Shoal off Stallingborough, awaiting high tide. She had sailed downstream from Gainsborough, where her master had picked up passengers. He had stopped at several other creeks and havens on the way, and was now carrying eighty to a hundred passengers instead of his usual cargo of coal. Another vessel, a Dutch hoy (a small, single-masted ship, possibly even smaller than the *Francis*) was anchored off, awaiting transhipment of the *Francis*'s probably coal-blackened, prayerful payload. A boat from the *Francis* had just successfully transferred sixteen men to the Dutch ship, when armed men were spotted moving quickly in their direction. The Dutch skipper hoisted sail immediately with the sixteen, leaving behind the *Francis*, with the men's possessions, not to mention their fellow travellers. The remaining Separatists separated, the able-bodied men fleeing, everyone else left to the mercy of the Grimsby magistrates.

James I was a stern lawmaker. On the A18 near Melton Ross there is (usually) a gallows, ordered by him as a warning that a local feud going back to 1411, between the Ros family of Melton Ross and the Tyrwhitts of Kettleby, must stop. The gallows have been maintained since, a reminder of the crepuscular Jacobean outlook, and a legal obligation on the landowner (although they rotted and fell down in 2020, and as of December 2021 have not been replaced). But the Grimsby magistrates do not seem to have been looking for Separatists as such; ironically, they may have feared this mysterious body of men loitering so conspicuously in the middle of the marsh were Papists on their way to join exiled Irish earls. Stallingborough was also a notorious smuggling spot, and since April 1608, there had been a ban on travel by sea unless the traveller first swore allegiance to the King. The arrests proved an embarrassment to the government, because they had committed no obvious crime. The arrestees were also a nuisance, as suggested mawkishly by the Separatist leader William Bradford,

> ...poore women ... in distress ... weeping & crying on every side, some for their husbands, that were carried away in ye ship ... others not knowing what should become of them, & their little ones; others againe melted in teares, seeing their poore little ones hanging about them, crying for fear, and quaking with could.[24]

The detainees were eventually released, and most made it eventually to the Netherlands, and many subsequently to Massachusetts. Probably the government was glad to be able to export these troublesome elements. One historian speculates that the Lord Treasurer and Secretary of State, Robert Cecil, 'let the pilgrims go because nothing was to be gained by making them stay, and because he did not want to give them a platform for oratory.'[25] Later, Charles I would write 'a good riddance' on a report of the exodus of Independents to Massachusetts.[26] One would-be Separatist, Francis Hawkins, was sick when he got to Immingham, and died before he could board, his body left behind in his Godforsaken England. Other members of his cohort are remembered in Immingham streets—Brewster, Winslow, Alden, Weston and Blossom. Americans recall these connections, or did; there is an imposing 1924 monument across the road from the church, topped with a piece of Plymouth Rock. The 1608 sailors and their descendants would not have approved of the church's Royal Arms, which is a rarity—James II's arms, set up in the year of William of Orange.

Immingham became essential to national security leading up to World War One, as a port and oil depot, and after 1912 Royal Flying Corps and Royal Naval Air Squadron scout planes, seaplanes and Sopwith Schneiders (unaffectionately nicknamed 'Spinning Jennies' because of their habit of going into uncontrollable spins) were based here, to carry out anti-Zeppelin and anti-U-boat operations, as well as pilot training. Immingham also became the Royal Navy's East Coast Command base, and a submarine depot. St Andrew's has modest memorials to some of the sailors who set out from here, or were coming here, aboard HM Ships *Blackwhale*, *Cotsmuir*, *Doon*, *Itchen*, *Bat*, *Legion*, *Fairy*, *Dee*, *Asia*, *Mekong*, *Valpa*, *Gaul*, and *Epworth*. What were they like, these men 'who go down to the sea in ships,' then went down with them—Deck Hands Joe H. Card, Wm. H. Rook or Victor J. Tumber, Trimmers Jas. E. Blowers and Samuel Gungey, Act. 2nd Hand Samuel Greep, Able Seaman Reginald G. Maund? Military men can be simultaneously brutal and profane, child-like and sentimental. What would they have made of the stunned platitudes that sign off their inadequate stew-hued memorials—'None untimely die who die for England' or 'There shall be no night there'? Did the bell that 'rang out for Agincourt' also ring out for Armistice?

Even the 1989 plan of the port issued by the proudly modern, pushily Thatcherite Associated Britain Ports is a museum piece, with its British Coal Corporation jetty and Britannia Gas tanks—antediluvian corporate identities for outgoing industries, another attempted alliance of modernity with tradition. That 1989 map feels almost as ancient as the 1906 photograph commemorating the cutting of the first sod of the deep water port, the formidable-looking cutter Lady Henderson (wife of the chairman of the railway company) surrounded by top-hatted and bonneted dignitaries, and St Andrew's vicar, behind an elaborate miniature wheelbarrow and spade made specially by Mappin & Webb. Future reboots of the British identity will rely less on historical imagery, now all history is argued over, and 'Great Men' outdated.

Brocklesby is a rare thing to come across in these un-chic postcodes (DN, for Doncaster)—a planned landscape and great house, home still to Pelhams, the Earls of Yarborough, surrounded by a sea of trees planted by public-spirited, scientific forestry-interested proprietors.

The first Baron Yarborough planted 12,552,700 trees between 1787 and 1823, and the fourth Earl (who died in 1936) planted almost 15,000,000. The species range from ash and oak to Caucasian wingnut and sequoia, and even though they are managed carefully, they lend this otherwise un-treed area a welcome bosky lushness. The Pelhams are more commonly associated with Sussex, and national politics, but a cadet branch has been prominent here since the 1560s, as employers, High Sheriffs, and Justices of the Peace.

They were also famous Masters of Foxhounds. Lincolnshire was never optimal hunting country, but the Brocklesby Hunt claims origins going back to 1590, when the Tyrwhitts, the Viners and the Pelhams combined their packs. There are hound lists going back to 1746, which gave the Brocklesby venery celebrity. One hound, Brocklesby Ringwood 1788, was painted by George Stubbs, and another, Brocklesby Ranter 1790, was in huge demand as a stallion hound. A descendant, Brocklesby Rallywood 1843, was described as the 'father' of the modern foxhound, and the pack called 'almost unique in their adherence to the Old English lines.'[27] Fox hunting was a bizarre and unedifying pastime, yet something in some English psyches seems to miss all that colourful charging across the landscape, with its horn-blowing and lore, 'the sport of kings, the image of war without its guilt, and only five-and-twenty per cent of its danger.'[28]

193

Georgian Earls of Yarborough brought South Country-like rational order to the area, with a Hall holding works by Titian, Lely and Reynolds, a Capability Brown-designed parkland with a mausoleum by James Wyatt, a Gothic Revival bridge and 'Hermitage,' kennels, an orangery, pigeon cote, the monumental Pelham's Pillar, stable blocks, urns to beloved horses, an Anglican church brimming with family monuments, and neat estate houses. The second Earl had a train station built in 1848, in the culturally reassuring Tudor-Gothic style—a personal convenience as Chairman of the Manchester, Sheffield & Lincolnshire Railway. The Manchester, Sheffield & Lincolnshire became the Great Central Railway, the Great Central the London and North Eastern, and that was incorporated into British Rail in 1948—but occasional trains stopped as late as 1993. The eighth and current Earl of Yarborough, born Charles Pelham in 1963, is now called Abdul Mateen, whose conversion meant that Lincolnshire had England's first Muslim High Sheriff when the Queen appointed him to that role for 2014–15.

Between unexpected aristocracy and industry, North Lincolnshire is a long-shadowed country of ironstone churches with flamboyant waterspouts and Roman-numbered clocks, and naves patched up with green sandstone, chalk and cement. Churchyards are neatly cut around the recent cremation tablets, and half-wildflowered around Georgian-to-Edwardian gravestones leaning increasingly away from the perpendicular. Some stones strike home, such as that to John and Abigail Ferraby of Wootton Hall, who lost children in infancy, and at the ages of six, ten, sixteen, seventeen and twenty-two. Abigail joined these six, aged only forty-six herself, in 1883, perhaps with relief, hopefully in hope.

At Thornton Curtis, reached down increasingly empty roads, which if local newspapers are to be believed are padded by demonic dogs, there is a Tournai marble font, as the village sign proclaims proudly. Tournai marble, quarried in what is now the Walloon part of Belgium, is actually a carboniferous limestone, but it gives off a striking black sheen when highly polished. It was widely used in Romanesque churches, even used as paving, but is much rarer in England. This is one of only seven Tournai marble fonts in the whole country (another is in Lincoln Cathedral).

A couple of miles away are the remains of Thornton Abbey, with its imposing barbican gatehouse of 1382 (naturally, also 'haunted'), whose gateway frames Immingham chimneys. Abraham de la Pryme was hugely impressed by the 'vast stupendious fragments of the buildings that have been there,' especially 'the gait-house yet standing, of a vast and incredible bigness, and of the greatest art, ingenuity, and workmanship that ever I saw in my life.'[29] Henry VIII rode over this brick bridge once, in 1541, clattering in under the no-longer-seeing eyes of effigies of Mary, John the Baptist and Augustine, and was entertained for three days at what had become a college. Six years later, the Dissolver was dead, his college was suppressed, and 400 years of faith had become a source of building stone.

This isolated assemblage is served surreally by a train station, with 1930s signs, which combines Ealing Comedy quaintness with North Lincolnshire functionality. Little two-carriage passenger trains (often empty) run by the East Midlands Railway whirr through here four times a day on the Barton branch of the Leicester–Cleethorpes line. On the Leicester–Cleethorpes line proper, these *Titfield Thunderbolts* alternate with rumbling, slow thirty-carriage freight trains bound for Drax and the 'Northern Powerhouse,' whose armoured impressiveness belies their breezy slogans about renewables. Between trains, the rails bake in the heat between deserted platforms, and all around arises the smell of grass and a symphony of birdsong, as if your train has just stopped at 'Adlestrop.'[30]

Goxhill has a medieval hall and a church with a fifteenth-century Crucifixion painting, and a sad remembrance of the Skinner siblings, who died in 1669—the boy on a Monday, then his sister 'bewailing ye loss of him even to admiration, followed him on ye Sunday.' Here Henry Welby 'retyred himself into the countrye' in the 1560s, to lead a studious life, interspersed with arguments with his dissolute younger brother, whom he tried constantly to reform. Eventually, possibly understandably, his brother attempted to shoot him, and this appalled Henry so much that he left Goxhill (and his wife and child) forever in about 1592 and went to London.

Here, for the rest of his life, he lived in complete seclusion, never leaving his house or seeing another human except for an old maidservant. He even tried to avoid seeing her by moving into an adjoining room while she cleared the table or made his bed. In 1598, his daughter came from Goxhill to get married near his house; he didn't even leave it on that occasion, or even see her. Welby was so notorious a sociopath that after he died in 1536, a biography was put together by well-known versifiers, including John Taylor, mentioned above, called *The Phœnix of these late Times, or the Life of Mr. Henry Welby, Esq.* (1537):

> *Arabia yeilds a Phenix, and but one. / England, This Phenix, and besydes him none, / To solitary Desarts, boath retyr, / Not mindinge, what the World doth most admire. / His Face, though it was much desyr'd by many / In forty foure years was not seene by any.*[31]

John Harrison was more socially engaged, even a kind of nation-builder—or at least a navy-builder, trade-booster, and science-advancer, which then amounted to the same thing. Born in Yorkshire in 1693, he was brought to Barrow upon Humber when he was about four and lived there until 1736. He spent much of his childhood and young adulthood watching ships on the Humber, or the smaller ones that came in and out along Barrow Haven.

Barrow had once been spiritually important—St Chad was granted monastery land there around 669—and strategically important to the Normans, who built a motte and bailey at the Haven. But for the young John, a self-taught maker of top-quality clocks—the tower clock at Brocklesby is his, built around 1722—and surrounded by sailors and sailing talk, thoughts turned to practical problems. How could ships find their locations and plot their courses more easily and safely? Latitude could be measured from the equator, using stars or the sun, but there was no way of measuring how far east or west a ship was, because there were no reference points once out of sight of land. Sailors had to resort to dead reckoning—calculating a ship's position from a previous 'fix' by combining its course, direction, speed and time, using a compass, an hourglass, and a long rope with a wooden float—a flawed methodology at best, and even more difficult at night.

The longitude difference between two locations being the difference between local times (as marked by the sun), it was essential that some means be found of reconciling these times with a reliable chronometer. A clock that lost time during the day—as all clocks did—would clearly be of limited utility and could even be dangerously misleading. It was especially difficult to devise a means of keeping stable time aboard ships, whose movements obviously played havoc with pendulums. Europe's naval powers all knew that the first country to master this would be at a huge advantage in economic terms, and in its ability to project power and expand empire. Many ships and sailors' lives would also be preserved. Sometimes dead reckoning was literally deadly, as was demonstrated on 22 October 1707 when Admiral Sir Cloudesley Shovell ran four of the five ships of his fleet ashore on the Scilly Isles, with the loss of almost 2,000 men.

The British Parliament passed the Longitude Act in 1714, setting up a Board of Longitude, offering up to £20,000 for solutions. In 1717, Harrison produced a high-performing long-case wooden clock, and by 1720 he had entered the longitude lists. He won several £500 grants, experimenting first on the Humber, then in London, and eventually at sea, with a succession of highly technical innovations and refinements—self-lubricating clocks, clocks that could withstand air pressure and temperature changes, the gridiron pendulum (made of strips of two different metals, so as to minimise temperature-related contraction or expansion), the grasshopper escapement (the clock's pacemaker, which 'kicked' like a grasshopper's legs), secondary springs, dumbbell balances and yet others. His most remarkable advance came in 1726, when he announced an astonishingly accurate clock with a variation of only one second a month. It took another nine years for it to be ready for sea trials, and by the time he died Harrison had spent an astounding forty-eight years on the task.

Harrison was considerate and kind, and socially active, much involved with the church when at Barrow, ringing and tuning the church bells and even becoming the choirmaster. But when it came to his work, he was obsessive, refusing to read distracting literature (even Shakespeare), and seems to have alienated the Commissioners of the Board of Longitude through his excessive secrecy. The Commissioners were also biased against mechanical solutions to a problem they saw as more likely to be solved through astronomy. Harrison's refusal to read anything other than mathematics and natural philosophy texts must surely help explain his notorious inarticulacy and prolixity; the opening sentence of his last published work is twenty-five pages long. Perhaps no one could blame the Longitude Commissioners for getting annoyed.

Yet it is ludicrous that it took the personal intervention of George III to ensure Harrison eventually got full credit, and most of the available reward. This is typical of England's attitude towards innovators; also typically, the government neglected to capitalise fully on the new technology, swiftly allowing its secrets to be exported. For Harrison, of course, the money and the geopolitics were always incidental.

* * *

The river bends on northwest deliberatively, rounding pleasingly forlorn (for decadently melancholic unengaged outsiders) New Holland—supposedly named in honour of all the Dutch gin (Hollands) once smuggled through here. A former ferry embarkation point—the paddle-steamer *Tattershall Castle*, now a restaurant ship on London's Embankment, was used here between 1934 and 1973—it is now one of the smallest ports on the North Sea, used to import wood from Scandinavia. A riverside path threads between the river and a nature reserve and 'Country Park' to Barton-upon-Humber, once bigger than Hull, but now feeling like a town whose last coach left two centuries ago.

There is a history-choked creek, and a boatyard crammed with sleek handmade craft and miniature galleons made for Hollywood versions of the past. There are large Georgian houses with wisterias that could be in Sussex, and other streets that owe more to Worksop. Horse head finials snort down their noses from the gateposts of Baysgarth Park, old home of the Nelthorpes—yet more fierce Lincolnshire Protestants, one a judge of Charles I, his son Richard involved in the Rye House Plot, and later executed for his part in the Monmouth Rebellion. A gentler power is evident at the Wilderspin National School, model school of Samuel Wilderspin (1791-1866), an influential advocate of education for the poor, and who, amongst much else, pioneered school playgrounds.

Barton was always vulnerable to attack, on the north coast of the Kingdom of Lindsey, then on the long front line between

Mercia and Northumbria. From the mid-800s it became an important Viking trading town. But old consequence is made clearest by Old St Peter's.

The church is one of the most impressive legacies of the Saxon twilight, the tower base circa 970 AD, its upper stages completed just before or, even more piquantly, just after Hastings. Lincolnshire has a lot of Saxon stonework,[32] and St Peter's was in fact the first building ever to be described as 'Saxon,' by Thomas Rickman in his influential 1817 study *Styles of Architecture in England*. Before Rickman, the very existence of a distinctively 'Saxon' building style was doubted. His studies contributed to a growing sense of awareness of England's Anglo-Saxon heritage, and a burgeoning pride in actual or supposed ancestral vigour, which in turn was used to legitimise imperial expansion. The term is imperfect because the period is imprecise, and historical records fragmentary; Nikolaus Pevsner always preferred 'Saxo-Norman.'

The tower is memorable for its height (70 feet), and two unusually tall tiers of blank arcading. These arcades are composed of primitive-looking pilasters—shallow relief representations of classical columns—called lesenes. Lesene means literally 'a mean thing,' because these pilasters have neither bases nor capitals. The effect is both impressive, and naïve. The clumsy attempt at classicism combined with massiveness of execution have a touching effect, like a folk-memory of departed Roman greatness combined with a proud desire to make their own mark. The woodwork-style mitred joints on the triangular door-heads show that the builders were more accustomed to carpentry than masonry. The squared blocks of gritstone had probably come from abandoned Roman buildings.

The porch on the west end may be even older than the tower; such structures are more usually associated with Orthodox, Carolingian and Ottonian churches (where they are called narthexes). The main body of the church is fourteenth century and is now given over to an exhibition on Anglo-Saxon England, including skeletons found in the area—the Church become a catacomb. When the nave was excavated, burials found varied from a medieval priest with a chalice and paten resting on his pelvis, to an eighteenth-century post-mortem with a neatly sawn-through skull. The church was declared redundant in 1972, almost exactly a millennium after work started on the tower. Bartonian Chad Varah, founder of the Samaritans, whose father was vicar here, would not have approved.

The animal painter Thomas Weaver (1775-1844), 'staunch friend to the shorthorns,' painted a magnificent example of a shorthorn bull at Hill Farm above Barton in 1809.[33] The bull, Patriot, was posed to show off his vast bulk and meatiness and— for a time of war—the perennial goodness of England's grass and English rustic virility. Beyond Hill Farm, the farm falls away to windmills and ships, other symbols of industry, big trees and the towers of churches, symbolising secure possession and national continuity. The implication is that 'Boney's' starveling France could show nothing so fine and prosperous, that England was not the 'nation of shopkeepers' Napoleon had laughed at, but a well-fed Arcadia of ordered liberty and sturdy yeomen. That vista is radically different now.

From everywhere around here can be seen the twin towers of the Bridge, at 510 feet like the tallest of tall ships. When it was built, it was the longest single-span suspension bridge in the world, at 1.38 miles. It is now the eleventh-longest, but still impresses as near-miracle. In this ultra-open place, any bridge would look insubstantial, but the Bridge's grace belies its functionality. It contains 44,000 miles of suspension cable and 400,000 tons of concrete, the whole maintained constantly by teams in high-vis jackets cleaning, de-rusting, painting, filling holes in the blacktop, or giddily halfway up the great wires checking for fraying, in little window-cleaning hoists that must quiver with every zephyr or far-below truck. Solid though it seems, and really is, it is designed to bend over 10 feet in 80 miles per hour winds. The vistas from the walkways on either side are as good as those from Grimsby's Dock Tower, but perhaps especially to the west on a warm evening when it has been raining, with the sun going down in splendour, and backlit air and water so full of each other that it is like being inside a pearl. Sometimes the cement works at South Ferriby could be a celestial city.

But vistas of the Humber are not invariably uplifting. Hull MP and poet Andrew Marvell looked out over the river with personal as well as political impatience. In certain lyrically melancholic, very seventeenth-century moods, the tides outside looked to him like tides of time, flowing terrifyingly quickly as looks, and love, faded:

> Had we but world enough, and time, / This coyness, Lady, were no crime. / We would sit down, and think which way / To walk, and pass our long love's day. / Thou by the Indian Ganges' side / Shouldst rubies find: I by the tide / Of Humber would complain...[34]

Marvell's father had drowned in the river in 1640. A consequence of this tragedy was that Andrew was adopted by a local family, the Skinners, who introduced him to John Milton. Marvell became Milton's assistant during the Interregnum, and was able to protect the proud older man from repercussions after Restoration.

Wide watersheds encourage wide-ranging ruminations—about the currents of existence, the brackishness or clarity of memory, the cruelty of fate, the unexpected survivals. 'Mud is the dust of water,'[35] like ashes are the dust of fire, and dissolution and regeneration are equal parts of awareness. The Humber Bridge is a marvel to most, but for a few it is instead a fatal attraction, a launching point into eternity. Every year, Humberside Police attend dozens of reports of people threatening to cast themselves into the abyss, and some of these 'succeed.' In April 2021, the footpaths were closed after six people killed themselves in the space of a month.[36]

When self-harmers stand on the ledge and regard the brown bath below, they mustn't see grandeur or human ingenuity, but a river flowing to paradise, or at least away from purgatory. What delusions, ecstasies, hopes, panics, realisations or regrets must race through their heads in the thronged milliseconds between leap and entry into the ocean of unity...

*   *   *

This is the beginning of a 147-mile peregrination, the 'Viking Way' (as if Vikings would have walked when they could sail), towards cosily unimaginable Rutland. Weekend walkers start to drop away, and increasingly you are by yourself. The hawthorns seethe with tits and yellowhammers, the reeds with sedge warblers and wheatears, and shelduck slop over the mud to find safe distance. Swifts scream and arc overhead like the seaxes of Essex. A fisherman in search of sole pulls out a flounder, and puts it back with contempt.

I find an ultramarine Christmas tree bauble lodged amazingly intact in mud as caressing as the cardboard it came in from China, swirled down from some hopefully happy Humberside festivity, perhaps many years ago. The tiny shiny convex globe reflects a tiny bulging Bridge, grotesquely swollen sedge and a fish-eye version of myself—an unflattering reflection, a reminder of John Ashbery's observation that 'the soul has to stay where it is / Even though restless.'[37] A sign that hasn't been in the river long advertises mysterious 'Markets 10-4 Sat/Sun,' an arrow helpfully pointing the way.

On one farm, guinea fowl parents call harshly for their young, and the anxious keets contend to keep up, almost invisible except as running ripples in the ankle-length sward. Bulls look out short-sightedly over crew yard fences, probably wishing they were out in the lush fields with the long eye-lashed Lincoln Reds. Other farm signs warn walkers 'Smile—You're on CCTV'—and there are aggrieved-sarcastic signs asking, 'Why are you tossing litter around here?' followed by ticked check-boxes reading 'I'm lazy,' 'I don't care about this community' and 'I think other people should pay to clean up after me,' climaxing with 'Don't be a tosser.' A few plastic bottles nevertheless lounge in field furrows, reflecting the sun slickly, evidence of human irredeemableness. Almost undercut concrete steps lead down through trees to a little beach where all the chalk pieces are of one size, and rusty wire cables stick out weirdly from clay cliffs. A fence emblazoned 'DANGER' surrounds the secretive, densely wooded Humberside Police Training Range.

Ships chug past steadily for the railhead at Goole, or up the Trent to Axholme, often close enough to the shore to be framed by hedges, swinging wide enough at some of the bends to look briefly miles from anywhere. Near South Ferriby, huge trees grow from old sloping pasture that gains a different kind of interest because of the less than perfectly bucolic backdrop—an austere three-storey farmhouse in the Dutch style, passing ships, the cement factory chimney, and sprawling Read's Island. The semi-industrial prospect is reminiscent of those early nineteenth-century engravings of Birmingham or Manchester, before the real start of the satanic mills, when the skyline was still spires, unbuilt-on farmland rolled up to sparkling new factories, and women washed clothes upstream of the first slums.

In South Ferriby itself, an iron cut-out caricature of an axe-waving Viking signals the route, up to the red-bricked, St George-flagged parish church in its sloping buttercup-brightened graveyard, many of whose 'residents' are higher than the nave roof. The nineteenth-century stone of one Snowden (Christian name obliterated), who died at Christmas one obliterated year, suggests a prickly personality:

Farewell vain world, I've seen enough of thee / Therefore am careless of what thou sayest of me / Thy smiles I court not, nor thy frowns I fear / My cares are past, My bones lay quiet here / What faults you saw in me take care to shun / Look at home enough there is to be done.

What was he like, this South Ferribian with his naïve philosophy? Or has he been posthumously misrepresented? Was this inscription even his idea? Descendants probably still live in the village. Do *they* 'look at home'?

A Norman tympanum of St Nicholas, patron saint of mariners, looks benignantly over the bend. This was a significant place, with a famous well, later called Chad's Well, into which Humber-crossers from the Romans on dropped coins, presumably in gratitude at heaving been delivered. So potent were and are the groundwaters that they caused the church to collapse in the sixteenth century, and as late as the 1990s washed away part of the graveyard.

The riverscape is full of humanising touches, attempts to make bearable the burdens of life. Read's Island, where German prisoners-of-war once built walls and which was halved by floods in 2008, is neighboured by the friendly sounding Pudding-Pie Sand. A nineteenth-century riddle acknowledges the river's blind force, but also makes horror homely:

As I was goin' over Humber / I heard a great rumble; / Three pots a boilin' / An' no fire under

Making horror homely is the chief benefit, perhaps purpose, of such riddles, but they can also make the homely horrific. Other

Lincolnshire riddles signify a richly strange inner existence, the humorous wordplay suffused with superstition and worry:

As I was going over London Brig / I spies a little red thing; / I picks it up, I sucks its blood, / And leaves its skin to dry

When I was going over a field of wheat, / I picked up something good to eat, / Neither fish, flesh, fowl nor bone, / I kep' it till it ran alone

Grows i' the wood, and whinnies i' the moor, / And goes up an' down our house-floor.[38]

One can 'hear' these rhymes being chanted by children, passed on over late-night firesides, chairs turned in and collars turned up against the chilly mystery of the great dark lands just outside the door.

John Rennie's Ferriby Sluice of 1844 pents up and then releases millions of gallons of water siphoned from the flats to the south. Standing on the swing bridge looking upstream, the New River Ancholme arrows south to Brigg and beyond. On hot days, the green-brown waters haze with rising fly, and ripple with mouthing bream. Looking back to the Humber, a heron probes surgically for sustenance, while keeping instinct's eye out for Grimsby-imported gyrfalcons. The bird's reflection stands almost as still as him; obscenely brown mudbanks exude faint expectancy and old odours; a wormy wooden trawler kedged among reeds won't essay the estuary again.

Up the hill, a battered dusty pipe funnels quarried chalk down to the cement works, and a board points out the salient features of a land given over to power of one kind or another—the lazy strength of the river, the might locked up in cement, distant views of Drax, Eggborough and Ferrybridge power stations and the Bagmoor Wind Farm, their combined massive force carried along double lines of pylons straddling combed and scraped fields. Pylons were named because their shape resembled the entrances to Egyptian temples, oddly appropriate for these vaguely sinister transporters of enigmatic energies and implicit fire. Countryside is always conditional, with changes in economies and technologies swiftly rendering the once-essential redundant—like the eighteenth-century post windmill at nearby Wrawby, once an engine of growth but now a quaint backdrop for geese. One day these pylons will no longer be needed either, but will stand here ages afterwards, slowly perishing in the unending wind.

Fat countryside leads down 1,200-year-old drove roads to Horkstow, famous for a folk song, *Horkstow Grange*, about a fight between a farm foreman, John Bowling, and a waggoner nicknamed 'Steeleye Span,' from which the influential folk band derived its name. Long before the Grange was ever built, Horkstow was home to at least one wealthy fourth-century Roman, who commissioned a floor mosaic showing a dramatic chariot race, probably at Lincoln, the only representation of its kind in Britannia. One chariot has overturned, spilling out the charioteer, who is being rescued while another man tries to catch the panicking horses—while two of the other three racers look in imminent danger. Horkstow's church is dedicated to St Maurice—legendarily a martyred legionary, massacred with 6,665 others in 286 CE. Opposite, fatting lambs tear the long grass on top of mounds marking Templar cells, and a line of poplars points down to Ancholme and Trent.

At the end of yellowhammer-loud Bridge Lane, John Rennie's 1834-5 suspension bridge has wisely been closed to traffic, but still arcs walkers over the deep brown East Drain into the green dream of the Ancholme Valley, former brickpits now a nature reserve of high hazels and hawthorns, hemlock and bramble, followed by fecund fields. Industrial architecture dates especially quickly, like visions of the future in literature. Rennie's bridge, so radical in its time, looks like Romans built it.

Maybe some real Roman mounts were remote ancestors of the ones George Stubbs dissected here fourteen centuries afterwards, spending almost two years obsessively working up his technique-honing, reputation-making 1758 folio, *The Anatomy of the Horse*.

Since the fourteenth century, Lincolnshire had been famous as a horse-breeding district, the Wolds producing chargers and hunters, and the Fens the Lincolnshire Black (progenitor of the shire horse), and the much smaller Lincolnshire Fen Pony, under thirteen hands in height, with a large head, straight back, and large feet, unlucky animals much in demand as pit ponies. Lighter Blacks were used as cavalry horses during the Civil Wars, and in peacetime there was the fourteen hands or higher Lincolnshire Trotter, used for pulling coaches. Trotting, when the horse moves its legs in diagonal pairs—front left and rear right at the same time, as opposed to pacing, when both legs on the same side move as one—appears originally to have been 'a peculiarity of horses bred on marshland.'[39] It was probably easy availability of animals that drew Stubbs to Horkstow, although he was also friendly with members of the Nelthorpe and Thorold families.

Stubbs lived alone in Horkstow, except for one Mary Spencer—the nature of their relationship is unclear—in a temporarily repurposed farmhouse. He had rigged up an iron and wood apparatus on which horses could be displayed in different poses, held in place by hooks. The animals were brought to him alive, and he would then cut their jugulars to bleed them to death. The veins and vessels were then filled with liquid wax which hardened to preserve their shape. Then he began the laborious business of cutting and skinning interspersed with painstaking drawing and note-taking, as he peeled away layers of skin, muscle and soft tissue to get to the bone—a very eighteenth century (or Da Vinci-like) attempt to get down to the truth of things, disgusting work as the flesh decayed, but made bearable by a fierce desire to *understand* what horses were made from and how they moved, and through that understanding gain insight into all Nature.

He would have worked mostly in winter, when the carcasses would have lasted longest, so those must have been frigid, silent days of too soon deteriorating light—alone in his studio, with the horse he had recently killed, and outside the brooding silence of a big country clasped in cold. But the forty-one drawings now in the Royal Academy of Arts library display a lucid knowledge of mass, power and structure that had never before been seen in British art, and was rare even in Europe. They even give his victims an *écorché* immortality—reproachfully staring at us with liquid eyes, spirit of the English horse in elegant equipoise, or trotting endlessly down the years.

Late in his career, Stubbs would paint a nationally celebrated example of Lincolnshire livestock, a painting which may have inspired Thomas Weaver's painting of Patriot—the Royal Lincolnshire Ox, which its owner John Gibbon had won in a cockfight at Long Sutton. The Ox was 6 feet, 4 inches tall, and weighed just under 3,000 pounds. Gibbon had him brought to London in 1790, and Stubbs painted him in St James's Park, standing with the Ox and the fight-winning cock—a rustic assemblage for central London. The Ox was sold to a showman, and for months was shown in the Strand, alongside ostriches and a rhinoceros, where his docility and 'Sagacity' were much admired. The poor Ox was advertised to be slaughtered to celebrate the King's birthday on 4 June 1791. Two weeks later, there were advertisements offering the opportunity to view 'a conspicuous PART of the late Royal LINCOLNSHIRE OX, which was slaughtered at the Lyceum in LONDON' for a shilling.[40] It was an undignified end for a phenomenon.

* * *

At Dragonby, there is a locally famous rock formation, formed by a petrifying spring, that vaguely resembles a dragon—a 'firedrake' for a place later famous for furnaces.

The 44-feet-long feature—very noticeable in a district not renowned for prominent stones—has a dragonish wedge-shaped 'head,' arched 'body,' and curving 'tail.' There have been suggestions that the stone may have been venerated in pre-Christian times, because at some stage in the rock's history a long groove, about 2 inches wide, has been carved carefully all along the 'spine' and 'neck.' Antiquarian Abraham de la Pryme (1671-1704) didn't see a dragon at all. When he was there, in 1696, Dragonby was called Conesby Cliff, and the dragon was called the Sunken Church, allegedly having sunk into the ground because of the inveterate Catholicism of the congregants. Pryme didn't see a church either, saying, perhaps disappointedly, it was 'most manifestly nothing but a natural rock.'[41] The name Dragonby was a 1912 coinage of local landowner Lady Winifride Elwes to give an air of romance to the houses she had built for workers at Scunthorpe.

This was an area of relatively dense prehistoric settlement—relatively, because the main prehistoric routes seem to have bypassed the county, making it a backwater even then. The Jurassic ridgeway was the most important for Lincolnshire, running from southwest Britain to Yorkshire—entering the county somewhere near Stamford, continuing via the vicinities of Grantham and Lincoln to the Humber. One famous local relic of prehistory is the Brumby Shield, made during the seventh or eighth century BCE, but Palaeolithic flint hand axes, Mesolithic microliths, Neolithic awls, Bronze Age metal 'hoards' (the kits of travelling smiths) and fragments of Beaker Folk pottery have all been dug out of rabbit warrens, or mines. Steel Age archaeologists have unearthed Iron Age settlements at Dragonby and Kirmington, possibly co-existing with Bronze Age cultures and later Roman settlements (who may have smelted iron ore in this area). After the Romans, Anglo-

Saxons strewed modern archaeology with pottery, spearheads, brooches and bells resembling those from Celtic monasteries.

Scunthorpe is the recent past's outdated idea of the gloriously shining future—Harold Wilson's 'white heat of technology,' Edward Heath's Humberside metropolis *par excellence*, epicentre of a Ruhr-rivalling economic 'northern powerhouse.'

'Escumetorp' is mentioned in *Domesday*, but the town of today is a twentieth-century conglomeration of five hamlets—Scunthorpe, Frodingham, Asbhy, Brumby and Crosby—a steel equivalent of Staffordshire's pottery Five Towns. The town, although only formally incorporated in 1935, grew swiftly after 1859, when thick layers of Lower Lias ironstone—the stone used to build so many local churches—were found in this part of the Cliff, below layers of sand left there by long ago seas. The first ironworks opened in 1862, and since then the town's fortunes have flared and flickered like its furnaces—incandescent in good times and in wars, fading in recessions and slumps, increasingly losing out to international competition. After 1979, a woman from Grantham was up in London, itching to shrink the state, save money, un-cushion uneconomic industries, and confront unions whose practices she deplored on principle. The 'Iron Lady' could see there were problems with steel.

It is possible the industry would have died altogether had nothing been done but, as with mining and shipbuilding, the reforms that were plainly necessary were not seen in their communitarian context. Monetarists reduced the world to 'market forces,' and didn't think through what might replace these industries, which had psychological as well as economic importance.

Just like the miners and shipbuilders, or (earlier) Grimsby's trawlermen, Scunthorpians were grittily proud of their demanding and often dangerous work—in June 1974, twenty-eight were killed when a chemical plant exploded at nearby

Flixborough, England's biggest ever peacetime explosion. They had built ways of life around the omnipresent works, these fiery fortresses ranging their horizon, armouring their country. The old arms of the town showed a grounded pride, realism gilded with romance—a wheatsheaf for agriculture, two *Gryphoea incurva* shells ('devil's toenails,' an oyster fossil frequently found in ironstone), a knightly helm and 'the top of a blast-furnace issuant therefrom Flames all proper,' with the scrolling motto 'The Heavens Reflect Our Labours.' The present North Lincolnshire Council logo is so easy to understand that it is almost empty of meaning—a stylised black scrap-heap with noxious-looking yellow and green clouds.

Sacked steelworkers were understandably often unwilling to take up jobs in call centres, retrain for other jobs which often didn't exist anyway, or leave for London. Executives and shareholders benefited greatly, but for many in 'Scunny' introducing market forces mostly meant introducing more uncertainty. 1988's privatisation of British Steel, the town's major employer, was part of a bewildering process of asset-stripping, cheapening, rebranding and trivialisation, as the United Kingdom started to metamorphose into a bathetic 'UK PLC.'

British Steel was merged into the Anglo-Dutch Corus in 1999, and taken over by India's Tata Steel in 2007. Tata floundered for years, but eventually Scunthorpe's 'long products' (wire, rod, rail, bars, structural sections, girders) operations were salvaged, and bought by a private investment firm in 2016. The business was promptly relaunched, confusingly, as British Steel Limited—which just three years later was insolvent. This by now considerably less 'British' company was eyed up by, of all potential purchasers, a Turkish Army pension fund, but in 2020 was eventually bought by China's Jingye Group. For now, British Steel still operates in Scunthorpe, and there are other steel companies in the area—but in a globalised marketplace there is no security, and little space for sentimental local or even national considerations. Thatcher's sincere wish to bring prosperity and stability has in some ways had the opposite effects. Maybe one day the steel will go for good, and the furnaces of Scunthorpe will be almost as mythical as Dragonby's 'firedrake.'

Relatively late development meant that squalid, Lancashire-like, back-to-back housing never came to Scunthorpe, and 1930s-1970s borough councils tried to retain some greenness and openness, especially in the west of the town. They put in playgrounds, a paddling pool, a golf course, cycling clubs and big-windowed schools, and grassed over piles of gosson (decayed ore). They retained some old buildings and added some good new ones, and honoured elements of the past in the museum and the 1963 Civic Centre, whose then strikingly contemporary entrance hall displays a fourth-century Roman pavement from Winterton, a representation of Ceres as a tribute to the wider district's way of life. But there were bad decisions too, and the town looks tired and dispirited, an almost extinct volcano. Smoke still spumes out along the ring road, above B&Q, McDonald's and Next—while hard-faced men do things to cars, or wander out onto the carriageway carrying cans of lager. Unused units are shuttered up; signs give old phone numbers and lapsed domains. Great swathes of elder and nettle bulge behind fencing, poppies blaze on banks, and dandelions poke up through concrete. A blackbird spinks from the top of a hawthorn, briefly audible over the car noise; a glossy rat charges for cover; a buzzard on a lamp-post looks out for roadkill—the small things always waiting for our downfall.

*　　*　　*

The little town of Brigg is globally known for *Brigg Fair*, a folk tune collected in the town in 1907 by the Australian composer Percy Grainger (1882–1961). Grainger was there at the invitation of his

213

friend Gervase Elwes—whose wife Winifride would later establish Dragonby—and revelled in its hitherto ignored rich seam of song.

He recorded farm bailiff Joseph Taylor singing *Brigg Fair* on wax cylinder—the first folk singer ever recorded—and later made a choral arrangement. It seems ironic that this so-English song's survival is attributable to an Australian (Grainger later took American citizenship)—or perhaps not, because Grainger was a Nordicist, on a mission to show that Anglo-Saxons were capable of music as good as anything from Italy. He even strove to purge musicology of Italian terminology, for example writing 'loudenlots' on scores, instead of 'crescendo.'

Joseph Taylor rendered the melody perfectly, but could only remember two stanzas (he was in his seventies), so Grainger added three further stanzas taken from other folk songs. The original lyrics were probably more plangent, but Grainger turned it into a paean to undying love.

It was on the fifth of August
The weather fair and mild
Unto Brigg Fair I did repair
For a love I was inclined

I got up with the lark in the morning
And my heart was full of glee
Expecting there to meet my dear
Long time I'd wished to see

The simple sentiment also seems at odds with Grainger's own sexual practices, which tended towards un-simple sado-masochism, but clearly Lincolnshire was a huge influence on him, and so the whole English folk tradition. 1937 saw the first performance of a sixteen-minute piece of six movements (one movement is based on *Horkstow Grange*), uniting them under the title *Lincolnshire Posy*, often considered Grainger's greatest work.

Brigg Fair is also beloved of classical fans because of a 1907 orchestration by Frederick Delius, as *Brigg Fair: An English Rhapsody*. The resultant combination of innocent sentiment and Delius' characteristic lush treatment give the song a prelapsarian air strongly at odds with the actual town, with its weeded river, roar of through traffic, and long history of rabbit-skinning. When I was last there, in June 2021, the streets were almost empty, yet the town was aurally alive, with wildly pealing church bells and the raucous cheering of football fans coming from the *Dying Gladiator* pub watching England beat Croatia 1-0. It was difficult to reconcile *Brigg Fair*'s sweetness with the sometimes brutal swiftness of sport—or is sugary sentiment the inevitable obverse of action?

Brigg Fair is in marked contrast to Lincolnshire's other celebrated folk song, *The Lincolnshire Poacher*. This lively melody, with its infectious refrain, is generic, but it has been associated with the county since at least the 1770s, when the following lyrics were published at York:

> *When I was bound apprentice,*
> *In famous Lincolnsheer,*
> *Full well I served my master*
> *For more than seven year,*
> *Till I took up with poaching,*
> *As you shall quickly hear:*
> *Oh! 'tis my delight of a shiny night,*
> *In the season of the year.*

> *As me and my comrades*
> *Were setting of a snare,*
> *'Twas then we seed the gamekeeper*
> *For him we did not care,*
> *For we can wrestle and fight, my boys,*
> *And jump o'er everywhere:*
> *Oh! 'tis my delight of a shiny night,*
> *In the season of the year.*

As me and my comrades
Were setting four or five,
And taking on him up again,
We caught the hare alive;
We caught the hare alive, my boys,
And through the woods did steer:
Oh! 'tis my delight of a shiny night,
In the season of the year.

Bad luck to every magistrate
That lives in Lincolnsheer;
Success to every poacher
That wants to sell a hare;
Bad luck to every gamekeeper
That will not sell his deer:
Oh! 'tis my delight of a shiny night,
In the season of the year.

Poaching was always one of those crimes, like cat burglary, highway robbery, piracy or smuggling, which could be regarded indulgently even by 'respectable' members of society—because of the courage and skill required, or because the 'victims' (in the case of poaching, rich landowners) were unpopular. There is an added 'national' dimension in that poaching was traditionally carried out by actually or supposedly dispossessed Anglo-Saxons against actually or supposedly oppressive Normans. Robin Hood and other folk heroes had no qualms about taking deer belonging in law to the Sheriff of Nottingham or other rich dignitaries, because to them that law was unfair and 'un-English.' There was a confused, often convenient, conceptual elision between zealously guarded Common Law rights and the 'ownership' of game, and the land itself—anti-aristocratic, often anti-monarchical theories absorbed by religious dissenters, secularised in the Whig 'Ancient Constitution,' influencing eighteenth- and nineteenth-century Radicalism, the early Labour movement and groups like the Kibbo Kift.

Real-life poachers saw their predations as bodily essential, but sometimes also as a kind of game—a test of their strength and wits against the powers that were. Sometimes poaching was a bitter business, pitting people of the same class against each other; at Well, near Alford, is the grave of 31-year-old William Dadley, a gamekeeper who was 'hurried to his Redeemer's presence by the hand of a murderer' five days after his wedding (a crime never officially solved). But the romance persisted of poaching as a 'sport,' and this particular form of illegality as an excusable, or at least understandable, assertion of necessity and pride. Folk songs are frequently subversive, but 'The Lincolnshire Poacher' has made it into state-sponsored respectability, co-opted by the army as a quick march—the 10th Regiment of Foot, the Royal Lincolnshires, eventually the Royal Anglians.

In the 1940 film *Tom Brown's School Days* it was used to assert Tom Brown's courageous stand against the drawlingly aristocratic bully Flashman and the brutal order he represents. Benjamin Britten arranged it for his *British Folk Songs*. With altered lyrics, the tune was also used to rally Union regiments during the American Civil War, as an Irish folk song, and even as a hymn. There are pubs named in honour of the song, and an unpasteurised cheese made near Ulceby in the eastern Wolds, not far from Dadley's grave.

Grainger is unlikely to have been subjected to the Lincolnshire bagpipes, whose last-known player (John Hunsley, from nearby Manton) had died several decades before. By the mid-nineteenth century, 'Lincolnshire bagpipes' had become a joking reference to frogs, but pipes of some basic kind had been enjoyed in the county since at least the fifteenth century. There is a medieval oak boss of a piper in the Cloister at the Cathedral, and at least two other church carvings showing the instrument. Several writers referred to the instrument as characteristic of the county—unsurprising, because pipes were always a rustic instrument, strongly associated with shepherds and herdsmen. In 1612's *Poly-Olbion*, Michael Drayton's 'Blazons of the shires' include 'Bean belly, Leicestershire her attribute doth bear. / And Bells and Bagpipes next, belong to Lincolnshire.'[42] In 1622's *Worthies of England*, Thomas Fuller writes:

> I behold these [pipes] as most ancient, because a very simple sort of music, being little more than an oaten pipe improved with a bag, wherein the imprisoned wind pleadeth melodiously for the enlargement thereof. It is incredible with what agility it inspireth the heavy heels of the country clowns, overgrown with hair and rudeness, probably the ground-work of the poetical fiction of dancing satyrs. This bagpipe, in the judgement of the rural Midas's, carrieth away the credit from the harp or Appollo himself; and most persons approve the blunt bagpipe above the edge-tool instruments of drums and trumpets in our civil dissensions.[43]

In 1984, the Marsh-based pipe-maker John Addison was commissioned to make a set of Lincolnshire pipes, based on the sketchy evidence of those church carvings and rare textual references, often disparaging. Five years later, he produced them, with a conical chanter and a single bass drone. These can be heard occasionally at recitals by the City of Lincoln Waites, a recreation of the official bands of medieval mayors of the city (Lincoln was one of the last English cities to do away with their Tudor Waites, in 1857). Conjectural though this instrument is, and however unlovely its sound, it is hard to hear the pipe and not be quietly stirred, taken back to some long-drowned soundscape.[44]

* * *

North of Scunthorpe is another dimming power base—Normanby Hall, in its 300-acre estate. The Hall was built between 1825 and 1829 by British Museum architect Robert Smirke for the Sheffields, courtiers, poets, politicians and soldiers hereabouts since the time of Elizabeth I. There are political connections even today—David Cameron's wife Samantha is the daughter of the eighth Baronet, and grew up on the estate—although the Hall has been owned by the council since 1964.

Not long after we came to Lincolnshire, we toured the Hall. The grounds have a herd of red deer, which in mating season attracts nearby wild stags, and the park has sometimes to be closed, lest walkers fall afoul of these impressive animals.[45] The Hall is less impressive, in fact dispiritingly institutional with its roped-off, sun-shaded interiors and yellowing-labelled cutlery set out on dusty tables, as the guide says, 'as if for a ceremonial banquet.' In recent years, the council has tried to refresh the visitor experience, but using other exhausted clichés.

A different kind of burnout can be detected at Winterton, where an eighteenth-century resident called William Teanby carved his wife's gravestone with what feels unpleasantly like gloomy relish, her 'sordid atoms' noted on the stone he used as his table, a cold companion-piece to his own coffin, which he used as a cupboard. The engraver William Fowler (1761-1832) was working in Winterton about the same time on spectres of a different kind, his painstaking colour representations of locally found Roman antiquities. Martial and other Roman satirists would have been amused or irritated by the unusual apparition at Winterton Old Hall, described by mystified early 1800s ladies (or, more likely, ladies' maids) as 'a ghostly powder-box,' with a powder puff that, however often it was removed from a particular dressing table, would eerily reappear—a ghost ephemeral even by ghostly standards.

Winteringham, where Romans crossed the water on boats from a timber jetty sometimes still visible, had another significant visitor in 672—Northumbrian queen turned saint Etheldreda (St Audrey), who crossed the Humber here on her way south to avoid distasteful conjugal duties, and seed Christianity and English unity. She founded a church at nearby West Halton and farther away at Stow, and ultimately an abbey at Ely, whose Cathedral eventually arose around *her* sordid atoms. Through an unjust transmogrification, Etheldreda/Audrey, exemplar of purity, became associated with almost opposite ideas. Her cult sparked a hugely popular annual fair, and the poor quality of cloth sold at this event—this 'St Audrey's lace'— ineluctably became 'tawdry lace' and then just plain 'tawdry,' doubtless to the delight of iconoclasts. But there is nothing tawdry about the view of the Humber as seen from the north-westernmost corner of the county.

Small roads wind round for miles to Alkborough, and the meeting of many waters, and an enticing enigma. This is the tip of the high Cliff, the end of the Edge, overlooking the great commingling of Humber, Ouse and Trent in a glittering blue-green-white hugeness. Alkborough is a place of inchoate excitement. The sea-going yachtsman shows there can also be a river-longing:

> The source of the Humber could be the cruising yachtsman's Holy Grail ... Only Neptune himself could turn around at Trent Falls and go back to the sea.[46]

This is not just a magnificent prospect forty miles or more into Yorkshire (York Minister can sometimes be seen), but one with a captivating puzzle. Cut into the turf is 'Julian's Bower,' a 44-feet-wide, eleven-ring labyrinth of unknown age. This is Lincolnshire's sole surviving labyrinth, although there are records of another here, two at nearby Appleby, and single ones at Louth and Horncastle. Alkborough is technically a labyrinth rather than a maze, because it has only one entrance and one way through, but the words are generally used interchangeably. The labyrinth/maze motif is ancient, complex and almost universal— an archetype which binds classical myth with Christian, European origin-legends with Arcadian games, hermetic philosophy with sexual symbolism.

'Julian's Bower' refers to Julian, grandson of Aeneas of Troy, and brother to Brutus, Britain's legendary founder. The Troy allusion is because that city's walls were supposed to have been designed cunningly to confuse attackers. Other mazes are or were actually called Troy Town, although they were sometimes named after other lost or destroyed cities, like Babylon, Jericho, or Nineveh. 'Bower,' though now it usually means a bedroom, stems from the same etymological root as *burg* and borough.

There are labyrinths in cultures from Afghanistan and Arizona to Sardinia and—especially—Scandinavia. Lincolnshire's mazes may be a reflection of long Scandinavian influence. There are many mazes across the British Isles, from prehistoric stone-cut designs to modern creations, but only eight surviving turf mazes. Yet they are incised into the national imagination. There are only three others in the world, all in Germany. Julian's Bower enters records as late as 1697, described by Pryme, at a time when there was great curiosity about 'sacred' geometries,[47] but it is likely medieval, because of the relatively complex layout.

Walking labyrinths may have been a religious penance, or as a substitute for a pilgrimage to the Holy Land, especially during wartimes when Palestine was inaccessible; the famous thirteenth-century pavement maze in Chartres Cathedral is called the *Chemin de Jerusalem*. The contrast between what is to be found at the centre of Christian labyrinths and that entered by Theseus is stark—light rather than darkness, salvation rather than Asterion.

221

Fishermen and travellers may also have walked the maze before voyages as a good luck charm. The confluence of the rivers below is not just dazzling, but dangerous, as indicated by a local saying recorded by Pryme—'Between Trent-fall and Whitten-ness / Many are made widdows and fatherless.' In lighter hours, turf mazes were used for processional dances and village sports; Titania bemoans the loss of rustic vigour:

> The nine men's morris is fill'd up with mud;
> and the quaint mazes in the wanton green,
> for lack of tread are undistinguishable.[48]

A Scandinavian turf-maze game called Maiden's Ring involved a girl standing in the centre of the maze while a boy had to dance or run towards her without stumbling. With their obvious womb symbolism, turf mazes must also have been used for nocturnal trysts. Perhaps the young woman who was sitting heavily by herself on the Bower when I last visited, and was still there two hours later, was missing her swain, and ruing the loss of England's potency.

This little-known conundrum at the end of a county is kept up with quiet pride, the pattern frequently re-cut, the pattern repeated on a gravestone, in the church porch, on stained glass and the village sign—a permanent record of its plan, a defence against the fear of forgetting. The shaft of a medieval cross stands headless in the churchyard, used as a sharpening stone for centuries, so organically worn that it might have been made by Henry Moore.

The Cliff slopes steeply below the maze, through the smell of sheep and thistle onto Alkborough's aptly-named Flats, now only patchily pastured because flood defences have been selectively removed to give floodwaters room. This was a World War Two bombing range, convenient for the 'Bomber County'; parts of observation posts still stand, and unexploded bombs had to be destroyed during the defence realignment. Now the defenders of the realm, and even the defenders against floods, have departed, and the Flats feel like some fen of the ancient world. Rare birds are watched by rare walkers, tiny twitching movements among all the whispering grass and reedmace—solitary sojourners threading lonely paths towards the site of the old Apex Light, which must have been Britain's furthest-from-the-sea lighthouse.

High up in a bird hide with shutters that opened along each side, a large and suddenly spotlighted spider was vibrating to herself in a web—another Greek myth, another maze with a brooding monster at its core. I felt guilty disturbing her dark dreams. Outside, a blackcap on a hazel carolled his evening alarums, a moorhen chirped and splashed unseen, and a buzzard trying to enjoy a last day's golden updraught was being buzzed by jeering crows. The sun was nearly gone, the breeze sprang suddenly cold, and I remembered all the miles between here and home. I closed the hide quietly and turned my face east, my shadow streaming in front.

7

THE EAST'S WEST

'So Nature, the cleere Trent doth fortunatly lay
To ward me on the west'—Michael Drayton, *Poly-Olbion*

The Isle of Axholme—Haxey—Epworth Gainsborough—Kettlethorpe—Doddington

Crows were bursting up out of black earth, like a lithograph by M. C. Escher, under a baroque blue sky. The effect was eccentric, even by the standards of the Isle of Axholme.

The warping of this particular field had given it a darkly rich topdressing. Warping is an old agricultural technique which involves the controlled admission of waters into a particular area and then emptying them out again, using a careful system of entrance and return drains, to enrich the soil with sediments. Sometimes, as with this field, it meant near-sable soil. In others, it could mean sandy silt. In yet others, cart warping would be followed in the spring by a spontaneous growth of white clover—gleaming flowers of good omen, revealing the re-nitration taking place below. Some fields here have 20 feet of warp on top of their original surfaces, the residues of centuries of rinse and repeat. For hundreds of years, Axholme's agriculturists have used these soils shrewdly to make their odd little Isle the 'garden of Lincolnshire,' a place renowned both for fecundity, and fey abstraction.

This is Lincolnshire-over-Trent, a Lincolnshire with a motorway running across its middle, that yet manages to be askew to the universe—a byword, even within its home county, for sequestration. Until the seventeenth century, the Isle was hard to reach from anywhere, cut off from the rest of Lincolnshire by the Trent, and from everywhere else by the Don, the Idle, and the Torne, and the quaggy hugeness of Hatfield Chase. Axholme was a wooded mini-realm sticking up slightly above the surrounding terrain, 10 miles tall by 6 miles wide, with a north-south slightly higher spine, rolling into rivers on each side in a profusion of bog-cotton and cranberries, orchids and sedge, alder and willow. The foliage would have been stiff with birds, and its waters busy with bream, dace, perch, pike and rudd—and 9-feet-long sturgeons, specimens of which could still be caught in the Don into the 1860s. Overfishing, pollution and flood defences between them thereafter stymied this spectacular fossil fish, although one was caught in the Humber in 1953, and presented to the Queen, in accordance with a statute of Edward II.[1]

The Isle's early inhabitants are elusive—perhaps rare seasonal visitors, descending from Yorkshire or Derbyshire to fish and fowl, then moving on, perhaps feverishly, leaving little to know them by except very occasionally their ochre-coloured carcasses, cousins to Denmark's better known Tollund Man, or the multiple bog bodies of Ireland. In 1747, the Crowle antiquary George Stovin (d. 1780) went to see one, and handled it with a blend of rough jocosity and scientific curiosity:

...in the moors belonging to Amcotts, was found by John Tate of Amcotts, who was digging turf, the entire body of a woman. He first cut of one of her feet with his spade, on which was a sandall; but being frighted, left it. I being informed of it, went with Thomas Perfect, my gardener, and others, and we took up the whole body; there was a sandal on the other foot; the skin was like a piece of tanned leather, and it stretched like a fine doe skin; the hair was fresh about the head and privy parts, which distinguished the sex; the teeth firm; the bones was raled black; the flesh consumed; and she lay upon her side in a bending posture, with her head and toes almost together, which looks as tho' she had been hurled down by the force of some strong current of water, and though a great part of this moor had been formerly graved of she lay seven foot deep from the present surface. I took the skin off one arm, from the elbow to the hand, and shaking the bones out, it would have made a ladies' muff. The other hand not being cut with the spade, as we dug for it, I preserved it, and stuffed it, first taking out the bones, which my son, James Stovin, now has in his possession ... the nails are firm and fast on the fingers. He also has one of the sandals... This lady's skin and the sandals were both tanned by the same tanner (to wit) by the black water of these moors ... I buried the remains of this lady in Amcotts chapel yard [Stovin was a Quaker]... I showed the hand and sandal to my worthy friend Thomas Whichcote, of Harpswell, esq. knight of the shire for the county of Lincoln in parliament, who was pleased to put the sandal on before I sent them to the Royal Society.[2]

George Stovin's case proves the power of local patriotism, strong in Axholme still:

It is related of Mr. Stovin that he scarcely ever left the Levels, living in Crowle and its vicinity, and with the true feeling of a native antiquary thinking no part of England comparable to the Isle of Axholme, and no town equal to Crowle.

But even he eventually succumbed to wanderlust:

In the latter part of his life, however, he crossed the Trent, and fixed his residence at Winterton.[3]

Another relic of old Axholme can be seen in in St Oswald's church in Crowle—the Anglo-Saxon Crowle Stone, a seven-feet-high shaft, a millstone monolith carved crudely (millstone is coarse-grained) with two birds facing each other, above two men facing each other (one of whom may be about to draw a sword), a third man on horseback and part of a badly damaged runic inscription. On the back are interlacing ornamentation and a snake.

The monument may have been set up to commemorate the passage of St Oswald's body through Crowle after he had been killed by King Penda, the last pagan king of Mercia, at the Battle of Maserfield. The well at nearby Lower Burnham was long believed to have been the locale of the battle, although the consensus modern opinion is that it was at Oswestry in Shropshire. But as late as the 1960s there was Christian interest in the well, and even a pilgrimage.[4] British Academy specialists believe the Crowle Stone is more likely to represent scenes from Norse myth, the Isle long attractive to Danes, who clung on here even after the Norman invasion.[5]

Axholme was later a stronghold of the Mowbrays, whose rampant lion is still the area's emblem, between the Conquest and the time they rashly decided to oppose Henry II; the mounds of their motte and bailey, captured by the king's men in 1173 in an amphibious operation, can be seen at Owston Ferry. Even after that they remained prominent in local affairs, until they moved away in the fifteenth century. One of England's surviving medieval customs (maybe its oldest) may be part of their legacy—the Haxey Hood game, which takes place every 6 January at Haxey.

Eleven 'Boggins,' a 'Lord' and a 'Fool' try to keep hold of the 'Hood'—a long leather bolster—while the rest of the town's population ('the sway') try to take it from them and bring it to one of Haxey's pubs, where it will stay until the next New Year's Eve. The ritual is said to derive from a real fourteenth-century incident, when Lady de Mowbray's riding hood blew off as she rode through the town, and was chased comically around the field by thirteen farm labourers. One caught the hood, but couldn't bring himself to approach Lady de Mowbray, so he asked another to hand it to her. She thanked them graciously, smilingly called the shy labourer a 'fool' and the other a 'lord,' and donated thirteen acres of land for the use of the people on condition that they re-enacted the chase each year.

This story may be based on fact, because there was a real 1359 donation of land to tenants *in perpetuum*—the Mowbray Deed, a source of fierce local pride, 'the palladium of the commoners of Axholme.'[6] Even now, the Isle is deeply proud of its association with one of England's most eminent families. Early twentieth-century stories about an Axholme cryptid—the outsize white 'Commonpiece Cat'—may conceivably derive from subconscious memories of the Mowbray lion, as much as any hoax, intoxicant or trick of light.

For several weeks before 6 January, the Boggins (one designated the Chief), the Fool and the Lord tour the district in costume, collecting for charity, singing traditional songs like 'John Barleycorn' and 'Drink Old England Dry.' The Lord and Chief Boggin wear hunting pinks, and top-hats festooned with badges and foliage, the other Boggins red jumpers. The Lord also carries a 'wand of office,' made up of thirteen willow wands (one upside down). The Fool is dressed in parti-colours and wears a hat covered with feathers, flowers and rags. His face is striped with black and red, and he has a whip and a sock full of grain, with which he can hit anyone who comes close.

On the day, work stops at midday. The little streets are crammed, the roads out double-parked, and a couple of thousand good-natured people clutching cans or camera phones, a mix of excitement-seekers and players from outside the area, mingle with journalists and interested observers, and (probably rather often) academic folklorists.

The principals tour the pubs, getting free drinks at each. The Fool goes in front, and has the right to kiss any women he encounters. He mounts the Mowbray Stone near the church and makes a speech of welcome, while damp straw is ignited behind him ('smoking the Fool'). He concludes with 'hoose agen hoose, toon agen toon, if a man meets a man knock 'im doon, but doan't 'ot 'im' ('house against house, town against town, if a man meets a man, knock him down, but don't hurt him'), then heads for the field where the game begins.

It starts with practice runs for children, then finally the Sway Hood is thrown into the air. It cannot be thrown by anyone else, nor carried, but has to be 'swayed'—pushed and pulled, with the people around it—in the direction of whatever pub the participants favour. The game is arduous, slow, and sometimes destructive of hedges, walls or unwisely-parked vehicles. People sometimes fall down and get trampled, but are swiftly extricated by Boggins. Eventually, often hours later, the Hood is touched by a pub landlord, and the Hood is in his keeping for the year; each of the town's pubs have Hood hooks behind the bar.

It is piquant to think a stray gust of wind 700 years ago may have given rise to this substantive thing—almost as if the lady's laughter is still audible after almost 700 years. The game's longevity is suggestive of little more exciting ever happening here, and long isolation from ominous 'interesting times.' It has weathered the disapprobation of magistrates, who always distrust volatile folk customs, and eighteenth to twentieth century dislikers of 'vulgarity.' Will it survive today's more insidious enemies—indifference and irony?

Aristocratic Isleonians regaled themselves on bittern, curlew, grebe, lamprey, perch, sturgeon and swan; the un-aristocratic dug turf, eeled, fowled, pannaged pigs, pastured cattle, planted barley, punted and reeded, often probably left largely to themselves. Rare eminent visitors enjoyed strange slaughter. In 1609, the 15-year-old Prince Henry and his retinue boarded boats on Thorne Mere close to the Isle—to pursue 500 deer that had been driven up to their necks in water,

> ...their horned heads raised themselves so as almost to represent a little wood. Here being encompassed about with the little fleet, some ventured amongst them, and feeling such and such as were fattest, they either immediately cut their throats, or else tying a strong long rope to their heads, drew them to land and killed them.[7]

To mark the new century, nine years previously the far-distant Queen signed into law 'An act for the recovery and inning of drowned and surrounded grounds and the draining dry of watery marshes, fens, bogs, moors and other grounds of like nature.' Her successor, James I, had continued to consider the question. It probably all seemed academic to Isleonians. Since Roman times, there had been talk and even half-hearted attempts at riverbank repair and straightening, land drainage and reclamation, which had not greatly affected the Isle, or anywhere else. It was not until the accession of Charles I in 1625—younger brother of the hunting Henry, who had died in 1612—that reality came home. The following year, the Dutch engineer Cornelius Vermuyden turned up with a team of mostly Dutch and Huguenot 'Participants,' armed with orders to impose economic efficiency and classical order on these 'wastes.'

The Dutch, of course, were preeminent in the management of waters, with centuries of experience in banking, bridging, channelling, culverting, delving, draining, gating, poldering, sluicing and warping. Their Golden Age was fundamentally based on their ability to expand their land—land to feed their growing numbers, to make fortunes from, on which to establish elegant estates, to paint prosperous peasants toiling in, and huge clouds passing over. Much of their conveniently close country had once been very like the Isle; their (safely Protestant) expertise could surely be utilised to turn the wastes into a wonderland, and all that 'empty' space into Exchequer specie. Vermuyden was besides known to the King through previous work along the Thames at Dagenham and Windsor, and in the 'Great Fen' that joined northern Norfolk and Cambridgeshire with the Holland parts of Lincolnshire.

The King's agreement with Vermuyden spoke piously of 'the good and welfare of his subjects inhabiting near or about the places,' but Isleonians, not just the poor ones, rightly saw a land-grab—dispossession of what they had, the enrichment of others, including *foreign* others, at their expense, the erasure of ancient rights of common, as enshrined in the Mowbray Deed. Vermuyden on the other hand needed to pay his imported workforce, and give returns to his investors.

As always in politics, private motivations mixed with public protestations, old grudges with new. Local distrust of royal intentions was mirrored at the highest London levels, with Lincolnshire MPs prominent among the King's opponents, refusing to pay forced loans or support his demands for ship money, and always paranoid about 'Popery.' As in the Fens, drainers soon found they needed to surround their Axholme operations with guards. There were disruptions and destructions of dykes and banks, accommodation and chapels built for the workers, and eventually assaults on the workers themselves. The work continued nevertheless, driven by cupidity but also professional pride, and maybe even the 'Protestant work ethic,' which existed long before that term was coined in the twentieth century.[8] It seems appropriate that one of those Dutch works should be called Idle Stop.

But the work was rushed—just eighteen months—and not always successful. That Vermuyden was granted extensive lands and then a knighthood, made him only more hated, and no less foreign. He sold up and moved on, to drain the Bedford Levels, go to debtors' prison, and ultimately die in obscurity. A slew of ethnic insults grew into being about this time—double-Dutch, 'talking Dutch as Daimports's dog' (to speak affectedly), Dutch auction, Dutch comfort (when something could have been even worse), Dutch concert (a terrible noise), Dutch courage, Dutch feast (when the host gets drunk before the guests), Dutch gleek (drinking too much), Dutch gold (an alloy of copper and zinc), Dutch nightingales (frogs), Dutch reckoning (an inaccurate account), Dutch uncle, and Dutch widow (a prostitute). English people who wanted to express a strong refusal would exclaim 'I'll be a Dutchman if I do!' As with Germans, the Dutch were too much like the English for comfort. The enterprise was nevertheless driven determinedly by the King, desperate for revenue and as zealous of his prerogatives as Isleonians were of their rights. The ill-will caused by these vast schemes helped greatly in creating the conditions of the Civil War.

During that war, Parliamentary troops broke down sluices, re-flooded reclaimed land for defensive purposes, and reinstated some rights of common. Ecstatic Isleonians lauded Cromwell as 'Lord of the Fens'—even though there were renewed attempts at drainages. The Isle's mood soured; a 1646 House of Lords order designed to suppress renewed rioting on the Isle was greeted by commoners who said,

...they did not care a Fart for the Order which was made by the lords in Parliament and published in the Churches, and that notwithstanding that order, they would pull down all the rest of the Houses in the Level that were built upon these Improvements which were drained and destroy all the Enclosures.[9]

The Rump Parliament of 1648-53 was especially loathed for having validated pre-war drainage agreements, and the Levellers John Lilburne and John Wildman led riotous protests on the Isle. In October 1651, protestors destroyed eighty-two houses and a mill. When a protestor was shot dead by a guard, the murder was winked at by the authorities, one of them hoping 'it might procure conformitie in the people to permitt him to goe on with his worke.' Cromwell came down especially hard after 1656. Yet folk memories of Interregnum indulgence persisted long after Restoration, especially as the returning Royalists fined the commoners for wartime damage. Drainage efforts resumed, and accelerated, fuelled by new cultural attitudes towards Nature and 'messy' wildness, as suggested by Alexander Pope:

Bid Harbours open, Public Ways extend; / Bid Temples, worthier of the God, ascend; / Bid the broad Arch the dang'rous flood contain, / The Mole projected, break the roaring main; / Back to his bounds their subject sea command, / And roll obedient rivers through the land.[10]

These works continued to cause a huge amount of bad feeling, from legal cases to lethal force. Samuel Smiles lauds a legal counsellor-turned-tax collector named Nathaniel Reading who fought 'thirty-one set battles with the fen-men' and, when he died in 1716 at 100 years old, had passed fifty years 'in constant danger of physical violence.'[11] Even some modern Isleonians can still refer to Reading as a 'turncoat barrister.'[12] Isleonians would later be predictably opposed to Enclosure, and gallantly yet perversely farmed in inefficient strips into the twentieth century.

Cromwell was still in living memory when the Isle's most influential son bawled into life in Epworth. John Wesley, born in 1703, was the son of Epworth's vicar, Samuel. In 1709, he nearly died in a fire at the Rectory. The fire may have been arson directed against his father, locally unpopular for being a Royalist, a Tory, and a detester of Dissenters (perhaps exaggeratedly so— he had been one himself). Although he had a good private sense of humour, his public manner was variously described as 'authoritarian', and 'choleric'. Whatever the cause, John often afterwards referred to himself as 'a brand plucked from the burning,' an allusion to Zechariah 3:2 9—'And the LORD said unto Satan, The LORD rebuke thee, O Satan; even the LORD that hath chosen Jerusalem rebuke thee: is not this a brand plucked out of the fire?'—and from an early age seems to have been determined to set the Church of England alight.

He lived at the rebuilt Rectory until going up to London's Charterhouse in 1714 (founded by another west Lincolnshire man, Thomas Sutton of Knaith)—and thus was absent for the great sensation of December 1715–January 1716. Extraordinary stories sprang up that the Rectory was haunted by 'Old Jeffrey,' a highly active poltergeist who knocked on doors at midnight, made noises of cackles, footsteps and groans, and set cradles rocking and peppermills turning by themselves. Family prayers would be interrupted by furious knockings, especially when they mentioned the King, and then things started to be seen—beds levitating, an old man in a white gown, a white rabbit, a headless white badger. Samuel reported being shoved, as did the visiting vicar of Haxey. The haunting was spoken of in London salons, and sensation-seekers streamed to Epworth just to see the outside of the house. Old Jeffrey became one of England's most famous ever apparitions, in a country proverbially said to have 'more ghosts per square mile' than anywhere else in the world.

'Old Jeffrey' was clearly a product of the often unhappy atmosphere of this house in its remote and often hostile town. Fourteen of the couple's nineteen children died in infancy, and Samuel and his much-tried wife Susanna both had strongly different views on such matters as William of Orange's legitimacy as king. Samuel had once moved out for a year when she refused to say 'Amen' to a prayer for King William. That the poltergeist often rapped hardest when there were prayers for the King was adduced as evidence for her as culprit.

Their daughter Mary (nicknamed Molly) was also suspected of attention-seeking; she had been crippled by a childhood accident, and this weighed gravely on her, as she wrote in 1726—'I have lived in a state of affliction ever since I was born, being the ridicule of mankind and the reproach of my family.'[13]

Another sister, Mehetabel (called Hetty) was formidably clever, frustrated, and poetically inclined. She could not have carried out the hoaxing by herself, because she was sometimes asleep during the loudest manifestations—but even then she was obliquely suspected, for sleeping obviously uneasily, flushed and muttering, as if she was somehow projecting energy. She certainly had the imagination, later lauded by Samuel Richardson and others for deeply personal poems, drawn from her poignant private history of having suitors rejected by her father, eloping then becoming pregnant, being forced into marriage with an illiterate and violent plumber, seeing all her children die in infancy, and being shunned by most of her family. When she died in 1750, after almost a decade of illness, only John's brother Charles attended her funeral.

The Old Jeffrey stories were circulated credulously by both Samuel and John, who may have diverged doctrinally, but were united in their belief in the existence of demons—John maybe even more so than his more widely read father. His *Journals* brim with out-of-the-world encounters with angels, convulsions, divine retribution, 'holy laughter,' prophecies, being 'slain in the spirit,' speaking in tongues, trances, tremblings and visions, testaments to the reality of which have ever since nourished not only Methodists and Primitive Methodists, but Bible Christians, Charismatics, Nazarenes, Pentecostalists, and others. The plodding, ratiocinative 'method' from which his sect derived its name was built on irrational foundations, like many other logical schemes. His 'Arminian' theology, derived largely from the ideas of the Dutch theologian Jacobus Arminius (1560-1609), yet another Dutch influence on Axholme, was based on belief in original sin, disbelief in predestination, the possibility of atonement and 'Christian perfection,' and the existence of prevenient grace—divine grace which predisposes a person to seek God prior to any initiative on the part of the recipient.

His theology was kinder than Calvinism, and more conformable to custom. Wesley would never actually leave the Church of England, although by the time of his death in 1791, Methodism's separation was all but complete—but it still aroused bitter controversy from Anglicans and scorn among the educated. But hundreds of thousands of people, often the poorest in society, came to hear Wesley speak at frequently huge outdoor meetings everywhere from Aberdeen to Cornwall. His message unnerved the Church of England hierarchy, always conscious that Anglicanism was an uneasy balancing act between extremes, and which was simultaneously under siege by scepticism.

On one occasion in 1742, John was refused communion at Epworth, so addressed the crowd from his father's tomb in the churchyard. Churchmen generally did not care for his large assemblies, with their highly charged or even hysterical atmosphere, which emphasised highly subjective 'Experience' at least as much as those other three, slightly less subjective, parts of the Methodist Quadrilateral—'Scripture,' 'Tradition,' and 'Reason.' Educated Whigs chortled at the upstart faith, like Horace Walpole, who called Wesley 'as evidently an actor as

Garrick,' and was greatly amused by the 'opera' and 'ugly enthusiasm' of a Methodist meeting, and the 'pure rosy vulgar faces' of congregants.[14] The nineteenth-century poet Robert Hawker was so disgusted by the ecstasies of converts that he called Methodism 'the mother of the brothel ... of modern England,' and Wesley 'that father of English fornication.'[15] Wesleyanism also had political subtexts disliked by Tories— egalitarianism, suspicion of authority, and utopianism. It is no coincidence that many of the first trade union leaders emerged from the Methodist movement, giving English radicalism a unique flavour; the British Left, it has been observed, 'owes more to Methodism than Marxism.'[16]

Methodism is presently the fourth-largest Christian denomination in the UK, and there are an estimated 70 million Methodists worldwide—all this from a little town in Axholme. It has been undergoing a 'journey of reconciliation' with the Church of England since 2003. But Wesley's extraordinary energy seems increasingly otiose, even here in its heartland. Axholme's Methodist chapels look little visited, albeit still neatly kept, part of a greater dwindling. Wesley's statue in the town is still garlanded, there are 'Wesley Day' markets, and Methodist pilgrims come to see the Rectory and its relics. But his epitaph in Epworth's churchyard is weathering, and in the decade to 2016, the numbers of Methodists in Britain fell by 3.5% every year.[17] Behind the now usually shut-up parish church, the rest of the graveyard is a lawn, except for two surviving urned monuments—too heavy for anyone to bother moving?—silent except for swishing limes framing misty vistas of trees, a water tower, a long decline towards far distant power lines.

* * *

Westbound traffic comes onto the Isle at the Lilliputian port of Keadby. The bridge, which used to open for ships, was built in 1916, and looks every inch of that year—when the first tanks were being built at William Foster & Co. in Lincoln—clumsily colossal, olive-green, and ponderous, maybe even menacing. Or was that the effect of the caged walkways, the bickering crows, and the Samaritans plaques screwed to the metalwork? The bridge seems too low to jump from, however desperate—although the Trent flows superficially smooth, and throws back brilliant cranes and cloudscapes. A 1920s car was rattling over the bridge as I did—a reminder of the puniness of those who forged this bridge, and the rickety construction of the world then and now.

Nearby, under the B3192, five waterways become three, and these enter the Trent here, complex and powerful currents making this reach almost as perilous to the unwary as 'boggart'-haunted Jenny Hurn Bend, not far away south. 'Jenny' was a long-lived Trentside legend, a water sprite called a 'boggart,' diminutive but dangerous, here 'described' by the pioneering folklorist Ethel Rudkin (1893-1985):

> The pygmy propels the dish rapidly across the stream by means of a minute pair of oars, the size of teaspoons. It is said, that having reached shore this being crosses the road and proceeds to browse in the field. Or again it is said that a 'thing' is known to come crawling out of the water, having large eyes, and long hair, and tusks like a walrus. It goes into the fields to feed. The river bank here curves in the shape of a horse-shoe, consequently a short-cut footpath has been used for years to counteract this bend.[18]

Rudkin was personally hag-ridden—half-fabulist, half-researcher, making *Wünderkammers* of vernacular objects and stories that would otherwise have vanished, and seeing the connections between things—like the phantoms of folk memory and the phantom of her husband, a decorated Machine Gun

Corps officer who died in France in 1918 after what her obituarist described as a 'blissful but tragically brief marriage.' She never remarried, but dedicated herself to the lore of this particular land, eventually needing to buy an old windmill to house her collection. Museums at Lincoln and Scunthorpe now have many of the objects she saved from Lincolnshire's abyss—eel spears, hobby horses, medieval pottery, music, photographs, witch bottles—and her handbag, holding the flowers she wore in her hair at her wedding, and letters from her husband. Elsewhere in western Lincolnshire, the connections between folk memory and real life are made explicit. At Eagle, historically linked with both the Knights Templar and the Knights of St John of Jerusalem— one St John's officer still has the title 'Bailiff of Egle' (*sic.*)—the memorial to eight villagers who died in France between 1914 and 1918 is a stone gateway with effigies of a Knight Templar and a Knight Hospitaller.

Lieutenant Gonville Bromhead from Thurlby probably saw himself as some kind of Christian knight, as he stood with the other 137 men, mostly of 'B' Company, the 2nd Battalion, 24th Regiment of Foot, against 4,000 Zulus at Rorke's Drift on 22 January 1879. In the 1964 film *Zulu*, Bromhead was portrayed by Michael Caine as a drawling and elegant fop, but in fact he was so deaf that he missed commands during drill, so he and his men were usually relegated to unglamorous secondary roles, like guarding supply depots. Despite this, Bromhead was described by a comrade as 'beloved in his regiment'; perhaps this was because his incapacity kept his men out of harm's way.

Bromhead played only a secondary role in the defence of the Drift, but undoubtedly it took great courage for anyone to stand against a numerically superior (if technologically inferior) force described by one terrified soldier as 'black as hell, and thick as grass.' Yet the eleven Victoria Crosses that were awarded for the action were thought by some even at the time to be excessive—

perhaps a means of glossing over the same day's debacle at Isandhlwana, where 1,300 British troops were killed. Lieutenant John Chard's vivid account of the battle was hugely popular at home and helped shape the frantic jingoism that was the prelude to the following century's inevitable hubris. Bromhead can be seen as faintly comical, typified by his later failure to meet the Queen, because he was on a fishing trip in Ireland and got the invitation too late. But he was also lucky—someone who was thrust into history's most cinematic front lines and comported himself creditably.[19]

Back on the thick-grassed Isle, silence soon sinks down as you cross the Sheffield and South Yorkshire Navigation and head north, with fields and little woods unfolding on the left and the wide bank walling out the Trent on the right, a direction pointer and reminder of both humanity's and Nature's might. In many directions are pylons, long lines looping out of sight, carrying sagging cat's cradles of megawatts to charge up the iPhones of England, but they are mostly in the slightly misty distance—the Isle too empty and inconvenient to string them across, making it an emerald eye in an electric storm. Back roads off these back roads throw up backwater names—Boskeydyke, Warpland, Amcotts Hook, Paupers Drain, Lover's Ground, Dirtness Levels, Godnow, Medge, Crook o' Moor—insignificant to the casual passer, deeply interesting to those who live or have lived there and gave them their affectionate or despairing names.

At Eastoft and Garthorpe, one side of the road used to be in Yorkshire, and you can stand on the old bed of the Don. You walk in a Dutch dream-time of titanic engineering, shifted rivers, sunken roads, efficient fields, occasional Zealand-style gabling on older houses—but emptier than the actual Holland, less ruthlessly functional. Villages are buried in fields which might once have been rivers. Children play near war memorials to Isleonians who joined the Belgian dream-time in 1914, and were followed by their children a generation later. Will any of these children ever go out on such terrible errands?

Old trolley buses await new passengers at the museum in Sandtoft (annexed from Yorkshire)—representative of that very English obsession with defunct vehicles, from trolleybuses and steam trains to vintage cars and warplanes. If the English love a trolleybus, they even more 'love a lord.' Axholme was never renowned for great architecture, but older Isleonians mistily remember Temple Belwood—Axholme's grandest house, standing on a site romantically held to have been sacred to Druids, and certainly inhabited by near-legendary landowners. The Mowbrays gave the site to the Templars, and after their suppression, the Hospitallers. After dissolution, it passed to the Vavasours—lawyers, but liked nevertheless, because one of them ruined himself taking out lawsuits trying to protect the Commoners from Vermuyden.

The house was rebuilt with Georgian opulence, with Gothick gatehouses that would be a loved landmark until the 1960s. But by 1900, the house had become a 'high class boarding establishment' offering 'charades, card parties, private theatricals, tableau vivants, and good concerts.' Sadly, these enticements failed to attract sufficient numbers of 'high class' guests, and so the house slid into less high-class establishment, school, borstal, part of the property portfolio of the fraudster Ernest Terah Hooley ('The Splendid Bankrupt'), magnet for lead thieves, and finally foundations for the M180 in the age of Humberside.[20] The only remnants are an eighteenth-century obelisk, commemorating the death of a horse called Sir Solomon, to mark whose demise the squire oddly shot his two best hounds—and a walled garden, at the heart of the walled garden of the Isle.

Samuel Wesley combined his duties at Epworth with being the incumbent at Wroot, where John served as his curate. Wroot is Lincolnshire's farthest west village, so far west even by Axholme standards that Isleonians joke getting there means going 'out of

England.' Wroot means roughly 'snout,' or spur of land, and going there does feel like being out on a promontory, with wide views east over Axholme, and west over the Chase. The snout has been lived in since at least Neolithic times; in the museum at Scunthorpe is a jade axe found at Wroot by Ethel Rudkin, where someone let it fall 12,000 years ago.

It is easy to imagine what journeying to Wroot must have been like in the Wesleys' time, especially with wintry winds picking up across the peaty plain, as they clip-clopped past little landmarks with names like Folly Drain, Tunnel Pits and Ninevah Farm. Today's unclassified, uneven, zig-zagging roads would have been a little busier, and the fields fuller of life, but the long and oft-repeated journey must often have been dreary, especially when they were heading towards rather than away from Wroot, a place Hetty described as 'devoid of wisdom, wit or grace,' whose residents were 'As asses dull, on dunghills born' with heads 'impervious as the stones.' For the Wesleys, Wroot was probably always associated with disagreeableness—and later with much worse.

In 1734, Samuel gave the Wroot incumbency to John Whitelamb, a poor man he had taken up and educated against the strongly held feelings of the rest of the Wesleys, who regarded Whitelamb as a freeloader, libertine and possible Deist. Whitelamb had already spent four desperately unhappy years living at the rectory in Epworth, maltreated by most, and had just become 'family' by marrying John's sister Mary. Matters might have improved after he and Mary moved to Wroot, but just months after their marriage, Mary and her stillborn child died, and were buried in its churchyard.

When Whitelamb died in 1769, the still unforgiving John wrote, 'Oh, why did he not die forty years ago, while he knew in whom he had believed?'[21] It is an unflattering sidelight on a man capable of magnificence, ancient bile now sunk in the warped earth of the Isle.

*   *   *

I came back 'into England' by way of Westwoodside, left Axholme over the Mother Drain, and crossed into Nottinghamshire, feeling sorry for the people who have to live here rather than in Lincolnshire.

No one knows why the Trent is called the Trent. Izaak Walton was engaging in wishful thinking when he surmised it was because of the thirty different kinds of fish to be found in it. It *may* derive from Romano-British words signifying 'flooding strongly,' or 'trespasser,' or 'great thoroughfare,' and any of those would be appropriate. River names are one of the biggest riddles in English etymology, some of them with ur-names that go back to the pre-Celts. A few of these persist—Don, Tamar, Wye—but others were altered by imperialists laying claim to the land by giving it *their* name, to harness its productivity and mystical forces in accordance with their values or ethnic interests, just as modern revolutionaries name or rename roads.

Between East Stockwith, northwest of Gainsborough, and Newton-on-Trent, the river's winding wideness marks the boundary between Lincolnshire and Nottinghamshire. Before that, it was the western frontier of the Kingdom of Lindsey, until being absorbed in Mercia after 679's Battle of the Trent; as usual with Anglo-Saxon battles, the location of this epic clash is unknown.

Gainsborough was an Anglo-Saxon foundation, the *burgh* of the Gaini, and King Alfred came here in 868 to marry Ealhswith, daughter of their chief. But it is better known for un-English reasons. The Trent's tidal bore, the Aegir, is named after the Norse god of the oceans, and in 1013, Denmark's king came likewise up the Trent, rather like a vengeful god himself. Sweyn 'Forkbeard' moored his fleet at the Morton bend north of Gainsborough, and set up camp on Thonock Hill—determined to extend the Danelaw into the recalcitrant west. Seven miles away, on the chancel arch at Stow Minster, is a contemporary graffito of a longship, hinting at the trepidation of those times. Gainsborough became Danish England's capital, even minting coins, but Sweyn did not linger long. He graciously accepted the submission of Lindsey, Northumbria and the Five Boroughs (Derby, Leicester, Lincoln, Nottingham, and Stamford), then set off on a royal harm offensive, leaving his son Cnut in charge.

Trentside romancers claim the legend about Cnut and the inexorability of the tides stems from a real incident on the river bank, but Cnut may have been too busy to make future clichés. King Æthelred tried to conquer Lindsey, but was thrown back easily, and the chief effect of his attack was that Anglo-Saxon hostages taken by his father in London had their ears, hands and noses cut off in retaliation. Cnut went on to outlive Æthelred, trounce Edmund at Assandun, be proclaimed King of all England, visit Rome, and die with the soubriquet 'The Great.' The town's time as English epicentre had lasted about a year.

For most of the long centuries since, Britain's most inland port existed on unglamorous industry. Its more abstractly-inclined sons often opted to live elsewhere. There were religious thinkers, like William of Gainsborough (d. 1307), Edward I's emissary to the French court, and reader in theology to the Pope—or the Patrick brothers, John (1632–95) and Simon (1626–1707), John a noted Protestant controversialist in the time of James II, the other Bishop of Ely and a founder of the Society for the Promotion of Christian Knowledge.

There were littérateurs, like Thomas Miller, born in poverty in 1807 and apprenticed to a basket-maker, who later moved to London and launched on a literary career after he had daringly sent the Anglo-Irish authoress Countess Blessington poems in some of his baskets. Miller's relentlessly sentimental novels and verse, with titles like *Dorothy Dovedale's Trials* and *Songs for*

British Riflemen, are strongly of their time, and even then were not always appreciated. He once asked Dickens for financial assistance to further his career, but as Dickens commented to Edward Bulwer Lytton, 'I fear [Miller] has mistaken his vocation.' His next-door neighbour in Gainsborough, Thomas Cooper (1805–92), was a less frivolous sort, devoting his life to the twin causes of Chartism and Creationism; his cheerily titled 1845 'prison rhyme' *Purgatory of Suicides* runs to a self-harm-provoking 944 stanzas.

But real literary immortality for the town can be found in *The Mill on the Floss*, written after George Eliot had visited in 1859. Her Floss is the Trent, which at the end floods disastrously, reuniting siblings Tom and Maggie Tulliver in death, after frequent differences in life. Gainsborough becomes St Ogg's in Eliot's imagination:

> ...one of those old, old towns which impress one as a continua-
> tion and outgrowth of nature, as much as the nests of the bower-
> birds or the winding galleries of the white ants; a town which
> carries the traces of its long growth and history like a millennial
> tree, and has sprung up and developed in the same spot between
> the river and the low hill from the time when the Roman legions
> turned their backs on it from the camp on the hillside, and the
> long-haired sea-kings came up the river and looked with fierce,
> eager eyes at the fatness of the land.[22]

The 'long-haired sea kings' are vaguely remembered in modern Gainsborough—the Sweyn Forkbeard and Canute pubs, Gainsborough Trinity FC's crest of a crown—but the once-frantic river frontage is almost devoid of life now, its eighteenth- and nineteenth-century maltings, mills and warehouses mostly repurposed as flats, plus others still awaiting conversion, and odd gaps brimming with rosebay willow herb. Impressive flood defences were opened here in 2000, part of a massive regeneration of the quays, which had been as derelict as the Isle of Dogs. The energy and money seem to have run out.

The Trent alone remains always the same—broad and brown, a 'great thoroughfare' indeed, far more powerfully flowing than the traffic on the bridge. One can easily envision it rising as at the end of Eliot's story to drown the guilty and innocent alike, and 'trespass' disastrously across an infinite plain. Like the little ports of the Humber, Gainsborough badly misses its barges, keels, lighters, sloops and long strings of 'Tom-pudding' tub boats. The few streets back from the river seem even less purposeful—subdued, sun-baked, a bit run-down, the classical parish church seemingly always closed, and England flags drooping from windows in hope of a breeze whenever some cup is at stake. The classical toll booths on the bridge, spruced up in 2000, have since had a toll taken from them, their cream stucco gritty with car exhaust particles, the damp gardens at their base deep in briar and litter.

But the town has the Old Hall, one of England's best Tudor buildings, a rare black-and-white oak-timbered edifice to find in this country of red brick. As George Eliot noted, 'It is all so old we look with loving pardon at its inconsistencies.' The oaks came from the estate; the owners came from France, and went everywhere.

The Burghs were a typically restless eleventh-century clan branching out from Normandy to England, Ireland, Scotland, Flanders and farther, omnipresent in British and wider history as crusaders, kingmakers, nobles, princesses and soldiers—and, at a *very* distant remove, the Anglo-Irish balladeer Chris de Burgh, notorious for 'Lady in Red.' By the fifteenth century, Thomas Burgh would be Edward IV's Master of Horse and chief supporter in Lincolnshire, who had fought at both Barnet and Tewkesbury. After Edward died, Burgh initially supported Richard III, who came to stay in 1483, but not long afterwards the family cannily altered their allegiance to the Tudors. Henry VIII would stay here with Catherine Howard in 1541.

Sir John Burgh (1562–94) was a quintessential Elizabethan soldier—half-idealist, half-opportunist, who brought troops from Lincolnshire to fight for the Protestant cause in Holland and France, and commanded the naval squadron which captured the famous Portuguese treasure ship the *Madre de Deus* off the Azores in 1592. That ship's un-Trent-like cargo, which included ambergris, cinnamon, cochineal, ebony, nutmeg, pearls, and pepper, aroused powerful emotions. Burgh himself died in a duel over the plunder, euphemised on his monument in Westminster Abbey as an 'untimely death,' although the nature of his demise is hinted at the end—'My sword shall not save me, Psalm 44:6.' The monument to this supreme swashbuckler was swept away during the eighteenth century by a grateful nation.

His house has a beamed long hall, a kitchen with two fireplaces big enough to roast whole oxen, and a castellated tower from where you can almost see the Humber. Evening sunshine gives monumentality to the lofty long hall, and slants reminiscently into the kitchens, briefly gilding dust, and highlighting the humps and bumps of the scullion-worn brick floors. English Heritage information panels oddly dangling on ropes show the plumb line, and highlight the drunken leaning of wall timbers.

John Wesley preached here several times, after one 1759 visit, recording 'I preached in the Old Hall to a mixed multitude, part civil, part rude as bears.' By then, the Burghs had long since left for bigger stages, and the Hall had become part pub, part flophouse, part possibly worse. It would become a linen factory, a theatre, a machine workshop, and an auction room—lucky not to be knocked down itself. English Heritage speculates that William Rose, who was born here in 1856 and would go on to invent wrapping machines, may have been the inspiration for the Cadbury's Roses chocolate brand. It seems a come-down from Crusaders.

The area has had bitterer tastes of history. During the Civil Wars, much of Lincolnshire was Parliamentarian, but its western side was always vulnerable to attack from the Royalists across the river. In January 1643, a Royalist raiding party captured Gainsborough and held it for six months. Responsibility for the retaken town's defence was given to the Earl of Kingston-upon-Hull, who before the War had endeavoured to remain neutral. His garrison was surprised by Parliament's Lord Willoughby, and he was captured. As he was being taken downstream to imprisonment, a chance shot from a Royalist battery sliced him in two. A surely too apt to be true story was that he had once said that before he took up arms for either side, a cannon ball would divide him between them.

Willoughby's forces were promptly besieged in their turn by Charles Cavendish, son of the Earl of Devonshire, but help came in the formidable shape of Cromwell. This was the battle that would cement Cromwell's military reputation. He overran Cavendish's advance guard at Lea, south of Gainsborough, then battled uphill at Foxby to the east, their ascent hampered by numerous rabbit warrens. At the top, there was a brisk exchange, as Cromwell recalled:

> We came up Horse by Horse, where we disputed it with our swords and pistols a pretty time, all keeping close order, so that one could not break the other. At last, they a little shrinking, our men, perceiving it, pressed in upon them and immediately routed the whole body.[23]

After this 'pretty time,' Cromwell eventually managed to take the Royalist reserve from behind. The Royalists were routed, and Cavendish himself was killed by a sword thrust to the chest by a former ironworks clerk named James Berry—a great survivor, who was later a member of Cromwell's House of Lords, and after the Restoration Commander of the Royal Horse Guards—in a swamp near the river that was long afterwards known as Candish Bog, near Graves Close and Redcoats Field. The town was secured, but the following morning the Earl of Newcastle was seen advancing from the north, with the main Royalist army. Cromwell withdrew to Lincoln through difficult country, losing only two men in a masterful retreat that augmented his military reputation as much as his victory over Cavendish.

The town went Royalist again—was retaken by Parliament in December—was evacuated in March 1644 as Prince Rupert approached—and secured again for Parliament in the summer of 1644. Gainsborough came into the Civil Wars one last time, in 1648, as a crossing place for a Royalist force advancing from Axholme, and then for Parliamentary armies going the opposite way, to inflict a final defeat of the Royalists at Willoughby near Nottingham.

All these once-urgent manoeuvres have left few traces, except for some road names, and the atmospheric façade of Torksey Castle. Torksey overlooks the Trent beside its important junction with the Foss Dyke, Britain's first canal, that links the Trent to the Witham at Lincoln. In 873, the Great Heathen Army had overwintered at Torksey, and later lords had the lucrative right to levy tolls on Trent traffic. The Elizabethan manor house (it was never a real castle) had been the home of staunch King's man Henry Jermyn, commander of the Queen's bodyguard, who had to leave suddenly on the outbreak of hostilities. His service was at first poorly requited, because in 1645 a Royalist flying column from the west bank set fire to his house. It would never be rebuilt. After the Restoration, the newly-created Earl of St Albans opted for London and Paris over Lincolnshire, with a dazzling career as Lord Chamberlain, Ambassador to France, patron of Abraham Cowley, and designer of St James's, after whom Jermyn Street is named.

Carolean town planning and once-fashionable tailoring seem equally far from Torksey under rain, where there were grasshoppers bounding among dripping bindweed, a fleeing female sparrowhawk, and the sharp tang of sheep dung in the former fireplace. The eight concrete towers of Cottam Power Station, begun 1964, when I was born, and decommissioned in 2019, stand on the Nottinghamshire shore, as cold now as Torksey's flue, as pointlessly picturesque. A thick 20-feet bough was flowing upstream faster than I could walk.

I watched a converted barge negotiate the hand-operated lock leading from the Foss Dyke out into the Trent. Rushing, smelling brown waters were raised so the inner gates could be opened, then lowered again once the gate had been closed, to let the boat sink to river level. Thunderheads piled up overhead as the lock-keeper and the barge skipper sustained an age-old, amiable conversation about weather conditions and moorings. The thundery showers resumed with increased force as the outer gate opened and the barge chugged out into the silver-brown Midlands, the drenched, hunched skipper probably having the time of his life—a twenty-first century man steering a nineteenth-century craft through an eighteenth-century lock on a second-century canal. It was an encapsulation of innovation and obsolescence, like the Torksey Viaduct, an engineering landmark of 1849, a rusting nuisance now.

The tidal Trent comes to its end a few miles farther on, at Newton-on-Trent. Here the A57 crosses on a little toll-bridge with tiny booths, each carload costing forty pence each way—a Ruritanian contrast to the Humber Bridge, right for this riparian remoteness. An oystercatcher passed unexpectedly over, calling in alarm to see me watching the traffic for Nottinghamshire—a bird much more of beaches, a sonic link to the shore.

* * *

Strong seas of belief sluiced across this area in the seventh century, strewing churches and fantastical legends indiscriminately. Cromwell marched and counter-marched through a landscape sodden with superstition. It is not certain at which Stow St Etheldreda founded her church as she passed through to Ely; 'stow' is a generic place name, signifying either assembly place or holy place. But hagiographical tradition maintains it was at Stow Minster she planted her ash staff, which burst into leaf to shelter her while she slept. The church erected to commemorate this 'event' is solid enough—an austere tenth-twelfth-century structure, almost fortress-like, that suffuses the whole area with magical force. Over centuries, real places have seeded themselves around the tree of faith, and sprouted in reverential reference—Coates by Stow, Normanby by Stow, Stow Park, Stow Pasture, Sturton by Stow and Willingham by Stow. Even the Cathedral may have branched off from Stow, which long styled itself 'Mother-Church to Lincoln.' Legends piled on legend, and folk tradition was augmented by national events. As well as Etheldreda's ash, the Minster remembers the Great Heathen fleet, the generosity of Godiva, the fate of Thomas à Becket and, especially, St Hugh of Lincoln with his swan. It was at Stow that Hugh was said to have tended lepers, and where he was 'adopted' by the fierce swan that would follow him around, and eventually became his symbol.

Swans were coincidentally flying over at Kettlethorpe, above a haunted gateway. All old gateways are unquiet, touched by memories of everyone who has ever gone through them, especially if they never came back, or if the house beyond has gone. They are entrances and exits, the starting and ending points of journeys, and thresholds, marking changes in consciousness, changes in state. This particular portal, with its worn mounting block, framed by summer foliage, connects Kettlethorpe to great events. There is a Georgian/Victorian house through the archway now, but once it framed the home of Katherine Swynford (1350?–1403), Lancastrian duchess, governess to John of Gaunt's daughters, later his mistress then wife, sister-in-law to Chaucer, mother of Cardinal Beaufort and the Chancellor, ancestress of Henry VII and so Elizabeth II.

The Swynfords were as brash and tough as the swine whose tusked heads form their rebus—earthy counterpoint to St Hugh's swans, perfect partners for Plantagenets. Katherine's extra-marital liaison with Gaunt attracted contemporary contumely, but she overcame the scandal through sheer intelligence. John had appointed her as governess to his daughters more because of her accomplishments and serious nature than her sexual allure. When she eventually married him, the chronicler Jean Froissart, the chief contemporary arbiter of correct courtly behaviour, was so impressed by her address and alertness that he defended her against all critics.

This opening teleports us in space and time to Hainault, whence Katherine's father came with Queen Philippa, and through Philippa to the Burghers of Calais, the Battle of Neville's Cross, and the chronicles of Froissart. It takes us forwards through the *Canterbury Tales*, and the eventful life of John of Gaunt—campaigning with the Black Prince, war with Scotland, high-level politics—and further still to the death of Richard II at Pontefract in 1400, allegedly starved to death by Katherine's son Thomas. This ivied archway onto emptiness is a strait gate from lower to higher estate, a way station on the English crown's long journey from 'long haired sea kings' to MBEs for milkmen.

A locally mythologised murder lay in front as I drove along the A57, with Lincolnshire on my left and Nottinghamshire at right. As one author notes, 'Otter is a name in the annals of Lincolnshire crime with a special and haunting resonance.'[24] Tom Otter was a casual labourer in 1805, from Tresswell just over the river, who had been working as a 'banker' (drainage navvy) at Lincoln's Swanpool. Bankers had a reputation for roughness, and Otter a bad name amongst bankers. He had left a wife and child in Nottinghamshire, and now made local woman Mary Kirkham pregnant. Parish officials had the right to issue 'bastardy bonds' to force men to pay maintenance to unmarried pregnant partners, and marry them in what were called 'knobstick weddings,' from the staffs carried by beadles. So Otter was taken to the church in a cart, accompanied by two constables, who of course had no idea the wedding would be bigamous. Following what must have been strained proceedings, the newly-weds walked the six miles from Lincoln to Saxilby's Sun Inn, probably also an exercise in marital tension. Later, they went to a quiet place called Drinsey Nook, where Otter found a hedge-stake and smashed in her head.

Unluckily for Otter, the body was swiftly found, and he was arrested the next day. The trial took place at the Sun Inn, and he was sentenced to death. He was hanged from the Cobb Tower of Lincoln Castle in March 1806, and his body encased in pitch and displayed in a 30-feet-high iron gibbet at Saxilby until 1850, when the last chains rusted away—a terrible local landmark, except to blue tits which legendarily nested in his skull. A children's rhyme recalled this folk-horror sight—'There were nine tongues within one head / The tenth went out to seek for bread' / To feed the living inside the dead.'

Bits of the gibbet are kept in Doddington Hall, incongruous on a marble fireplace, and the hedge-stake was displayed in local pubs. The murder, as if not horrible enough, accumulated supernatural trappings, thanks largely to the testimony of a labourer called John Dunkerly, or Dunberly (taken after the trial), who claimed to have seen the whole thing. His account of the killing has a terrible vividness:

I heard this man say, 'sit down you can rest here.' I climbed through a gap and got into the stubble close: nowt but the hedge divided us. I could have touched Tom Otter if I had put my arm out when he came and tore a stake out of the hedge, he must have been a strong man from the way he pulled out the hedge-stake, which was two feet into the ground; the moon shined into his face at the time and his eyes frightened me, for there was a fiery look in them such as a cat's eyes when seen in the dark. I heard him say to his-sen [himself], 'This will finish my knob-stick wedding'; then he made three strides to where she was sitting with her head hanging down, and swinging the hedge-stake with both hands, hit her a clout on the head. She ged [gave] but one scream, and called on God for mercy then tumbled with her head on the ground. He hit her head again as it lay on the grass that grew by the lane-side, and that time the knock sounded as though he had hit a turnip. I saw her legs and her arms all of a quiver like for a minute, and then she was as still as a cobble-stone.[25]

Dunkerly claimed he had picked up the bloody hedge-stake in bewilderment, then fled for fear of being accused. After this, his testimony becomes less plausible.

Doubtless encouraged by many interlocutors, Dunkerly (and others) piled on dubious detail. Otter's dead hand had grasped his when he was helping erect the gibbet. He had had conversations with the kicking corpse, and how Otter would come to him in his dreams every anniversary of the killing, and make *him* re-enact the murder, afterwards leaving the hedge-stake at the scene. 'It was a kind of misty twilight we seemed to be walking in...' he would say, and many of his listeners were probably equally befogged.

Mary's blood had dripped onto the floor of the Sun, and the stains could not be washed out, people gasped. It was said the Foss Dyke turned the colour of blood when the murderer's body had passed over it, and the bridge broke. Spectators had been injured in the crush to view the body. The weather on the day the gibbet was erected was unnaturally wild and windy, and one of the men erecting it had died when Otter's body fell on him, the moment after he had said sneeringly, 'He'll never come down any more.' The very hedge-stake could not be restrained, but every year on the murder's anniversary would always be found on the scene of the murder. The sound of a crying child was reported from the room Mary's body had occupied, and people wouldn't walk alone down the lane after dark. Cathedral clergy were eventually enlisted to lay the spectre, and the hedge-stake was burned secretly at night in the Minster Yard.

The Bishop doubtless wanted to destroy the stake for rational reasons, irritated by its unsettling effects as a symbol of superstition, but paying it such attention must have given an impression that he was giving all this 'misty twilight' credence. The sad affair became solidified in local folk-belief and turns of phrase—for years afterwards, farmers would say of a rope or wire that it needed to be strong enough to tie down Tom Otter's stake. It lingers even now, in field and road names; part of the B1190 is Tom Otter Lane, leading to Tom Otter Bridge, past a field once called Murder Close. The murder will eventually fade from memory—the gibbet is shown on an 1824 map, but has become just Gibbet Wood by 1903; in the meantime, it seems a shame it is not poor Mary Kirkham we remember.

But then evil is always more interesting. At Doddington, visitors most want to see the gibbet, and the scold's bridle, the 'haunted' Holly Bedroom, and the pierced armoured breastplate and correspondingly holed shirt of John Hussey, who fell to Parliament fire at Gainsborough. Hussey's portrait, which hangs beside, is unflattering, his flushed cheeks an odd contrast to his supercilious expression and the otherwise sombre palette, but we should allow for his possible aversion to the procedure, and the conventions of seventeenth-century portraiture. It must have been more than aristocratic self-interest that made him throw in his lot on the King's side, here in this strongly Puritan borderland. Was there also an element of chivalric nostalgia that made him go out through that gatehouse—some yearning for epic colour? What was the last thing apple-cheeked John saw or thought during that 'pretty time' at Gainsborough, when Cromwell made his name, and the future of England was shaped?

A bed in the Tiger Bedroom, which came from Seaton Delaval, once bore the slumbering lump of the Duke of Cumberland— the 5-feet-high, 23-stone son of George II, called 'Butcher Cumberland' because of his brutality after Culloden. Sometimes old horrors really do crowd close—in display cabinets in old houses, the toponymy of tiny places, the ascent of families, the emergence of nations, and the spreading of ideals. Like John Hussey, John Dunkerly, Hetty Wesley, or Ethel Rudkin, sometimes we see terrible things in dreams, and nations stir and mutter in their sleep.

8

THE CITY ON THE CLIFF

'Thou Lincoln, on thy sovereign hill!'
—William Wordsworth, *Ecclesiastical Sonnets*

THE CATHEDRAL—ST HUGH OF LINCOLN—BISHOPS PAST AND
PRESENT—THE LIBEL OF LINCOLN—GEORGE BOOLE—
LINCOLN AT WAR

We'd been travelling for hours, through bad traffic, heading from London to Holderness. We were getting tired, the light was already failing, and the snow that had begun to fall an hour before had suddenly become thick. We needed petrol. We needed to stretch. Coffee called, and food—and we were wearily aware of the long road still to travel tonight, up the long straight A15 (Ermine Street!), over the Humber, then far into the East Riding's east, already late, and with the weather worsening. But then we came over the hill, and saw the City on the Cliff.

The foreground was a mess—a brutal flyover over a dismal gulf of closed factories and industrial units, the railway, the crawling cars ahead wiping, wiping their windscreens, their brake lights twinkling on and off as they threaded the suddenly slippery downwards slope. The middle ground rose higher, with infinitely better architecture—but who could look at even those buildings, when the farthest height was crowned by one of the great monuments to the Middle Ages, a pale and otherworldly wonder floodlit beyond the flying snow, a doubly blanched vision of extravagant beauty? We cannot have been the only drivers distracted by *those* towers, *that* west front, that supreme example of Anglican-Gothic ordering. It was the first time I'd seen the Cathedral, and twenty-five years on I remember details as well as the immensity of that impression.

A little later, we had the darkling Close to ourselves, the Cathedral's west front soaring from our feet, a cliff on top of the Cliff—bathed in powerful uplights, snow swirling around the heads of saints like an encapsulation of 'Northness.' More snow lay companionably across our shoulders, made crisp cut-outs of trees, made old walls sparkle with crystals. Everything was muffled, muted—except the beating of our hearts and the creaking of shoes through the snow on the stones; the city beyond the gateway, itself hushed, might have been in some other dimension. Lights in the precinct's elegant drawing rooms showed where the Dean and Chapter were preparing to dine, and curtains were being drawn—curtains, when you could gaze at *that*...

The Cathedral's doors were being locked by wardens, as the great building put up its defences against the dangerous night, another day of Christian witness completed, with winter coming down hard. A late pigeon swooped across a beam of light, searching for shelter in some crevice—like Bede's bird that flew through a window into the warm hall and then back out again into the night, a metaphor for the soul and the brevity of life.

Away from the floodlights, around the sides, the air struck bitterly chill, among the buttresses and down pipes and gargoyles, the tracery and colours of the windows un-illuminated from behind, the stories traced in glass gone black. These sides were not always seen by visitors, slightly more prosaic places, where maintenance men could work largely unnoticed on fabric repair and Victorian vents, walking on dead citizens whose markers have been removed so as not to impede ride-on mowers. Tourists usually only come round the sides to pass through the precinct, or to see George Frederick Watts' fine 1903 bronze of his old friend Alfred Tennyson, who had died in 1892—one of the sculptor's last works, finished when he was eighty-six, the year before he died.

The Lincolnshire-born Poet Laureate is shown in flowing Victorian long coat, Ulster cape and carrying a floppy hat, with his dog Karenina, who is looking up at him worshipfully while he ponders a flower. This alludes to 'Flower in the crannied wall,' a verse of 1869—

Flower in the crannied wall. / I pluck you out of the crannies, / I hold you here, root and all, in my hand, /

Little flower—but if I could understand / What you are, root and all, and all in all, / I should know what God and man is.

Watts' statue captures the poet and his period well, and Tennyson's audience—their religiosity and sentimentality, their blend of curiosity and concern about the speed of their own changes. It seemed a suitable statue to come across around the shadowy side of a closed cathedral, with snow settling on his scalp, and the frozen nose of his hound. Behind the Green (that evening white) on which the statue stands, the city started up again, lights on in houses, a hurrying chorister, and a bright bus negotiating narrow streets with care.

Lincoln Cathedral is probably the only building in Lincolnshire that is world famous. Even in a county noted for its churches, it attracts superlatives alike from architectural historians and uninformed visitors. For over two centuries, between 1311 and 1548 when its spire collapsed, it was the tallest building in the world, and even now stands in a category of its own. It exists on a different plane altogether from Lincolnshire's seaside attractions, but probably even those who so sturdily bypass Lincoln on their way to caravans in Skegness or Mablethorpe register its stately presence from the ring road, are vaguely glad it's there—a symbol of old England continuing, and a promise of *something* above the mundane. Arthur C. Benson, lyricist for Elgar's *Coronation Ode*, lived in Minster Yard as a child. Perhaps he was thinking partly of this supremely elevated building when he wrote the solo part for 'Land of Hope and Glory':

> *Dear Land of Hope, thy hope is crowned, /*
> *God make thee mightier yet! /*
> *On Sov'ran brows, beloved, renowned, /*
> *Once more thy crown is set.*

The site on which it stands was noteworthy before the Cathedral was thought of, and prominent before Lincoln was named. The Cliff has always been a strong place, a redoubt, dominating the surrounding ground, a magnet for people of the plains. It is a narrow escarpment of yellowish limestone, which starts at Alkborough, encompasses Scunthorpe, comes to a point at Lincoln, then broadens out again on the far side of the Witham valley as the Lincoln Edge, to encompass large parts of Kesteven, eventually faltering somewhere near Kettering. The stone's gold tones colour the city itself and the older buildings in outlying villages, and its oolites act as foundation for both prehistoric trackways and the Romans' Ermine Street (part of which is now the A15). Lincoln's site, dominating the strategically valuable Witham gap, has made it irresistible alike to faith-builders, fort-makers and town-founders. It is the county's biggest urban centre, with around 115,000 residents, and its only prestigious one, not just physically dominating the landscape, but psychologically colouring the whole county.

Before the city was named, before there were towns, before there was even a 'Britain,' the Corieltauvi (or Coritani) tribe lived in this area. The famous fourth-century BCE Witham Shield, now in the British Museum, was found in the Witham near Washingborough in 1826, where it may have been thrown as a votive offering to a river god. A Celtic carnyx—a bronze trumpet shaped like an elongated S, with a stylised animal's head outlet, used in battles—was found in the Witham in 1768 and drawn for Joseph Banks, but got melted by him accidentally in 1796, in an unfortunate experiment to test the strength of early bronze. Had it survived, it would have been only the second known British example.[1] There was a first-century BCE settlement at Brayford Pool, a natural lake formed by the Witham now in the middle of the city. The local Celtic word for this pool was *lindo*, etymologically related to the Irish *linn* (pool)—as in Dublin (*dubh linn*, 'dark pool'). The Romans who came *circa* AD 48 Latinised *Lindo* and added *Colonia*, to which post-Romans added laziness, gradually turning *Lindum Colonia* into Lincoln.

The Coritani seemingly offered little resistance to the determined Romans, with their military might, civic organisation and harshly rectilinear buildings—although 2,000 men from Legio IX marched out from here in AD 60 to relieve Boudicca's siege of Colchester (*Camulodunum*), and never returned. Luckier IXers died in Lindum beds, although their tombstones attest to brief, tough lives: Gaius Saufeius from Macedonia, who died at forty, after twenty-two years' service; Lucius Sempronius

Flavinus from Spain, who died at thirty; standard-bearer Gaius Valerius, thirty-five; trooper Quintus Cornelius, forty; and an unknown legionary of unknown age, found at an unknown site in the city on an unknown date.[2] A roof tile has also been discovered, stamped *LEG IX HISP.*, HISP signifying Hispania, where the Legion had once fought well.

The IXers were replaced in AD 71 by Legio II *Adiutrix*, to counter a perceived threat from the Brigantes to the west; that threat obviated, the *caster* became consolidated as a *colonia*, a home for retired legionaries, with Colchester, Gloucester and York one of just four in all Britannia. Legio II included unlucky Lucius Licinius Saliga, who died at just twenty, and Titus Valerius Pudens, thirty, from Savaria in Pannonia Superior (now Szombathely in Hungary). A decurion of the Second Cavalry Regiment of Asturians also signed off here, forgetting to leave us his name. A decurion was an officer commanding ten horses, but the term was also used to describe local officials responsible for public works, and one was Lincoln's Volusia Faustina, who died aged twenty-six, perhaps unexpectedly a woman. Countless journeys and innumerable intense experiences lie locked up in these tantalisingly few lapidaries, although the legions tramp on in model form in the city's museum, and forever across national myth.

The imperialists turned their *lindo* into an inland port, linking it to the Trent and so the sea via the Foss Dyke. Parts of the 9-feet-thick city walls are still visible here and there, as are a well, and the landmark third-century Newport Arch, once the northern gate and now the oldest arch still used by traffic in Britain. The arch used to be over 6 feet taller than it is today, because the road surface has been raised; lorries became stuck under it on at least three occasions in the go-ahead twentieth century. Lindum boasted piped water, sewers, a bath house, mosaic pavements, pottery kilns, a mint, an imperial cult, and guilds of Apollo, Mercury and the Fates. Altars have been found dedicated to Mars and to the *genius loci*, sculptures of the three 'Mother Goddesses' (a cult common in the Rhineland) and small statues that probably once decorated house altars. One especially fine statue, to Mars, found in the Foss Dyke in the eighteenth century, is nearly 11 inches tall, showing the helmeted but otherwise unclothed god holding up a hand that would have held a spear, and the names of its donors and coppersmith clearly marked on its base, along with the amounts they paid.

A haunting funerary sculpture of a boy holding a hare was found when St Swithin's Church was being built in the 1870s. The bronze life-size leg of a horse was discovered at an unknown location in the city on an unrecorded date in either the eighteenth or the early nineteenth century, suggesting there had been at least one imposing equestrian statue—a teasing hint of how grand Lincoln's public spaces might have been at their height. Just outside the city, at Nettleham, was found an ecumenical section of archway, honouring both the Emperor and an otherwise unknown Celtic god, Rigonemetis ('King of the Grove').

At the bottom of the town, the medieval St Mary's Guildhall on the long, straight High Street conceals old Roman road surface in its basement, on which can be seen contemporaneous cart tracks. *Lindum*'s carters could have carried exotica from the ends of empire or been engaged in more local trade—Trentside agricultural produce along Till Bridge Lane, Humber salted fish down Ermine Street, timber from the Witham valley, iron ore from the north Cliff, and beef, dried fish, mutton, reeds and salt along the minor roads that ran out east across fens and over wolds to the summer pastures and salterns of the coast.

The Romans withdrew from Britain in the fifth century; the last regular military units probably left in 407, when Constantine III took troops from Britain to assist his play for the throne. Sometime between 430 and 449 was Bede's *Adventus Saxonum*, when Saxons, according to his story, initially invited to settle by the British king Vortigern in return for military service, started to descend in large numbers all along the no longer defended Saxon Shore. Britain began to abandon imperial administrative and legal usages, and even literacy, and Roman cities and rural settlements alike fell into decay.

But Lincoln long adhered to old forms; the city still had a *praepositus* or *praefectus civitatis* in charge of civic affairs in the 620s. Modern Lincoln is proud of its imperial prestige, with the lines of barbicans and walls marked out on modern road surfaces; less assured cities might not tolerate having a central street called Occupation Road. Even where the Roman heritage has been treated ungently, the old occupiers can be seen as 'worthy adversaries' it is an honour to have overcome. The badge of the Royal Air Force station at Scampton, home of No. 1 Air Control Centre and the Red Arrows, is a longbow with a drawn arrow— the bow representing how Ermine Street was bent to accommodate the even more ruthless arrow of the runway.[3] The Romans would have admired such directness.

The dearth of early Anglo-Saxon cemeteries near the city implies it may have remained a centre of British power long after the departure of the Romans. But Anglo-Saxons were in the area, some high-status; a seventh-century burial mound excavated in 1849 at Caenby contained the skeleton, sword and shield of a 'princely burial.'[4] By the mid-Saxon period, the Anglo-Saxons had arrived in earnest, judging from the huge cemetery (over 700 skeletons excavated, many more left *in situ*) that was examined between 2016 and 2018 during work on the city's eastern bypass.

The city contains two imposing late Saxon church towers, tall and solid even if made of rubble—St Peter-at-Gowts halfway down the High Street, and St Mary-le-Wigford, that sticks up unexpectedly in a rather unloved location at the bottom of the hill, between the railway station and a traffic-laden road. St

Mary's has a time-travelling tablet built into its wall, part of a Roman tombstone whose surviving inscription reads, 'To the departed spirits and to the name of Sacer, son of Bruscus, a citizen of the Senones and of Carssouna, his wife and of Quintus, his son.'[5] Above this is other writing, from much later—'Eirtig had me built and endowed to the glory of Christ and of Saint Mary XP'—a proud and devout Saxon, wanting to make a permanent mark in a society not especially skilled with stone.

The first mention of Vikings in connection with Lincolnshire was in 841, when the *Anglo-Saxon Chronicle* mentioned in passing that 'many men in Lindsey, East Anglia and Kent were killed by the enemy.' The Vikings made Lincoln one of the Five Boroughs of their Danelaw, with Derby, Leicester, Nottingham and Stamford. They established a market and a mint by the ninth century. Few Viking artefacts have been recovered from Lincoln, but street names like Flaxengate and the many villages around the city with the Viking endings 'by' and 'thorpe' are evidence of long and mostly placid settlement. By the middle of the eleventh century, Lincoln in combination with Stamford would produce a quarter of England's coins. The city may have had as many as 12,000 inhabitants just before the Norman invasion, a size it would not attain again until the nineteenth century.

* * *

On the modern road bridge that spans the Witham beside Brayford Pool, there are signs for the benefit of philosophical boaters. Those entering the Pool are asked 'Where are you going?' and those going out, 'Where have you been?' One might have expected the signs to be the other way round, but the questions work whichever direction you're going. Questions of this kind have been asked in Lincoln for centuries.

There may have been a cathedral church at Lincoln as early as the eighth century, belonging to the Diocese of Leicester, which had been founded in 679. Confusingly, there was a See of Lindsey covering some of the same territory, founded in the seventh century, likewise with an unidentified cathedral site ('Sidnacester'—possibly Stow). The See of Leicester was forced to relocate to Dorchester-on-Thames following the Viking invasions, and stayed there until 1072, when the territories of both (plus Oxford and Peterborough) were transferred to Lincoln by Lincoln's new Bishop Remigius, a Benedictine monk from Fécamp in Normandy who had contributed men and ships for the invasion. His new Diocese of Lincoln was the biggest in England, extending from the Thames to the Humber, and despite subsequent losses is still one of the largest—reportedly described by one twentieth-century bishop as '2,000 square miles of bugger all.'

It was Remigius who began the Cathedral we see today, and his chief legacy is the severe west front with its three enormous arches; other work was subsequently damaged, replaced, or is hidden from view. Remigius' Cathedral was designed for defensibility as much as divinity, described by Henry of Huntingdon as 'a strong church with very strong projecting towers, and, as befitting the times, invincible to enemies.'[6] The building was a statement of right to complement the might of the castle erected in 1068 a few hundred yards away, and Remigius would also be deeply involved in the compilation of the *Domesday Book*. He also gave the Cathedral its constitution, and a library (one of these volumes survives).

Henry of Huntingdon describes him as charming and 'great of heart' (a piquant detail is that he was just 4 feet, 6 inches tall)— but he was also an active intriguer, constantly fighting off land grabs by the Diocese of York, and once, apparently, even being accused of treason. After his death in 1092, there were attempts to have him canonised, but these met with coolness, and were gradually abandoned after the canonisation of Hugh in 1220 as Lincoln's first saint. Remigius' once-prominent tomb itself disappeared from reckoning, only rediscovered by chance in 1927.

St Hugh was born in Avalon in Burgundy around 1140, and became prominent in the Carthusian Order, an order noted for its mysticism and strictness. In 1175, he was recruited by Henry II to administer England's first Charterhouse, at Witham in Somerset, which Henry had endowed as part of his expiation for the murder of Thomas à Becket. Hugh did such a good job that in 1189, Henry entreated him to become Bishop of Lincoln, which for most of the preceding nineteen years had had no incumbent, and where the great Cathedral had been damaged by fire and an earthquake in 1185, thought to have been one of the most powerful ever experienced in England.

Hugh was an inspired choice, managing the diocese well, caring for lepers and the poor, and standing up against kings when necessary, at least once playing a constitutionally significant part when he refused to grant Richard I money for military purposes. He appointed the renowned scholar William de Montibus as Master of the Cathedral School, which attracted students who would become renowned scholars in their own right. He was careful in his judgements, qualifying sentences with things like 'that is only as far as I can recollect,' and would never seal any letter that contained a questionable statement. He was greatly admired for his asceticism and dedication, every year going on retreat to Witham—and for having a devoted swan that followed him when he visited the outlying church at Stow. He also had a disarming turn of phrase and logic, once admonishing immoderate mourners, 'What are you about? What are you about? By Saint Nut, by Saint Nut, it would indeed be a great misfortune if we were never allowed to die.'

Hugh started the great post-earthquake rebuild, using the See's money and even helping personally. The thirteenth-century hagiographer Henry of Avranches marvelled, 'often he carries in a pannier the carved stones and the sticky lime.' His grand, cruciform vision in local limestone and blue-black marble, with its experimental style of vaulting, and aborning Chapter House, deeply impressed the man from Avranches, who like most educated men of his period, knew something about architecture:

> With the value of the material, the design of the art well agrees, for the stone roof talks as it were with winged birds, spreading its wide wings, and like to a flying thing strikes the clouds, stayed upon the solid columns. And a sticky liquid glues together the white stones, all which the workman's hand cuts to a nicety. And the wall, built out of a hoard of these ... seems not to exist by art but rather by nature; not a thing united, but one. Another costly material of black stones props the work, not like this content with one colour, not open with so many pores, but shining much with glory and settled with firm position ... That stone, beheld, can balance minds in doubt whether it be jasper or marble ... Of it are the columns, which so surround the pillars that they seem there to represent a kind of dance. Their outer surface more polished than new horn, with reflected visions, fronts the clear stars.[7]

Hugh travelled to France in the last year of his life, his eyesight failing, partly for nostalgic reasons, but also on the hunt. Visiting Meulans in the Île de France, he approached the altar of St Nicasius, an eighth-century martyr, and made a generous donation—then picked up the saint's skull and tried to wrench out one of its teeth. Failing to free one, he put his fingers into the nostrils and secured himself a small bone instead. St Nicasius' nasal bone joined St Benedict's tooth and a nerve from the arm of St Oswald in his reliquary, described as a substantial ring of gold and jewels, four fingers broad, with hollow compartments for relics, whose smith had been told of its need in a dream.

Making his way eventually to Remigius' home town of Fécamp, Hugh asked to see its famous bone of St Mary Magdalen, which was sewn up inside linen and silk. The shocked monks demurring, he took out a penknife, cut off the cloth and gazed at and kissed it reverently. He then tried to break off a bit, and then to nibble some fragments away, before finally bringing his molars into play and biting hard. He spat out two bits and gave them to his servant, saying 'Excellent man, keep those for us.'

He died in Westminster in 1200, and was transported back to Lincoln through wind and rain, along roads lined with crowds at times so dense his cortège could not proceed. At Stamford, while his body rested in the church, a pious cobbler was said to have begged to die at just that moment, and did (Hugh became patron saint of shoemakers). At Lincoln, the powerful, including King John, vied to help carry his coffin up the hill, and the town's Jews came out in respect for a prelate who had been a rare protector. The cheap vestments he had stipulated for his funeral were appropriately torn away by relic-hunters.

Hugh was canonised two decades afterwards, whereupon his cult became second only to that of Thomas à Becket. In 1280, his remains were moved to a new gold-laden and bejewelled shrine in the presence of Edward I and Queen Eleanor; 'the head came away and sweated wonder-working oils,' and was placed in its own shrine. When Eleanor died just over the Nottinghamshire border in 1290, her grieving husband had her entrails interred in the Cathedral, while the rest of her was taken on its disconsolate road to London, leaving a trail of 'Eleanor Crosses' from Lincoln all the way to Charing. Hugh's shrine remained intact until the Reformation, when one of his teeth, clothed in beryl with silver and gilt, was enumerated among the riflings—a singular survival from the man who bit Mary Magdalen.

*   *   *

But Lincoln was not just a sacred locus; it was also a strategic location, one of the keys to central England. There had been a Roman fort on the site—probably an Iron Age fort beneath that—and the Conqueror had constructed a linchpin castle to guard the Witham Gap and Ermine Street/Fosse Way crossroads.

In 1135, after the death of Henry I, Stephen of Blois, the Conqueror's grandson, seized the throne. Henry's superbly connected daughter Empress Matilda—widow of the Holy Roman Emperor, wife of the Count of Anjou, and niece of the King of Scotland—naturally resented this cousinly coup. This was the beginning of 'The Anarchy' of 1135–53, eighteen years, according to a contemporary saying, 'When Christ and his angels slept.' The south of the country divided along royal or rebel/Angevin lines, with French and Scottish interventions, in a war in which neither side could get a decisive advantage. Meanwhile, the barons of the Midlands and North looked on, fighting amongst themselves, and using the confusion of the times as cover for their own depredations. The pro-Stephen *Anglo-Saxon Chronicle* gives a picture of 'all dissention, and evil, and rapine,' with the 'wretched men of the land' oppressed with 'castle-works … filled with devils and evil men' who tortured loyal subjects in ingenious ways.

In 1140, Ranulf, Earl of Chester, and his brother William, took Lincoln Castle from Stephen's side, using a cunning stratagem. On a day when the garrison was largely engaged in sports, the brothers' wives went to the castle, ostensibly to pay a courtesy call on the commandant's wife. A little later, Ranulf, attended by just three men-at-arms, all of them unarmed, arrived as if to collect the ladies. As soon as they got inside the gate, they overpowered the skeleton guard and opened the gates for William's detachment. Incensed, Stephen came in person to besiege it, successfully capturing seventeen of Ranulf's knights, but Ranulf got away to Chester to fetch help, while his wife held the castle successfully. In the meantime, Stephen availed of the Cathedral's fortress-like architecture and fortified it further. Omens ensued, noted the anti-desecration, pro-Angevin William of Malmesbury with grim satisfaction; as Stephen offered a wax candle in the minster, it broke just as the Bishop reached out to take it. The chain by which the pyx was suspended snapped and the sacred vessel fell to the floor. On 2 February 1141, Ranulf was back, and the First Battle of Lincoln began.

The Angevin forces were made up of Ranulf's own tenants, plus Welsh mercenaries, and a column of men 'disinherted' by the King, led by the Earl of Gloucester, Ranulf's father-in-law, anxious to rescue his besieged daughter. Stephen had more men-at-arms, but fewer cavalry. His retinue of mounted earls had also come unprepared, 'as if to a conference, not a battle.' So unprepared were the earls for war that the battle afterwards was nicknamed the 'Joust of Lincoln.' Inevitably, says William of Malmesbury, 'the earls to a man ... consulted their safety by flight.' The King's forces were surrounded, Stephen himself fighting grimly, 'grinding his teeth and foaming at the mouth like a boar.'[8] When his sword broke, Stephen fought with a two-handed axe, and then a stone hit him on the head. A knight called William of Caimes grabbed Stephen's helmet and shouted 'Here, everyone, here! I have the King!' Only about 100 were killed in the fighting, but hundreds of citizens seem to have died in the city's subsequent sacking. Stephen was carried off to gilded captivity in Bristol, Matilda attempted to take the throne, Stephen was released in a prisoner exchange, Matilda left England for ever, and the monarchical merry-go-round ended with Matilda's son becoming Henry II after all.

The Second Battle of Lincoln (20 May 1217) seems almost seriocomic. It may even have seemed slightly so at the time, although great events hinged on its outcome. King John, who in 1214 had lost England's old possession of Anjou at the Battle of

Bouvines, was so politically weakened by this disaster that he was compelled to affix his seal to the *Magna Carta*. He then made matters worse by refusing to implement it, adding faithlessness to weakness. This caused many nobles to revolt against the crown—the First Barons' War—made even more dangerous by the invasion of Prince Louis of France, who speedily conquered much of England.

In 2016, John's son Henry III inherited this mess at the age of nine—plus an empty Exchequer, not helped by John's loss of his treasure in The Wash. Henry was lucky his regent, William Marshal, was both loyal and one of the greatest soldiers of his time, called by Archbishop Stephen Langton 'the best knight that ever lived.' He is one of the best-remembered of medieval knights, because of his prowess, but also because his proud son commissioned a romance-biography about his father's life, *L'Histoire de Guillaume Marechal*, which in its language and style resembles an Arthurian saga, albeit one based on real events.[9]

Sir William Marshal, first Earl of Pembroke, obtained his rank through marriage to Isabella, daughter of Richard de Clare ('Strongbow'), famous in Irish history of one of the island's Norman conquerors. Despite being around seventy years old, he mustered an army and marched on Lincoln, where Louis of France's forces had just taken the city, although the Castle was still being held for the King by the sexagenarian Nichola de la Haye, hereditary Constable of the Castle and Sheriff of Lincolnshire.

Thomas, Comte du Perche, in command of Louis' besiegers, was aware of Marshal's approach, but unsure in what numbers. Marshal's numbers were in fact substantial—estimated at 400 knights, 250 crossbowmen, and many more infantry. Sir Falkes de Bréauté, in charge of Marshal's crossbowmen, was scorned by contemporary chronicles as 'common stock,' reputed to have first come to attention by murdering a man with a scythe—but then few to the manor born would have cared to be associated with crossbow fighting, seen as militarily *infra dig*. Perche opted for a defensive strategy, holding Marshal's forces at bay while he continued the siege of the Castle.

Bréauté's crossbowmen proved decisive in the quarrel, taking the north gate, then taking up positions on roofs from where they could hail bolts onto the heads and horses of the rebels. Then Marshal unleashed his horse and foot, leading personally— so excited to fight that he galloped off without his helmet, and a page had to be sent running after him—and the rebels broke and started to flee. Marshal scoffed that rebel knights 'ever foremost in the Tourney, hide themselves at our appearance.' One who did not hide was Perche, who chose to fight on despite being called to surrender. He was pierced by a spear through the eyehole of his helmet, but managed to buffet Marshal three times over the head with his sword before falling dead, while the rest of his army surrendered, or fled towards the London road. The allegedly treacherous city was promptly pillaged by the forces of legitimacy, in what became sardonically known as 'The Lincoln Fair.' Although the numbers who died seem to have been very small—some say as few as five knights—it was a turning point for French ambitions, and when reinforcement ships were sunk in the English Channel, it meant the end. In September 1217, Louis renounced his claim on the English throne, and returned the Channel Islands to England.

Thanks largely to his exploits at Lincoln, William Marshal, who died two years afterwards, has a fictional half-life, featuring in many historical novels, and films like *The Lion in Winter* (1968) and *A Knight's Tale* (2001). Nichola de la Haye was honoured for her role in the siege by Henry III and is increasingly remembered today as a rare, and rarely successful, female combatant—even though, or because, her constableship was taken from her four days after the battle. The snobbishly scorned Falkes de Bréauté has the strangest immortality of all. He married cleverly, acquiring new estates in London, which became known as Fawkes Hall, then Foxhall, and so eventually Vauxhall, first home of the car company. The company's griffin logo is derived from the crossbowman's putative coat of arms.

*   *   *

The Cathedral continued to grow, its architecture as renowned as its sanctity. But there were also problems, like when the central tower fell down, around 1237—according to the ever-creative Matthew Paris, immediately after one of the canons had said, 'If we should hold our peace, the stones should cry out.' The 'Lincoln Imp' emblem that is seen all over the city, from the Lincolnshire County Council logo to the shirts of Lincoln City FC players, is based on a thirteenth-century carving high up in the Angel Choir erected over St Hugh's shrine—a fairly generic demon, with a toothy grin, hairy body, clawed hands, cloven hooves, and a crossed-over leg—but universally known as Lincoln's, at least since the nineteenth century, when a shrewd jeweller called Usher secured the sole right to use the image on tourist wares. Usher transmuted tat into gold by giving generously back, becoming a major donor to the city's museum and art gallery, the latter named after him.

The damp, dark and disconsolate Franciscan undercroft down the hill on Greyfriars Passageway would have been a new building, possibly not even complete, when Robert Grosseteste became the tenth Bishop of Lincoln in 1235. It was one in which he would have taken a special interest, as an admirer of that then still newish order (founded 1209), with its emphases on popular preaching and missionary activities. He probably saw the cold-dewed undercroft alive with earnest friars seeking sanctity by eschewing property, not just as individuals but corporately for the order—an aspiration increasingly impossible to live up to with the Franciscans' expansion, and consequent need for expensive buildings like this one. There was always an innate tension within the order which would soon lead to violent dissensions and affected the Franciscans into the nineteenth century. But in 1235 all this was unforeseeable—and even more so the undercroft's future as school, house of correction, mechanics institute, museum and a 2020s 'intermittent exhibition space' (a telling trajectory).

Grosseteste had been appointed to this senior post as a compromise candidate. He was known to be formidably clever; he had written highly regarded books of philosophy, science and theology, made painstaking translations of Greek and patristic texts, and been the director of the Franciscan school at Oxford. He was a major influence directly and indirectly on other major influencers, like Adam Marsh, Roger Bacon, Duns Scotus, John Gower and Simon de Montfort. The first line of his widely admired allegorical poem, *Chasteau d'Amour* ('The Castle of Love')—'*Ky bien pense bien poet dire*' ('He who thinks well speaks well')—hints at a rare articulacy both in books and speech. Even his name, derived from *grosse tête* ('great head'), implies above-normal brainpower. But he lacked social connections, and was getting old (about sixty). He wasn't expected to interest himself much in administrative matters.

However, those who had seen him as a sinecurist would be surprised, as he began a thorough visitation, in the first year alone deposing eleven heads of religious houses for laxity or corruption. He completed the Cathedral's famous rose windows, the 'Bishop's Eye' and the 'Dean's Eye.' He wrote and spoke vigorously against secret marriages, goods being sold in sacred precincts, games being played in church, fights between guilds over precedence in processions—and table manners, and why small children should not sleep in beds with their mothers, in case they were crushed by accident. He also argued with

Archbishop Boniface, Henry III and eventually Pope Innocent IV, who kept sending non-English-speaking Italians to rich English benefices, and had 'requested' that his nephew be inducted into a Lincoln canonry. Grosseteste's outspoken opposition to papal abuses probably prevented him from being canonised. But this, and the fact that he had been much admired by John Wycliffe, would later move John Foxe to portray him as an ur-Reformer, a principled proto-Protestant. Matthew Paris' description gives a flavour both of Grosseteste's activity and his personality:

> ...a manifest confuter of the pope and the king, the blamer of prelates, the corrector of monks, the director of priests, the instructor of clerks, the support of scholars, the preacher to the people, the persecutor of the incontinent, the sedulous student of all scripture, the hammer and the despiser of the Romans. At the table of bodily refreshment, he was hospitable, eloquent, courteous, pleasant, and affable. At the spiritual table, devout, tearful, and contrite. In his episcopal office, he was sedulous, venerable, and indefatigable.[10]

Whilst out on his arduous visitations across the eight counties of his diocese, the sexagenarian somehow found time to learn Ancient Greek, symbolic of his lifelong interest in Aristotle—a thinker who, although then being rediscovered, was still sometimes controversial in the thirteenth-century Church. Aristotle's emphasis on the importance of 'Matter' as well as 'Form' (a doctrine called hylomorphism), and interest in biological classifications, had always made some Christians suspect him of materialism. He had furthermore argued that the world had always existed, while of course the Church maintained it had been created by God, and at a particular time.

The emerging doctrine of the 'Great Chain of Being'—the universe as a divinely ordained hierarchy, with huge implications for medieval society and which even influences modern biology—borrowed from both Platonism and Aristotelianism. Grosseteste read and wrote so copiously that he devised a subject-ordered *Tabula* (table) to keep track of all this information. Literary historian Dennis Duncan claims Grosseteste as one of two inventors of the index.[11]

Grosseteste's legacy remains integral to English reflection. The zoologist Alastair Crombie thinks him:

> ...the real founder of the tradition of scientific thought in medieval Oxford, and in some ways, of the modern English intellectual tradition.[12]

He wrote learnedly on many subjects, but above everything else, on light. He was one of the first to think about the properties of light—as magical power, but also physical force, a gift from God at least partly explicable through algebra, geometry and mathematics. His starting point was Genesis—'And God said, Let there be light: and there was light. / And God saw the light, and it was good; and God divided the light from the darkness.' As yet, there has been no finishing point, his works absorbed by thinkers from Newton to the 'Big Bang' theorists. As one historian of science notes:

> From a philosophical point of view ... [Grosseteste's] use of the notion of light in his account of the basic structure and origin of the physical universe is of fundamental importance and the greatest originality.[13]

Light to Grosseteste was lovely—but it was also logic. Grosseteste's worldview was as highly coloured as the stained glass in the building from which his influence radiated out, and as significant. Windows were casements onto a brilliant kingdom, and even the plain glass of alchemical vessels was filled with new ways of seeing. He even foresaw the telescope:

[Glass] shows us how we may make things a very long distance off appear as if placed very close, and larger near things appear very small, and how we may make small things placed at a distance appear any size we want.[14]

Where, Grosseteste wondered, did colour come from? How does light work? What does it *mean*? What might be its connections to matter, numbers, harmony, proportion, rhythm, the Chain of Being, and most importantly our relationship with the Light's great Giver? Light, in his sight, was multi-dimensional and infinite, condensing to make matter, simultaneously reaching into our hearts and radiating out into the firmament as 'rarefied' force, ultimately uniting Heaven with Earth. Earth could almost *be* Heaven, because 'all the higher lights come together in it.'[15]

It was a subject to which he kept returning, with ruminations on the Sun, the rotation of the Earth, heat and light, movement and light, and rainbows. He must have mused on these luminosities out on his episcopal rounds, riding his caparisoned palfrey under the canopy of Lincolnshire's sky, noticing the way the sun lay on some slope, or rose redly out of the flatlands. His was a holistic and searching intelligence, whose rays have not yet been extinguished.

* * *

The main road up to the Cathedral from the lower town is called Steep Hill for excellent reasons. Buses bound upwards ascend complainingly around the back, carrying the heavily laden, the infirm, the lazy, and the old. Other Lincolnites and tourists toil up and, more dangerously, down its one-in-seven gradient, holding onto handrails and frequently stopping to gasp and take selfies. Steep Hill does not fit the Lincolnshire stereotype, but is more like somewhere in the South Country, with its topography, cobblestones, twelfth- to nineteenth-century buildings housing little shops and twee tea rooms, and a flourishing fig tree that gives a little hint of the Levant—or perhaps the Medieval Warm Period, when grapes were grown for the Bishops.

Another hint of the Levant is the Jew's House, adjacent to the Jew's Court, built of local stone in the 1150s, in the then still-exotic Norman style. This was probably the home of the city's rabbi—an important man, head of the second-largest Jewish community outside London. It has been continually occupied since its erection, perhaps by Aaron of Lincoln (c.1125–86), who is thought to have been the richest man in liquid assets in England and had financial links across much of Europe.[16] Lincoln's Jews, as elsewhere, were often the objects of dangerous resentments and dark suspicions.

Sometimes Jews were protected by the Crown, or by nobles, or the Church. At other times, the authorities acquiesced in nativist prejudice, or persecuted Jews vigorously for private reasons—whether out of twisted principle, or because they were in hock to them. Aaron once took in pledge the Cathedral's plate, which cannot have endeared his community to true believers. On the other hand, he and others also raised money to help build the Cathedral and other churches, and advanced money to monasteries seeking to expand their acreage and income from the wool trade.

There was an attempted pogrom in Lincoln in 1190, with damage to property, although most of the targets escaped with their lives. In 1194, Lincoln was compelled to send twenty to forty contributors to the Northampton *Donum* set up to levy taxes on Jews to pay for the ransom of Richard I. There were more attacks in 1220 and during the Second Barons' War in 1265, perhaps to destroy evidence of money the barons owed to moneylenders (compromising information, which could also have been useful to the king). But before that came the most infamous episode in all of England's Jewish history.

Jews had occasionally been accused of ritual murder even in ancient times, notably by the first-century AD obsessive Apion of Alexandria, but the idea that they routinely murdered Christians, especially children, and used their blood in occult ceremonies, gained bitter force after the start of the Crusades. The first English case in which Jews were accused of killing a human child was in Norwich in 1144, and there were similar allegations in Gloucester (1168), Bury St Edmunds (1181) and Winchester (1192). The deaths seem to have been real enough, but the authorities took no action in any of these cases, presumably because there was no evidence of Jewish involvement. Yet the prejudice became rooted amongst the population, sometimes encouraged from the pulpit, because 'the martyrdom of the lads ... proved a considerable source of attraction to the cathedrals and abbeys of these towns.'[17] The 'Libel of Lincoln' took on even more serious tones, and has passed into folklore.

During 1255, a rumour grew in Lincoln that a young boy named Hugh, after the city's beloved Bishop who had been canonised in 1220, had been murdered by a Jew named Copin, who had then thrown his body down a well—or cesspit, to add even more disgust and horror. Copin was arrested and tortured, then confessed and hanged, after implicating ninety-one other Jewish inhabitants of the city. These were duly arrested and sent to the Tower of London, where eighteen were executed. The rest were eventually freed by order of Henry III, seemingly reluctantly, after representations by Franciscan friars and Henry's brother Richard. That the King had taken such an interest gave the story credence, and his terrible miscarriage of justice also swiftly developed supernatural dimensions. The boy's body was buried inside the Cathedral, and his tomb rapidly became almost a rival shrine to that of St Hugh. The boy was frequently styled 'Little

Saint Hugh,' even though he had never been canonised, and he and the real saint became confused in the popular imagination.

Influential writers played a crucial role in the dissemination and embellishment of the legend, like Matthew Paris (c. 1200–59) whose *Historia Anglorum* and *Chronica Majora* told of a mock trial of the boy held by a secret conclave of Jews, followed by tortures including beatings, crowning with thorns, and piercings 'with a wood knife,' culminating in crucifixion.[18] Chaucer's 'Prioress's Tale' is set 'in Asie, in a greet citee,' but at the end of her tale, the Prioress refers to 'Yonge Hugh of Lincoln, slayn also / With cursed Jewes, as it is notable, / For it nis but a litel whyle ago.' Even had she not, the English credulous would have mentally transferred the action to their own 'greet citees,' caught up in his shockingly vivid tale of how 'the Jewes han conspyred' to kill a hymn-singing-seven-year-old Christian boy—'This cursed Jew him hente and heeld him faste / And kitte his throte, and in a pit him caste.' In Chaucer's telling, 'mordre wol out' magically—the murder was discovered when the corpse 'with throte y-corven lay upright, / He *Alma Redemptoris* gan to singe / So loude, that al the place gan to ringe.' The only true-to-life part of his tale tells of how the provost punished the guilty parties—'with wilde hors he dide hem drawe, / And after that, he heng them by the lawe'—which parallels the fate of poor Copin.[19]

A folk ballad, 'Hugh of Lincoln,' tinged the legend with both Christian tropes and dark sensuality, making the murderer a woman who tempts the boy with an apple, and murders him bloodily in the luxurious interior of the 'Jew's castell:'

She's led him in through ae dark door, / And sae has she thro' nine; /
She's laid him on a dressing table / And stickit him like a swine. /
And first came out the thick, thick blood, / And syne came out the

thin; / And syne came out the bonny heart's blood; / There was nae mair within.

She then encases him in lead, and throws him into 'Our Lady's draw well.' His distraught mother makes a winding sheet, 'and at the back o' merry Lincoln / The dead corpse did her meet.'[20]

This combination of blasphemy, boy-child, eeriness, exoticism, gore, mystery, out-of-control women, well-poisoning and (ill-gotten by implication) wealth appealed greatly to the more crepuscular side of the medieval imagination. The sorry calumny undoubtedly encouraged Edward I when he banished all Jews from England in 1290, and has tainted Christian-Jewish relations ever since. The boy's folk cult declined after 1290, and his monument was eventually swept away. When the tomb was opened in 1791, Hugh's body—drawn hauntingly by the Swiss artist Samuel Hieronymous Grimm[21]—was found to have been preserved in pickling fluid, which the scientifically minded Joseph Banks tasted. The body of course showed no sign of mutilations.

Christopher Marlowe, Thomas Percy and many others duly reinvented or repeated the story, and an enterprising nineteenth-century owner of the house made a fake well in the basement, to which he charged admission. A version of the ballad still crops up in modern folk music, albeit now shorn of Jewish references, famously 'Little Sir Hugh' by Steeleye Span.[22] The story gives the city a faintly disquieting undercurrent, even though Jews returned during the Commonwealth, and have been present since.

* * *

John de Dalderby became Bishop of Lincoln in 1300, so far its only Lincolnshire-born one, with a reputation for learning and liberality—and restoring speech to Rutlanders who could only bark like dogs. He also acted against errant clerics, like vicar-choral Robert Coty, described in 1307 as:

...a public and notorious dicer ... several times [he had] lost his clothes and other goods and ... at St Yves he had lost a horse which he had [borrowed] from his kinsman ... Having lost ... all his clothes dressed [only] in his shirt he ran through the street of Wycford [now St Mary-le-Wigford] Lincs by night [with] the dogs following ... with great noise and ... was arrested by the watchman.[23]

The Chapter House played host to English Parliaments in 1301, 1316 and 1327, and it was also the venue for the trials of the Lincolnshire branches of the Knights Templar, during which Dalderby acted as Papal commissioner. He also added to the fabric—most notably, the upper stages of the central tower, at 271 feet the highest of any English cathedral. Until one night in 1548, there was a spire on top of that, giving a total of 525 feet. Although Dalderby was never canonised, his tomb became the centre of a popular cult, and a place to transact canonical business—so persistent a cult that in 1540 it yielded 2,621oz. of gold and 4,285oz. of silver to the sticky fingers of the Commissioners.

John Gynewell, Bishop of Lincoln between 1347 and 1362, earned a different kind of sanctity. His episcopate coincided with the Black Death, a catastrophe he met with extraordinary energy. He did not allow a mere deadly pestilence to prevent him making his visitations across the vast space for which he had sacred responsibility; if anything, the ever rising death toll made him more determined to bear witness and comfort his flock. He rode almost constantly around this enormous area, covering hundreds of miles some months, sometimes averaging twenty-one miles per day—seemingly superhumanly immune to the disease, aiding and comforting villages without benefit of clergy or anywhere to inter their dead. Between March 1349 and March 1350, he made 1,025 appointments of new clergy to replace those who had died, or resigned in anticipation of death. When he heard that the abbot of Louth Park, whom he had met a week ago, had just died of the disease, he turned his horse round to give his blessing to the new incumbent.

Somehow during this period, work continued on the Cathedral, exemplified by the misericords in the choir stalls that show the typically medieval intermeshing of the sacred and the profane, idealism and fatalism, with subjects ranging from the Adoration of the Magi to an arrow-pierced knight toppling from his horse—and the Ascension to a man beating acorns out of a tree.

Lincoln's livelihood had long depended on its wool staple—the right to levy taxes on wool exports—and associated industries. Robin Hood's 'Lincoln green,' incidentally, was really red—an early modern misreading of the medieval name 'Lincolne greyne,' a reference to the grains of carmine used to make sumptuous scarlet. But the Black Death affected the city's weavers drastically, and then in 1369 the city lost the staple to Boston.

Its plight was very long ignored, because it was so far from London—it was the most north-easterly county directly governed from London (the Council of the North governed north of the Humber), and difficult to reach, even by water, because the Witham and Foss Dyke were prone to silting. The monks or nobles who were supposed to maintain the King's Highway often chose not to, or could not afford to. The higher roads across the heath from Sleaford to Lincoln were bleakly exposed and wearisome, an eerily empty country of gorse and rabbit warrens with a reputation for lawlessness.

In Henry VII's time, the common council wrote to the King asking for financial relief, claiming that the city was 'eight or nine parts fallen to ruin.' When John Leland visited five decades later, he crossed over the 'Highe bridge' that still spans the Witham, still with its range of Tudor buildings—a unique survival, known as the 'Glory Hole'—and noted new water conduits and some 'goodly' buildings. But he also notes the ruins of churches and monasteries, and the blocked Foss Dyke. The Cathedral had not been despoiled, but churches had been getting pulled down as early as the 1490s, because derelict churches both reflected badly on the faith, and their materials were a source of much-needed income. Many private houses were also falling down or in disrepair. In 1515, the concerned Council had forbidden private persons to pull down even empty houses or take building materials out of the city. Over the course of that century, the Council tried to raise money in all kinds of creative ways—forced loans, rents charged in advance, reversionary leases, sales of exemption from office, selling freedoms of the city, enclosure of common lands, and the felling and selling of trees— but nothing seems to have worked.

Cardinal Wolsey *did* take an interest—he was a former Bishop of Lincoln—and there were updates to guild charters and repairs to bridges and roads. But his attention made little difference, and became almost a disadvantage once Wolsey fell from grace. By the 1530s, churches were being demolished or secularised regularly. A population of perhaps 6,000 at the time of the Conquest had dwindled to around one third of that by the Tudor period, and the city had become effectively a medium-sized market town, whose yearly fairs and occasional grand civic occasions probably only served to remind citizens of more expansive times.

The Chapter House that had hosted kings and parliaments was also the meeting place of the Lincolnshire Rising leaders in 1536, and it was there that Henry VIII's uncompromising reply to their demands was read out by the city's Recorder. The Recorder censored Henry's reply, considering it likely to inflame the jostling crowd. The king had apostrophised the whole county, more in anger than sadness:

How presumptuous then are ye, the rude commons of one shire, and that one of the most brute and beestelie of the hole realme and of leest experience, to fynde faut with your Prynce?[24]

The Recorder's redaction made the crowd suspect that the Rising's leaders had misled them about the king's nature; they were lucky to escape with their lives. Perhaps if the Recorder had not omitted those phrases, local resolve might have been stiffened instead of weakened, with history-altering consequences. Several Rising leaders were later hanged, drawn and quartered in the city, within a few hundred yards of the Chapter House.

In 1540, Cromwell's commissioners at last turned their attentions to the Cathedral, with a royal order to remove 'a certain shrine [St Hugh's] and divers feigned relics and jewels, with which all simple people be much deceived and brought into great superstition and idolatry,' but other adornments were spared, for a time. When Henry VIII passed through Lincoln the following year, he was greeted in the greatest possible state, and thereafter there was a general process of Protestantisation (except during the Mary Tudor irruption)—more church furnishings removed, plays banned, Elizabeth's Act of Uniformity enforced, increasingly acrimonious divisions between Puritanical and more easy-going churchmen, and dark rumours of Jesuit spies, 'Popish colleges,' and weapons being stashed in the remote Recusant countryside north of the city. These rumours were not wholly without foundation; John Wright, one of the Gunpowder Plotters, lived at Twigmore Hall, near Kirton Lindsey. The famous Cathedral bell, 'Great Tom o' Lincoln,' a proverb for powerful volume, was tolling for everyone.

By some way of compensation, the Cathedral was resounding to great new music, particularly that of William Byrd (1539/40-1623), organist and choirmaster at the Cathedral between 1563 and 1572. Byrd's origins are obscure, although his biographer

Edmund H. Fellowes postulates Fenland origins.[25] He became organist at the Cathedral at just twenty years of age, and was married in the city five years later. Byrd was, and remained, a Catholic, but this did not cause him difficulties at Lincoln—only much later, when associated with Thomas Tallis (1505?–85) and the Chapel Royal in London.

Tallis and Byrd had a unique working partnership, as teacher and pupil with a forty-year age gap who became artistic collaborators—and an ambivalent cultural rôle, as Catholics whose music is now regarded as the acme of Anglican musical genius. A more cynical kind of genius was shown by Elizabeth I and Archbishop Cranmer, who saw they could make use of these talented recusants to consolidate the new national religion. The Queen granted the unlikely pair a 21-year-long monopolising patent for all printings of polyphonic music, sole use of the paper used for writing musical scores, and a lease of Crown lands.

Tallis has been called the 'Father of English Church Music,' and Byrd, who wrote stirring anthems and plangent madrigals as well as settings for the new rites, the even wider title of *Britannicae Musicae parens* ('Parent of British music'). One well-known music critic calls Byrd 'the most imposing figure of the English Renaissance' after Shakespeare, 'the English Lassus,' citing the 'sombre grace of his Masses' and 'noble and human tone' of his English music.[26] To Lang, Byrd's religious music, strongly influenced though it was by Italian and other traditions, is 'English' because his contrapuntal parts are overlaid with top melodies deriving from more conventionally English accompanied solo songs. Byrd's transcending joy in melodies shines through his 'Reasons briefly set down by th'auctor, to perswade every one to learne to sing,' the introduction to his collection *Psalmes, Sonets, and Songs of Sadnes and Pietie*:

There is not any Musicke of Instruments whatsoever comparable to that which is made of the voyces of men, where the voices are good, and the same well sorted and ordered. The better the voice is, the meeter it is to honour and serve God there-with: and the voice of man is chiefly to be imployed to that ende.[27]

The twentieth-century Belgian musicologist C. J. Van den Borren enthuses:

Byrd is a pastoral poet who loves misty distances, graduated tints, softly undulating landscapes ... a rustic whose rural lyricism decks itself in the most exquisite graces.[28]

Perhaps some of Byrd's 'good' voices were first heard under the arches of the Cathedral, some of his 'misty distances' seen from the top of the Cliff.

Lincoln's Members of Parliament were members of the interlocking Ayscough, Clinton, Grantham, Monson, St Paul, and Wray families who used their influence to appoint officials and the 'right' (Puritan) kind of preachers, intrigue at council level, and question the royal prerogative when up in London. Despite this, James I liked Lincoln, raising money to scour the Foss Dyke, and spending eight days in the city in 1616, cockfighting, fencing and hunting on the heath outside the city. The Venetian Ambassador told the Doge the king thought Lincolnshire 'the most delightful county in his kingdom.'

James' successor, Charles I, was unluckier with Lincoln. Quite apart from the hostilely Puritan cultural climate and the unpopularity aroused by his drainage schemes, his reign coincided with outbreaks of plague and rising food prices. After the King's standard was raised, Lincoln was immediately associated with the northern Parliamentary counties, and even if it had not been, its location guaranteed a torrid wartime.

In February 1643, troops from Lincoln were sent to attack the royalist stronghold at Newark. In March, a royalist column advanced from Newark to the gates of Lincoln, and they tried again to take the city in May and July. The Earl of Newcastle finally took it for the king in August, and the famous city preacher Edward Reyner had all his goods stolen and narrowly escaped being shot in his own church. Newcastle was expelled in his turn in October. 'Lincolnshire,' exulted a parliamentary newspaper,

> ...is at liberty. The Lord Willoughby, Sir John Wray, Sir Edward Ayscough, Sir Christopher Wray and Sir Anthony Irby, are now by an orbicular providence, by an admirable revolution, reinstated, re-entered, relincolnshired again.[29]

But the conduct of the war at Lincoln caused bitter disagreements between the Parliamentary commanders. In January 1644, Cromwell launched a Commons tirade against Willoughby for having permitted cannon to fall into the hands of the King at Lincoln, and employing 'verie loose and profane commanders,' one of whom had allegedly ordered a parish constable to procure women. Cromwell was unassailable, but a few days later, the still seething Willoughby would challenge the Earl of Manchester to a duel.

The Parliamentary pamphleteer had written too soon, because in March 1644, the 'relinconshired' city was taken back by Royalists with characteristic flair by Rupert of the Rhine—who then with equally characteristic lack of planning had to abandon the city quickly, leaving Sir Francis Fane to conduct a doomed defence with a wholly inadequate garrison. Six thousand Parliamentarians fought grimly up slippery Steep Hill in heavy rain, and when they tried to mount the castle walls with tooshort ladders were bombarded with rocks that did more damage than any ordnance. Fane eventually surrendered, with 650 men. Fierce though the battle had been, only about fifty Royalists were killed, and just eight Parliamentarians, but the upper town was pillaged angrily. In the Cathedral, Roundheads tore up over 200 brasses and destroyed monuments including the shrines to St Hugh's head and body, the altar tomb of Queen Eleanor, and the monument to Robert Grosseteste. Cromwell spent most of that August in the city, although allegations that he ordered the stabling of horses in the Cathedral and considered demolishing it were fabrications.

But there were expulsions of the diocese's royalist clergy, dangerous criminals like Hugh Barcrofte of Welbourn, whose indictment lists such transgressions as 'Hee is scandalous in his life in absentinge himself from the society of all Godly ministers haveinge lived within a mile of Boston by the space ofive years now last past but neuer came to the Lecture there.'

Thomas Gibson of Horncastle 'hath frequently used creingeings [cringing] outward Adoracions and boweing at the name of Jesus,' and 'scandalized Orthodox and godly men, with nicknames of Zelotts, Annabaptists, Puritans, Brownists.'

Dr Hurst of Barrowby and Leadenham compared the Earl of Essex, Lord Fairfax, Sir William Waller and Cromwell to the four horns of the Book of Daniel 8, Cromwell singled out as 'the greatt and terrible horne ... not worthie of the name of Christian.'

William Underwood of Hareby was accused of:

> continual frequenting of Ailehouses ... keeping Companie theire with men of ill faime (vizt) Coblers and Pedlers and such as spend that they gett in drinkinge and Tiplinge in Ailehouses and thereby hath made himself a skorne & derision to others in havinge the backside of his clothes besmered over with creame by those that keepe him Company.[30]

Lincoln had a respite after the surrender of the King (who was accompanied by yet another Lincolnshire clergyman, Michael Hudson of Uffington) to the Scots at Southwell that May—but was again taken by royalists as they passed through in 1648. The unlucky preacher Edward Reyner, back in the city after two years' absence, was again the special target of royalists, who chased him with drawn swords into the Minster library, shouting they would have him dead or alive. He opened the door, was robbed of his coat and money, and led away for likely execution. Luckily for Reyner, one of the royalist captains had been one of his pupils when he had taught at Market Rasen, and secured his release—one of those paradoxes of civil wars, which like all family quarrels can combine the most vindictive cruelties with redemptive unexpected mercies born of long intimacy.

During the Protectorate, the city became a nest for non-conformists, many of them further to the left than the government. The Quakers George Fox and John Whitehead preached in the county, Whitehead being 'buffeted and most shamefully intreated, being often knocked down by the Rude and Barberous people,' who were being egged on by the city magistrate. The long-suffering Edward Reyner was libelled as a 'Lyar' by another Quaker, Martin Mason, who could not understand why so many in Lincoln preferred the 'Garlic and Onions of Egypt' to the milk and honey of Canaan. As well as the paid clergy, Mason also sparred with other freelance fanatics, in an exchange of pamphlets with titles like *The Boasting Baptist Dismounted, and the Beast Disarmed and Sorely Wounded without any Carnal Weapon*, and *The Quaker Quashed and his Quarrel Queld*. Restoration may have been a relief to Lincolnites.

Lincoln had been badly damaged by all this war, and despite brave pre-Restoration promises, Charles II's Exchequer was not up to the task of indemnifying all the nobles and gentry who had suffered materially in his cause. Robert Sanderson was, however, appointed Bishop in 1660, reward for a man long devoted to both the royal family as chaplain to Charles I, and to the Cathedral, who had before the war donated books to the library and assisted Dugdale to record the minster's ornaments in what is known as the *Winchelsea Book of Monuments*, still an invaluable resource for art historians. Puritan clergy and officials were replaced by royalists, who included the decidedly un-aristocratic James Yorke, a Lincoln blacksmith who before the war had issued a genealogical and heraldic book called *The Union of Honour*, and was now made mace bearer to the mayor. Yorke was highly regarded as a historian by writers like Thomas Fuller and Walter Scott, and his pictorial records of the arms of Lincolnshire's pre-Civil War gentry are still a useful compendium of lore that might otherwise have been forgotten.

Presbyterian Dissenters were granted indulgence—Edward Reyner even got a pension—but other outspoken Dissenters, including the aforementioned Martin Mason, were imprisoned. There were so many Quakers in Lincoln Castle that a room was set aside for them, and the Monthly Meeting paid for a loom so the prisoners could earn some money. A hugely expensive restoration of the Cathedral commenced, and in 1674, Christopher Wren built a new library. But still the city stayed a backwater, exemplified in the slightly ludicrous career of Thomas Barlow, Bishop between 1675 and 1691, a violent anti-Catholic who yet professed allegiance to James II, and seems never even to have visited Lincoln.

The old saying, 'Lincoln was, London is, and York shall be,' seemed still applicable in early Georgian times. Daniel Defoe found Lincoln:

> ...an antient, raged, decay'd and still decaying city; it is so full of the ruins of monasteries and religious houses, that, in short, the very barns, stables, out-houses, and, as they shew'd me, some of the very hog-styes, were built church-fashion; that is to say, with stone walls and arch'd windows and doors. There are here thirteen churches, but the meanest to look on that are any where to be seen; the cathedral indeed and the ruins of the old castle are very venerable pieces of antiquity ... this cathedral is in itself a

very noble structure, and is counted very fine, though I thought it not equal to some ... an old dying, decay'd, dirty city.[31]

But there were always impressive individuals associated with Lincoln, like yet another Bishop, Edmund Gibson (in office 1716–23)—a noted translator from Anglo-Saxon and Latin, and the compiler of *Codex Iuris Ecclesiastici Anglicani*, still the most complete collection of English ecclesiastical statutes. He was also a High Church Whig who worked hard to reconcile Tories to the house of Hanover—and the instigator of the Regius Professorships of Modern History at Oxford and Cambridge.

Beyond the Bishop's study, the Cathedral was in sorry state. The spires on the two western towers were weighing down the whole west front, threatening the whole building, but when in 1726 the authorities decided to remove them there was a conservative riot, with a mob forcing open the Close gates to fight the workmen and constables, making the Cathedral's dignified Prebendary dance to the chant 'High Church or Low, Jump again, Conington!' For three days, some workmen were locked into the Cathedral, and peace was only restored by a public promise to restore them instead. (They were eventually removed in 1807.)

Grosseteste's tomb was opened twice in 1782, the second time so Joseph Banks could see it. He left a detailed record and a poignant drawing of the great man in his modest sepulture— bones 'little decay'd' in a yellowish fluid, the flesh of his feet impressed into lead 'corroded and crack'd, as if eaten by a menstruum [solvent],' his pastoral staff 'almost annihilated,' its lamb's head finial resembling 'soft cheese,' and no trace of shroud or vestment, except a small piece of gold brocade adhering to a finger bone on his left hand.[32]

Outside the precinct gates, Lincoln was a city of poverty and tough law, its Castle notorious as it must have been in Norman times as assizes, barracks, prison and overlooking the place of public executions. A pub just outside the Castle, The Struggler's Inn, links to those times—located across from the old Hangman's Ditch, a place for desperate last orders, before the doomed men and their sometimes drunken escorts embarked on the maudlin final stage. Later, the Castle's Cobb Tower would be the place of public executions—the last in 1859—with thousands of thrilled Lincolnites turning up to see miscreants' last kicks against an infinite blue backdrop.

The Castle took pride in the nineteenth century as liberal executioner, pioneers of the 'long drop,' a quicker and more reliable hanging technique devised by Horncastle cobbler William Marwood. Marwood's ingenuity would be rewarded when he was appointed public executioner, dispatching 176 people within nine years, including Irish nationalist 'Invincibles' and the notorious burglar Charlie Peace. The last execution at the Castle was in 1961.

The Victorian jail and chapel survive, other legacies of what once passed for humane reform—prisoners kept in solitary to consider their souls' well-being, even in chapel, when tall vertical partitions were placed between seats to prevent prisoners from talking to or even seeing each other, or anyone except the preacher. The effect seen from the pulpit is one of vertical coffins, a living death by sermon. For some, such conditions must almost have felt worse than execution. The Gothic courthouse by Robert Smirke, built in the Castle courtyard in 1823, is still in use today as Lincoln Crown Court—barristers and defendants mingling with tourists, distinguishable only by being better dressed.

*　　*　　*

In 1847, a 31-year-old school master in Pottergate, the highly religious son of a Lincoln cobbler, published a book with an uninviting title, and unlimited ramifications.

The Mathematical Analysis of Logic, Being an Essay Towards a Calculus of Deductive Reasoning was no page turner, but its author, George Boole, was a prodigy, despite having little or no formal education—multilingual since childhood and qualifying as a teacher at sixteen. He was also a celebrity, at least in the world of mathematics, having three years previously won a Royal Society medal for a paper on differential equations (equations that examine the relationship between a physical quantity and its rates of change).

The book sets out Boole's attempt to analyse the logic of categorical propositions (propositions like 'All A is B'), on a principle of fundamental dichotomy. Modern mathematicians find dismaying flaws in his methodology, accusing him of poor definitions and inconsistency:

> ...anyone unacquainted with Boole's works will receive an unpleasant surprise when he discovers how ill constructed his theory actually was and how confused his explanations of it.[33]

Non-mathematicians are likely to find the whole subject unintelligible in any case. But this flawed booklet nevertheless was a first hesitant step towards what we now know as 'Boolean logic,' further developed by Boole in his *Laws of Thought* of 1854. Boolean logic is a form of algebra which defines every value as either 'True' or 'False.' This allows a machine to select whether to move onto the next stage, or to make a single pass through a set of instructions. This basic ability to compare values, whether numbers or text, was integral to the development of computers.

In 1948, the American mathematician Claude Shannon's paper 'A Mathematical Theory of Communication' relied on Boole's thinking to propose a linear schematic model of a communications system—the possibility of transmitting bits of information (including pictures, words and sounds) in the form of 1s and 0s along a wire. Boolean logic is therefore the basic building block of all programmes, all computer circuits, all mobile phones.

Boole could never, of course, have dreamed of such applications, but simply felt constrained to answer mathematics' call as Samuel repeatedly answered the Lord in Boole's favourite passage of the Bible. His unique contribution to modernity's architecture is remembered in a stained-glass window in the Cathedral, and on 2 November 2015 he was the object of one of Google's famous home page Google Doodles, due gratitude from a company that would not exist had it not been for him.

Lincoln in the nineteenth and early twentieth centuries was also a centre of engineering. Robey & Co made coal-mining gear and the lift for Blackpool Tower, before moving on to aircraft, frigate engines and landmines in the World Wars. Ruston & Hornsby, founded in 1918, was a noted maker of narrow-gauge steam locomotives, which were exported all over the British Empire; I saw one in southern India, rusted and stained but toiling on through broiling heat between banana trees, pulling a train covered with people clinging on for life to the outside.

William Foster & Co started life in 1856, making threshing machines and mill gear, moving on to traction engines and eventually the world's first tanks (then called 'landships'), the first ones of which rolled off the production lines in 1916, to harvest Germans at the Somme.

'It is a source of great satisfaction to us to know that our efforts in the peaceful city of Lincoln reacted with such splendid success on the battlegrounds of Europe,' enthused Sir William Ashbee Tritton, Foster's Managing Director, in a lavish corporate brochure filled with pictures of the 'glorious tanks' being tested in a park at Lincoln that the firm published in 1920, the same year the Cenotaph was raised. The 'glorious' subject-matter is oddly relieved by childish cartoons of a centipede and a tank, the first outraced by the second:

> The Tank, another Centipede,
> Was certain how to run,
> HE understood that right was might,
> Without ado he meant to fight,
> Spontaneous he went, on sight,
> Baldheaded for the Hun.[34]

Modernity certainly could have unpleasant aspects—something all too well understood by the city's most famous MP. Sir Charles de Laet Waldo Sibthorp (1783-1855), who was MP between 1826 and 1832 and again between 1835 and 1855, was one of England's greatest nineteenth-century eccentrics, and a half-serious hero to the long-time twentieth century *Daily* and *Sunday Telegraph* satirist Michael Wharton, who wrote those papers' proudly reactionary 'Way of the World' columns under the name of Peter Simple.

'Over thirty years,' smiles the former Conservative MP Neil Hamilton,

> ...[Sibthorp] set a standard of reaction, nationalism and xenophobia unrivalled in Parliamentary history ... If he had been present at the Creation, he would undoubtedly have urged God to think again and conserve the formless void.[35]

Between 1841 and 1855, *Punch* referred to Sibthorp satirically no fewer than 345 times. In *Sketches by Boz*, Dickens calls him 'a militia-man, with a brain slightly damaged and (quite unintentionally) the most amusing man in the House.' Even the understated *Dictionary of National Biography* describes him 'an able but eccentric speaker.'

Sibthorp was forty-three when he first took his seat in 1826, and was immediately distinguishable by his Regency sartorial sense—long coat and big boots, a huge gold quizzing glass on a long chain, his eyes gleamingly intense amongst a mess of whiskers, his hands copiously beringed. 'Can anything be more absurd,' Dickens enquired, 'than the burlesque grandeur of his air, as he strides up to the lobby, his eyes rolling like those of a Turk's head in a cheap Dutch clock?' Sibthorp told the agog House that reform was a thing he detested, as he detested the Devil, and innovation was 'at best a dangerous thing,' resulting in a revolution, railways 'and other dangerous novelties.' Railways were 'steam humbug,' he said, and he never travelled on one, successfully opposing routing the main line to London through the city.

The extension of the franchise, the scrapping of rotten boroughs, secret ballots and the banning of political bribery would all encourage unrest: 'I wish to see more expense and merriment at elections ... Give a man some genial liquor to drink and he will open his heart to you.' He bitterly opposed Catholic emancipation and denounced the government for granting money to the seminary in Maynooth, whose users were 'little better than devils incarnate' (ironically, his brother would later convert *twice* to Catholicism). He also hated free trade, telling the house that Lincolnshire's farmworkers were 'perfectly content with everything but the movements of the Anti-Corn Law League.'

He also denounced the new-fangled water closets and sanitary boards, barrel organs, and the proposed new National Gallery, and disapproved of a levy to encourage the building of free libraries, because, as he told the delighted house, he had always disliked reading when at Oxford. Foreigners, too, were menaces, singling out foreign opera dancers and singers who took money out of the country: 'I am sorry to say that the higher classes encourage foreigners, whether of character or not, male or female.' There was no reason for anyone to go abroad, he felt, except in times of war, and those who did travel should be taxed. Other tax rises were, however, unacceptable, public servants were paid too much, and the state should be pared to the bone.

He disapproved of Queen Victoria's German husband, and for that reason proposed that the consort's £50,000 annuity should be reduced to £30,000. His proposal unexpectedly won, and Victoria never forgave him, nor the city that elected him eight times, refusing to visit while he was still its MP. Albert's Great Exhibition, Sibthorp said, was 'an absurdity and a wild-goose chase,' which meant the cutting-down of trees in Hyde Park, and would bring domestic criminals as well as foreigners 'talking all kinds of gibberish' in order to sell 'foreign stuff of every description.' There might also be racial tensions:

> Suppose a case: a foreigner called a cabman and told him to drive to a certain place; the cabman could not understand him and before he knew what he was about, he would have something like a stiletto in him.

This 'treasonous' government, he expostulated, should be shipped to Botany Bay, and he hoped the Crystal Palace would be destroyed by hail. When he finally realised he was beaten on this one, he issued a sharp warning to householders near Hyde Park to look out for your 'silver forks, spoons and servant maids.' The new House of Commons was 'a piece of mere frippery and flummery ... more suitable in style for a harem.' His last intervention in that House was in 1855, when he accused Lord John Russell of misappropriating funds. He died not long afterwards, incandescent to his larger-than-life last, a caricature of the conservative instinct.[36]

*   *   *

Lurking in the city background were old doctrinal disputes, with occasional outbreaks of sectarian unpleasantness. In 1889, a ritual prosecution was taken out against Bishop Edward King (whose predecessor in the post had been Christopher Wordsworth, nephew of the poet and a noted hymnologist). King was generally agreed to be the nearest thing nineteenth-century Protestant England could come to saintly, but he happened to be a High Churchman and friend of the Tractarian E. B. Pusey.

A churchwarden from Cleethorpes complained that King had dabbled in what were still called 'Romish' practices during services, such as having lighted candles on the altar and facing towards the altar—away from the congregation—during prayers. The case became national news, as it was an anachronism even in 1888. The case was eventually found against the complainants, except on one small technical point. So ritual persisted, albeit with constant subtle changes in response to social developments, the Church for the last century much more a reflector than a shaper of culture—a comfy church for a decent, easily embarrassed and pragmatic nation.

Even now, even when you know its messy history, despite the bathos of the modern liturgy and the *New English Bible*, Anglican ritual can entrance—allowing us into the world of Hugh and Grosseteste, giving a connection with ancestors, and alchemizing inchoate aspirations and the institutions of State into conformity with each other, at least for the duration of the service.

In 2011, we attended the enthronement of the seventy-second Bishop of Lincoln, the Most Reverend Christopher Lowson. It was the grandest occasion in the city for years, bringing out a cross-section of the English elite—that unique blend of what Walter Bagehot called the 'dignified' and 'efficient' parts of the English Constitution.[37]

First up the long nave advanced a vanguard of vergers, Dean's vergers, readers, visiting readers, sub-deans, and *canonici emeriti*. Then came the representatives of temporal power—the Chairman of the County Council, the Mayor of Lincoln with attendants bearing the civic regalia, Her Majesty's Judges in robes and horsehair perukes, the High Sheriff of Lincolnshire, and the Lord-Lieutenant. They came to musical accompaniment, the Bedel stalking in front with his staff of office, then lines and lines of chanters, chantresses and choristers, choral scholars and lay vicars, more vergers and readers, a priest-vicar, the heads of schools connected to the Cathedral.

The transepts disgorged endless gorgeously attired celebrants, increasing in seniority and sumptuousness as they came on like a High Church high tide—canons' verger, the Chapter Cross, the *Clericus Fabricae*, Deacons of the Rite, prebendaries, registrars, chancellors, archdeacons, the Bishops of Grimsby and Grantham, the Canterbury Vesturer, the Precentor and the Dean. The processors seemed transfigured by the simple expedient of wearing robes which brushed the nave pavement as they moved in precedence set down centuries ago, looking very serious as they flowed towards the choir, clasping orders of service in spotless hands. Sartorial splendour, in a world of grunge—albs, cassocks, surplices, stoles, copes, dalmatics, chasubles, embroideries of Hugh's swan depending from the sleek necks of canons, mitres crowning the minor bishops. The Dean spoke at last: 'In the name of the Father and of the Son and of the Holy Spirit' and the audience rumbled 'Amen,' a deep and grateful sound, and an ancient one.

Legal officials read out and approved then-Archbishop Rowan Williams' *Mandate*, their wigs nodding as they approached and retreated in gowns and buckled shoes. The preliminaries satisfactorily completed, there was a fanfare of trumpets and the organ rolled into powerful life, while we sang out John Henry Newton's hymn:

> *Glorious things of thee are spoken, / Sion, city of our God; / He whose word cannot be broken / Formed thee for his own abode: / On the Rock of Ages founded, / What can shake thy sure repose?*

As the hymn echoed itself away into the resounding drum of the building, fading around the spandrels and corbels, there came three loud blows. *Thud. Thud. Thud.* Everyone turned to see. The Great West Doors were thrown open dramatically to reveal St Hugh's successor silhouetted by sunlight, wrapped in an aura of the otherworld as well as all the trappings of state. 'In the name of the Lord we greet you' we said together on the Dean's cue, and many present were not just being polite. The bringing in of a Bishop is like a new chapter in a long and much-loved book, and while he knelt to pray the choir sang a Bruckner motet, 'Locus *iste a Deo factus est, aestimabile sacramentum, irreprehensibilis est*' ('This place was made by God, a priceless sacrament; it is without reproach').

On call-and-response cue, we answered the Archdeacon of Stow and Lindsey (a title from legend as well as the landscape), to assure him that we had turned to Christ, repented of our sins, renounced evil and believed and trusted in God the Father—our voices rising and falling, rising and falling again in solemn creed and cadence, while grotesque carvings smirked down as if they knew us better than we knew ourselves. The Bishop splashed water from the black Tournai font—muscled into place by Norman henchmen nine centuries before—over himself and adjacent others, and we rendered an Englished *Gloria in excelsis*. In that moment all probably *did* wish 'Peace to His people, peace on earth'—while many must certainly have believed that the new Bishop signified better times. The lady next to me had moist eyes as schoolchildren lisped through readings.

The Bishop-Elect listened to the Declaration of Assent, which reminds him of all those historical compromises made by his predecessors. Then came the Oaths of Allegiance to the Queen, and that of Due Obedience to the Archbishop of Canterbury. The Oath of Fidelity was followed by his procession to St Hugh's Choir where he was inducted and installed at last in his *cathedra*. Although he was concealed from almost everyone's view by lovely masonry, these sacred mysteries were beamed onto on the large TV screens placed at strategic points while we sang, to a tune written for Westminster Abbey, a translation of a seventh-century Latin text, *Christ is made the sure foundation*, with a powerful final stanza that sets out the Church's final stance on the Trinitarian controversy:

Laud and honour to the Father, / Laud and honour to the Son, / Laud and honour to the Spirit,

Ever Three and ever One, / One in love and One in splendour / While unending ages run.

The Bishop was enthroned, the Anglican order reaffirmed, England itself. The choir struck up *Te Deum Laudamus* to a score by Haydn, while the Bishop exchanged the Peace with the College of Canons and clergy. The Bishop finishing at last, the episcopal entourage returned to the nave, while we sang 'O Holy Spirit, Lord of grace' to a tune by Byrd's friend, Tallis. He ascended the pulpit to preach his first sermon, and I had a fantasy that he was going to stand there for a long silent moment and fix us all with staring eyes before telling us that he had spent the previous night fasting, and striving to pierce the veils of the universe. But no, he told us winningly—he was going to watch *Strictly Come Dancing*. I cannot have been the only person who winced. The Church of England in an instant became the Church of Empty. The Order of Service read 'After the sermon, silence is kept for a few moments,' and it was, but not necessarily for the right reasons.

The rare ceremony over, we passed out eventually beneath ancient fanes and through Remigius' door, back out into dazzling light and a babble of Americans and Japanese excited to see such quaint pomp of Old England, and as we walked we smiled at each other, and shook off the semblance of a spell.

9

THE WIND ON THE HEATH

'*Such sweet-clothed valleys or aspiring hills*'
— William Browne, *Britannia's Pastorals*

WOLDS AND VALLEYS—CAISTOR—HORNCASTLE—
SOMERSBY—SPILSBY—LOUTH

At Hibaldstow, people were falling from the sky.

High above the heat haze could be seen the gaudy dots of parachutes—clients of the skydive club at the former RAF base, hurtling earthwards from 15,000 feet at 150 miles per hour. It felt appropriate to see aeronauts above the resting place of seventh-century sky-pilot St Hybald, called by Bede 'a most holy and continent man, who was an abbat in the province of Lindsey.'[1] Hybald is elusive even by seventh-century standards—all we know, other than his name and Bede's high opinion, was that he once went to Ireland to 'discourse of the life of the former fathers ... rejoicing to imitate the same' with one Father Egbert, a friend of St Chad. Even the locus of Hybald's abbacy is unknown, although it was probably Bardney, southeast of Lincoln. But this insubstantial man landed here at least, with his body awaiting eternal uplift in the chancel at Hibaldstow, and three other churches dedicated to him nearby, at Ashby-de-la-Launde, Manston and Scawby—the only ones dedicated to him anywhere.

Those skydivers must have a good view of Gainsthorpe, although they are probably too busy to take it in. It is possible that the soon-to-be Saint Hybald knew the place, if it existed in his time. Hybald must at least have met some of the people who toiled hereabouts thenabouts, and would have had a truer opinion of local people's nature than the seventeenth-century legend-makers who told Abraham de la Pryme the village had been burned because of the thievishness of its inhabitants.

Hybald may have walked where I walked in 2021—along the lines of the streets of the later village when it *was* a village, and not just a large field full of bumps. Aerial photographs show the shapes of house platforms, dovecotes and a pond, raised up slightly from the grass like old scar-tissue. On the ground, in July, the lines are not easy to see, but it is an evocative kind of exercise, conjuring up structures and vanished lives from numinous heat haze, while harebells nod, cardinal-red soldier beetles couple on thistles, and inquisitive cows crowd round to stickily lick my hand. Someone still farms here, someone has probably always farmed here. Not far off, huge barns loom out of the shimmer, like cathedrals to Ceres.

No one knows why Gainsthorpe was abandoned, sometime during the fourteenth century, but it was probably because of the gradual switch to pasturage, with the Black Death as another possible factor. Lincolnshire has over 130 identified deserted village sites.[2] This is comparable to other places in England, but they seem more visible here somehow. Gainsthorpe is the best known; it was in fact the first deserted village ever identified by aerial photography, captured in 1925 by O. G. S. Crawford, 'the founding father of modern landscape history.'[3] But there are traces to be found all over the county—oddly regular dips and hollows, short courses of stones in unexpected locations, the chalk arch of the church at Calceby, changes in vegetation, the slightly darker stripes of cultivation strips, that have somehow survived later cultivations. Armtree, Beasthorpe, Burreth, St Matthias at Skinn, Sythesby, Tatebi—names sound out of the ground, as quietly plangent as the names of villages stolen by the sea. We hear in them whispers of Goldsmith's lost village of his Anglo-Irish childhood, 'Sweet Auburn, loveliest village of the plain,'[4] Cobbett's bluff outrage on behalf of English peasantry, and Scottish nationalist mourning for crofts lost to English Clearances. Lost villages can make us feel simultaneously radical anger at their erasure by exploiters and conservative nostalgia for imagined Arcadias.

The unspectacular fall of Gainsthorpe is counterbalanced at Redbourne by a spectacular *near*-fall, followed by a notable rise. The near-fall was that of the six-year-old Charles Beauclerk, who according to a famous if apocryphal story, was held out of a window by his mother, Nell Gwyn, who threatened to drop him unless Charles II both acknowledged that he was his father and gave him a peerage. The King legendarily replied, 'God save the Earl of Burford!' The Beauclerks/Burfords soared out of their Drury Lane dubiousness to become Dukes of St Albans, Grand Falconers of England, and in-laws to Spencers and de Veres. Charles Beauclerk's grandson, Topham, would be a close friend of Bennet Langton and Dr Johnson.

In 1776, Stubbs painted the family of the Reverend Carter Thelwall, vicar of Redbourne, paragons of respectability, in front of their inherited Hall, with the tower of his church in the background.[5] In 1791, the seven-years-older girl from that painting married the eighth Duke of St Albans, adding a coronet to her coach and Restoration-era raffishness to the family tree. The Beauclerks took an interest ever after in the village, adding *Alice in Wonderland*-type Hall gates on the main road, with prancing lions and fake arrow slits, and other Tenniel-like buildings, including a colonial style smithy with a leaping horse finial.

Inside the church from the painting, there are coloured chevrons on the piers, an extraordinarily lurid 1840s window showing the opening of the Sixth Seal, enjoyably bad paintings of Biblical scenes, and funerary memorials ranging from rough to rococo. There are also newspaper cuttings about a 1930s incumbent, the Rev. A. R. Tremearne, who was being boycotted by his parishioners because they didn't like him covering the Sixth Seal with one of his own artworks. The church guide—written by Henry Thorold, a well-known county historian and member of one of Lincolnshire's oldest families—devastatingly calls these 'idiosyncratic decorations.' In one clipping, Tremearne is pictured on top of the beetling church tower (a striking 90 feet), defiantly raising a yellow flag, the international naval signal of having infectious disease on board. In its combination of peculiar church furnishings, perverse parsons, louche aristocratic connections and indignant arguments over insignificant things, Redbourne is a little ampoule of English eccentricity.

* * *

A much grander kind of obstinacy had been manifested in this airy region centuries before. Between 1361 and 1368 Fillingham's vicarage was occasionally occupied by John Wycliffe, who spent those years fretting about the state of the faith, and telling the many people who were prepared to listen such things as that CARDINAL stood for 'Captain of the Apostates of the Realm of the Devil, Impudent and Nefarious Ally of Lucifer.' Churches generally, he added, were 'dunnus of thefis and habitacionis of fendis,' the Pope's adherents were 'daughters of the diabolical leech,' and Scripture should be the only guide.

After he went up to Oxford, he increasingly loudly rejected the sale of indulgences, confession, absolution, vows of celibacy, papal excommunication, pilgrimages, image worship, and the existence of Purgatory. In 1381, he would formally deny the 'Miracle of the Mass'—transubstantiation, when communion bread and wine were transformed magically by the priest into the body and blood of Christ. From 1382 on, there began to appear his own translations into English of the Latin Vulgate.

All this was regarded with coolness by the Church, who mocked him and his followers as 'Lollards'—probably from a Dutch word, *lollen*, meaning babblers or mumblers—and more dangerously called him heretical. His ideas were met more warmly by many English, who had reason to be cynical of corrupt and worldly prelates, and furthermore had a nationalist resentment of Rome, especially when it came to sending money there. There was a generic social malaise in England, largely caused by the Black Death, while the Church more widely was in trouble. In 1378, a tumultuous Vatican Conclave elected *two* Popes, and then in 1409 the Council of Pisa elected a third, officiating respectively from Avignon, Rome and Pisa.

Wycliffe, who had learned theology from Thomas Bradwardine and philosophy from William of Occam, could hold his own in scholarly disputes; Church courts set up to try him 'broke up in confusion.'[6] He simultaneously spoke to deep instincts among the uneducated, like the Lincolnshire blacksmith who averred he could make 'as good a sacrament between ii yrons as the priest doth upon his altar.'[7] And he was bitterly committed. There had been many reformers, but 'Wycliffe's hatred could be satisfied only with the complete extinction of his opponent.'[8]

He was also personally ambitious, according to medieval historian May McKisack:

> Determined pursuit of his own material interests comes out unmistakeably ... the harsh censoriousness of much of his writing reflects unpleasantly upon the author ... his narrowly theological outlook, his distaste for music, art, romance—'jeestis of battles and fals cronycles'—and for all secular learning, is none the less repellent for having been shared by many of his orthodox contemporaries ... It is hard to believe he was amiable.[9]

This un-amiable visionary was fortunate to have influential protectors, like Joan of Kent (Richard II's mother) and John of Gaunt, who may have been persuaded by his message, but in any case could use it to their advantage. But as Wycliffe would have understood, principalities and powers are not to be relied upon. John of Gaunt became preoccupied elsewhere, and his indulgence petered out. Then, during the Peasants' Revolt in 1381, it transpired (or was believably alleged) that John Ball, one of its most radically egalitarian leaders, was a Lollard. But the Lollards were still treated oddly gently, at least by the standards of the fourteenth and fifteenth centuries. Wycliffe lived out his last years (he died in 1384) in Leicestershire, with just one ally remaining, obsessive to the unsatisfied end, a pale, ill, emaciated figure consumed by his work.

The Church fought back eventually. Two Bishops of Lincoln endowed Lincoln College in Oxford in 1427 to rescue theology from 'ignorant layfolk, who profane with swinish snouts its most holy pearls.'[10] In 1428, Wycliffe's bones were dug up and tossed into the River Swift. But by then his work had long been, and was still being, done—influencing Jan Hus in Bohemia, Martin Luther in Germany, and ultimately English churchmen like Cranmer, who disliked Lollardy yet availed of some of Wycliffe's ideas to make the case for breaking from Rome.

The highly educated Catherine Parr must have read some of Wycliffe's writings, perhaps during the three years she spent at nearby Kirton-in-Lindsey between 1530 and 1533, whilst married to Lord Burgh. Her religious writings are marked by strong anti-Popery, and nationalist descriptions of her more famous later husband as the English Moses, set to free his people from servitude.[11] The Anglican controversialist John 'Bilious' Bale would hail Wycliffe as the 'Morning Star of the Reformation.'[12]

Wycliffe never aspired to be the leader of any movement and would have been incapable of leading one. There would probably have been a Reformation of some kind if he had never existed. But from an English perspective at least, it is difficult to picture that Europe-upturning event without this adamantine, un-amiable man, dreaming prophetic thoughts in his Lincolnshire vicarage.

* * *

This is the least Lincolnshire-like part of Lincolnshire—the contoured county that gives the lie to the old 'calumny' of flatness.

There are parts of the Cliff that could be in the West Riding—almost Brontë country, with their high, undulating expanses, deceptive distances, fields of scrubby grass and gorse, and beds of glacial sand, divided by drystone walls and wind-sheared thorns. Cars speed along lonely roads as if eager to get gone, dogs bark and bark from gated farms, while sheep stand grumpily backwards on to the prevailing. RAF jets often overfly from nearby numerous bases, more sky-pilots taking a godlike view of dangerous ground—hopefully more successfully than the Airborne planners at Fulbeck who in 1944 planned the great parachute drop on Arnhem immortalised in *A Bridge Too Far*.

The heathland is almost as lonely as the deepest Fenland, despite its relative proximity to the county capital. Ermine Street still traces its imperious course as the A15 north of Lincoln heading for the Humber—surfing the sunny tops of the Cliff exhilaratingly, a panopticon road unrolling under untrammelled skies, where at night bright planets ride close by, or from which rain or snow fall unremitting, as your wipers sweep away so you can see the signs for Watering Dyke Houses, Grange de Lings, Caenby Corner, or Spital in the Street, and in between wan almost-emptiness.

This is a country of iron purposes as well as stone. The crusading Knights Templar owned forty-seven estates in Lincolnshire, many clustered around here, grim warriors turned builders of beautiful round churches (imitations of the Church of the Holy Sepulchre in Jerusalem), farmers and financiers of such successfulness that they were taken down by Rome in 1307, with the reluctant assistance of Edward II. They are remembered in place names and in the desolate remains of one of their preceptories (subordinate communities) at Temple Bruer.

Subordinate community though it was, Temple Bruer was important to the order, established in the 1160s where the roads between Lincoln, Sleaford and Stamford converged. The Templars and their tenants (who were sometimes coerced, shunted around like livestock) grazed sheep and pigs, gathered bracken to sleep in and gorse to burn, and ate birds, boar and deer. By the end of the thirteenth century there were hundreds of sheep here, and the estate had a reputation for premium-quality wool. The foundation had a 52-feet-wide round church (almost as big as London's Temple Church), walls and a crenelated gatehouse, there was a market and an annual fair, and Henry III and Edward I overnighted.

But by 1312, the Order was dead, sunk by mendacious accusations of black magic and the envy of a king of France, and the Knights Hospitallers took over the buildings until they too fell afoul of kingly avarice. In the 1530s, there were still 'greate and vaste buildinges but rude at this place,'[13] and the church was visible until the eighteenth century. Now, there is just the tower, rising incongruous out of a neat complex of barn conversions (are the farmers descended from Templar tenants?), its exterior showing high-pitched old rooflines, stigmata of old structures roughly handled by the hands of history. There are six steps up to a round-topped door, and two rooms within, one with contemporaneous carving, the other incised with the names of graffitists going back to the eighteenth century. Outside, a tractor powers up and out of the yard, the unglamorous realities of earth as always outlasting millenarian dreams.

At Glentworth, Sir Christopher Wray lies adjourned by a Saxon tower, Lord Chief Justice and Speaker of the Commons, who presided over some of the great, sometimes show, trials of the sixteenth century—Anthony Babington, who had plotted to murder the Queen, the Jesuit martyr Edmund Campion, and William Davison, the privy councillor who became the scapegoat for the execution of Mary Stuart.

South Carlton leads off from here too, with its chapel to the Lords Monson, centuries present in the county, falling out on both sides in wars—one imprisoned for life by Charles II, every year on the anniversary of Charles I's death-sentence being dragged on a sledge from the Tower to Tyburn and back, with a noose around his neck—for better or worse the family always adhering to their motto 'Ready for my Country.'

The church at Willoughton holds another kind of imperative call—an early nineteenth-century vamping horn, or shawm, 6 feet long, the earliest kind of megaphone of a type first demonstrated to Charles II in St James' Park (audible 850 yards off) and subsequently used for naval defences, but here blown in peace—calling gleaners to and from fields, warning trampling cowherds off the commons, giving notice of marriage banns. It is a reminder of a lighter side to Cliff life, exemplified for me by a May Day morning at Hemswell, and schoolchildren dancing around a Maypole at bright noon, with blossom in their hair.

In the seventeenth and eighteenth centuries, the countryside here was still lonely and crepuscular, frequently dangerous because of the uncertainty of the road and the predations of criminals. A late seventeenth-century geologist riding from Lincoln to Caistor described the fifteen solitary miles as 'Arabia Deserta,' an impression reinforced by finding out that houses were at times overwhelmed by flying sand. Dunsby Hill near Sleaford was so notorious for highwaymen that local insurance policies specifically exempted 'accidents of Dunsby heath.'[14] In 1751, Sir Francis Dashwood of Nocton Hall erected the Dunston Pillar, a 100-foot limestone land lighthouse to illuminate the heath between Lincoln and Sleaford. There was an assembly room at the Pillar's base, and it is possible it was used by Sir Francis' notorious 'Monks of Medmenham Abbey,' better known as the 'Hellfire Club.' It would have been a suitably drear location for their mock-Satanic drinking games and rituals.

When Dashwood became Chancellor of the Exchequer in 1762, his Nocton estate was let to a Lincoln physician with equally unorthodox *bon-ton* connections—Dr Francis Willis, who attended George III during his bouts of mental illness, which involved the use of straitjackets and tying the monarch to the bed, much to the monarch's disgust (although Willis' approach towards mental illness was much more enlightened than almost any of his medical contemporaries). A courtier recorded a testy dialogue between patient and physician:

'Sir, your dress and appearance bespeaks you of the church. Do you belong to it?'

'I did formerly, but lately I have attended chiefly to physick.'

'I am sorry for it. You have quitted a profession I have always
loved, and you have embraced one I most heartily detest.'

'Sir, Our Saviour Himself went about healing the sick.'

'Yes, yes, but He had not £700 [a year] for it.'[15]

A Coade Stone statue of George III was loyally placed on the
Pillar in 1810 by one of Sir Francis' descendants, the third Earl
of Buckingham; the architect in charge was killed by falling from
the Pillar during the raising of the statue, and buried at
Harmston with a stone that reads: 'He who erected the noble
King / Is here laid low by Death's sharp sting.' The King was also
'laid low' in 1941, because the statue posed a potential danger to
low-flying bombers, and it now stares slightly dyspeptically over
the courtyard at Lincoln Castle.

* * *

The highest point between Kent and Yorkshire is the trig pillar
of Normanby-le-Wold, 551 feet above sea level, mostly hidden
by a hedge, but its general location unmistakable thanks to 'The
Golfball,' the white sphere of the National Air Traffic Control
Radar Installation at Claxby. The little pillar, erected in 1936,
speaks to history in its way—part of the Ordnance Survey
mapping-military nexus during an increasingly tense period, a
wayside marker for that decade's tweed-clad walkers, rising out
of the cities of the plain for a time, to contemplate continuity
from the crown of eastern England.

Today those cities are only geographically far, their best and
worst aspects beamed constantly close from the TV transmitter
at Belmont, which when erected in 1965 was the tallest guyed
tubular steel mast in the world, at 1,272 feet, and the tallest
structure of any kind in Britain. It became Britain's second-
tallest in 2008, when the signal went digital, which is roughly

when we finally gave up TV. But even in its slightly curtailed guise, its Barad-Dûr-like column of red lights can be seen on clear nights from everywhere in the county, from the far side of the Humber and sometimes even from Derbyshire.

In the plashy and unpolluted Bain valley not far from the transmitter's base, cattle wallow in the little river, signifying their approval of this accommodating vale by copiously decorating the ground with rich and sloppy pats, which in summer are beaded with gemmy dung flies. The animals are excluded from the ivy-mounded graveyard of Biscathorpe's church by a ha-ha. The little building is a last gasp of Strawberry Hill Gothic, built in 1844 and luckily avoiding the attentions of the heavy-handed Victorian 'restorer,' James Fowler of Louth—outdated while still being built, an essay in perverse antiquarianism with its pointed arches, mellow coloured windows and gallery of unsentimental heads. It could be a backdrop for the picnic in *Pickwick*—or maybe a folk-horror story, because that so-scenic Bain hides Lovecraftian horrors, leggy and writhing creatures under its stones.

Since its introduction in the 1970s to bolster the food industry, the American signal crayfish (*Pacifastacus leniusculus*) has largely replaced the European crayfish *Astacus astacus* in many rivers—like the grey squirrel they are larger, faster breeding and more aggressive than their British counterparts, and carrying the fungal pathogen their introduction was supposed to ameliorate. They also undermine river banks and eat the eggs of the Miller's Thumb (*Cottus gobio*), a primitive-looking fish with a very large head, large fins and a brown tapering body, that shares their liking for fast-flowing waters with gravelly beds. Male Bullheads guard their eggs, but they cannot always prevail against signals the same size as themselves, and which are present in infinitely larger numbers.

The Lincolnshire Wildlife Trusts have an eradication programme, but conventional trapping does not work, because the meshes only trap the largest specimens and moving nets around in any case spreads eggs and the pathogen, while hand-catching is laborious, time-consuming, and can even be quite painful (the largest males are 8 inches long and formidably pincered). The best hope for *Astacus astacus* might be the ongoing re-expansion of otters across the old Lincolnshire ranges.

The Wolds also host larger, but much less substantive, monsters—wild men, a leitmotif of medieval and early-modern culture, represented in Lincolnshire by the 'Wild Man of Stainfield,' a hairy semi-human said to have wandered in the woods between there and Wragby, terrorising the district until slain by Francis Tyrwhitt-Drake. It combines all the tropes of these stories—the sinister forest, a dangerous half-seen creature (or outlaw) moving in its depths, frightened villagers, a gallant champion who slays the beast, the 'truth' of the tradition allegedly corroborated by the symbology of a great family's coat of arms, or inexplicable artefacts found in churches—in the case of the Tyrwhitt-Drakes, a coat of arms featuring a wild man crest, a helmet, gauntlets, a dagger and some tattered pieces of cloth.

The name Tyrwhitt is also a local onomatopoeic term for the lapwing (*Vanellus vanellus*), and is said to have been taken by Francis in gratitude to the bird, which alerted him to the presence of the beast. Over centuries, such stories become densely embroidered until ultimately any tiny bit of truth there may once have been—some possible real hermit, some real outlaw once hunted down—has been erased. Even the artefacts that seem to have given rise to this legend have vanished, stolen in 1995. As one version of the Tyrwhitt 'family motto' goes, 'Tyme Trieth Truth'—or perhaps it just shows that people will always see strange creatures where the light is uncertain. Another wild man, 'Shag Boy,' was supposed to haunt the hills about Ruckland, whose rector George Hall may well have given credence to such stories. He was a prominent member of the Gypsy Lore Society, founded in 1888 by David MacRitchie, who believed fairy stories were based on folk memories of pre-Celtic inhabitants.

Wild men also feature in the heraldry of the Willoughbys. The architectural writer John Harris was curiously moved by these. In Spilsby church, he had smirked at the crudely carved wild man effigies on the Willoughby tombs, before going to visit where the family had lived. Eresby Hall was begun in the 1530s by Charles Brandon, Duke of Suffolk, after he married Catherine Willoughby, heiress to the last Lord Willoughby d'Eresby. Their son, said John Leland in the 1560s, 'intendenth to build sumptuously,'—and by all accounts did—a large H-shaped house, with an orangery, parterres, stables and ornamental reflecting waters. But by the eighteenth century, the family, now Dukes of Ancaster, rarely came so far north, and it burned in 1769, leaving no drawings or detailed descriptions, only a rumour of luxury. The shapes of garden features can be seen up close, and from the Spilsby bypass, a long avenue of trees, and at the end a solitary gate pier. Harris collapsed mysteriously walking back down this avenue, and could not stand up again, needing to be carried to an ambulance—afterwards half-believing it was 'revenge' of the Willoughby wild men.[16]

Walking one dusk on the beach, I came unexpectedly across a neighbour—a shrewd and tough woman, uncharacteristically panic-stricken and sweating, who pointed breathlessly back into the black tunnel under the thorn trees and gasped, 'There's a hairy tramp in there, staring at me!' I found none under there, of course, and some part of me couldn't help being disappointed. Other people have stronger imaginations, like those who stubbornly report big cats in their back gardens—the 'Lindsey Leopard' which slinks in and out of local headlines, a ghost-pain of wildness.

* * *

A geologist walking west to east across the uplands would see geology gradually change. The ironstone heath with its limestone walls, patches of Kimmeridge clay and blown sands would be increasingly interspersed with fields of thin and flinty soil over red and white chalk, the westernmost end of a chalk ridge that runs south-eastwards across the county to near Burgh le Marsh, then ducks under the Wash, to re-emerge in Norfolk.

Caistor was founded by the Romans on a western spur of these Wolds, on a site still known for its springs. But Caistor is best known today (insofar as it *is* known) for the Gad Whip—a wicked-looking implement with a 6-foot stock and a 7-foot lash, kept in a case in the church. A leather purse attached to the stock once contained silver coins, including an Edward I silver penny. Until 1846, the whip was used every Palm Sunday as part of a strange ritual surrounding the rental of nearby fields.

The tenant was required to send a man and the whip to the church, the man detailed to crack the whip three times in the porch during the first lesson of Matins. During the second lesson, the whip was held over the head of the vicar, following which the lash was folded around the stock and the whole thing placed in the pew of the landowner to show who really had the whip hand. Some of the splendidly named people awaiting resurrection in the graveyard must often have shaken their heads or smiled at this foolish custom—Keturah Hanson Green, Sydney Mudd, Kennington Keats, Harriet Quickfall, Dimmack Moody, John Spittlehouse, Alice Turtle, Lois Ogg and Mahala Rawlinson.

Caistor's Roman connections would have most interested Grammar School pupil Henry Newbolt (1862-1938), whose much-anthologised 1892 poem 'Vitaï Lampada' is derived from a phrase by Lucretius, 'the torch of life.' The poem starts with a cricket match in a hushed cathedral close, and goes onto a Gatling gun in a blood-soaked desert, these differing situations united and at least partly uplifted by the public-school sporting ethos, the team captain and the regimental subaltern alike inspired by sportsmanship, the overriding need never to let the side down, whether a Gentleman's Eleven or a Redcoat square. At the lowest ebb of military fortune, on the hinge of fate, when 'England's far, and Honour a name, / The voice of a schoolboy rallies the ranks,' with the message that none who hear it 'dare forget,' and 'Bear through life like a torch in flame, / And falling fling to the host behind—'Play up! play up! and play the game!'[17] Newbolt wrote many poems, of which the best remembered is 'Drake's Drum' of 1896, which refers to the old belief that Francis Drake was not dead, and would return if needed by the nation:

> *Take my drum to England, hang et by the shore, / Strike et when your powder's runnin' low; / If the Dons sight Devon, I'll quit the port o' Heaven, / An' drum them up the Channel as we drumm'd them long ago.*[18]

It is too easy to write off Newbolt's work as risible period piece. He was not heedless of the attrition of war, even wars made more bearable by gentlemanly comportment. His hugely popular 1899 collection *The Island Race* was also not uncritical of his country, as suggested in 'Vigil':

> *Know'st thou what is Hatred's meed? / What the surest gain of Greed? / England! wilt thou dare to-night / Pray that God defend the Right?*

The supposed anachronism would also be a highly successful editor, novelist and playwright, and a friend to Yeats and Eliot. In 1914, he was given the job of producing war propaganda, and was given responsibility for all telecommunications—high-tech trusts that would never have been entrusted to a naïve throwback.

These chalky hills are the nearest Lincolnshire gets to the South Country, although much smaller and without emblematic chalk figures or stone circles—or traffic. Some of the slopes here are startlingly steep, if not high, as dramatic as eastern England gets—although none would have impressed Lincolnshire's best-known alpinist, Charles Hudson, vicar of Skillington, who in July 1865 was in the first expedition that conquered the Matterhorn—only to die in a fall on the way down.

There are side roads here where every car feels like a small event, highways humming for the next, silent except the tread of your boots, the panting of dogs, the soughing of wind, the whistlings of curlew and lapwing amid furrowed fields and little clumps of trees, and sometimes in the distance folk-horror scarecrows with outstretched arms and chemical drums where their heads should be. Asparagus, winter barley, beans and linseed tremble in fields scattered with tiny flints, and just occasionally coins lost by some medieval or modern.

There are vantage points from where and weathers in which you can simultaneously see the towers of Lincoln and in the other direction an equally otherworldly suggestion of sea. The prehistoric Bluestone Heath Road draws you inwards and on, plodding stoically as so many have plodded stoically this way, on the move between yesterday and tomorrow, between elemental landscapes and zones of being. Desultory digs have daylighted patches of Roman road surface, sometimes following the conjectured route of the Bluestone, sometimes diverging, lost roads criss-crossing earlier lost roads, all much later overlaid by railways that have become lost in their turn—a palimpsest of public transport of yore, with even the public now echoingly absent.

* * *

For many middle-aged or older British, especially English, men, 'Dr Beeching' is deeply unlikeable—his surname a kind of shorthand for out-of-touch officialdom, of Whitehall arrogance and callousness. The main road into the industrial estate that grew up around Alford's closed station is named Beeching Way, in wry remembrance of his allegedly brutal axe.

There have been train romancers since the start of trains, but especially since the lines began to be dieselised, and the sleek old locomotives superseded. Their ranks were long regenerated by the likes of the famous 1936 GPO film *The Night Mail*, featuring Auden's verse and Britten's music, the Rev. Awdry's *Thomas the Tank Engine* stories, and whimsies like the 1953 Ealing comedy *The Titfield Thunderbolt*, starring Stanley Holloway and Sid James, in which villainous bus drivers try to crush the plucky people of Titfield, led by their squire and vicar, who want to keep their line open in the face of Whitehall rationalisation.

Lincolnshire is no exception, with a standard gauge steam line run by hobbyists from Ludborough along part of the old route towards Grimsby, which they dream about reopening all the way. That line had a long history indeed, opened in 1848 and only closed in 1980—with years of hauling Grimsby fish up to London, and grain from Louth to Immingham, and even a brief military interlude between 1940 and 1941, when it was patrolled by an armoured train. For the final decade it was a freight-only service, as passenger traffic had been dwindling for decades, with small stations being shut as early as the 1930s. In total, Lincolnshire has lost 334 miles of standard gauge train track, which is a lot of distance to be nostalgic about.

But steam trains were dirty and inefficient, and not enough people wanted to use them outside the tourist season; there was a station in our village on the Louth-Mablethorpe line, and locals have told me they were relieved when it shut, because it frightened livestock and brought the 'wrong kind of people' into the area.[19] But still hundreds of thousands yearn for the days of steam, talk lovingly about rolling stock, smell romance in smuts, and collect memorabilia of times when Britain was ingenious and self-confident, if not *the* workshop of the world, at least one of them. England is seen through magic smoke as the land of excellence and restraint, the land of *Brief Encounter*. Steam nostalgists' ancestors probably deplored the end of the stagecoach at the hands of the inhuman iron road.

Lost railways can be better than real ones, because the cinder beds have become wonderfully overgrown nature corridors, a refuge for animals and for me from intensively farmed fields and primped gardens, passing over or under old brick bridges rustling with leaves and budded with stalactites, restless with bats and specialised spiders. I like the raised views of the country, the backs of people's houses, the traces of old industries, the intriguing tunnels, the unexpected meetings with creatures from lizards to woodpeckers, and the ghosts of former travellers. Steam trains are better viewed from the guard's van of history. As Compton Mackenzie reflected almost a century ago:

> In the far future, when they cease to serve man's purpose, their platforms covered then by grass will no doubt diffuse a magical atmosphere like the still discernible contours of Roman camps.[20]

Train travellers in any case travel through time rather than inside it. Probably only walkers in the Wolds are really travelling properly, penetrating at their own pace into steep-sided glacial valleys, old quarries with abandoned tools, vanished village streets, seeing shadows, seeing life—ridge and furrow, packhorse tracks, a still-used Tudor dovecote, a muntjac peering from the middle of a hedge like a trophy head upon a wall, jays crashing and laughing through a combe, a red kite straying further east than usual, Scots pines sticking up suddenly by themselves, the most evocative of evergreens. The slowness of walking allows you to think about the swiftness of history, its chances and fates, its wonders and waste.

Wonders as at Thornton, where there is one of the oldest organs in the country, an early eighteenth-century or maybe even late seventeenth-century masterpiece of the carpenter's art, including the pipes, diapasons and six stops. It is the kind of instrument Purcell could have played, repaired, or tuned while still an apprentice in London, perhaps sometimes even making noises as squeakily alarming as the ones I make when I try a couple of chords. But behind my racket lurks a suggestion of the instrument's transportive potential, its warmly rich timbre—the organ as Purcell's 'Wondrous Machine'—the first of his songs I ever heard, the first music that made me want to cry.

Waste like at Burwell. In 1957, *Country Life*'s John Harris went to see Burwell Hall, a famous Georgian jewel of 1760, only to find it abandoned in the middle of a brambled lawn, with sheep in the hallway, and heaps of grain and potato sacks under Palladian plaster ceilings and the eyes of still-hanging portraits. The following year, he returned just in time to see workmen hacking down the last of the plaster with pickaxes, and the 'superlative' mahogany stairs smouldering on a bonfire. He was 'black with rage' at Lincolnshire's 'philistine farmers.'[21] The pleasure of ruins can sometimes be a kind of pain.

* * *

Horncastle is a town of antique shops, which are set among remnants of Rome. Here, the crayfish-beset Bain meets the bream-filled Waring at the foot of the Wolds, around the horn-shaped promontory that gave the town its name.

We used to spend Saturday afternoons here, as we had a huge-feeling house to fill, and here we could find, among the retro trash and 'collectible' trinkets, Victorian, Georgian and even older things at a fraction of the price we would have paid in London. Our unlucky cars ground complainingly up and down steep hills weighed down with beds, books, bricks, chairs, lumps of stone, pictures, sculptures, tables and all kinds of impulse buys, some ill-advised, but many still doing service two decades on, in a house that now feels much too small. We were always foolishly hoping we might find a lost work by either of Horncastle's celebrated painters—Thomas Sully (1783-1872), 'the prince of American portraiture' who painted Thomas Jefferson and Queen Victoria, and a famous patriotic work *The Passage of The Delaware*—or miniaturist Annie Dixon (1817-1901), who depicted Victoria's children.

In between Roman consequence and its post-1960s decline into knick-knacks, Horncastle had long been a place of equestrian significance. The Duke of Wellington's horse Copenhagen was said to have been foaled near Market Rasen. By the Middle Ages, it was renowned as a place to buy and sell horseflesh, and by the nineteenth century it was England's biggest equine market by far, attracting buyers from Europe's royal families—mingling with a multifarious array of aristocrats, breeders, conmen, farmers, horse-whisperers, military men, racers and touts, over weeks that could, and sometimes did, become riotous. It also had even more anarchic undercurrents; Arthur Thistlewood, leader of the 1820 Cato Street Conspiracy to murder the Cabinet, was born in Tupholme, studied at Horncastle Grammar School, and owned a farm locally before moving to London.

A key component of the horse-mad townscape were the gypsies, and it was their annual presence that drew George Borrow (1803–81) here in the mid-nineteenth century, trying to sell a horse, pursuing a gypsy girl, and more generally a dream of life on the open road. Borrow was a fantasist and serial show-off, the argumentative, brilliant, didactic and pedantic scion of a respectable Norwich family, who was fanatically dedicated to three things—the Church of England, philology and gypsies. He had toured Spain in the early 1840s, a strikingly tall figure with a green umbrella, trying to persuade the people to join the

Church of England, writing vividly and often to archly comic effect about his doomed quest in 1843's bestselling *The Bible in Spain*. He would later try to convert the chapel-going people of Wales, with an equal lack of success.

In between came *Lavengro* (1851) and *The Romany Rye* (1857), highly spiced accounts of time spent among Britain's distrusted, distrusting gypsies—living in caravans or sleeping under the stars, cooking over fires, horse-coping and odd-jobbing, and learning the Romany tongue, chiefly by showing off his real, or perceived, prowess—at once trying to be one of them and seeing himself as an educated cut-above. The semi-fictional books have a cast of strong recurring characters, like 'The Flaming Tinman,' love-interest Isopel Berners, and the charismatic Jasper Petulengro, with whom Borrow's alter-ego has an evocative exchange, the key passage of both books.

Petulengro is sitting down, 'his eyes fixed intently on the red ball of the setting sun,' thinking about his recently deceased parents. He does not believe in an afterlife, he tells Borrow, and is sorry he cannot, because:

'Life is sweet, brother.'

'Do you think so?'

'Think so! There's night and day, brother, both sweet things; sun, moon and stars, brother, all sweet things; there's likewise a wind in the heath. Life is very sweet, brother, who would wish to die?'

'I would wish to die...'

'You talk like a *gorgio* [non-gypsy]—which is the same thing as talking like a fool. Were you a Romany *Chal* [native-born] you would talk wiser. Wish to die, indeed—a Romany *Chal* would wish to live for ever.'

'In sickness, Jasper?'

'There's the sun and stars, brother.'

'In blindness, Jasper?'

'There's the wind on the heath, brother; if I could only feel that, I would gladly live for ever ... we'll now go to the tents and put on the [boxing] gloves; and I'll try to make you feel what a sweet thing it is to be alive, brother!'[22]

Petulengro's extolling of the 'wind on the heath' and pugilism are perfectly of their place and time, capturing the essence of upland Lincolnshire, and a passionate yearning for freedom and rustic vigour—at least as seen through the eyes of Borrow, who is out under the stars by choice. (The people at the Gordon Boswell Romany Museum near Spalding had never heard of Borrow.) But *The Romany Rye*'s evocations of Horncastle's horse fair captures something of English rural life just before the machine age, filled with colour but also discontents—injustice, old rivalries and resentments, poverty, sickness, Cobbett-style nationalist radicalism, and the missionary utopianism of burgeoning Nonconformist sects.

Borrow puts his horse through its paces to show it off to a crowd of potential purchasers. When one asks to be allowed to try the horse, Borrow declines,

'Lest you should be a Yorkshireman.'

'Yorkshire?' said the man; 'I am from Suffolk—silly Suffolk—so you need not be afraid of my running away with the horse.'

'Oh! If that's the case, I should be afraid that the horse would run away with you.'

The ensuing long haggle is followed by a near-fight between potential purchasers, eventually a successful sale, and then in the evening a long conversation with new acquaintances, one of whom is a Hungarian who smokes a pipe 6 feet in length. When Borrow's new interlocutors find out that he is the Romany Rye they have heard about, they are delighted and order champagne, then throw two full bottles through the closed window. They open more and the exchange becomes ever more tipsy, yet somehow always returns to Borrow's expertise as gypsy, historian, linguist, and generally as an Englishman, with the Church of Rome always in the background as enemy of all that is good and true. The following day, Borrow meets the sexton of the church, whose father had known an elderly countryman who remembered the Battle of Winceby—and an Irish thimble-rigger, who offers yet more opportunities for anti-Catholic points. It is a strange farrago, utterly unreliable—yet similar unexpected encounters, wide-ranging connections and conversations, and woozily-remembered evenings were probably always part of the fair experience.

At West Keal, deep-carved dragons chase their tails around the tops of columns, and the opened church door frames fen, with Boston Stump as coda. Elizabeth Shaw would have seen that view many times during 106 years of living in the village, between 1693 and 1800. A drawing of her at the Spalding Gentlemen's Society shows the phenomenon of nature in the last year of life, slumped in shawls before her brazier, a bellows on her knee, last breaths for a dying fire.

There are memories of a King and Dauphin of France at the remains of Somerton Castle—John II and his son Philip, captured by the Black Prince at the Battle of Poitiers, and imprisoned here in luxurious style between 1359 and 1360, beguiling exile with a personal astrologer and band. Old Bolingbroke is even more regal, home of John of Gaunt and the future Henry IV, often hosting Geoffrey Chaucer, in its last military action (1643) defended for the king, replying to calls of

17. St Wulfram's, Grantham

18. The once-important port of Saltfleet

19. St Peter's, Barton-on-Humber

20. One of the oldest brasses in England—an unknown knight in Croft church

21. The Fens near Midville

22. On the shores of the Humber

23. Low tide

24. Lincoln Cathedral, or Lincoln Minster—West front and Exchequer gate

25. Lincoln Cathedral, Lincoln Castle and the Bailgate area

26. The MV *Nimrod* and old sea-dogs

27. Former trawler at Grimsby

28. Grimsby Royal Dock

29. A sea serpent

30. The Trent at the old Roman ford at Marton

31. A road in the heathlands between Lincoln and Sleaford

32. One of the Willoughby monuments in Spilsby church

surrender with the defiant 'Bug-bear words must not winne castles' (although in the end they did). A more successful soldier—from a career point of view—was Welbourn's Sir William Robertson (1860-1933), who rose from trooper in the 16th Lancers to Field Marshal and Imperial Chief of Staff, a promotional trajectory that has never been bettered (although his generalship has).

Scrivelsby is connected with ceremonial soldiers, the Dymokes, hereditary King's Champions going back in England to Richard II, who are themselves connected to the Marmions, who performed similarly for the Dukes of Normandy, and became stock-figures of Walter Scott's powerful chivalric nation-shaping.

The Dymokes' job was to send an armoured, mounted knight to every coronation at Westminster Hall. After the first course of the banquet, the Champion had to ride into the Hall in full armour, preceded by two trumpeters, with esquires holding his shield and lance, and escorted by the Lord High Constable and the Earl Marshall. The Lancaster Herald then called on anyone who wished to dispute the new monarch's claim to declare themselves and fight. The Champion would throw down his gauntlet, which would be handed back by the Herald after a pause. This was done three times—at the entrance to the hall, in the middle, and in front of the king's table. After the third time, the king would drink to the Champion from a gold cup which he then handed to the Champion, who would drain it, and keep the cup as fee. The Champion would then shout 'Long life to his Majesty the King,' bow to the monarch and back his horse out.

At the coronation of James II in 1685, the Champion flung his glove to the ground so energetically that he fell off too, and lay on his back in the middle of the hall—making the queen snort and the king laugh. At the Coronation of William and Mary in 1689, the Champion had lost his gauntlet, stolen by a mysterious elderly woman. A male stranger, reputed by gullible Jacobites to have been Bonnie Prince Charlie, was supposed to have done the same at George III's coronation in 1761. The ceremony was abandoned for Victoria's accession, counterintuitive at a time of Gothic Revival, but in the longer term a sign of prosaic things to come.

The Dymokes' house has been several times replaced, and the stone gateway, with its prancing lions, is more suggestive than what it leads to, and their parish church across the road is surrounded by fields of kale. Cabbages and kings—England through the looking glass.

* * *

At Somersby, even a house possibly by Vanbrugh is outdone in interest by the Rectory next door, and the church across the road. The Rectory was home-base to Alfred Tennyson for his first twenty-eight years, his father the rector of Somersby and Bag Enderby, Alfred a dreamy wanderer along the district's flowery verges and winding lanes, amid a traditional haze.

Alfred added to this haze greatly over the course of his hugely successful public life, with generations of Tennyson scholars ascribing personal significance to just about every bridge, field, house, mill or road in the triangle between Horncastle, Louth and Spilsby. The lamprey-full River Lymn is often claimed to be the 'Brook' of his late poem of that name,[23] although the Bain is perhaps a more likely source.[24] Tennyson always denied he had any particular watercourse in mind, but when he wrote it he was living in London, with few possible other models for his little hilly stream that goes 'on for ever,' as he knew *he* would not.

Clear memories of countryside not just seen but imaginatively inhabited cluster in his work, from his jaunty salute to 'The Grasshopper'—'Bayard of the meadow'—to the most plangent parts of 'In Memoriam.' Somersby or Bag Enderby must surely have the seeded the 'Old Yew, which graspest at the stones /

That name the under-lying dead, / Thy fibres net the dreamless head, / Thy roots are wrapt about the bones,' as the poet famously mourns his friend Arthur Hallam, now walking by himself in 'the eternal landscape of the past.' The Danish shield boss nailed to the door of Bag Enderby would have been a constant reminder to an impressionable boy and man of violent waves that once raced across this anciently peaceful place, iron truths and blood salts always being spilled into its thirsty earth.

The poet's uncle, Charles Tennyson d'Eyncourt, had an equally lush sensitivity. He dreamed up a royal pedigree for himself and, to wide ridicule, turned a small Tudor house at Tealby into a battlemented, drawbridged Gothick extravaganza called Bayons Manor, designed by architects including Anthony Salvin (1799-1881), who had studied under John Nash, and was starting to make a reputation designing and restoring statement, Jacobean and Tudor Gothic-style buildings, from Windsor Castle to private houses for clients with Romantic tastes and deep pockets.

It was an English Abbotsford—with fake ruins in the grounds, and diamond-paned rooms crammed with antique costumes, furniture, paintings, *papier-mâché* panelling, statuary, stone chimneypieces, the Westminster Abbey canopy from Victoria's coronation, and cod-suits of armour and weapons forged for the 1839 Eglinton Tournament, a famously costly attempt to recreate a medieval joust in Scotland. When the Duke of Northumberland visited about 1845, he said to the gratified d'Eyncourt, 'At Alnwick I have only three gateways, *you* have five.'

D'Eyncourt's ambition was to be raised to the peerage, and every time he was overlooked he would add angrily to the building. It was a Teutonic *tour de force*, an ideal atmosphere in which his friend Edward Bulwer-Lytton could immerse himself during the 1840s while writing hugely profitable novels about the last days of Barons or Saxons, which gave English letters 'the great unwashed,' 'the pen is mightier than the sword' and 'It was a dark and stormy night.' D'Eyncourt's relations with his sons—all of whom hated the house—were as tensely dysfunctional as anything the novelist could have imagined, referring to them bitterly as The Sot, The Snob and The Stone.

The last days of the d'Eyncourts came the following century, with only the smaller rooms still lived in by the 1930s, then only the gardener's cottage. The army moved in, the contents were sold, and a farmer turned part of it into a flat. By 1949, according to a local newspaper, 'A damp mustiness floats up and permeates the onlooker ... Dust forms the carpets in the bare rooms ... fungi grow in the cupboards. Stuffed boars' heads have fallen from their pegs.' Pieces of armour remained rusting on the walls, which were caving in to weather, vandalism and the weight of the copings. In 1963, two statues of English kings from the old House of Commons were sent to Westminster Hall, and as if they had been its last guardians, the park was drained and ploughed, and the 'ancient' confection finally blown up after just a century. Bayons' huge footprint now boasts—a bungalow.[25]

* * *

Another of Tennyson's uncles (by marriage) was an obsessive of a different order, and the most epic of all of Lincolnshire's explorers—the Arctic's equivalent of Captain Scott. John Franklin, born in Spilsby in 1786, became a naval midshipman at fourteen, and fought at the battles of Copenhagen and Trafalgar. He spent the four years between these sailing in the Pacific with Matthew Flinders (his step-cousin) and defending East India Company vessels in the South China Seas. After being wounded off New Orleans in 1815, he decided he had had enough of sultry climes for a while, and by 1818 commanded a ship in David Buchan's expedition to find a passage around the north of the American continent that would allow entry into the Bering Straits.

The following year, he was back with his own Admiralty expedition, and spent three years on the same quest. The terrible privations he experienced during those years seem merely to have encouraged him, especially as he was publicly lionised on his return as the 'man who ate his boots.' He came back for two years in 1825, promoted and now also a member of the Royal Society, to explore the waterways between New York and Montreal. He was knighted in 1829, captained a frigate in the Mediterranean, and in 1837 became a Lieutenant-Governor of Van Diemen's Land, where he and his second wife Jane introduced a more liberal regime for the penal colony.

By 1845, he was back in Arctic mode, charged with another attempt to find the elusive North West Passage, in command of two ships, *Erebus* and *Terror*—whose names hint at the way the 'white hell' was regarded by most, even at the Admiralty. At the age of fifty-nine, overweight and in indifferent health, he had lobbied hard to be given the command, which whatever happened seemed likely to be his last. On 19 May, *Erebus* and *Terror*, which had been specially reinforced against ice, set sail from Greenhithe in Kent amid much patriotic anticipation of success. The expedition was excellently equipped; it was one of the first voyages of discovery to be equipped with cameras, and lavishly provisioned with tinned food. Franklin even took his pet monkey, Jacko, one of only two famous monkeys associated with the county—the other being the one which, in 1723, reputedly threw the son and heir of Culverthorpe Hall from the roof of the house to his death.

Previous Arctic expeditions, including some of Franklin's, had mapped most of the north Canadian coast, leaving only around sixty miles utterly uncharted; it was surely only a question of time before the stolid Franklin filled in the gaps. 'The name of Franklin alone is, indeed, a national guarantee' said the president of the Royal Geographical Society. Franklin was liked by his men; one of his officers, James Fitzjames, wrote home:

> We are very happy, and very fond of Sir John Franklin, who improves very much as we come to know more of him. He is anything but nervous or fidgety: in fact I should say remarkable for energetic decision in sudden emergencies.[26]

Five crewmen were discharged with illness when the ships got to Greenland, and may have lamented being left behind. On 26 July, his ships met whaling vessels at the entrance to Lancaster Sound (north of Baffin Island), and Franklin spoke cheerfully of having enough supplies for five years or even longer. After several days within sight of each other, the ships went their separate ways. Those whalers were the last Europeans to see the expedition. What happened after that was pieced together painfully over many years, and there are still riddles.

Three crew members died of unknown causes and were buried on Beechey Island in the Barrow Strait. In September, the ships got stuck in ice off King William Island and were borne slowly south down its west coast. In May 1846, ship's officer Lieutenant Graham Gore left a note in a cairn on King William Island— stone cairns were used to mark messages and supplies, where there were no other landmarks—giving their route up until they had been frozen in, and ending 'Sir John Franklin commanding the expedition. All is well.'

Events became less well. Their ships stayed stubbornly frozen in, in unusually severe conditions. Their stocks of canned food may have been contaminated, because they had been supplied by an unscrupulous canner who a few years later would be implicated in a major scandal for supplying the Navy with putrid meats. Franklin's crews seem to have suffered from botulism, malnutrition, scurvy and, some think, lead poisoning. Franklin died at King William Island on 11 June 1847, and on 22 April

1848, the increasingly desperate crew decided to abandon the still trapped ships. Later, 105 men made it back to the cairn where Lieutenant Gore had left his as yet uncollected note, and added a postscript, saying they would strike out for the Back River, hoping that way to reach Hudson Bay trading posts. None got there.

Erebus and *Terror* had been expected to get to the Bering Straits by the spring of 1846, but it was not until two years after that the Admiralty started sending out search ships—and then only after insistent pressure from Franklin's wife-widow. Jane Franklin had by now become a kind of national heroine, thanks to her unceasing campaigning and fund-raising to get the Admiralty to try to find her husband. She was sought out by celebrities, and the subject of a hugely popular ballad, 'Lady Jane's Lament:'

> *I wonder if my faithful John / Is still battling with the breeze; / Or if e'er he will return again, /*

> *To these fond arms once more / To heal the wounds of dearest Jane / Whose heart is griev'd full sore.*

Eventually, the embarrassed Admiralty sent two ships under the experienced Arctic explorer Sir James Ross to Lancaster Sound, two men-of-war to the Bering Straits, as well as an overland expedition, and also offered a 100 guinea reward, while Lady Franklin offered £1,000. The graves on Beechey Island were found in 1850, then there was nothing until 1854, when a Hudson's Bay surveyor named John Rae discovered that a party of Inuit had encountered about forty half-starved white men dragging a sledge during the winter of 1845/6. The Inuit had found other bodies in the same area, and had artefacts to prove it—spoons and forks, and a silver plate engraved 'Sir John Franklin, K.C.H.'

There was even grimmer news: Rae also found evidence of cannibalism among the crew. The suggestion scandalised British public opinion. Charles Dickens was just one of many who refused to countenance that *Englishmen* could have done such a thing. They must surely have been killed by 'the Esquimaux,' he raved in *Household Words*, because they were 'covetous, treacherous, cruel.' In 1859, bones were found, a boat with skeletons, and the note in the cairn.

A total of forty expeditions—governmental, international, and private—were to go in quest of the missing man, even after Franklin was officially declared dead in 1854. Lady Jane not only campaigned constantly by day, but at night searched for her husband using less orthodox methods, carrying on an extensive correspondence with ladies and 'sensitives' across Britain who claimed to have been vouchsafed information through dreams or spirit guides. One of these letters is fairly typical:

> My lady, I have took the liberty of thus a-Dressing you with a Line through whose hands I hope will forward to you this remarkable dream which I have often found too true ... I saw in my dream 2 air Bloons a great distance off rising just like the moon—I said in my dreams to myself There's Sir J. Frankland.[27]

Franklin's reputation rose and sank like 'air Bloons' over the years, from national hero to blunderer, then tragic victim. British naval exploration generally has been blamed for being dismissive of native knowledge, over-reliant on technology, and taking a negative attitude toward the landscape.[28] One of the expedition's boats was found to have contained such useful items as slippers bound with red ribbon, delftware teacups, and a copy of *The Vicar of Wakefield*. Francis Spufford portrays the whole expedition perishing among an 'English cloud of unknowing.'[29]

The search expeditions, however, led to the first really accurate mapping of some of the Arctic Islands, and (in 1852) the first successful navigation of the Northwest Passage. Evidence found in the 1980s—bones with knife marks, skulls with no faces— would prove there really had been cannibalism, and the Inuit could not have been responsible. The 1980s forensic anthropologists also exhumed the bodies on Beechey Island, finding them eerily well-preserved, down to eye and hair colour. It was not until 2014 that the *Erebus* was found sunk in Victoria Strait, while *Terror* eluded searchers until 2016. Franklin's body has never been located. His statue brings a hyperborean hint to the placid market place at Spilsby, and a link to Westminster Abbey, where his equally lionised nephew by marriage wrote the verse for his monument:

> *Not here: the white North hath thy bones, and thou / Heroic Sailor Soul / Art passing on thine happier voyage now / Toward no earthly pole.*

* * *

Some corners of the Wolds could be Rupert Bear's 'Nutwood'— soothingly settled, sheep-smelling and sounding tracts with stereotypically English architecture and little lanes. Coming off the A16 between Ulceby and Partney, itself a quiet road, Langton-by-Spilsby is a Mary Tourtel dreamscape of thatched *cottage orné*, substantial farmhouses, and a red-brick classical church that could be in Cambridge.

Bennet Langton's (1737-1801) family had been seated here since the twelfth century. As a very young man, he read Samuel Johnson's magazine *The Rambler*, and was so impressed he went to London to meet its author. His initial astonishment at Johnson's scruffy and shambling figure—he had expected a 'remarkably decorous philosopher'—was dispelled the moment Johnson began to speak. Johnson for his part always liked the company of intelligent young men. He was also snobbishly proud of his connection with 'Lanky'—Langton was unusually tall and skinny, jokingly likened to a stork by Raphael[30]—saying of him, 'Langton, Sir, has a grant of free warren from Henry the Second; and Cardinal Stephen Langton, in King John's reign, was of this family.'

The Cardinal Johnson referred to was Stephen, born at Langton-by-Wragby, who became so famous that he was nicknamed 'Stephen with the tongue of thunder.' As a student in Paris, he had distinguished himself by dividing up the Bible into chapters, and his system became ubiquitous across Europe. As Archbishop of Canterbury between 1207 and 1228, he became a key mover in forcing the passing of the *Magna Carta*. He was the Great Charter's first signatory as witness and helped assure its reissuance in 1225. He was also a shrewd administrator, overseeing the translation of Thomas à Becket's relics to Canterbury, asserting English rights against Rome's, and passing still-binding canon law decrees at the 1222 Osney council, 'which is to the ecclesiastical history of England what the assembly at Runnymede in June 1215 is to her secular history.'[31] This was the start of a lifelong friendship between Johnson and the Cardinal's connection, during which Johnson would often visit Langton in Kent, London, and Lincolnshire. Langton was unusually intense. Johnson said to Langton's tutor, 'His mind is as exalted as his stature. I am half afraid of him; but he is no less amiable than formidable.' He was a highly respected classicist, easily eligible to become one of the nine original members of Johnson's celebrated Club, but could get verbosely tangled up when speaking. Johnson once impersonated Langton's nervous eloquence:

> ...assuming [Langton's] manner, [Johnson], in in a connected speech on a familiar subject, uttered a succession of sentences, in language resembling the style of metaphysics, but, though fluent,

so obscured by parentheses and other involutions that [Johnson's friend, Sir John Hawkins] was unable to collect from it a single idea.[32]

In old age, Johnson entrusted Langton with a precious list of his projected studies (Johnson always fretted that he should have been more systematic), which Langton later gave to the King. In the last year of his life, Johnson remarked, 'I know not who will go to Heaven if Langton does not.' When Boswell mentioned somebody else as also being virtuous, Johnson rejoined, 'Yes, Sir; but ＿＿ has not the evangelical virtue of Langton. ＿＿, I am afraid, would not scruple to pick up a wench.'[33]

The Johnsonian scholar John Wain wrote:

> Johnson deferred to Langton as 'a man whom God had made effortlessly good', even if at times he decried Langton's poor management of his income, and lax family discipline, saying Langton had his children 'too much about him'.[34]

Johnson could relax in Langton's company, not feeling obliged to be brilliant. Once when he went to dinner at Langton's he only spoke two words before the meal, saying 'Pretty baby!' to one of Langton's children. Once in London, Langton and Topham Beauclerk banged drunkenly on Johnson's door at 3am, and got him to join them for 'a frisk' (which he did)—a liberty few would have dared to take. When Johnson visited Langton in Lincolnshire, he could be even friskier, visiting rustic relations and playing skittles in the bar at Tetford. Even more remarkably, the man who was called reverently 'Dictionary Johnson' and 'The Great Cham of Literature:'

> ...took it into his head to take a roll down a very steep hill behind the house. Bennet Langton and his father attempted to dissuade him; but he was determined to do it, insisting that he not had a roll for a long time. So, emptying his pockets of keys, pencil,

purse and penknife, he lay down at the summit, turned himself over it and rolled over and over to the bottom.[35]

* * *

'Louth,' noted one of its mid-twentieth century vicars, 'has always lived a self-contained life, and so it has not figured largely in the history of the nation.'[36] The little red-brick town on the Lud (from *Hlude*, an Old English name meaning 'the loud one, the noisy stream'), from which the town gets its name, has early but obscure origins.

Roman coinage has been found, the Saxon Archbishop of York laid claim to the town, and there was certainly a monastery in 792, whose abbot, Æthelheard, became Archbishop of Canterbury. There may have been a shrine here to a Bishop of Lindsey, who may have been called Herefrid, who may have been martyred by the Great Heathen Army. The town is in *Domesday*, and King John may have visited in 1201. But by 1247 there was certainly a notable church here, dedicated to St Herefrid, a few of whose relics were still in possession of the rebuilt church (now dedicated to St James) in 1486—an ivory comb and an altar cloth painted with his portrait. A triumphal spire went up between 1501 and 1515, one of the tallest on any parish church in England, at 295 feet, which was topped off originally by a copper weathercock made from a basin that was part of the booty from Flodden. It is a suitably Perpendicular landmark for a town precisely on the Greenwich Meridian. In 1844, intrepid artist William Brown sketched the Louth Panorama from the steeple, one of the earliest aerial pictures—a giddying vista from small familiar fields to tiny ships adventuring the curvature of earth.

Below this pointer to Heaven was a grand, rich church with a deeply conservative congregation in love with ceremonial seen as indissolubly linked to the land. There were Corpus Christi pageants and plays at Louth in the 1510s and 1520s, in which costumed actors played the parts of Christian knights or monsters against backdrops of painted cloth. Lincolnshire churches generally were noted for their 'plough lights,' kept burning in churches, sometimes on ploughs taken into the building, maintained by special guilds. The custom of Rogation, when clergy paraded the parish boundaries with banners, crosses and holy water and blessed the fields, lasted in some parts of Lincolnshire at least into the late 1540s. The Holy Ghost Himself appeared in St James' in 1500 and 1518, in the guise of a white dove let through the ceiling.[37] Congregants were naturally perturbed to learn of Henry VIII's plans for their beloved church.

By 1536, Thomas Cromwell's commissioners had closed down thirty-six of Lincolnshire's fifty-two monasteries, and confiscated huge amounts of Church money, driving monks and nuns out in the fields to starve. On 1 October that year, Louth's vicar, Thomas Kendall, informed the church grimly that there was to be a visitation by Cromwell's commissioners. At the end of the service, as three silver crosses were being carried around inside the church, a man named Thomas Foster jumped up and called out, 'Masters, step forth, and let us follow the crosses this day: God knoweth whether ever we shall follow them hereafter or nay.' That evening, fuelled by rumours that the church's jewels were to be taken the following day, 'the poor men took the keys of the church' from the unresisting wardens, instigated by a cobbler named Nicholas Menton, who would become known as 'Captain Cobler'.

On the Monday, an angry crowd surrounded the Bishop's representative and prevented him from entering, and only reluctantly allowed the frightened man to depart. Soon afterwards, two of Cromwell's servants were put into the stocks, the Bishop's Registrar's account books were burned, and he only just avoided being hanged. The swollen crowd marched towards Caistor, in response to news of a general muster against the Dissolution plans. This was the start of the Lincolnshire Rising, the first and only time Louth 'figured largely in the history of the nation'.

There were about 30,000 pilgrims, as they called themselves, by the time they got to Lincoln, picking up people—usually the poorest—everywhere they went, bringing whatever weapons they could find. They carried banners showing five crosses for the wounds of Christ, a chalice and horns, the last an allusion to a rumoured planned tax on livestock. They brought what weapons they could find; in the church in Horncastle are scythe blades said to have gone with the town's contingent. Some gentry joined in out of sincere feeling, or were constrained to join the rebels (often, their own tenants) in order to prevent attacks on their lives or damage to their property. At Boston, Lord Hussey had to escape from his own house in disguise, while longer-sighted Sir Anthony Irby decamped, taking 150 of his dependents to join the king's forces. There was wild talk of an army of 40,000 'harnessed and naked men' assembling at Ancaster, but this never materialised, and within a few days those who had gathered at Lincoln or elsewhere were quietly slipping off home.

Henry VIII's wily commander, the ubiquitous Duke of Suffolk, negotiated with the marchers, and made lavish promises to the marchers to induce them to go home, leaving their weapons and their leaders in his hands. The pilgrims indeed saw some of their leaders once more—on the following 10 March, being executed in the marketplace at Louth. Thomas Kendall was given special treatment at Tyburn—hanged, cut down alive, disembowelled, having his entrails burned while still alive, and finally decapitated. Unlucky Lord Hussey found himself in the Tower of London, his trial delayed multiple times, until finally he was executed at Lincoln in 1541. One hundred and seventy-eight would be executed altogether. Henry's anger was rooted in fear; Louth's example had sparked off the more dangerous 'Pilgrimage of Grace' in Yorkshire, and later the Bigod Rebellion in the northwest.

Lincolnshire yielded, but resentfully. In the 1560s, despite repeated stern warnings, there were still altars and images in many county churches, and as late as 1688, a seemingly still smarting St James' paid for the privilege of ringing bells to mark the birthday of James II.

Although the Holy Ghost was no longer permitted to descend, a different ghost took a liking to the Tudor town, giving England one of her best-known supernatural stories.

The tradition says Sir John Bolle of Thorpe Hall was on the 1596 raid on Cadiz and was put in charge of a ransomed family of Spanish gentlefolk, whose daughter, Donna Leonora Oviedo, fell in love with him, and offered him money to become her lover. But Sir John was married already, and refused to dally dishonourably. In due course, he made his way back to Louth, while the still besotted Donna Leonora retired to a convent, where she died miserably lovelorn. But at least her ghost was able to be with him. For a long time afterwards, her spirit was reported at Louth, walking the Hall and crossing the tree-overhung road outside, and the Bolles would set an extra place at meals in case she came—an archetypal 'Green Lady' in a gown, lending period interest to a quiet town, and offering evidence not just of an afterlife, but the superior moral character of the English gentleman.

One of Sir John's descendants also loomed large in Louth: Sir Charles Bolle, noted for his courage during the 1630s plague outbreaks in visiting the infected to leave them medicines, then making a doomed attempt to defend the town from the Parliamentarians. He was heavily fined for recalcitrant royalism, but paid a much higher price in the life of his son. On 13 December 1643, at far-away Alton in Hampshire, the young Richard Bolles, a royalist colonel, led a defence of the churchyard and then the church against a much larger force of Parliament men, climbing on scaffolding inside the church and firing determinedly from the windows. However, as one Parliamentarian veteran recalled, 'By this time the Church-yard was full of our men, laying about them stoutly with their Halberts, Swords, and Musquet-stocks, while some threw hand-granadoes in the Church windows.' When several hours later the Parliamentarians finally burst into the church, the royalists continued to fire from behind the bodies of horses they had piled up in the aisles. Bolle, having killed six or seven Parliamentarians personally, was finally brained by one of these 'musqueteers,' purportedly in the pulpit. The still bullet-marked church's memorial to 'this Renowned Martialist' from 'Linckhorne Shiere' tells of Charles I's reaction:

> His Gratious Soveraigne hearing of his death, gave him his high Comendation in ye passionate Expression, Bring me a Moorning Scarffe, i have lost one of the best Comanders in this kingdome.

A battle of more direct relevance to the county, and that could have altered the whole course of the conflict, had been fought earlier that year, at Winceby near Horncastle. On 11 October 1643, Parliamentary forces commanded by the Earl of Manchester, with Cromwell to assist, drew up against Sir William Widdrington's Royalists on opposite sides of a natural amphitheatre. Dragoons raced downhill from both sides and clashed on the lowest ground, after which both front lines charged, Parliament's shouting the field-word 'Religion!' and exchanging fire at close range. During hand-to-hand fighting, Cromwell's horse was killed and he got trapped under it, and was called to surrender by a Royalist, Sir Ingram Hopton. But then Hopton died, and Cromwell barely escaped himself, as other Parliamentary horses tore into the fray and routed the Royalists, trapping them against high hedges, whose only gate opened the wrong way. Even now, the place is called Slash Hollow, and Winceby is remembered as the battle that stopped the royalist advance, and where Cromwell could have died, with incalculable consequences.[38]

Louth would become an increasingly quiet market town once those tumults had died down, a harmoniously red-bricked reservoir of sturdy national stock, and sometimes restless young men who would leave its Edward VI-founded grammar school to make all kinds of marks—Captain John Smith, Sir John Franklin, Lord Tennyson—and the now forgotten Vice-Admiral Augustus Hobart-Hampden (1822–86), who battled slavers off South America and Russians in the Baltic and Black Sea, ran blockade-runners to help the Confederacy during the American Civil War, and most improbably of all ended up in charge of the Ottoman Navy, known as 'Hobart Pasha.'

Louth's long quietude, and the grandeur of its cathedral-like church, gradually gave the old town centre an air that visitors still call 'Trollopean'—although it is much less so now than when we first knew the town. The cattle market that was founded in the early 1600s—now Lincolnshire's only one—coexists with many small shops, including a department store founded in 1781. While it has always had some crime, malodorous industries, pockets of poverty and drinking dens—in the nineteenth century there used to be a hostelry called the Rat and Louse, on a street called Aswell Hole—from the eighteenth century it increasingly attracted admirers like John Betjeman, in search of agreeable middle-class living amid decorous architecture.

Rare interruptions came in the twentieth century, with almost eighty Ludensians killed in the World Wars, including some killed in Louth itself, when German planes bombed and machine-gunned the town. On 20 May 1920, there was a disaster, when a cloud burst high in the Wolds, and the hills funnelled a wall of water along the Lud, now really a 'loud one' and 'noisy stream,' through the centre of town, killing twenty-three and making hundreds more homeless.

Like Lincoln's Colonel Sibthorp, or Boston & Skegness's long-serving representative Sir Richard Body, Louth's former MP, the late Sir Peter Tapsell (1930-2018) was a strongly self-willed Lincolnshire Tory, who really knew something about the countryside, and instinctively preferred landed interests to liberal. Tapsell was once Anthony Eden's personal assistant, but ever afterwards confined himself to representing his constituents at Westminster, eventually becoming 'Father of the House' between 2010 and 2015, when he retired. He was an old-school, independent-minded, un-bribeable Tory with substantial private means derived from stockbroking, who wore hand-made, three-piece suits, and went to opera rather than football games.

He also had a BA in Modern History, and would lecture un-historically-minded ministers about the dangers of whatever policies they were espousing that week. Outdated though he was in many ways, he far-sightedly opposed intervention in Iraq and Afghanistan. He was always heedless of Central Office prescriptions or whips' instructions, and immune to fashion. When we first saw his election posters they were still in the old Conservative red, perhaps even the very same posters he had used when first elected for a Lincolnshire seat in 1966. He was so electorally secure that he rarely campaigned anyway, despite boundary changes which briefly allowed a certain Jeffrey Archer to represent the town, a politician who could be said to epitomise the new breed of Conservative.

He was, however, unfailingly generous to even the smallest constituency causes, for instance eagerly assisting a campaign I organised, against a proposed new town for the Marsh. He didn't like the European Union, capital punishment, wind turbines, or monetarism, and supported Michael Heseltine's bid for leadership. Although he was on friendly terms with Mrs

Thatcher, she wasn't his kind of Conservative. As he once said cuttingly, 'I knew her before she was blonde.'

When he died, the *Guardian*'s obituarist gave a generous tribute, half-admiring a man who had never played the party game:

> Each time Sir Peter Tapsell, the veteran Conservative MP, rose to speak in his later years, it was almost as if the Commons had been transported back five decades. Wearing his double-breasted pinstriped suit and with his ponderous and orotund oratory delivered with a drawling lisp, he seemed the embodiment of the last of the Tory knights of the shires, a figure from another age.[39]

10

PERIOD DRAMAS

'You go, to the drum and fife
To taste the colour and the other side of life'
—R. L. Stevenson, *Mater Triumphans*

Stamford—Grimsthorpe—Belton—
Harlaxton—Woolsthorpe—Grantham

The youngling had been grizzling all the way to Stamford and when we got there was thoroughly out of sorts. As soon as we'd parked, he ran off sulkily, down a covered alleyway, while we shook our heads in annoyance and hastened to catch up. Then he reappeared unexpectedly, his mouth hanging open, sulk forgotten as he stared at the unlikely figure advancing out of the alley's gloom—a tall and slender silhouette, made look even taller by a military shako, extravagantly whiskered, wearing a red coat with white facings, white breeches and knee-length boots, and toting a musket. The twenty-first century had been brought up sharp by the eighteenth. The grim reenactor stepped out of the gloom, suddenly smaller, and smiled and winked at the boy, before striding away creakingly, incongruous among the cars along the London Road.

Stamford's occasional Georgian Festivals may be the best times of all to see that town, known for its stone architecture—'the best stone town in England,' according to John Betjeman—as seen in many period dramas. Stamford's superbly preserved streets of Ancaster, Barnack, Casterton, Clipsham, Collyweston, Ketton, Weldon and Wittering Pendle stone—there are over 600 listed buildings in the town, thanks to a 1967 conservation area designation, the first in Britain—have acted as sumptuous backdrop for adaptations of *Middlemarch*, *Pride and Prejudice*, Henry James' *The Golden Bowl* and others. In the course of 2021, film crews were in the town and neighbouring Burghley House, rumoured to be filming both the next series of *The Crown* and, less predictably, the next film in the *Batman* franchise.

During Georgian Festivals, fencibles, militiamen and public hangmen vie with clergymen, potboys, smallpox-scarred wenches and smiling moderns for pavement space, while the Meadows along the River Welland are studded with fires and tents for camp followers, stocks, pillory and gallows, stacked muskets, old-fashioned fairground rides, sweetmeat stalls and a Punch and Judy theatre. England has an over-abundance of 1940s-themed festivals; this admittedly highly subjective distillation of the 1740s is infinitely more interesting. In such a setting, the Festival offers at least a limited idea of what Georgian England might have looked like, in its combination of rational prosperity and underlying darker currents—a combination that might stand for the history of Stamford itself.

The south-western corner of Lincolnshire is the part of the county that has been longest and most directly affected by national affairs—the part of Lincolnshire nearest to major transport routes from prehistory to today, and so most convenient for London. Lincolnshire meets Cambridgeshire, Northamptonshire and Rutland here; Lincolnshire's border with Northamptonshire is just twenty yards long, the shortest county boundary in Britain. It is mostly attractive and fertile countryside, hilly and frequently bosky—offering a combination of agricultural income and good hunting, as well as commanding situations on which to site statement houses, which are otherwise rare in Lincolnshire. The seventeenth-century antiquarian Thomas Fuller is supposed to have said that 'there is nowhere that has better churches than Lincolnshire, or worse houses.'

But Stamford has Burghley, one of the most historically important and palatial houses in England. Although the house itself is just over the county border, its parkland borders Stamford on two sides, and for centuries the proximity of the great estate provided not just prosperity (at times) for the town but also reflected prestige, and connections with the highest levels of statecraft. William Cecil (1520–98), the first Baron Burghley and builder of the house, was secretary of state under both Henry VIII and Elizabeth, and then the latter's Lord High Treasurer, responsible for the execution of Mary Queen of Scots. His son Thomas (1542–1623), later made the Earl of Exeter, served in the Low Countries and against the Armada, and was President of the Council of the North. Another son, Robert (1563–1612) was also a secretary of state, and secured the accession of James VI of Scotland to the English throne. Robert would have known of, although possibly not been friendly with, fellow Stamfordian aristocrat Sir Everard Digby (1578–1606) who was executed for his part in the Gunpowder Plot.

One of Robert's descendants, another Robert (1830–1903) was a renowned conservative intellectual and three times Prime Minister during the nineteenth century. Yet other Cecils were (and are) also MPs, ministers and peers, patrons of the arts, endowers of universities and respected writers, like David Cecil. Many members of the family have been deeply committed to Stamford, erecting buildings, contributing towards bridges, churches and roads, aiding charities and generally engaging in civic life. Burghley was a powerhouse of its day, and Stamford almost its satellite. Perhaps the family's greatest single influence was in keeping the main train line to the north away from the town in the 1840s, out of concern for its socially unsettling effects. This meant Victorian industrialisation and growth went elsewhere, so avoiding inevitably destructive alteration.

If ease of access to London's power has often been a boon to Burghley and Stamford, it also means greater susceptibility to the capital's complexes, whether political crises or religious spasms, or today's existential anxieties. In 2021, Historic England named Burghley House as one of four places in Lincolnshire that had a 'slavery past,' benefiting directly or indirectly from slavery, because an eighteenth-century Cecil married into a family of West Indies merchants.[1]

That individual and that generation may well have been guilty of cliometrics—crass historic quantification—or even wilful blindness to the source of their wealth. What is to be done about this is less clear. Slavery, after all, has historically been carried out by many, perhaps most cultures. Lincolnshire even has a native slave, Bourne-born John Jewitt, who spent 1803–05 enslaved on the Pacific North West coast (now British Columbia), and wrote a *Narrative* when he got home, regarded by Canadian historians as 'a classic of captivity literature,' and an indispensable source of information about the First Nations.

Another Bourne boy, Job Hortop, who in 1567 was press-ganged on one of Sir John Hawkins' execrable slaving expeditions, saw slavery in its whole inhuman context. He was compelled to help capture slaves in Africa for sale in the West

Indies, but he also witnessed African kings drowning their enemies in their thousands after a fierce battle in what is now Sierra Leone. After deadly storms, numerous battles with Africans, and Portuguese and Spanish vessels, encounters with 'sea-monsters,' and near-starvation, Hawkins simply dumped Hortop and ninety-five of his fellow-countrymen in central America so he could get his slaves to market safely—adding lack of concern for his countrymen to greed and racism. The stranded sailors were stripped of their clothes by local tribesmen, then captured by the Spanish and thrown into prison in Mexico City under constant threats of execution and Inquisition pressure to convert. Shipped to Spain, they were again imprisoned, and some burnt at the stake. Hortop was sent to the galleys, where he and his shipmates were chained 'four and four together ... our lodging was on the bare boards and banks of the galleys, our heads and beards were shaved every month; hunger, thirst, cold and stripes we lacked none.' He spent twelve years like this, a further seven in prison, before finally escaping in a boat. He didn't return to England until 1590.

But Stamford long predates twenty-first century angst, Georgian grace, or even Elizabethan heydays. Ermine Street forded the Welland slightly to the west of here, the Romans for some reason choosing not to build precisely here, but their 'stony ford' at least providing the town's later name. In 61 AD, the environs were the scene of an imperial embarrassment, when Boudicca pursued the Legio IX as it fell back towards Lincoln. It first features in the *Anglo-Saxon Chronicle* in 656, mentioned in a grant of lands to Peterborough Abbey. There was a Danish settlement on the site from the ninth century, one of the Danes' Five Boroughs, but in 922 'Stan-forda' appears again as having been conquered by King Edward the Elder (Alfred the Great's son), as part of his successful campaign to extend Anglian and Saxon power northwards. It became an English borough in 972.

Ermine Street declined in importance in favour of a new route linking Smithfield Market in London to Edinburgh, which came to be called the Great North Road. This famous thoroughfare bent through the centre of Stamford, its sharp angles still obvious today, and the town became increasingly important as a staging post, a centre of trade, and an inland port, navigable via the Welland to The Wash.

It was also a religious centre under the control of Peterborough Abbey, and some of these buildings survive—the oldest St Leonard's Priory of c. 1082, which is supposedly on the site of a seventh-century monastery founded by St Wilfrid. The town was badly damaged by Lancastrians in 1461, as John Leland noted— 'The northen men brent miche of Staunford towne'[2]—but there are still impressive churches.

St Mary's has the 'Chapel of the Golden Choir' with its roof of painted golden stars, and the monument to Sir David Phillip, a veteran of Bosworth and later Keeper of the King's Swans in Lincolnshire, Northamptonshire, Cambridgeshire and Huntingdonshire. In the graveyard of St John's, where the youthful Sir Malcolm Sargent (1895-1967) played the organ, is an eighteenth-century gravestone to a publican named Pepper:

> Tho' hot my name, yet mild my nature, / I bore good will to every creature, / I brewed fine ale and solid it too, / And unto each I gave his due.

All Saints has monuments to the long-established local family of wool merchants, the Brownes, who rebuilt the church and endowed Browne's Hospital in Broad Street, one of the best-preserved medieval almshouses in England. The remains of two Knights Hospitaller establishments were incorporated into the town's best-known hostelry, the George, still doing business with clients from kings to commercial travellers, a much-photographed landmark with its iron sign spanning the road to

London. King Charles I spent two differently flavoured nights at the George—on 15 March 1641, on a pre-war royal progress to Grantham, and again on 23 August 1645, heading from Newark to Huntingdon, the war and his cause obviously failing.

Stamford also had a less contemplative side, with a huge Mid-Lent Fair mentioned by Shakespeare, and bull-running. According to a persistent tradition, William de Warenne, the fifth Earl of Surrey (d. 1240), saw two bulls fighting on the Meadows, after which one broke away and ran through the middle of the town, tossing townspeople and trampling market stalls. He pursued on horseback, and enjoyed the incident so much that he gave the field to the town's butchers, on condition they donated a bull to be run through the town every St Brice's Day (13 November). The bull-running became as famous as Pamplona today, attracting huge and often drunken crowds to chase and taunt the poor animals down the streets towards the Meadows or into the river, after which they would be slaughtered and the meat given to the poor. The tradition attracted increasing criticism, especially in the latter part of the eighteenth century, although not out of concern about cruelty to bulls. The local paper, which incidentally claims a foundation date of 1695 as the *Stamford Mercury*, and therefore to be the oldest continuously published newspaper in England, had this to say at the apogee of the Enlightenment:

> What a pity it is so barbarous a custom is permitted to be contin-
> ued, that has no one good purpose to recommend it, but is kept
> as an orgy of drunkenness and idleness to the manifest injury of
> many poor families.[3]

The tradition was spasmodically suppressed, only to break out again, but was eventually banned in 1839, the ban enforced by soldiers who would have worn uniforms like those that frightened our boy, and who probably encamped in the same place.

Stamford was briefly a university town, when in 1333 disgruntled students and tutors from Oxford decamped and founded a rival, called the University of Stamford but known as the Brazenose, because one of the upstart university's instigators had been the maunciple (the official responsible for catering) of Oxford's Brasenose College.

The reasons for this 'Stamford Schism' are unclear, but it appears to have been a factional division between students from northern England and students from the south—Lincolnshire, as so often, neutrally neither one nor the other. The students are said to have brought a brass lion's head door knocker with them from Brasenose Hall, and fixed it to the gate of their new establishment. The outraged Oxford and Cambridge authorities lobbied Edward III hard to have the rival academy closed down, and two years later succeeded. But Oxford long felt sore on the subject; until 1827, all Oxford graduates were compelled to sign a declaration that they would never teach at Stamford. The brass lion's head knocker on the still standing gateway is a replica, the original removed by Brasenose College, Oxford in 1890, and displayed jealously on the wall behind the high table in the College Hall.[4]

But that foray into further education fed town pride. In the Stamford version of the medieval legend of the brazen head—an alchemist-made head of brass that issued prophecies—it was sometime Stamford resident Roger Bacon (1214?–94) who was the alchemist, and the Brazenose knocker that spoke the dread words, 'Time was. Time is. Time is past.'

The ubiquitous William Stukeley was therefore immersing himself in old tradition when he founded a learned society in the town in 1736, the Brazen Nose Society, 'in memory of that antient College of the once flourishing University here.' The Society's list of subjects for its meetings say more about

Stukeley's magpie curiosity than the University of Stamford's short-lived curriculum:

> ...astronomy and the latitude of Stamford, lunar maps, a remarkable wasp's nest, a 'stone as big as a walnut, taken out the bladder of a little Dutch dog', and a medieval seal ... experiments with an air pump and a microscope and, a great excitement, pictures projected by 'the Italian shades or magic lanthorn'.[5]

Stukeley was long committed to Stamford, writing about town history, campaigning for the Whig interest in elections, rescuing artefacts, refurbishing two houses, and building a fantastical rococo garden with a grotto, 'druidical circles,' and a Temple to Flora for his wife's pot plants. But the Brazen Nose Society languished, and when Stukeley tried to relaunch it in 1745, it was even worse. He started a special minute book, with a list of subscribers starting with the confident words 'We whose names are subscribed...'—but the only name on the paper would be his own. A little later, he noted hopefully that three carpenters had joined, but clearly this was not the august kind of academy he had envisaged. He told his journal that the town did not have 'one person, clergy or lay, that had any taste of learning or ingenuity, so that I was actually as much dead in converse as in a coffin.' In 1747, his cat Tit died, and this little sadness knocked him into pitchy depression:

> The creature had a sense so far superior to her kind; had such inimitable ways of testifying her love to her master and mistress, that she was as a companion, especially so to me when according to custom, I smoak'd my contemplative pipe, in the evening at six o'clock.[6]

When he discovered the gardener had buried Tit under the mulberry tree in the garden, he no longer 'car'd to come near that delightful place.' The following January, he left Lincolnshire for London, never to return.

In St Martin's on the south side of the river is the Burghley Chapel, filled with predictably dignified and grandiose memorials—while in its graveyard is the car-sized resting place of the rather less dignified Daniel Lambert, England's fattest man ever when he died in 1809 (an adipose achievement not beaten until 1984), and one of its leading raree-shows. Lambert, born in Leicester in 1770, was the son of the Earl of Stamford's huntsman, and until his twenties led an active life and was of normal weight. But by the age of twenty-three he had ballooned to thirty-two stone, and was compelled to swap his job as the keeper of Leicester's prison for a life in freak-showbiz.

He moved to London's Piccadilly, and reluctantly exhibited himself to a constant stream of gawpers—'receiving company', he called it—every day between midday and five, and became a nationwide sensation through images published in pamphlets and painted on pub signs. He was 5 feet, 11 inches tall, and measured 3 yards and 4 inches around his middle. Tiring at last of life in the fat lane, he went to Stamford in 1809 to watch the races, and died at the Waggon & Horses Inn. A window and part of the wall had to be removed so his body could be moved. His coffin, which contained 112 square feet of elm, had to be mounted on wheels, and it took twenty men to slide it down a ramp into the ground.

His tombstone combines generosity and wit with actuarial precision:

In remembrance of that prodigy in nature
Daniel Lambert a native of Leicester
Who was possessed of an exalted and convivial mind and,
In personal greatness had no competitor:
He measured three feet one inch round the leg and
Weighed fifty two stone eleven pounds
He departed this life on the 21st June 1809
Aged 39 years.

PERIOD DRAMAS

* * *

Eminent though the Cecils are, they are outdone in Lincolnshire antiquity by the Berties, whose barony of Willougby d'Ereseby was first founded in 1313, and whose name crops up again and again in country history, if only as vanished presence. The family has been most closely associated with Grimsthorpe near Bourne since 1516, when the tenth Lord Willoughby d'Eresby married Catherine of Aragon's cousin, Maria de Salinas, and was given the manor as a wedding gift from the King.

In 1533 their child Katherine, who had become Baroness on their deaths (the peerage could descend in the female line), married Charles Brandon, Duke of Suffolk. Brandon pulled down a no-longer-needed abbey and began to build a better house to reflect his expanded landed grandeur. The building was thrown up within eighteen months, and badly, in order to welcome Henry VIII and Queen Katherine in 1541. That royal stay was in the event ill-starred, Grimsthorpe later cited as the place where Katherine had allegedly been unfaithful with Thomas Culpepper.

After Brandon died in 1545, his widow became an ever stauncher Protestant, hosting Hugh Latimer over 1552/3, and sending him money while he was in the Tower of London before being burnt at the stake. She married Richard Bertie in 1553, but when Mary Tudor ascended the throne, she was in a vulnerable position. She particularly hated Mary's Catholic Bishop Stephen Gardiner (1483?-1555), and called her dog Gardiner 'so that I might kick him at least once a day!'

In 1554, she and her husband felt it wise to decamp to the continent, although it says much about her aristocratic insouciance that they took a leisurely five weeks to travel from London to Gravesend, and brought with them a major-domo, a 'gentlewoman,' a joiner, a brewer, a kitchen maid, a laundress, a

Greek rider of horses, and a fool. They remained abroad until Elizabeth came to the throne in 1558. When they came back, Grimsthorpe was in a parlous state, and Katherine was reduced to petitioning the Queen to send furniture and even cups.

Their son Peregrine, a soldier lauded for his defence of Bergen-op-Zoom against the odds in 1588, married the daughter of the Earl of Oxford, so bringing into the family the hereditary office of Lord Great Chamberlain, a role they still partly fulfil today—a rank just below the Lord Privy Seal, with the right and responsibility for robing the monarch on coronation days, investing him or her with the insignia, and serving water at the banquet. An allegorical portrait in the King James Room at Grimsthorpe shows the pale, blue-eyed, long-legged Peregrine wearing black armour with gold tooling lounging against a castled landscape, the Elizabethan image of the perfect gentleman—cultured, elegant, deadly.

His son, the fourteenth Lord Willoughby d'Eresby (and first Earl of Lindsey), would also become a soldier, mortally wounded at Edgehill in 1642. As Willoughby lay dying at Warwick Castle, the victorious Parliamentary commander, the Earl of Essex, sent officers to see him 'upon a little straw in a poor house, where they had laid him in his blood, which had run from him in great abundance ... only he had great vivacity in his looks.' The dying man seems to have inherited his grandmother's capacity for vituperation, scolding the Parliamentary officers, saying 'he was sorry to see so many gentlemen, some whereof were his old friends, engaged in so foul a rebellion.' He 'continued this kind of discourse with so much vehemence, that the officers by degrees withdrew themselves.'[7]

His heir, Montague Bertie, who had been captured at the same battle, was no less devotedly royalist. He was ransomed and rejoined the doomed monarch in the field, and also served as a Gentleman of the Bedchamber. Bertie and Charles shared wartime accommodation in Oxford, and a story of that time suggests the aura of magic that seemed to royalists to cling about their *Eikon Basilike*, even in intimate moments. Bertie, waking in the night on his pallet by the door, noticed that the lamp that had been alight in Charles' bedroom had gone out, but decided not to disturb him and fell asleep again himself. When he next awoke, he noticed that the lamp was alight, 'which so astonished him, that taking the boldness to call the king ... he told him what he had observed' whereupon the King replied that he had awakened himself in the night and likewise found the chamber dark, and likewise woke a second time to find it burning. When Bertie assured him that he had not lit the lamp, and that nobody else had been in the chamber, Charles took it as a good omen:

> The King then said that he did consider it as a prognostic of God's future favour and mercy towards him or his; that although he was at that time so eclipsed, yet either he or they might shine out bright again.[8]

When Charles was captured, Bertie volunteered to go into captivity with him. In January 1649, he and three other noblemen bravely offered to guarantee with their lives and estates any terms the Army or Parliament might make to release the King and restore his title, but this was refused out of hand. He was also refused permission to attend Charles I in his final hours but was left a gift by him—a French romance called *Cassandra*, about Alexander the Great. After the execution, he was one of the four pall-bearers at Windsor. He would later serve as Lord Great Chamberlain at the coronation of Charles' son, an occasion which must have elicited mordant reflections.

The family tradition of quixotic loyalty to kings was carried on by the third Earl's brother, who in December 1688 passed a message to James II on behalf of 'several chief officers of the army' that at twenty-four hours warning he could have 3,000–4,000 horses to 'march with him wherever he would command them'—a sincere offer, luckily for him not taken up.[9]

The family's women always played their parts too, as assured Duchesses of Ancaster, invaluable confidants to the arriviste Hanoverians. In 1761, George III married Princess Charlotte of Mecklenburg-Strelitz, who had an obviously upturned nose. When she first arrived in England, people in the street who saw her passing used to shout out 'Pug! Pug! Pug!' The puzzled princess asked the Duchess of Ancaster, 'Vat is dat they do say— *poog*? Vat means *poog*?' The Duchess replied, with impressive address 'It means, God bless Your Royal Highness.' One can easily understand their indispensability.[10]

Grimsthorpe, the house of these to-the-manor-born courtiers, is accordingly grand, designed in 1715 by a distant Bertie relation, John Vanbrugh, the preeminent baroque scenographer who had worked on Audley End, Blenheim Palace and Castle Howard, and perhaps Somersby Grange, next door to the Tennysons' rectory. Vanbrugh, a former military engineer, combined fortification-like mass and strength with classical detailing, in a style already regarded as slightly old-fashioned. After he died, Nicholas Hawksmoor may have worked on the internal decorations; Sir James Thornhill certainly painted grisaille portraits of kings for the entrance hall, and 'Capability' Brown landscaped the grounds. It is a monumental edifice to find in unassuming backroads.

The house has a sadly resonant place in the history of English music. One summer's day in 1778, a storm capsized a pleasure boat on the Castle's lake. One of its occupants, 22-year-old Thomas Linley, decided to swim to the shore whilst wearing his coat and boots, with inevitable consequences. Linley was a violinist and composer, and had been a close boyhood friend of Mozart when both were studying at Florence. The noted musicologist Charles Burney said of him, 'The *Tommasino*, as he is called, and the little Mozart, are talked of all over Italy as the most promising geniuses of the age.'[11]

The year before he drowned, Linley had written music for *The Tempest*, of which the opening air is sadly appropriate—the grandly exciting 'Arise! Ye spirits of the storm.' The little lake when I last saw it, a calm blue eye in a bee-loud landscape stretching towards lambent fields, looked an unlikely death-dealer—more evocative of Linley's other music, like his orchestration of Thomas Arne's 'Where the bee sucks, there suck I,' or the air 'Wrapt close from harm,' where horns, used by other composers to evoke the chase or war, waft gently Elysian instead, calling the young man home across 'Albion's beauty-blooming isle.'

Lady Charlotte Bertie (1812–95), who lived in another extraordinary family house at Uffington, became a talking point in 1822, when she married a much older iron founder, and prominent Dissenter, named John Guest. This chortlingly anticipated *mésalliance* was in fact a hugely successful union, Lady Charlotte acting as her husband's secretary while producing ten children, and after his death running his iron works near Merthyr Tydfil. She also learned Welsh (her eighth language), and between 1838 and 1845 published the first complete English translation of the *Mabinogion*, an enormous fillip for Welsh identity. She later became a noted expert on porcelain, fans, games and playing cards, and her collections are in the V&A and British Museums. It was fortuitous her collections were moved, because the house burned down in 1904—leaving only outbuildings, magnificent gates, and a lime avenue that leads past statues to nothing.

* * *

Belton's avenue still leads to something, luckily: another late seventeenth-century Carolean emulation of continental buildings in a grand Baroque style. The Brownlows, who still live here, emerged from obscurity in the sixteenth century—the first, Richard (1553-1638), a leading lawyer in London, so good he retained a law office at the Court of Common Pleas for forty-seven years. He bought large estates in Lincolnshire, which his sons inherited. One grandson, Sir John Brownlow, began to build at Belton in 1684 in Wren-like magnificence.

This great structure had to be filled with something, so he hired Grinling Gibbons to fill blank walls with cedar and limewood birds, flowers, fruits, leaves and ears of wheat—still-life subjects in his trademark crisp but swaggering style, with some of the birds' wings protruding a foot from the wall. The spaces between were gradually filled with paintings by Lely, Rembrandt, Teniers, Titian and Van Dyck, and looked down onto rooms carpeted by Aubusson, furnished by Chippendale, and made interesting by such items as furniture from the old House of Commons, and firedogs once owned by Marie Antoinette.

The Commons furniture was provided by Sir John Cust, who was Speaker between 1761 and 1770 (the Custs had married into the Brownlows in 1717). In the eighteenth century, Speakers received no pension upon retirement, but were granted a peerage instead, and allowed to take the contents of their official residence.

Later Custs helped carry the historical weight of three centuries—as fighters in the Peninsular Wars, masters of ceremonies to Queen Victoria, Surveyors of the King's Pictures, editors of journals, administrators in India, and Orientalist intellectuals, who combined firm colonial rule with a genuine and often deeply scholarly interest in the cultures of the ruled. The sixth Baron was a close friend of Edward VIII, and Belton accordingly has a unique collection of memorabilia, including the only portrait of Edward made while he was king, by the morally uptight society artist Frank Owen Salisbury (1874-1962), who would not have approved of Wallis Simpson, let alone abdication. What did he know about the King's private life, or mind? Edward looks as unready as Æthelred, quizzical, even worried, as if the wrong head has been put onto his magnificent uniform.

* * *

One last extravagant house is at Harlaxton, south Lincolnshire's answer to Charles Tennyson d'Eyncourt's Bayons. It is set on the Lincolnshire side of the Vale of Belvoir, picture-book countryside that yet contains a grimmer sensibility, derived in part from the striking appearance of the Earl of Rutland's skyline-dominating Belvoir Castle, but also from Lincolnshire's only famous witch-scare.

Lincolnshire generally escaped the worst paroxysms of witch fever, like those of Pendle or Matthew Hopkins' suspicious Suffolk, but Belvoir's 1618 outbreak, which spread through the whole Vale and up to Lincoln, became the stuff of contemporary ballads—including one with an impressive twenty-five verses, starting,

Of damned deeds, and deadly dole, / I make my mournfull song, / By Witches done in Lincolne-shire, / Where they haue liued long: / And practisd many a wicked deed, / Within that Country there, / Which fills my brest and bosome full, / of sobs, and trembling feare.[12]

The boredom-immune balladeer's 'Sobs, and trembling feare' are replaced in Tracy Borman's more recent book, *Witches – James I and the English Witch Hunts*, with indignation about what was done to Joan Flowers, and her daughters Margaret and Philippa, which she calls 'a murderous conspiracy that has remained hidden for almost 400 years.'[13] The daughters were in service at the Castle, until Margaret lost her job. About the same time, Joan, who had in any case always been suspected of having supernatural powers, was jilted, and she seems to have blamed the Earl and Countess.

According to the eventual indictment, the three joined forces with other local women, and vowed revenge with the help of Satan, never loth to assist in such cases. Margaret inveigled her way back into the Castle and stole items from the family's bedrooms—wool, gloves belonging to the two young heirs, a handkerchief belonging to their daughter. Joan rubbed one of the boys' gloves on her black cat familiar's back—the cat named in court as Rutterkin—and pricked it with pins, and buried the other boy's gloves in a dung-heap. Both died soon afterwards, and their sister suffered mysterious fits and illnesses. Their devastated parents were unable to have more children 'because' Joan had boiled wool from their bed with cockerel feathers and blood.

The women expanded their psychic operations against new targets, and made the mistake of bragging about their successes. Soon they were all charged with the murder by magical means of the boys and several others, and of holding covens across the Vale. As they were being taken to Lincoln Castle for trial, Joan, while protesting innocence, reportedly asked for a piece of bread, saying 'Should I not be telling the truth, may this bread choke me,' whereupon inevitably it did. The remaining women were incarcerated while awaiting trial, and whilst there Margaret admitted to having been visited by no fewer than four devils, including the always obliging Rutterkin.

It was the reign of the sorcery-sniffing James I, who had published a treatise entitled *Daemonologie*, and had had witches executed in Scotland before coming south to assume the English throne, and ginger up the backsliding Southrons. In 1604 he had passed the Witchcraft Act, designed to strengthen existing laws, inspired by his own book and the famous German fifteenth-century work the *Malleus Maleficarum*, relied upon by many national legal systems (especially in Protestant countries).

Macbeth was first performed around 1606, both reflecting and helping shape the culture. So the assizes at Lincoln had a good idea what to look for, and the alleged witches not much of a chance. Margaret and Philippa were hanged by 'strangling twist' on 11 March 1618, in front of thrilled crowds, while the wider nation had to make do with widely circulated lurid prints and song sheets.

This locale seems almost to expect over-the-top architecture. Even the name of Harlaxton's visionary builder is Byronic— Gregory Gregory, an obsessively secretive loner who inherited the estate in 1822, and needed somewhere to put his extensive art collection. He wanted to own a house that incorporated *every* feature and style of architecture he had encountered in his extensive travels. He also wanted to outdo Belvoir Castle, facing his site tauntingly from the far side of the Vale. And he had no heirs, or anything else on which to spend his considerable fortune.

It was the start of twenty years of building, rebuilding and changes of mind with the help of fashionable architects like Salvin, who worked on Bayons, and Burn, who designed Revesby. While the house overall was a thing of fantasy, it was also designed to be functional, with a special railway line to bring coal into the house on two levels. The result, says Pevsner, is 'the wildest and most fanciful mansion of the 1830s,' which 'must be seen to be believed.'[14]

'Rejoicings at Harlaxton Manor' was the heading of a poster produced to commemorate the raising of the roof in 1837, with a grandly bombastic ceremony one would like to have seen. 'The welkin resounded with acclamations, that were again and again reiterated,' as a procession was assembled, headed by a gatekeeper 'bearing a gigantic gilt key,' a watchman 'with insignia of office' and a post boy 'Carrying letter-box,' followed by two boys with masonic emblems on poles, stone sawyers carrying a 'beautiful polished steel cross-cut saw, decorated with festoons of flowers, ribbons and evergreens,' and so on down to phalanxes of artisans and labourers. When the procession got to the Golden Lion pub, 'a discharge of fire-arms took place,' followed by a grand dinner, and numerous toasts including 'Town and Trade of Grantham' and 'Success to the Village of Harlaxton and God Speed the Plough.'[15]

At the end, insofar as there ever was an 'end' to building, there stood a house like nothing else in Lincolnshire, for appearance, inconvenience and size—a huge and largely unpeopled hotchpotch of towers and turrets, gabling and grand doors, stone curlicues and sweeping staircases, cherubim and terms, lion statues and cloud-ceilings with celestial musicians. It was, John Piper later marvelled, 'a Victorian dream-palace.'

When Gregory died—he was so secretive that no one is quite sure where he is buried, while the only portrait of him was posthumous and has disappeared. His place was taken by a succession of distant relatives, some of whom seem to have shared Gregory's dislike of modernity. Electric light was installed for a charity ball, and removed again the following day, and there was only one bathroom.

It would probably have been demolished or fallen down in the 1930s had it not been purchased by Violet Van Der Elst in 1937, whose husband had made a fortune in toiletries like Shavex, the first brushless shaving cream. Mrs Van Der Elst was a woman of expansive embonpoint and pronounced views, although more amenable to modernity than previous owners. She put in twenty miles of electric cable, extra bathrooms and a huge chandelier, and campaigned so vigorously against capital punishment she sometimes ended up in prison herself—an indignant fixture outside London prisons on hanging days, in her antique Rolls Royce. At home, her chief recreation was contacting the late Mr Van Der Elst on the astral plane, in the black-carpeted Great Hall at the top of the black-carpeted stairs.

She moved out during the war in favour of the 1st Battalion of the Airborne Division, who left a Pegasus emblem behind them in the courtyard. In 1948, Mrs Van Der Elst had flown for good, and the house fell into the unlikely hands of the Society of Jesus, then two small American universities in succession—the University of Stanford and, since 1971, the University of Evansville, the latter purchase narrowly averting the house's conversion to the world's strangest dog stud.

* * *

In April 2021, Isaac Newton was described as a potential beneficiary of 'colonial-era activity,' an increasingly standard sort of accusation for a man who was anything but.[16] But Newton really did colonise the world in certain ways. In Grantham, he carved his name on a window-sill of the grammar school he attended between 1654 and 1659. In algebra, mathematics, optics and physics, his name is even more deeply incised.

Newton was born in Woolsthorpe, southwest of Grantham, on Christmas Day 1642. The son of a prosperous but illiterate sheep-farmer who had bought the manor, he was baptised at Colsterworth, where part of the font is proudly shown, although his first sundial (moved here from his house in 1877, while another went to the Royal Society) is largely obscured by the organ.

Newton went up to Cambridge and got his BA in 1665. But that year, plague broke out in the town and Newton returned hastily to the relative safety of Woolsthorpe—except for odd forays to Grantham, where he bought prisms at the market. He also spent that time at Woolsthorpe doing one or two other things—discovering the generalised version of the binomial theorem, differential calculus, integral calculus, and, as everyone knows, conceiving the idea of universal gravitation by seeing an apple drop from a tree in the garden. He was then, he recalled much later, 'in the prime of my age for invention, and minded mathematics and philosophy more than at any time since.'

A binomial being the sum or difference of two terms, a binomial theorem is a formula for the expansion of any power of a binomial. Differential calculus is related to determining how sensitive a quantity is to any changes in some other quantity ('differentiation'). Integral calculus looks at things like calculating the area under a curve, or the volume of some shape ('integration'). Integration is usually much harder than differentiation. It turns out the two operations are each other's inverses. This is called the 'fundamental theorem of calculus,' and Newton discovered this for himself, although there were other discoverers. Both operations rely on 'infinitesimals' (infinitely small quantities), a point which troubled many.

These are tools with almost infinite applications, and philosophical implications. It is easy to see why he was lionised in his lifetime, and why Pope felt moved to write as his Westminster Abbey epitaph,

Nature, and Nature's laws, lay hid in night: /
God said, Let Newton be! and all was light.

The epitaph is reproduced on the wall of the room in the house where Newton began—prematurely, not expected to live a day, said to have been so small that he could have 'fitted into a quart pot.' Woolsthorpe Manor is a modest seventeenth-century manor, but inside can be seen much of the home Newton knew, and some of the graffiti on its walls may be his—a church, a windmill, a pheasant, a man in a frocked garment. Above the front door (clearance 5 feet, 7 inches!), an historically-conscious eighteenth-century owner inserted a panel carved with cross-bones, one of the quarterings of the Newton coat of arms.

Upstairs in this cool-toned house is Newton's study, where he built bookshelves to accommodate his long-ago dispersed personal library, which apparently consisted mostly of works of divinity. There are contemporaneous or reproduction furnishings, busts, globes, gloomy prints, and a third edition of his 1687 masterwork *Philosophiae Naturalis Principia Mathematica*. These things were not Newton's; but they convey something of the atmosphere in which he would have worked (except for his death mask above the fireplace).

In an adjoining room, there is a reconstruction of his famous experiment with the prism, which was conducted on 21 August 1665. It was Newton's special insight into the way light could be split and recombined that inspired his reflecting telescope of 1669—the most powerful telescope yet seen, and the clearest, because he reflected the image seen through the lens in a mirror rather than through another lens. There are also letters to and from the German mathematician Gottfried Leibniz, with whom the easily offended and humourless Newton carried on an increasingly venomous correspondence—one of the great objective thinker's notorious feuds.

Woolsthorpe's garden is as famous as Archimedes' bath in the history of science and popular culture. Newton's Eureka moment was recorded by William Stukeley, who in 1726 visited Newton in Kensington:

> The weather being warm, we went into the garden, & drank thea under the shade of some appletrees, only he, and myself. amidst other discourse, he told me, he was just in the same situation, as when formerly, the notion of gravitation came into his mind. 'Why should that apple always descend perpendicularly to the ground,' thought he to him self.: occasion'd by the fall of an apple, as he sat I contempatve mood: 'why should it not go side-ways or upwards, but constantly to the earth's centre?' Assuredly, the reason is, that the earth draws it. there must be a drawing power in matter. & the sum of the drawing power in the matter of the earth must be in the earths center, not in any side of the

earth. therefore dos this apple fall perpendicularly, or toward the center. if matter thus draws matter; it must be in proportion of its quantity. therefore the apple draws the earth, as well as the earth draws the apple that there is a power like that we here call gravity wh extends its self thro' the universe.[17]

That homely anecdote literally grounded scientific speculations. As apple-enthusiast J. C. Pillans notes, the tree 'has achieved fame far beyond the realms of Pomology.'[18] There is still an apple tree in the garden, but what was claimed to have been the original blew down in 1820, although rootstocks were sold—so offshoots of the tree still bud somewhere.

Newton was briefly an MP in the Convention Parliament which met in 1689 to ratify William III's claim to the throne and establish the Protestant Succession, but his only recorded contribution to this great debate was to ask an official to close the window. But he fizzed with fiscal patriotic rectitude when made Warden of the Mint, charged with guarding the coinage against 'clippers and coyners,' of whom he had twenty-seven executed at Tyburn. He would become President of the Royal Society in 1703, which post he held for the rest of his life. He published his *Opticks* in 1704, was knighted the following year, and when he died in 1727, lay in state in Westminster Abbey. Some of this might have seemed overdone for a man known for modesty. 'I do not know what I may appear to the world,' he reflected famously,

...but to myself I seem to have been only like a boy playing on the seashore, and diverting myself in now and then finding a smoother pebble or a prettier shell than ordinary, whilst the great ocean of truth lay all undiscovered before me.

* * *

Newton's deep-seated if understated Protestantism, high achievement, and concern for 'sound money' calls to mind Grantham's second most-famous product. Margaret Hilda Roberts was born in the town in 1925, daughter of a Methodist alderman and several-times Mayor who ran two high-end grocers' shops, with the slogan 'If you get it from Roberts's—you get the BEST!' What her biographer Charles Moore calls her 'grand simplicities' began to be formed above the family shop, and listening to lay preachers. As she said late in life:

> As a Methodist in Grantham, I learnt the laws of God. When I read chemistry at Oxford, I learnt the laws of science, which derive from the laws of God, and when I studied for the Bar, I learnt the laws of man.

As Mrs Thatcher, she would also learn the laws of politics, and help cement liberal opinion's view of Grantham, and places like Grantham, as benighted backwaters. She was a complicated as well as a divisive person, whose instincts were strongly traditionalist, but whose governments had a paradoxically liberalising and modernising effect, and not just in relation to the economy. In her combination of long memory and brisk business, she is perfectly Granthamian.

Unlike Stamford, Grantham has often seen itself as modern and progressive. The subtitle of Michael Honeybone's 1953 *The Book of Grantham*—'The history of a market and manufacturing town'—says something about Granthamians' view of themselves. 'Trade dominated the town's life from the twelfth century,' Honeybone notes, and the town seems never to have had a castle, or walls, or even much agriculture within its bounds. A Granthamian wool merchant advised Edward II on international trade, and in the fourteenth century other town merchants were in nationally important positions in shipping, customs and tax collecting. Later, Granthamians were indifferent to the

Lincolnshire Rising, which they probably saw as a regrettable disruption of trade. Margaret Roberts must have learned some of this mercantile realism at school. But even Michael Honeybone starts with a picture of Grantham's greatest landmark, a building that makes all industry uninteresting.

The 282-foot spire of St Wulfram's church has beetled above Grantham since the early fourteenth century, marking where Anglo-Saxons and then Normans worshipped, a way-finder for miles around, standing beside Newton's school like a giant gnomon. Its spire, while shorter than St James' in Louth, seems even taller in its setting, and is so harmoniously conceived that John Ruskin (admittedly a highly susceptible person) is said to have almost fainted the first time he saw it.

After this aesthete-overwhelming exterior, the interior feels startlingly bare. However, above the south porch is the Trigge Chained Library, given by Francis Trigge in 1598, for:

> ...the better encreasinge of learnings and knowledge in divinitie & other liberall sciences & learning by such of the cleargie & others as well as beinge inhabitantes in or near Grantham & the soake thereof as in other places in the said Countie.[19]

It was the world's first public reference library, and is still housed in the same room, in some of the same bookcases, with volumes going back to 1472. This mercifully escaped Reformation iconoclasm, and Roundhead occupation in 1643, perhaps because Trigge had been a Puritan, although the rest of the interior was largely stripped. It also escaped George Gilbert Scott's almost equally brutal 'restoration' of 1866, when the screen, galleries, pews, pulpit and furnishings were yanked out, and auctioned off without reserve. In 1808, the church had also been robbed of all its silver plate.

King John came to Grantham in 1213 to convene a parliament at the Angel Inn, a hostel founded in 1203 by the Knights

Templar. That building was absorbed into the present part-fourteenth-century premises, but the Angel has carried on continuously, and is now the Angel & Royal Best Western Hotel. Some of its interior has been conserved, and a gilded angel carving still blinks out over a High Street hectic with cars. Edward I also stayed at the Angel when he stopped on his disconsolate journey from Lincoln to London with the carcass of his queen. Edward IV came in 1469, and Richard III in October 1483, who used the room now called the King's Chamber to receive the Great Seal of England, and start proceedings to execute the Duke of Buckingham. Charles I was here in 1633, and Cromwell in 1643. Edward VII, a man always fond of his food, was so impressed by his fare in 1866 that he graciously allowed the addition of the suffix '& Royal.'

Grantham served as market town for a huge area of premium-quality farmland and manorial estates. Some of those who toiled at Irnham in the fourteenth century and were immortalised in the illustrated *Luttrell Psalter*, now in the British Library, would have visited on market days, when they were not carrying, ploughing, scrumping cherries, or guarding geese against the comical-to-horrifying Hieronymus Bosch-style creatures stalking along the manuscript margins, on the edge of reality.[20]

Richard Foxe of Ropsley (1446?-1528) knew the town as a boy. He left Lincolnshire to pursue a stellar career—Lord Privy Seal to Henry VII, bishop of Durham and Winchester, as chief English envoy securing the 1492 Treaty of Étaples between England and France, in 1497 concluding peace with the Scots, negotiating both Margaret Tudor's marriage to Scotland's James IV and the future Henry VIII's marriage to Catherine of Aragon, and in 1508 facilitating the proxy marriage of Henry VII's daughter Mary with Archduke Charles of Austria, the future Holy Roman Emperor Charles V (the engagement was called off in 1513, after Foxe had fallen from favour). But he remembered where he came from—becoming Chancellor of Cambridge University, and founding both Oxford's Corpus Christi College and Grantham Grammar School, where two centuries or so later the young Isaac Newton would sit agog.

Grantham was always amenable to the latest industrial developments, whether the wool trade of the Middle Ages or the heavy engineering of the late eighteenth to twentieth centuries. It was also a busy coaching town by the mid-eighteenth century, with five turnpike roads radiating outwards. By 1797 there was a canal linking the Witham to the Trent. William Stukeley would have hated all this. His magnificent house is now gone, with even its site uncertain, in whose garden he buried the embryo of one of his wife's miscarriages, under a Roman altar.

The railway was relatively late to arrive, the Great Northern Railway not opening a station until 1850, although it soon made up for tardiness by turning Grantham into a major engine depot, magnetising trainspotters right up until the end of the steam era. On 7 July 1938, the famous *Mallard* engine set a speed record of 126 mph immediately north of the town. The rise of road transport brought a new kind of through traffic, and a new kind of engineering expertise. A company called Aveling-Barford made road machinery before the World War Two, and Bren-gun carriers during its course (one reason Grantham suffered bad bombing in the war, with seventy killed). Afterwards, writes Michael Honeybone wistfully, 'For a few exhilarating months during 1946 Grantham seemed destined to become a major car producing town.'[21] Providentially, this project proved a non-starter.

* * *

In Wyndham Park at Grantham is an unusual Great War memorial, to the Machine Gun Corps, with two bronze Vickers heavy machine guns muzzles down in the ground. The Corps was founded in Grantham in 1915, and the town hosted its administration centre, depot and training facility. The machine gun was widely considered at the time an 'unchivalrous' weapon, rather like the crossbow in the Middle Ages, and Corps personnel were known to rip off their regimental insignia if likely to be captured, in order to avert ill-treatment. Today, the machine gun still exemplifies the terrible mechanization of modern war; its 'celebration' at Grantham is reminiscent of Foster of Lincoln's tribute to their tank, and the countywide fascination with Bomber Command.

Grantham was never a fortress, but it was frequently a garrison town, important between 1642 and 1646 because of its proximity to the Royalist bastion at Newark. Colonel Rossiter's 8th Horse Regiment was stationed here from 1644 to guard against incursions from Newark, and also issued out, in June 1645 raising a royalist siege at Hougham, before galloping straight to Naseby, where they turned the tide of the battle. That October, they nearly captured Prince Rupert of the Rhine near Belvoir.

After the war, Rossiter's Horse metamorphosed into the North and South Lincolnshire Militia Regiments, in which Granthamians were liable for service, or into which they were pressed, often as the alternative to prison. They provided recruits to the regular army, many serving in the Peninsular War and the Crimea. The 17th/21st Lancers were also associated with this area, the 17th's Charge of the Light Brigade commemorated at Belvoir, not to mention in Tennyson's poem—perhaps he knew some of the men who rode into the 'Valley of Death.' The 21st won three Victoria Crosses at the battle of Omdurman in 1897, the last major battle where cavalry—including the young Winston Churchill—rode down the enemy.

The Lincolnshire Regiment was also present at Omdurman. It had been raised originally in 1685 as the Earl of Bath's Regiment, to help suppress the Monmouth Rebellion. Its Colonel, Sir Charles Carney, was a Catholic, and remained loyal to James II during the Glorious Revolution; he fled with him, and would later command the Jacobite reserve at the Battle of the Boyne.

It then saw action against the French in Flanders during the Nine Years' War, and during the War of the Spanish Succession, notably at Blenheim, Ramillies, Oudenarde and Malplaquet. In 1751, it was renamed the 10th Regiment of Foot, as part of attempts to professionalise the army, moving away from gentlemen-amateur Colonel-Proprietors who saw their regiments as personal property to be equipped (or risked) as they wished, towards a regulated command structure and greater uniformity. These attempts were not wholly successful. At the battle of Brandywine Creek on 11 September 1777, the British officers were described by one American witness as,

> ...rather short, portly men ... well-dressed and of genteel appearance, and [who] did not look as though they had ever been exposed to any hardship; their skins being white and delicate as it is customary for females who were brought up in large cities.[22]

The 10th nevertheless distinguished itself at the battle, earning the nickname 'The Springers' because of the alacrity with which they answered the command 'Spring up!' from their prone firing position.

In 1782, the regiment was allocated Lincolnshire as its recruiting ground, and there would have been many Yellowbellies at the Battle of Alexandria in 1801, during the Walcheren debacle of 1809, and at the siege of Tarragona in 1813. It fought at Sobraon during the first Anglo-Sikh War (1846)—during which the sight of Sikhs killing British wounded aroused the redcoats to equal fury, culminating in thousands of fatalities as Sikh soldiers trapped on the banks of the Satlej river fought to the death, while others who tried to flee were bayoneted, swept into the water and shot as they tried to swim away. The regiment's barracks in Lincoln was named after the battle, and for years afterwards, officers of the 10th and 29th Foot would greet each other as 'My dear cousin,' in allusion to their regiments' rendezvous in the middle of the fray.

The Victoria Cross was instituted in 1857, and that year saw the regiment's first awards, during the Indian Mutiny. Private Denis Dempsey, from Bray in Ireland, got the VC for carrying gunpowder through a burning village and under heavy fire to mine the enemy position. The following year, he was the first to enter Jugdispore 'under a most galling fire.' Lieutenant Henry Marshman Havelock got it for his actions at Cawnpore, when he led a leisurely advance in a hail of gunfire against the enemy's last field gun. At Benares, Private John Kirk got it for volunteering to help rescue a Captain Brown and his family trapped by rebels in the compound of their house.

Mooltan, Goojarat, Punjab and Lucknow were added to the regimental battle honours. The 10th, now called the Lincolnshire Regiment, relocated to Africa, fought against Mahdists at Atbara and Khartoum (both 1898), and then Boers. Paardeberg saw the day that became known as 'Bloody Sunday,' 18 February 1900, when incompetence caused the deaths of hundreds of British soldiers who had been ordered to advance on *laagered* Boers, while others died from drinking water deliberately contaminated by the Afrikaners.

From Mons in 1914 to the Second Battle of Bapaume (August–September 1918), the Lincolnshire Regiment was much in the Western Frontline. Corporal Charles Sharpe, a farm boy from Pickworth near Bourne, who had run away to join the army, won the VC for his actions on 9 May 1915, when he was the first to reach a German position at Rouges Banc and cleared a fifty-yard stretch with hand grenades. The rest of his party had been killed, but when assistance arrived he managed a further 250 yards. An ironic postscript is that he was injured in World War Two, when German bombs fell on the school at Bourne where he worked as a PT instructor.

On 2 September 1918, Lance-Sergeant Arthur Evans was awarded the medal for volunteering to swim a river and capture a German machine gun post. Having taken the post by shooting two and taking four prisoners, he was joined by an officer and another man, but the officer was wounded and Evans assisted him back across the river and to safety under winnowing fire.

The 'Grimsby Chums'—officially, the 10th (Service) Battalion—was one of the famous 'pals battalions' raised by Lord Kitchener. These battalions were made up of men recruited from the same locality who would theoretically be more cohesive than battalions of men drawn from different parts of the country. The theory was cogent, but it meant heavy battle losses would have a disproportionately devastating effect on the recruiting locations.

The Chums fought at the Somme, in the first wave, but got pinned down in a crater, bombarded by both sides' artillery. Second Lieutenant Harold Hendin managed to get five of the Chums as far as the German reserve trench, then held off attacks for several days until eventually being forced to retreat. There were 502 Chum casualties in a single day, only two officers and 100 men returning unscathed. The regiment would later fight at Vimy Ridge and Passchendaele and during the 1918 German offensive, by the end so depleted it was only fit to be a training battalion. A total of 810 Chums were killed or died on active service—although even that was dwarfed by the number (1,072) of Grimsby fishermen who were killed mine-sweeping or trawling.

The Regiment won a third VC at Gallipoli, Captain Percy Hansen racing across hundreds of yards of open ground several times to rescue six wounded men from burning. The same year, he won the Military Cross for a one-man reconnaissance at Suvla

Bay, swimming across and scrambling up rocks, wearing just a blanket and carrying only a revolver.

In World War Two, the Lincolnshires were sent to Norway, and so were among the first British troops to encounter the *Wehrmacht*. They encountered them again at Dunkirk, on D-Day, at Caen, Le Havre, the Venlo Pocket, the Rhineland and Bremen, amongst other places—while other battalions fought Rommel in North Africa and Kesselring in Italy. Yet others went to confront the Japanese Imperial Army for two years in Burma. Acting Major Charles Ferguson Hoey got the VC posthumously in 1944 for having taken a Japanese post single-handedly, outrunning his advancing company despite being wounded at least twice, and while firing a Bren gun from his hip.

In recognition for these and other services, in 1948 the King allowed the regiment to adopt the prefix 'Royal.' Twelve years after that distinction, the regiment was unsentimentally amalgamated into the 2nd East Anglian Regiment (Duchess of Gloucester's Own Royal Lincolnshire and Northamptonshire) which in 1964 became the Royal Anglian Regiment. Today, a single company of one battalion of the Royal Anglians 'continues the traditions' of the Royal Lincolnshires, including being nicknamed 'The Poachers'—while 674 Squadron Army Air Corps, based at Cranwell, uses the Lincolnshires' sphinx emblem within its crest, and marches to 'The Lincolnshire Poacher.' These are excellent formations, but it is difficult not to regret the loss of regimental colour and distinctiveness. Today's army feels very far away from Stamford's straight-backed Georgian certainties, like a long-running period drama ending in anti-climax.

11

TIME WAS—TIME IS—TIME IS PAST

'So in immensity my thought is drowned,
And sweet it is to founder in this sea.'
—Giacomo Leopardi, *'L'Infinito'*

People said I was making a mistake. 'Don't tell *anyone* about Lincolnshire!' a friend joked. 'They'll *ruin* it!' I thought about this before I began to write.

It really *is* a risk to tell people about a place that matters to you. Might not your personal demi-paradise suddenly fill with people who—however excellently intentioned—won't see it quite the way you see it, won't really *understand* it? When you find a place that fits, you develop a jealous and selfish sense of proprietorship—even though you were once a new arrival yourself, perhaps equally unwanted. Increased attention means increased change, and while change is frequently beneficial, it can have unexpected consequences. Even the most generous investments always come with conditions.

But the outside world is coming here anyway, fly-tipping over the imaginative and physical borders, altering loved landscapes, colonising the county's inner life. Lincolnshire is already less distinctive than when we first knew it, and every day it becomes a tiny bit more like everywhere else.

Lincolnshire always had less pleasant aspects—its drab, dispiriting and ugly places, its prospects ruined by planning decisions, or the 'improvements' of newcomers who probably should never have moved to the countryside. Every day, there seem to be more nondescript houses, more roads, more lights, and traffic. Local news headlines increasingly resemble the troubled headlines of big cities, and local attitudes and local manners are increasingly homogenised. There are fewer farmers, and you hear the accent less often. There are fewer small shops, fewer mouldering old buildings, fewer quiet places, fewer wild animals. There is a plan to build a huge nuclear waste dump on the coast. Every day, there is slightly less character, less friendliness, and less imagination.

These changes are incremental and subtle, and each one is individually explicable, or ignorable. They are nonetheless real, and cumulatively injurious to a unique identity. After over twenty years here, we finally feel ourselves to be a little like locals, and are becoming as fiercely nostalgic as the Fenlanders who resisted Vermuyden. The things we came here to find, and the unexpected things we found, are receding equally from us, and from everyone.

It is dauntingly difficult to address such amorphous tendencies, which are much bigger than Lincolnshire, or even England— which seem part of global movements towards agglomeration, dehumanisation, materialism, mechanisation and standardisation. But I eventually concluded that highlighting a few otherwise overlooked aspects of Lincolnshire just might encourage some residents to value what they have more highly, and make casual visitors a little less casual. This matters, because places that are taken for granted, places that take themselves for granted, are easily imposed upon or abused, whether by old aristocratic expropriators or modern politicians seeking to export problems from their constituencies.

Writing about Lincolnshire seemed suddenly necessary, maybe even a kind of public service. It would also be selfish catharsis for myself. I have never regretted that decision. Every time I look out of the window, which I do too often—to watch curlews piping past, rain curtains trailing across the field, a double rainbow, sunbeams on fourteenth-century stone—every time I hear the geese, or the toads, or the pounding breakers of Doggerland—every time I drive across the county to see it unfurling on all sides—I know I made the right choice. If all these things are destined one day to disappear, become something like myth, there seems all the more reason to write their stories now, commit the dream to 'memory.' As the Roman historian noted, 'These things never were, but are always.'[1]

For all its problems—past, present or projected—Lincolnshire is still a county like no other. This is an England time half-forgot, where you can still find an unabashed past inside an unpretentious present—and freedom and space on a little offshore island.

This is the England the rest of England half-forgot—a form of English life that is not yet archaeology, which still honours those who once so flourishingly autographed the arts, religion and science, and atlases from the Arctic to Australia. Twenty-first century angst, twenty-first century irony, and twenty-first century force have not yet made full landfall. For now, at least, Lincolnshire is still a place that has escaped—and still a place of escape.

If some of Lincolnshire lives on the sufferance of future seas, that just makes the threatened lands shine out all the more strongly, like the last vision of a drowning man when everything is encapsulated, or a final sight of Atlantis with the waves curling above. Whatever the crowding future brings, something like eternity can sometimes still be seen, here at the ever-changing edge of England.

NOTES

1. ANOTHER COUNTRY

1. Rev. G. S. Streatfeild, *Lincolnshire and the Danes*, Kegan Paul, Trench & Co, 1884, p. 1.
2. *Henry IV, Part 1*, Act 1, Scene 2.
3. James Howell, *English Proverbs*, 1659, cited in *The Oxford Dictionary of English Proverbs*, OUP, 1989, p. 466. John Aubrey heard the saying in Wiltshire.
4. Cited in Keith Thomas, *Pursuit of Civility—Manners and Civilization in Early Modern England*, Yale University Press, 2018, p. 370.
5. Thomas Fuller, *Worthies of England*, 1662, my edition *Fuller's Worthies*, Folio Society, 1987, p. 235.
6. Samuel Johnson, *Dictionary of the English Language*, 1755, my edition Studio Editions, 1994, p. 454.
7. Jack Yates & Henry Thorold, *Shell Guide to Lincolnshire*, 1965, Faber & Faber, 1965.
8. '19 April 1983: "Frightened! Frit!",' Democracy Live, http://news.bbc.co.uk/democracylive/hi/historic_moments/newsid_8185000/8185773.stm, accessed 15 December 2021.
9. John Donne, 'Devotion XVIII,' from *Devotions Upon Emergent Occasions*, 1624, https://www.gutenberg.org/files/23772/23772-h/23772-h.htm, accessed 11 April 2022.
10. John Bunyan, *Pilgrim's Progress*, 1678, my edition Cassell & Co., 1919, p. 15.

11. J. E. Cirlot, *A Dictionary of Symbols*, my edition Dover Publications, 1994, p. 204; Udo Becker, *The Continuum Encyclopaedia of Symbols*, 1992, my edition Continuum, 1994, p. 287.

12. Barnabe Googe, *Eglogs, Epytaphes, and Sonnetes*, 1563, https://archive. org/stream/barnabegoogeeglo014583mbp/barnabegoogee- glo014583mbp_djvu.txt, accessed 11 April 2022.

13. Francis Grose, *Dictionary of the Vulgar Tongue*, 1811, my edition Bibliophile Books, 1984.

14. *The Tempest*, Act 2, Scene 2.

15. *King Lear*, Act 2, Scene 4.

16. T. Chin, P. D. Welsby. 'Malaria in the UK: past, present, and future', *Postgraduate Medical Journal*, https://pmj.bmj.com/con- tent/80/949/663, accessed 22 April 2021.

17. Bishop (Mandell) Creighton, *The Story of Some English Shires*, Religious Tract Society, 1897, quoted in William George Smith (ed.), *Oxford Dictionary of English Proverbs*, Second Edition, Clarendon, 1935, my edition 1966, p. 20.

18. Edmund Blunden, 'The Landscape,' *The Legacy of England*, B. T. Batsford, 1935.

19. M. W. Barley, *Lincolnshire and the Fens*, Batsford, 1952, p. v.

20. George Crabbe, 'The Lover's Journey,' 1812, https://www.poetrynook. com/poem/lovers-journey-0, accessed 11 April 2022.

21. Elizabeth Jennings, 'In a Garden,' 1953, https://allpoetry.com/ poem/8495563-In-A-Garden-by-Elizabeth-Jennings, accessed 11 April 2022.

22. William Camden, *Britannia*, 1637, cited in James Boyce, *Imperial Mud—The Fight for the Fens*, Icon, 2020, p. 148.

23. Anonymous, 'Lincolnshire: A Poem,' 1720, quoted in Stuart Piggott, *William Stukeley—An Eighteenth-century Antiquary*, Clarendon Press, 1950, p. 19.

24. Bernie Taupin, interview with *Esquire*, quoted at https://www.stand- ard.co.uk/culture/music/bernie-taupin-songs-elton-john- 70-a4447726.html, accessed 15 December 2021.

25. See https://genome.ch.bbc.co.uk/schedules/service_bbc_two_eng- land/1997-03-19, accessed 28 April 2022.

26. Mark Brown, 'Video work reveals racism of Lincolnshire community,' *Guardian*, 19 August 2006, https://www.theguardian.com/uk/2006/aug/19/arts.race or Adam Lusher, 'Racism unleashed: 'Send the lot back' – on the road in post-referendum England,' *The Independent*, 28 July 2016, https://www.independent.co.uk/news/uk/politics/racism-brexit-immigration-eu-referendum-post-referendum-boston-least-integrated-town-a7150541.html, both accessed 12 December 2021.

27. Nicholas Fletcher, '"Lincolnshire is the most racist county in the country",' *Lincolnshire Live*, 15 August 2017, https://www.lincolnshirelive.co.uk/news/local-news/lincolnshire-most-racist-county-country-325508, accessed 12 December 2021.

28. Hilary Healey, *A Fenland Landscape Glossary for Lincolnshire*, Lincolnshire County Council, 1997.

2. SHADOWS IN THE WATER

1. Most likely a larger species of plesiosaur, like a rhomaleosaur.
2. Jacquetta Hawkes, *A Land*, 1951, my edition Collins, 2012, p. 5.
3. Victoria & Albert Museum, 'The Festival of Britain,' https://www.vam.ac.uk/articles/the-festival-of-britain, accessed 15 March 2021.
4. Benedict Anderson, *Imagined Communities: Reflections on the Origin and Spread of Nationalism*, 1983, my edition Verso, 1991; Eric Hobsbawm & Terence Ranger (eds), *The Invention of Tradition*,1983, my edition Cambridge University Press, 2012.
5. Zbigniew Herbert, *Mr. Cogito*, 1974, my edition Zbigniew Herbert, *Collected Poems 1956-1998*, Ecco, 1998.
6. See William Smith, *A Delineation of the Strata of England and Wales with Part of Scotland*, 1815, my edition Thames & Hudson, 2020.
7. Maev Kennedy, '850,000-year-old human footprints found in Norfolk', *Guardian*, 7 February 2014, https://www.theguardian.com/science/2014/feb/07/oldest-human-footprints-happisburgh-norfolk, accessed 10 June 2021.
8. José Francisco Correia da Serra, 'On a submarine forest on the coast of England,' *Philosophical Transactions*, 1799, https://www.jstor.org/stable/pdf/107029.pdf, accessed 11 April 2022.

9. 'The Double Vision of Manannan,' John Montague (ed.), *The Faber Book of Irish Verse*, Faber & Faber, 1974, p. 45.

10. Fin, humpback, minke and pilot whales are quite common in the North Sea, as are several species of porpoise and dolphin. Sperm whales are occasional visitors; one washed up on the Holderness coast in 1825, and is displayed at Burton Constable Hall. It may have been Herman Melville's inspiration for *Moby Dick*.

11. W. G. Sebald, *The Rings of Saturn*, Vintage, 1995.

12. Decommissioned in 2020. As of December 2021 the site is being considered for a nuclear waste dump.

13. D. H. Lawrence, *Etruscan Places*, 1932, my edition Penguin, 1950, p. 27.

14. Cathal Buidhe MacGiolla Gunna, 'The Yellow Bittern,' https://poets.org/poem/yellow-bittern-bunnan-bui

15. Geoffrey Chaucer, 'Wife of Bath,' *Canterbury Tales*, first published 1475, my edition Oxford University Press, 1976, line 870.

16. Les Murray, 'Cave Divers Near Mount Gambier,' 1990, *Selected Poems 1964-2010*. See https://marthebijman.files.wordpress.com/2019/04/les-murray_selected-poems.pdf, accessed 11 April 2022.

17. Julian of Norwich, *Revelations of Divine Love*, 1373, my edition Oxford University Press, 2015.

18. Thomas Traherne, 'Shadows in the Water,' *Oxford Book of Seventeenth Century Verse*, Sir Herbert Grierson and G. Bullough (eds), Oxford University Press, 1976, p. 914.

19. William Blake, 'Auguries of Innocence,' c. 1803, https://www.poetryfoundation.org/poems/43650/auguries-of-innocence, accessed 11 April 2022.

20. Cited in Michael Welland, *Sand—A Journey Through Science and the Imagination*, Oxford University Press, 2009, p. 30.

3. THE BRACING COAST

1. Herman Melville, *Moby Dick*, 1851, Chapter 42.

2. Algernon Swinburne, 'By the North Sea,' 1880, https://www.victorianweb.org/authors/swinburne/northsea.html, accessed 11 April 2022.

3. Matthew Arnold, 'Dover Beach,' https://www.poetryfoundation.org/poems/43588/dover-beach, accessed 11 April 2022.

4. Swinburne, op. cit.

5. Alfred Tennyson, 'Here often, when a child, I lay reclined,' 1850, https://thereaderonline.wordpress.com/2015/08/03/featured-poem-lines-here-often-when-a-child-i-lay-reclined-by-alfred-lord-tennyson/, accessed 11 April 2022.

6. Quoted in Rev. William M. Cooper, *An Illustrated History of the Rod*, Wordsworth, 1988, p. 430.

7. Quoted in William Henry Wheeler, *A History of the Fens of South Lincolnshire*, 1896, my edition Cambridge University Press, 2014.

8. Beard points out that John kept the Great Seal with him, and that he would have been unlikely to entrust equally valuable items to an army consisting largely of mercenaries. See Charles R. Beard, *The Romance of Treasure Trove*, Sampson Low, Marston & Co., 1933, pp. 110-7.

9. Cited in Joan Thirsk, *English Peasant Farming—The Agrarian History of Lincolnshire from Tudor to Recent Times*, Routledge & Kegan Paul, 1957, p. 19.

10. Hilaire Belloc, 'The Sea-Wall of the Wash,' *Hills and the Sea*, 1906, my edition Methuen, 1913, p. 92.

11. Piggott, op. cit., p. 21.

12. *Dictionary of National Biography*, Oxford University Press, 1992, p. 2,895.

13. Alain Schnapps, *The Discovery of the Past*, British Museum Press, 1996, p. 179.

14. Schnapps, ibid., p. 213.

15. Quoted in Stuart Piggott, *Ancient Britons and the Antiquarian Imagination: Ideas from the Renaissance to the Regency*, Thames & Hudson, 1989, p. 129.

16. Piggott, ibid., p. 127.

17. Stuart Piggott, *Stukeley*, p. xiii.

18. Frederick W. Haberman (ed.), 'Sir Norman Angell,' *Nobel Lectures: Peace 1926-1950*, Elsevier, 1972, https://www.nobelprize.org/prizes/peace/1933/angell/biographical/, accessed 15 December 2021.

19. Michael Meadowcroft & Liz Bee, 'Norman Angell (1872-1967),' https://www.beemeadowcroft.uk/liberal/angell.html, accessed 15 December 2021.

20. J. B. Whitwell, *Roman Lincolnshire*, Society for Lincolnshire History and Archaeology, 1971, p. 52.

21. John Leland, *Itinerary*, Vol. 4, edited by Lucy Toulmin Smith, Southern Illinois University Press, 1964.

22. Alfred Tennyson, 'Maud,' 1850, https://www.poetryfoundation.org/poems/45367/maud-part-i, accessed 15 December 2021.

23. A. J. Marriot, 'Laurel and Hardy at Butlins Skegness,' https://www.laurelandhardybooks.com/skegness.html, accessed 15 December 2021.

24. Edmund Vale, *The Seas and Shores of England*, B. T. Batsford, 1936.

25. Nikolaus Pevsner, *Buildings of England: Lincolnshire*, Penguin, 1964, p. 406.

26. Simon Jenkins, *England's Thousand Best Churches*, Penguin 1999, my edition, 2000, p. 365.

27. Arthur Mee, *The King's England: Lincolnshire*, Hodder & Stoughton, 1949, my edition 1970, p. 326.

28. UK Government, *2011 Census,* https://ukcensusdata.com/lincolnshire-e10000019, accessed 15 December 2021.

29. Dave Burke, 'Do you live in this town? It's the murder capital of England and Wales,' *Metro*, 23 January 2016, https://metro.co.uk/2016/01/23/do-you-live-in-this-town-its-the-murder-capital-of-england-and-wales-5640004/, accessed 15 December 2021.

30. The Newsroom, 'Campaign aims to tackle "significant negativity" about Boston', *Lincolnshire World*, 22 September 2021, https://www.lincolnshireworld.com/heritage-and-retro/heritage/campaign-aims-to-tackle-significant-negativity-about-boston-3391924, accessed 15 December 2021.

31. F. L. Cross (ed.), *Oxford Dictionary of the Christian Church*, Oxford University Press, 1957, p. 1,464.

32. John Warkworth, *Warkworth's Chronicle*, reproduced in *Three Chronicles of the Reign of Edward IV*, Alan Sutton, 1988, p. 30.

33. Warkworth, ibid.

34. Alfred Tennyson, 'The Palace of Art', https://www.poemhunter.com/poem/the-palace-of-art-2/, accessed 11 April 2022.

35. Quoted in James Lees-Milne & Hugh Montgomery-Massingberd, *Gunby Hall*, National Trust, 2000.

36. Cited in Laura Cumming, *On Chapel Sands*, Penguin, 2019, p. 20.

37. See Michael Pye, *The Edge of the World—How the North Sea Made Us Who We Are*, Viking, 2015.

38. Their son became Richard II.

39. Andrew Hoyle, '*Boston's Forgotten Crusade*', Boston Hanse Group, 2017, https://www.academia.edu/33842635/Bostons_Forgotten_Crusade, accessed 12 November 2021.

40. George Ripley, *Chymical Writings*, 1756, cited in Alexander Roob, *Alchemy & Mysticism*, Taschen, 1997.

41. J. W. F. Hill, *Tudor & Stuart Lincoln*, Cambridge University Press, 1956, p. 48.

42. John Leland, *Itinerary, In or About the Years 1535-1543, Part IX,* edited by Lucy Toulmin Smith, Southern Illinois University Press, 1964, p. 33.

43. Paul Henry Lang, *Music in Western Civilization*, J. M. Dent, 1942, revised edition 1963, p. 277.

44. Percy A. Scholes, *The Oxford Companion to Music*, Oxford University Press, 1950, p. 921.

45. Lang, op. cit., p. 279.

46. Thomas Morley, *Plaine and Easie Introduction to Practicall Music*, 1571, https://s9.imslp.org/files/imglnks/usimg/b/bc/IMSLP160042-PMLP09691-morley_1597.pdf, accessed 11 April 2022.

47. More recent studies suggest that Taverner was not as militantly iconoclastic as had been supposed. See, for example, Hugh Benham, *John Taverner: His Life and Music*, Routledge, 2017, p. 267.

48. Foxe accused a certain Grimwood of Hitcham of swearing a man's life away by perjury, but noted with satisfaction that Grimwood had been punished by instant death, when his bowels fell out of his body—an incident the alleged perjurer first heard about many years after the book's publication, when he was surprised to hear his name being used in a sermon against false witness.

49. A. M. Cook, *Boston (Botolphstown)*, Boston Church, 1948, p. 58.

50. Quoted in A. A. Garner, *Boston and the Great Civil War*, Richard Kay, 1992, p. 2.

51. Anne Bradstreet, 'A Dialogue Between Old England and New', 1650,

https://www.poetryfoundation.org/poems/43700/a-dialogue
-between-old-england-and-new, accessed 10 November 2021.

52. David A. Price, *Love and Hate in Jamestown: John Smith, Pocahontas and the Heart of a New Nation*, Faber & Faber, 2005, p. 233.

53. Sir John Wray, speeches of 12 November and 15 December 1640, quoted in J. W. F. Hill, *Tudor & Stuart Lincoln*, Cambridge University Press, 1956, p. 146.

54. Edward Parnell, *Ghostland—In Search of a Haunted Country*, William Collins, 2019, p. 59.

55. A new vineyard was planted in Lincoln in 1972, and produces wine from three varieties of white grape.

56. *Anglo-Saxon Chronicle*, translated by Rev. J. Ingram, 1823, my edition Studio Editions, 1993, p. 193.

57. *Louth Park Abbey Chronicle*, c. 1413; *Chronicle of Hagnaby Abbey,* early fourteenth century. See Caitlin Green, 'The drowned villages and eroding coastline of Lincolnshire c 1250–1600', https://www.caitlingreen.org/2015/05/drowned-villages-of-lincolnshire.html, accessed 2 July 2021.

58. See Basil E. Cracknell, *Outrageous Waves—Global Warming & Coastal Change in Britain Through Two Thousand Years*, Phillimore, 2005.

59. R. Holinshed, cited at https://www.caitlingreen.org/2015/05/drowned-villages-of-lincolnshire.html#fn12, accessed 10 November 2021.

60. Jean Ingelow, 'High Tide on the Coast of Lincolnshire,' 1863, https://www.bartleby.com/246/604.html, accessed 11 April 2022.

61. *Lincoln, Rutland and Stamford Mercury*, 16 November 1810, https://www.smarchive.org.uk/, accessed 10 November 2021.

62. 'Climate Central, Flooded Future: Global vulnerability to sea level rise worse than previously thought', 2020, https://www.lincolnshirelive.co.uk/news/local-news/worrying-predicted-map-shows-huge-4179417, accessed 7 November 2021.

63. Matthew Hollis, 'Stones,' 2016.

64. Da Serra, op. cit.

4. LITTLE KINGDOMS

1. Joseph Conrad, 'Karain: A Memory,' *Tales of Unrest*, 1898, https://conrad.thefreelibrary.com/Tales-of-Unrest/1-1, accessed 10 November 2021.

2. Mario Praz, *An Illustrated History of Interior Decoration from Pompeii to Art Nouveau*, 1945, quoted in Edward Hollis, *The Memory Palace—A Book of Lost Interiors*, Portobello, 2013, p. 6.

3. See 'The Seasonal Soundscape Project,' https://jackhalgh.github.io/The-Seasonal-Soundscape-Project/; Action Pyramid, 'A Ghost Pond Emerges,' https://soundcloud.com/action-pyramid/action-pyramid-a-ghost-pond-emerges, both accessed 11 April 2022.

4. John Betjeman, 'A Lincolnshire Church,' *Collected Poems*, John Murray, 1958.

5. Edward Peacock, *North Lincolnshire Dialect Dictionary*, 1889, quoted in Kevin Leahy, *The Anglo-Saxon Kingdom of Lindsey*, Tempus, 2007, p. 41.

6. Jabez Good, *A Glossary or Collection of Words, Phrases, Place Names, Superstitions, & c., Current in East Lincolnshire*, H. Fulford, 1900, my edition Skegness Publicity Service, 1973, p. 7.

7. Alfred Tennyson, 'Northern Farmer—Old Style', https://www.poetryfoundation.org/poems/45371/northern-farmer-old-style, accessed 1 December 2021.

8. Edward Campion, *A Tennyson Dialect Glossary*, Lincolnshire Association, 1972.

9. Jean Harrowven, *Origins of Rhymes, Songs and Sayings*, Kaye & Ward, 1977, my edition 1982, p. 35.

10. See http://farwelterd.co.uk/index.php

11. Edward Campion, *Lincolnshire Dialects*, Richard Kay, 1976, my edition 2001, p. 56.

12. Song of Solomon 2: 11-12.

13. See https://internationalbcc.co.uk/

14. John Gillespie Magee, 'High Flight', https://nationalpoetryday.co.uk/poem/high-flight/, accessed 3 July 2021.

15. Roger L'Estrange, 'A Pike and Little Fishes,' *Fables and Storys*

Moralized, 1699, quoted in Peter Ure (ed.), *Seventeenth-Century Prose 1620-1700*, Penguin, 1956, p. 219.

16. Geoffrey Hill, *Mercian Hymns*, included in *Selected Poems*, Penguin, 2006.

17. Robert Burton, *The Anatomy of Melancholy*, 1621, my edition Everyman's Library, 1964, p. 310.

18. Patrick Barkham, 'Kill them, kill them, kill them—the volunteer army plotting to wipe out Britain's grey squirrels,' *Guardian*, 2 June 2017, https://www.theguardian.com/environment/2017/jun/02/kill-them-the-volunteer-army-plotting-to-wipe-out-britains-grey-squirrels, accessed 10 November 2021.

19. Christopher Lever, *The Naturalized Animals of the British Isles*, Hutchinson, 1977, p. 106.

5. TALES FROM THE RIVERBANK

1. See https://assets.publishing.service.gov.uk/government/uploads/system/uploads/attachment_data/file/972103/regionalstatistics_overview_23mar21.pdf, accessed 21 November 2021.

2. 'Growth in the agri-food sector in Greater Lincolnshire is important not only locally, but for the whole of the UK,' https://www.greater-lincolnshirelep.co.uk/priorities-and-plans/sectors/agri-food-sector/, accessed 21 November 2021.

3. Health & Safety Executive, 'Workplace fatal injuries in Great Britain, 2021,' https://www.hse.gov.uk/statistics/pdf/fatalinjuries.pdf, accessed 21 November 2021.

4. 'Hare coursers warned as dispersal order issued in Lincolnshire,' BBC, 9 January 2022, https://www.bbc.co.uk/news/uk-england-lincolnshire-59927932, accessed 10 November 2021.

5. 'Experiencing the highs and lows,' BBC, 25 June 2004, http://news.bbc.co.uk/1/hi/england/3827507.stm, accessed 20 November 2021.

6. See https://www.britishmuseum.org/collection/object/H_1858-1116-4, accessed 17 July 2021.

7. Paul Kingsnorth, *The Wake*, Unbound, 2014, p. 93.

8. Bede, *Ecclesiastical History of the English Nation*, Everyman's Library, 1910, my edition 1930, Book III, Chapter XI.

9.   1 Corinthians 9.

10. Anonymous, 'Guthlac A,' *Exeter Book*, late tenth century, my edition Everyman's Library, 1926.

11. Felix, *Vita Guthlaci*, c. 740, Charles Goodwin (tr.), John Russell Smith, 1848.

12. Felix, ibid.

13. Felix, ibid.

14. Anonymous, 'Guthlac B,' *Exeter Book*, late tenth century, my edition Everyman's Library, 1926.

15. Anonymous, 'Guthlac B,' op. cit.

16. Ibid.

17. Llewellynn Jewitt, *Half-Hours Among Some English Antiquities*, Hardwicke & Bogue, 1877, p. 155.

18. Alfred Tennyson, 'In Memoriam - A. H. H. OBIIT MDCCCXXXIII: 106', https://poets.org/poem/memoriam-ring-out-wild-bells, accessed 7 July 2021.

19. See Frances M. Page, *The Estates of Crowland Abbey—A Study in Manorial Organisation*, Cambridge University Press, 1934.

20. Hubert Larken, *The Official Guidebook to Croyland Abbey and Triangular Bridge*, Crowland Abbey, 1925.

21. Peter Rex, *The English Resistance: The Underground War Against the Normans*, Tempus, 2004, p. 163.

22. Charles Kingsley, *Hereward the Wake, or Last of the English*, 1866, my edition S. W. Partridge & Co., no date.

23. R. E. Glasscock, *The Lay Subsidy of 1334*, British Academy, 1975, cited in J. V. Beckett, *The East Midlands from AD 1000*, Longman, 1988, p. 52.

24. Page, op. cit., p. 123.

25. Page, op. cit., pp. 139–44.

26. Ronald Hutton, *The Rise and Fall of Merry England, The Ritual Year 1400-1700*, Oxford University Press, 1994, p. xxx.

27. John Capgrave, *The Life of Saint Gilbert of Sempringham*, c. 1450, Chapter II, cited in Eric W. Iredale, *Sempringham and Saint Gilbert and the Gilbertines*, p. 57.

28. William Dugdale, *Monasticon Anglicanum, or, The history of the ancient*

abbies, and other monasteries, hospitals, cathedral and collegiate churches in England and Wales. With divers French, Irish, and Scotch monasteries formerly relating to England, 1693, cited in Iredale, op. cit., p. 115.

29. Capgrave, op. cit., p. 66.

30. 'R. I.,' *The History of Tom Thumbe, the Little, for his small stature surnamed, King Arthur's Dwarfe: whose Life and adventures containe many strange and wonderfull accidents, published for the delight of merry Timespenders*, 1621.

31. Sarah Allison, 'The Evolution of Tom Thumb', https://writinginmargins.weebly.com/tom-thumb-timeline.html, accessed 10 November 2021.

32. Anonymous, 'Antiquities in Nursery Literature,' *Quarterly Review*, Vol XXI, January 1819, https://bit.ly/3wzjQsJ, accessed 15 December 2021.

33. Kenneth Sisam (ed.), *Fourteenth-Century Verse and Prose*, Oxford University Press, 1921, my edition 1959, p. 3.

34. John Dyer, 'The Fleece,' Book I.

35. Dyer, 'The Fleece,' Book II.

36. Quoted in Bechhofer Roberts, *Paul Verlaine*, Jarrolds, 1937, p. 159.

37. Jacques Borel (ed.), 'Chronologie,' *Paul Verlaine, Œuvres Poétiques Complètes*, Editions Gallimard, 1962, p. xxviii.

38. Roberts, op. cit., p. 167.

39. Daniel Defoe, *A Tour Through the Whole Island of Great Britain*, 1724-6, my edition, P. N. Furbank and W. R. Owens (eds), Yale University Press, 1991, p. 221.

40. Arthur Young, *General View of the Agriculture of the County of Lincoln*, 1799, my edition Augustus M. Kelley, 1970, p. 246.

41. Sir John Sinclair, cited in J. M. Neeson, *Commoners: Common Right, Enclosure and Social Change in England, 1700-1820*, Cambridge University Press, 1993, p.31.

42. William Cobbett, *Rural Rides*, 1830, my edition George C. Harrap, 1950, p. 295.

43. Cobbett, ibid.

44. John Clare, 'The Fens', https://www.poetry.com/poem/22302/the-fens, accessed 7 July 2021.

45. *Prospectus*, J. B. Henson, 1818.

46. Quoted by Spalding Civic Society, https://www.spaldingcivicsociety. org.uk/projects-campaigns/blue-plaque-scheme/william-booth/, accessed 10 December 2021.

47. Stewart Turner, 'Barbeque 67—the bizarre story of the UK's "first ever rock festival",' UK Yahoo News, 24 May 2017, https://yhoo. it/3uowKHl, accessed 10 December 2021.

6. LIGHT ON THE HUMBER

1. See Robert Van de Noort, *The Humber Wetlands: The Archaeology of a Dynamic Landscape*, Windgather Press, 2004.

2. William Lambarde, 1580s notes on Lincoln and Stamford (unpublished), cited in Ivan E. Broadhead, *Portrait of Humberside*, Robert Hale, 1983, p. 13.

3. Department of Transport, 'UK Port Freight Statistics 2020', https:// assets.publishing.service.gov.uk/government/uploads/system/uploads/ attachment_data/file/1014546/port-freight-annual-statistics-2020.pdf, accessed 17 December 2020.

4. Alan Rogers, *A History of Lincolnshire*, Darwen Finlayson, 1970, p. 11.

5. Broadhead, op. cit., p. 12.

6. 'The First Discoveries,' http://www.ferribyboats.co.uk/discoveries. html, accessed 20 July 2021.

7. Assuming Hengist and Horsa existed. Marc Morris points out that alliterative heroes and three-ship flotillas are common tropes in many northern European origin stories. See Marc Morris, *The Anglo-Saxons*, Hutchinson, 2021, p. 26.

8. Rufus Noel-Buxton, *Westminster Wader, being an estimate of Westminster in All Ages, by one who longs for MUDDY WATER, and the return of the bittern to London Fen*, Faber & Faber, 1957, p. 19.

9. James Campbell, 'When a Hull man walked across the River Humber - it really did happen,' *Hull Live*, 19 August 2018, https://www.hull-dailymail.co.uk/news/history/hull-man-walked-across-river-1907357, accessed 22 May 2021.

10. Defoe, op. cit., p216.

11. Arthur Storey, *Trinity House of Kingston-upon-Hull*, Trinity House, 1967, my edition 1989, p139.

12. Entrance to Winteringham, detailed by Jack H. Coote, 'East Coast Rivers', *Yachting Monthly*, 1981, p. 89.

13. Danielle de Wolfe, 'Luton isn't the worst place in Britain - it's Grimsby (according to ShortList readers),' *ShortList*, 21 January 2016, https://www.shortlist.com/news/is-grimsby-really-the-worst-place-in-britain, accessed 10 October 2021.

14. Laurel Ives, 'UK's 'unhealthiest' High Streets revealed,' BBC, 2 November 2018, https://www.bbc.co.uk/news/health-46059306, accessed 10 October 2021.

15. 'Top 10 most deprived towns in England,' *iLiveHere*, https://www.ilivehere.co.uk/top-10-most-deprived-towns-in-england-2019.html, accessed 10 October 2021.

16. Davey Brett, 'In Defence of Grimsby,' Vice.com, https://www.vice.com/en/article/3bjkk3/in-defence-of-grimsby-the-worst-place-in-the-uk-to-be-a-man-193, accessed 10 October 2021.

17. Edward Gillett, *A History of Grimsby*, Oxford University Press, 1970, p. 5.

18. G. S. Streatfeild, *Lincolnshire and the Danes*, Kegan, Paul, Trench & Co., 1884, p. viii.

19. Gillett, op. cit., p8.

20. *Orkneyinga Saga*, Chapter 59, Judith Jesch (tr.), 2009. See https://emidsvikings.ac.uk/blog/a-poet-visits-grimsby/, accessed 4 July 2021.

21. Tom Blass, *The Naked Shore of the North Sea*, Bloomsbury, 2015, p. 184.

22. To take a random date, 38,800 kg were sold at Grimsby on 3 June 2021, http://www.grimsbyfishmarket.co.uk/fishprices/prices, accessed 3 June 2021.

23. Edward Trollope, 'Anne Askew,' *Reports and Papers of the Associated Architectural Societies*, 1862, quoted in J. W. F. Hill, *Tudor & Stuart Lincoln*, Cambridge University Press, 1956, p. 60.

24. William Bradford, *Of Plimoth Plantation*, 1630-1651, Chapter 2, https://www.gutenberg.org/files/24950/24950-h/24950-h.htm, accessed 5 August 2021.

25. Nick Bunker, *Making Haste from Babylon – The Mayflower Pilgrims and Their World*, Bodley Head, 2010, p. 201.

26. Cited in A. L. Rowse, *Reflections on the Puritan Revolution*, Methuen, 1986, p. 24.

27. Kay Gardner, 'Among the world's finest,' *Lincolnshire Life* magazine, February 2005.

28. The description of fox-hunting given more than once by the Cockney grocer John Jorrocks, in Robert Smith Surtees' 1843 comic novel *Handley Cross*.

29. Abraham de la Pryme, *Diary*, p. 130.

30. Edward Thomas' poem 1917, recalling a June 1914 train journey across rural England in summer. See https://poems.poetrysociety.org.uk/poems/adlestrop/, accessed 15 November 2021.

31. Edward Irving Carlyle, 'Welby, Henry,' *Dictionary of National Biography*, 1885-1900, vol. 60.

32. A map in the Lincolnshire volume of the British Academy's ongoing *Corpus of Anglo-Saxon Stone Sculpture* shows the wide spread of finds, https://www.thebritishacademy.ac.uk/documents/739/16-cramp.pdf, accessed 12 November 2021.

33. See https://i.pinimg.com/originals/84/1a/c8/841ac80c0cb8a8bd2adc2ddb565df0b0.jpg, accessed 12 November 2021.

34. Andrew Marvell, 'To His Coy Mistress,' 1680s, *Oxford Book of Seventeenth Century Verse*, 1934, my edition Oxford University Press, 1976.

35. Gaston Bachelard, *The Poetics of Space*, 1969, my edition Beacon Press, 1994.

36. Nathan Standley & Charles Gray, 'Heartbreak as six people die in one month after taking their own lives at the Humber Bridge,' *Yorkshire Live*, 5 April 2021, https://www.examinerlive.co.uk/news/local-news/humber-bridge-hull-deaths-toll-20322201, accessed 10 November 2021.

37. John Ashbery, *Self-Portrait in a Convex Mirror*, 1972, my edition Carcanet New Press, 1977.

38. 'Lincolnshire Household Riddles,' *Notes & Queries*, December 1865, cited in Mark Bryant, *Dictionary of Riddles*, Routledge, 1990, p. 199.

39. Anthony Dent & Daphne Machin Goodall, *A History of British Native Ponies*, J. A. Allen, 1962, my edition 1988, p. 231.

40. Robin Blake, *George Stubbs and the Wide Creation*, Chatto & Windus, 2005, pp. 251-3.

41. Pryme, op. cit., p. 106.

42. Michael Drayton, *Poly-Olbion*, 1612, Twenty-Third Song.

43. Fuller, op. cit., p. 234.

44. The pipes can be sampled here: http://www.lincolnwaites.com/lincolnshirebagpipe/sound_lincolnshirepoacher.mp3, accessed 10 November 2021.

45. 'Normanby Hall: Scunthorpe Parkrun cancelled due to rutting stags,' BBC, 15 October 2021, https://www.bbc.co.uk/news/uk-england-humber-58928452, accessed 20 November 2021.

46. Coote, op. cit., p. 91.

47. See, for example, Sir Thomas Browne, *The Garden of Cyrus or, The Quincunciall, Lozenge, Or Net-work Plantations of the Ancients, Artificially, Naturally, Mystically Considered*, 1658.

48. *A Midsummer Night's Dream*, Act 2, Scene 2.

7. THE EAST'S WEST

1. There is a welcome project to reintroduce the sturgeon to the waters around Britain. See https://www.bluemarinefoundation.com/2020/07/01/the-royal-fish-returns/, accessed 10 April 2021.

2. George Stovin, *The History of the Drainage of the Great Level of Hatfield Chase, in the Counties of York, Lincoln, and Nottingham,* unpublished, discussed by Charles Jackson, 'The Stovin Manuscript,' *Yorkshire Archaeological and Topographical Journal*, Vol. VII, 1882, https://archive.org/details/yorkshirearchae16socigoog/page/n211/mode/2up?view=theater, accessed 10 April 2021.

3. Stovin, ibid.

4. 'Holy Well, Lower Burnham, Haxey, Lincolnshire,' *The Northern Antiquarian*, 21 March 2014, https://megalithix.wordpress.com/2014/03/21/holy-well-lower-burnham/, accessed 10 April 2021.

5. See British Academy, *Corpus of Anglo-Saxon Stone Sculpture*, 1999, https://www.thebritishacademy.ac.uk/documents/739/16-cramp.pdf, accessed 10 April 2021.

6.   James Tait, 'Mowbray, John de,' *Dictionary of National Biography*, 1885-1900, https://archive.org/details/dictionaryofnati39stepuoft, accessed 12 November 2021.

7.   Malcolm Hobson, 'History of Thorne', http://www.historyofthorne.com/history.html, accessed 6 July 2021. See also Samuel Smiles, *Lives of the Great Engineers*, 1874, my edition, David & Charles, 1968, p. 21.

8.   By Max Weber, in *The Protestant Ethic and the Spirit of Capitalism*, 1905 (German), 1930 (English), https://resources.saylor.org/wwwresources/archived/site/wp-content/uploads/2011/08/HIST304-4.5-The-Protestant-Ethic-and-the-Spirit-of-Capitalism.pdf, accessed 12 November 2021.

9.   Quoted in James Boyce, *Imperial Mud—Fight for the Fens*, Icon Books, 2020, p. 81.

10. Alexander Pope, 'Epistle I', *Epistles to Several Persons*, 1735, https://quod.lib.umich.edu/e/ecco/004809098.0001.000/1:3?rgn=div1;view=fulltext, accessed 12 January 2021.

11. Samuel Smiles, *Lives of the Great Engineers*, 1874, my edition David & Charles, 1968, p. 29.

12. Collin Ella, *The Isle of Axholme: A Guide to the District and its Villages*, self-published, 2007, p. 12.

13. See *Proceedings of the Wesley Historical Society*, Vol XL, Wesley Historical Society, October 1976, https://biblicalstudies.org.uk/pdf/whs/40-6.pdf, accessed 1 June 2021.

14. Horace Walpole, letter to John Chute, 10 October 1766, cited in *The Faber Book of Church and Clergy*, A. N. Wilson (ed.), Faber & Faber, 1992, p. 83.

15. Piers Brendon, *Hawker of Morwenstow: Portrait of a Victorian Eccentric*, Jonathan Cape, 1975.

16. Morgan Phillips, speech for Denis Healey, delivered at the 1953 Socialist International Conference in Copenhagen. Cited in James Callaghan, *Time and Chance*, HarperCollins, 1987.

17. See https://www.churchtimes.co.uk/articles/2017/7-july/news/uk/methodist-church-ponders-decline, accessed 11 May 2021.

18. Ethel Rudkin, *Lincolnshire Folklore*, 1936, reprinted by Beltons, 1987.

19. See Ian Bennett, *Eyewitness in Zululand, The Campaign Reminiscences of Colonel W. A. Dunne, South Africa, 1877-1881*, Greenhill Books, 1989.

20. Terence R. Leach & Robert Pacey, *Lost Lincolnshire Country Houses*, Vol. 1, Society for Lincolnshire History and Archaeology, 2008, p. 18.

21. *Proceedings of the Wesley Historical Society*, Vol. XL, October 1976, https://biblicalstudies.org.uk/pdf/whs/40 6.pdf, accessed 1 June 2021.

22. George Eliot, *The Mill on the Floss*, 1860, Chapter XII.

23. Oliver Cromwell, letter 'To the Committee of the Association sitting at Cambridge', 13 July 1643, cited in John West, 'Oliver Cromwell and the Battle of Gainsborough, July 1643', http://www.olivercromwell.org/Cromwelliana_Archive/1993.pdf, accessed 10 October 2021.

24. Stephen Wade, *Lincolnshire Murders*, Sutton Publishing, 2006.

25. Anonymous, *The Lincolnshire Times*, 22 November 1859.

8. THE CITY ON THE CLIFF

1. There is one in the Museum of Scotland. See https://www.nms.ac.uk/explore-our-collections/stories/scottish-history-and-archaeology/deskford-carnyx/, accessed 7 September 2021.

2. J. D. Whitwell, *Roman Lincolnshire*, History of Lincolnshire Committee, 1970.

3. See https://www.raf.mod.uk/our-organisation/stations/raf-scampton/, accessed 7 September 2021.

4. See https://heritage-explorer.lincolnshire.gov.uk/Monument/MLI50430, accessed 11 April 2022.

5. The Senones were an 'uncivilized nation of Gaul' (*Lemprière's Classical Dictionary*), based in and around modern Sens, who fought Caesar in the first century BCE and thereafter vanish from view.

6. Henry of Huntingdon, *Historia Anglorum*, quoted in Peter Sawyer, *Anglo-Saxon Lincolnshire*, History of Lincolnshire Committee, 1998, p. 154.

7. Henry of Avranches, *Metrical Life of St Hugh*, 1220-1235, 'baldly

Englished in pedagogic patois' by Charles L. Marson, *Hugh—Bishop of Lincoln*, unknown publisher, 1901, pp. 120-1.

8. Henry of Huntingdon, op. cit.

9. See https://archive.org/details/lhistoiredeguill03meyeuoft, accessed 18 November 2021.

10. Matthew Paris, cited in A.F. Scott, *Every One a Witness: The Plantagenet Age*, Book Club, 1975, p. 245.

11. Dennis Duncan, *Index, History of the*, Allen Lane, 2021, pp. 49-52. The other is Grosseteste's contemporary, the Dominican friar and later Cardinal Hugh of Saint-Cher, who invented the word-index, or concordance.

12. Alistair Crombie, *Robert Grosseteste and the Origins of Experimental Science, 1100–1700*, Clarendon Press, 1953.

13. Neil Lewis, 'Robert Grosseteste,' *Stanford Encyclopaedia of Philosophy*, https://plato.stanford.edu/entries/grosseteste/, accessed 10 November 2021.

14. Robert Grosseteste, *Perspectiva*, cited in Alan Macfarlane & Gerry Martin, *The Glass Bathyscape—How Glass Changed the World*, Profile, 2002, p. 37.

15. Grosseteste, op. cit.

16. Marcus Roberts, 'Lincoln,' http://www.jtrails.org.uk/trails/lincoln/history?page=9, accessed 10 November 2021.

17. See Richard Gottheil, Hermann L. Strack, Joseph Jacobs, *Jewish Encyclopaedia*, 1906, https://www.jewishencyclopedia.com/articles/3408-blood-accusation, accessed 10 November 2021.

18. See https://archive.org/stream/matthewparisseng03pari/matthewparisseng03pari_djvu.txt, accessed 10 July 2021.

19. Chaucer, 'Prioress's Tale', *Canterbury Tales*, first published 1475, my edition, Oxford University Press, 1976.

20. James Kinsley (ed.), *The Oxford Book of Ballads*, Oxford University Press, 1969, my edition 1971.

21. 'Little Saint Hugh of Lincoln,' *Wikiwand*, https://www.wikiwand.com/en/Little_Saint_Hugh_of_Lincoln, accessed 10 July 2021.

22. See https://www.youtube.com/watch?v=VkZFx5SqfHY, accessed 10 July 2021.

23. 'Lincoln Cathedral,' *British History Online*, https://www.british-history.ac.uk/vch/lincs/vol2/pp80-96, accessed 10 November 2021.

24. Henry VIII, 'Ansvvere to the petitions of the traytours and rebelles in Lyncolnshyre', State Papers, 1536.

25. Edmund H. Fellowes, *William Byrd*, Oxford University Press, 1936, p. 1.

26. Paul Henry Lang, *Music in Western Civilization*, J. M. Dent, 1942, my edition 1963, p. 287.

27. William Byrd, *Psalmes, Sonets, and Songs of Sadnes and Pietie*, 1588, cited in Edward H. Fellowes, *The English Madrigal Composers*, Oxford University Press, 1921, my edition 1963, p. 84.

28. Charles Van den Borren, *Les Origines de la Musique de Clavier*, 1912, cited in Percy A. Scholes, *The Oxford Companion to Music*, Oxford University Press, 1950, p. 128.

29. Anonymous, *Mercurius Britannicus*, 28 December 1643.

30. J. W. F. Hill, *The Royalist Clergy of Lincolnshire*, Lincolnshire Architectural and Archaeological Society, 1938.

31. Daniel Defoe, op. cit., p. 215.

32. Sir Joseph Banks, private correspondence, published by J. W. F. Hill, 'The Tomb of Robert Grosseteste with an account of its opening in 1782', offprint from np nd.

33. Michael Dummett, 'A review of Studies in Logic and Probability,' *Journal Symbolic Logic*, 1959, pp. 203-09, cited in Stanley N. Burris, 'Annotated Version of Boole's Algebra of Logic 1847 as presented in his booklet *The Mathematical Analysis of Logic Being an Essay Towards a Calculus of Deductive Reasoning*,' University of Waterloo, 2019, https://www.math.uwaterloo.ca/-snburris/htdocs/MAL.pdf, accessed 10 November 2021.

34. Anonymous, *The Tank—Its Birth & Development*, William Foster & Co., 1920, reprinted 1977.

35. Neil Hamilton, *Great Political Eccentrics*, Robson Books, 1999, pp. 77-89.

36. William Donaldson, *Brewer's Dictionary of Rogues, Villains and Eccentrics*, Cassell, 2002, pp. 572-4.

37. Walter Bagehot, *The English Constitution*, numerous editions, first published 1867.

9. THE WIND ON THE HEATH

1. Bede, op. cit., 669 CE.
2. Paul Whitelam, 'Revealed - the 100-plus medieval Lincolnshire villages that were wiped off the map,' *Lincolnshire Live*, 27 October 2019, https://www.lincolnshirelive.co.uk/news/local-news/revealed-100-plus-medieval-lincolnshire-3463235, accessed 10 November 2021.
3. Richard Muir, *The Lost Villages of Britain*, BCA, 1985, p. 252.
4. Oliver Goldsmith, 'The Deserted Village,' 1770, https://www.poetry-foundation.org/poems/44292/the-deserted-village, accessed 4 July 2021.
5. See https://www.artfund.org/supporting-museums/art-weve-helped-buy/artwork/4760/the-reverend-thelwall-carter-and-family, accessed 15 November 2021.
6. *Dictionary of National Biography*.
7. 'Confession of William Ayleward', *Register of Bishop Chedworth of Lincoln*, Lincoln Archive Office REG 20, fol. 61r, https://religion.wikia.org/wiki/Lollardy#cite_note-2, accessed 5 July 2021.
8. David Knowles, *Saints and Scholars*, Cambridge University Press, 1962, p. 149.
9. May McKisack, *The Fourteenth Century, 1307-1399*, Clarendon Press, 1959, pp. 515-6.
10. Quoted in Laurance Goulder, *The Universities—Oxford and Cambridge*, Guild of Our Lady of Ransom, 1963.
11. Catherine Parr, *Lamentations of a Sinner*, 1547, quoted at https://tudortimes.co.uk/people/katherine-parr-religious-writings/the-protestant-queen, accessed 7 July 2021.
12. John Bale, *Illustrium maioris britanniae scriptorium*, 1548.
13. Leland, op. cit., Part I, p. 28.
14. J. W. F. Hill, *Tudor & Stuart Lincoln*, Cambridge University Press, 1956, p. 5.
15. Quoted in Elizabeth Longford, *The Oxford Book of Royal Anecdotes*, Oxford University Press, 1989, p. 324.

16. John Harris, *No Voice from the Hall—Early Memories of a Country House Snooper*, John Murray, 1998, p. 209.

17. Henry Newbolt, 'Vitaï Lampada', https://allpoetry.com/Vita-Lampada, accessed 6 June 2021.

18. Henry Newbolt, 'Drake's Drum,' 1896.

19. Grimoldby station on that line was incidentally the childhood home of the actor Donald Pleasance, whose father was its stationmaster.

20. Compton Mackenzie, *The Darkening Green*, 1934, quoted by Stewart E. Squires, *The Lost Railways of Lincolnshire*, Castlemead, 1988, p. xii.

21. Harris, op. cit., pp. 177-82.

22. George Borrow, *Lavengro—The Scholar, The Gypsy, The Priest*, 1851, my edition Everyman's Library, 1925, p. 160.

23. '"The Brook": A Poem by Alfred, Lord Tennyson,' *Interesting Literature*, https://interestingliterature.com/2018/11/the-brook-a-poem-by-alfred-lord-tennyson/, accessed 5 November 2021.

24. 'Tennyson's the Brook,' *Tennyson Country*, 21 April 2020, https://tennysoncountry.com/2020/04/21/the-brook/, accessed 5 November 2021.

25. Terence R. Leach & Robert Pacey, *Lost Lincolnshire Country Houses*, Vol. III, Old Chapel Lane Books, 1992.

26. Quoted in Owen Beattie & John Geiger, *Frozen in Time—The Fate of the Franklin Expedition*, Bloomsbury, 1987, p. 45.

27. Quoted in Frances Spufford, *I May be Some Time: Ice and the English Imagination*, Faber & Faber, 1996, p. 131.

28. See, for example, Barry Lopez, *Arctic Dreams*, Macmillan, 1986.

29. Spufford, op. cit., p. 231.

30. See Raphael's 1515 cartoon, 'The Miraculous Draught of Fishes', https://www.vam.ac.uk/articles/the-raphael-cartoons-the-miraculous-draught-of-fishes#slideshow=85409956&slide=0, accessed 7 July 2021.

31. *Dictionary of National Biography*, p. 1,723.

32. Christopher Hibbert, *The Personal History of Samuel Johnson*, Readers' Union, 1973, p. 90.

33. James Boswell, *The Life of Samuel Johnson*, 1791, my edition Everyman's Library, 1992, p. 1,134.

34. John Wain, *Samuel Johnson: A Biography*, Viking Press, 1974, p. 225.

35. Hibbert, op. cit., p. 203.

36. Humphrey W. Burton, *The Story of Louth Parish Church*, British Publishing Company pamphlet, nd (1930s).

37. Ronald Hutton, *The Rise and Fall of Merry England: The Ritual Year, 1400-1700*, Oxford University Press, 1994, p. 36.

38. See Richard Brooks, *Cassell's Battlefields of Britain & Ireland*, Weidenfeld & Nicolson, 2005; Peter Gaunt, *The Cromwellian Gazeteer*, Alan Sutton & The Cromwell Association, 1987.

39. Stephen Bates, 'Sir Peter Tapsell,' *Guardian*, 19 August 2018, https://www.theguardian.com/politics/2018/aug/19/sir-peter-tapsell-obituary, accessed 7 July 2021.

10. PERIOD DRAMAS

1. 'MP calls for Lincolnshire slavery report to be "shredded",' BBC, 18 March 2021, https://www.bbc.co.uk/news/uk-england-lincolnshire-56447347, accessed 6 July 2021.

2. John Leland, *Itinerary*, Part IX, 1535-1543, Southern Illinois University Press, 1964, Vol. 5, p. 5.

3. *Lincoln, Rutland & Stamford Mercury*, 18 November 1785, quoted in Clifford Morsley, *News from the English Countryside 1750-1850*, Harrap, 1979, p. 112.

4. 'The Brazenose Site in Stamford,' Stamford Local History Society, http://stamfordlocalhistorysociety.org.uk/brazenose-site-stamford, accessed 10 December 2021.

5. Piggott, 1950, op. cit., p. 140.

6. Piggott, ibid., p. 152.

7. Edward Hyde (Lord Clarendon), *The True Historical Narrative of the Rebellion and the Civil Wars in England*, 1702-4, my edition Oxford University Press, 1956, p. 281.

8. Account of Sir Thomas Herbert, quoted in Roger Lockyer (ed.), *The Trial of Charles I*, Folio Society, 1999, p. 54.

9. Robert Beddard, *A Kingdom Without a King—The Journal of the Provisional Government in the Revolution of 1688*, Phaidon, 1988, p. 34.

10. Quoted in Elizabeth Longford, *The Oxford Book of Royal Anecdotes*, Oxford University Press, 1989, p. 311.

11. Quoted in Percy A. Scholes, *The Oxford Companion to Music*, Oxford University Press, 1950, p. 516.

12. Roy Palmer, *A Ballad History of England from 1588 to the Present Day*, Batsford, 1979, p. 14.

13. Tracy Borman, *Witches—James I and the English Witch-Hunts,* Jonathan Cape, 2013, p. xviii.

14. Nikolaus Pevsner, *Buildings of England: Lincolnshire*, Penguin, 1964, my edition 1998, p. 363.

15. Reproduced in Russell Read, *Harlaxton*, Horsfall Davenport, 1978, p. 6.

16. Mark Bridge, 'Decolonisation plan will tell Sheffield students of Isaac Newton's slavery links,' *The Times*, 26 April 2021, https://www.the-times.co.uk/article/decolonisation-plan-will-tell-sheffield-students-of-isaac-newtons-slavery-links-z89djfml5, accessed 1 December 2021.

17. William Stukeley, *Memoirs of Sir Isaac Newton's Life*, 1752, https://en.wikisource.org/wiki/Memoirs_of_Sir_Isaac_Newton%27s_life/Life_of_Newton, accessed 10 December 2021.

18. J. C. Pillans, *Lincolnshire to the Core, An Introduction to the Apple Varieties Originating from the County*, leaflet, Lincolnshire County Council, 1992.

19. 'History,' Discover St Wulfram's, http://www.discoverstwulframs.org.uk/history.aspx, accessed 3 December 2021.

20. 'The Luttrell Psalter - Introduction,' British Library, https://www.bl.uk/onlinegallery/ttp/luttrell/accessible/introduction.html#content, accessed 10 December 2021.

21. Michael Honeybone, *The Book of Grantham—The History of a Market and Manufacturing Town*, Barracuda Books, 1953, p. 59.

22. Quoted in Christopher Duffy, *The Military Experience in the Age of Reason*, Routledge & Kegan Paul, 1987, my edition 1998, p. 85.

11. TIME WAS—TIME IS—TIME IS PAST

1. Sallust, *Concerning the Gods and the Universe*, Part I, first century BCE.

SELECT BIBLIOGRAPHY

R. W. Ambler, *Ranters, Revivalists & Reformers*, Hull: Hull University Press, 1989

C. L. Anderson, *Lincolnshire Links with Australia 1788-1840*, self-published, 1988

Martin Andrew, *Francis Frith's Lincolnshire*, Salisbury: Frith Book Company, 2001

Anon, *A Guide to Tennyson's Lincolnshire*, Skegness: Skegness Publicity Service, 1973

Anon, *Gunby Hall*, London: National Trust, 2000

Anon, *Woolsthorpe Manor*, London: National Trust, 1984

M. W. Barley, *The Face of Britain: Lincolnshire and the Fens*, London: Batsford, 1952

Richard Barnes, *Coasts and Estuaries*, London: Book Club Associates, 1979

T. W. Beastall, *Agricultural Revolution in Lincolnshire*, Lincoln: History of Lincolnshire Committee, 1978

Owen Beattie and John Geiger, *Frozen in Time: The Fate of the Franklin Expedition*, London: Bloomsbury, 2004

J. V. Beckett, *The East Midlands from AD 1000*, London: Longman, 1988

John Beeler, *Warfare in England, 1066-1189*, New York: Cornell University Press, 1966

Stewart Bennett and Nicholas Bennett (ed.), *An Historical Atlas of Lincolnshire*, Chichester: Phillimore, 1993

SELECT BIBLIOGRAPHY

J. D. Birkbeck, *A History of Bourne*, Bourne: Lanes, 1976

Julia Blackburn, *Time Song: Searching for Doggerland*, London: Jonathan Cape, 2019

Tom Blass, *The Naked Shore of the North Sea,* London: Bloomsbury, 2015

Alan Bloom, *The Fens*, London: Robert Hale, 1953

James Boyce, *Imperial Mud – The Fight for the Fens*, London: Icon, 2020

Charles Brears, *A Short History of Lincolnshire*, London: A Brown & Sons, 1927

Ivan E. Broadhead, *Portrait of Humberside*, London: Robert Hale Ltd, 1983

Lynne Broughton, *Interpreting Lincoln Cathedral: The Medieval Imagery*, Lincoln: Lincoln Cathedral Publications, 1996

John Bruce, *Historie of the Arrival of Edward IV*, London: Camden Society, 1830

John Bygott, *The County Books: Lincolnshire*, London: Robert Hale Ltd, 1952

G. Edward Campion, *Lincolnshire Dialects,* Boston: Richard Kay, 1976

M. H. Carré, *Phases of Thought in England,* London: Oxford University Press, 1949

Peter Chambers, *The Wrecks and Wreckers of Mablethorpe*, Horncastle: F W Cupit, 2001

——, *Images of North Lincolnshire*, Derby: Breedon Books, 1993

——, *Grimsby: The Story of the World's Greatest Fishing Port*, Derby: Breedon Books, 2007

Daniel Codd, *Haunted Lincolnshire*, Stroud: Tempus, 2006

——, *Mysterious Lincolnshire*, Derby: Breedon Books, 2007

A. M. Cook, *Boston (Botolph's Town),* Boston: Church House, 1948

G. H. Cook, *Portrait of Lincoln Cathedral*, London: Phoenix House, 1950

William M. Cooper, *An Illustrated History of the Rod*, Ware: Wordsworth Editions, 1988

Jack H. Coote, *East Coast Rivers from the Humber to the Swale*, London: Yachting Monthly, 1981

Basil E. Cracknell, *Outrageous Waves: Global Warming & Coastal Change in Britain through Two Thousand Years*, Chichester: Phillimore, 2005

SELECT BIBLIOGRAPHY

Eric Croft, *Lincolnshire Railway Stations*, Keyworth: Reflections of a Bygone Age, 1993

S. E. Crooks (ed.), *Nature Reserves Handbook*, Horncastle: Lincolnshire and South Humberside Trust for Nature Conservation, 1989

F. L. Cross, *The Oxford Dictionary of the Christian Church*, London: Oxford University Press, 1958

G. J. Crossland and C. E. Turner, *Immingham: A History of the Deep Water Port*, Watlington: T&C Publishing, 2006

Linda Crust (ed.), *Billy Paddison of Soloby*, Louth: Louth Naturalists, Antiquarian and Literary Society, 2000

Laura Cummings, *On Chapel Sands*, London: Chatto and Windus, 2019

David Cuppleditch, *Joseph Willey: A Victorian Lincolnshire Photographer 1829-1893*, Cheddar: Charles Skilton Ltd, 1987

——, *Around Louth in Old Photographs*, Gloucester: Alan Sutton, 1989

——, *Pocket Images Around Louth*, Stroud: Nonsuch, 1995, my edition 2006

——, *Lincolnshire Photographic Collection: The Lincolnshire Coast and The Lincolnshire Wolds*, Stroud: Sutton Publishing, 2003

Susan Davies, *Quakerism in Lincolnshire*, Lincoln: Yard Publishing, 1989

Dennis Duncan, *Index, A History of the*, London: Allen Lane, 2021

Colin Ella, *The Isle of Axholme: A Guide to the District and its Villages*, self-published, 2007

Ros Evans, *Nature Guide to East Anglia & Lincolnshire*, London: Usborne, 1981

Felix of Crowland, *Vita Guthlaci*, Charles Goodwin (tr.), London: John Russell Smith, 1848

Edmund H. Fellowes, *The English Madrigal Composers*, London: Oxford University Press, 1963

——, *William Byrd*, London: Oxford University Press, 1936

Naomi Field, *Louth: The Hidden Town*, Lincoln: North Lincolnshire Archaeological Unit, no date

Roy Fisk, *Reflecting Lincolnshire*, Market Rasen: Imprint, 1981

Thomas Fuller, *Fuller's Worthies*, London: The Folio Society, 1987

Prisca Furlong, *Aesthetic East Lindsey*, Louth: Imp-Art Publications, 1989

SELECT BIBLIOGRAPHY

A. A. Garner, *Boston and the Great Civil War 1642-1651*, Boston: Richard Kay, 1972, my edition 1992

Edward Gillett, *A History of Grimsby*, London: Oxford University Press, 1970

Jabez Good, *Jabez Good's Lincolnshire Glossary*, Long Sutton: C. H. Major, 1973

Laurance Goulder, *Church Life in Medieval England*, London: No. 8 Pilgrimage Pamphlets, 1965

Adrian Gray, *Hidden Lincolnshire,* Newbury: Countryside Books, 1994

——, *Lincolnshire Headlines*, Newbury: Countryside Books, 1993

——, *Lincolnshire Tales of Mystery & Murder*, Newbury: Countryside Books, 2004

——, *Tales of Old Lincolnshire*, Newbury: Countryside Books, 1999

Herbert Green, *Forgotten Lincoln*, Wakefield: EP Publishing, 1974

Geoffrey Grigson (ed.), *About Britain No. 8: East Midlands and the Peak*, London: Collins, 1951

Meg Gwynne, *Ghosts and Legends Galore*, Louth: Allinson & Wilcox, 1976

Meg Gwynne and J. Kendal Bourne, *The Green Lady of Thorpe Hall and Local Ghostology*, Louth: Allinson & Wilcox, 1974

Neil Hamilton, *Great Political Eccentrics*, London: Robson Books, 1999

Owen Hamilton, *Lincolnshire Landscape*, London: Robert Hale, 1939

T. H. Hancock, *Bomber County: A History of the Royal Air Force in Lincolnshire*, Lincoln: Lincolnshire Library Service, 1978

John Harris, *No Voice from the Hall: Early Memories of a Country House Snooper*, London: John Murray, 1998

Jacquetta Hawkes, *A Land*, London: Collins, 1951

Victor Head, *Hereward*, Stroud: Sutton, 1995

Hilary Healey, *A Fenland Landscape Glossary for Lincolnshire*, Lincoln: Lincolnshire County Council, 1997

T. Hennell, *Change in the Farm*, Wakefield: EP Publishing, 1977

J. W. F. Hill, *Tudor & Stuart Lincoln*, London: Cambridge University Press, 1956

——, *The Royalist Clergy of Lincolnshire*, Lincoln: Lincolnshire Architectural and Archaeological Society, 1938

SELECT BIBLIOGRAPHY

Gervase Holles, *Lincolnshire Church Notes*, Lincoln: Lincoln Record Society, 1911

Edward Hollis, *The Memory Palace: A Book of Lost Interiors*, London: Portobello Books, 2013

Clive Holmes, *Seventeenth Century Lincolnshire*, Lincoln: History of Lincolnshire Committee, 1980

Diana & Michael Honeybone (eds.), *The Correspondence of William Stukeley and Maurice Johnson 1714-1754*, Woodbridge: Boydell Press, 2014

Michael Honeybone, *The Book of Grantham: The History of a Market and Manufacturing Town*, Buckingham: Barracuda Books Ltd, 1980

John Howard (ed.), *Facets of Tealby*, Caistor: Tealby Society, 2002

Eric W. Iredale, *Sempringham and St Gilbert and the Gilbertines*, self-published, 1992

A. S. Ireson, *The Stones of Stamford*, Stamford: Stamford Town Council, 1986

Anthony Jennings, *The Bourne Identity*, Bourne: Bourne Civic Society & Shaun Tyas, 2019

——, *The Old Rectory: The Story of the English Parsonage*, Durham: Sacristy Press, 2018

Llewellynn Jewitt, *Half-Hours Among Some English Antiquities*, London: Hardwicke & Bogue, 1877

Julian of Norwich, *Revelations of Divine Love*, Oxford: Oxford University Press, 2015

David Kaye, *Lincolnshire*, Princes Risborough: Shire Publications, 1995

——, *Lincolnshire and South Humberside*, Princes Risborough: Shire Publications, 1984

A. F. Kendrick, *The Cathedral Church of Lincoln*, London: George Bell & Sons, 1898

John R. Ketteringham, *Lincolnshire People*, Barnsley: The King's England Press, 1995

——, *A Lincolnshire Hotchpotch*, self-published, 1989

Winston Kime (ed.), *The Skegness Date Book 1850-2000*, Skegness: Skegness Town Council, 2006

Sophia Kingshill and Jennifer Westwood, *The Fabled Coast, Legends and Traditions from Around the Shores of Britain & Ireland*, London: Random House, 2012

Paul Kingsnorth, *The Wake*, London: Unbound, 2014

Malcolm Knapp, *Lincolnshire Living Memories*, Salisbury: Frith Book Company, 2004

David Knowles, *Saints and Scholars – Twenty-Five Medieval Portraits*, Cambridge: Cambridge University Press, 1962

Tim Knox, *Grimsthorpe Castle*, Grimsthorpe: Grimsthorpe and Drummond Castle Trust, 1996

Paul Henry Láng, *Music in Western Civilization*, London: J. M. Dent, 1963

Richard Larn, *Shipwrecks of Great Britain and Ireland*, Newton Abbot: David and Charles, 1981

Kit Lawie and Michael Richardson (eds.), *East Keal: The Story of a Village*, Spilsby: Marden Hill Press, 2000

M. K. Lawson, *Cnut: England's Viking King 1016-35*, Stroud: The History Press, 1993, my edition 2011

Terence R. Leach and Robert Pacey, *Lost Lincolnshire Country Houses*, Vols 1–5, Burgh le Marsh: Old Chapel Lane Books, 1990-2002

Kevin Leahy, *The Anglo-Saxon Kingdom of Lindsey*, Stroud: Tempus, 2007

Peter and Gemma Leak, *Washed In, Washed Out, Washed Away*, North Somercotes: East Coast Grafix, 2011

John Leland, *Leland's Itinerary in England and Wales*, Vols 1–5, Southern Illinois: Centaur Press, 1964

Lincolnshire Federation of Women's Institutes, *The Lincolnshire Village Book*, Newbury: Countryside Books, 1990

Elizabeth Longford (ed.), *The Oxford Book of Royal Anecdotes*, Oxford: Oxford University Press, 1989

Evelyn Lord, *The Knights Templar in Britain*, Harlow: Pearson Educational 2004

Basil Lubbock, *The Arctic Whalers*, Glasgow: Brown, Son and Ferguson, 1937

F. H. Ludlam and R. S. Scorer, *Cloud Study: A Pictorial Guide*, London: John Murray, 1957, my edition 1966

E. Mansel Sympson, *Lincolnshire*, London: Cambridge University Press, 1913

Christopher Marlowe, *Legends of the Fenland People*, Wakefield: E P Publishing, 1976

Hugh Marrows & Glen Hood, *100 Walks in Lincolnshire and Humberside*, Marlborough: Crowood Press, 1996

Walter Marsden, *Lincolnshire*, London: Batsford, 1977

Charles Marson, *Hugh of Lincoln*, London: Edward Arnold, 1901

May McKisack, *The Fourteenth Century 1307-1399*, London: Oxford University Press, 1959

Arthur Mee, *The King's England: Lincolnshire*, London: Hodder & Stoughton, 1970

——, *Lincoln*, London: St. Hugh's Press, no date

A. D. Mills, *Oxford Dictionary of English Place-Names*, Oxford: Oxford University Press, 1998

Dennis Mills (ed.), *Twentieth Century Lincolnshire*, Lincoln: History of Lincolnshire Committee, 1989

Derek Mills, *A Covey of Tales: The Memoirs of a Lincolnshire Gamekeeper*, Grimsby: Ashridge Press, 1999

F. J. Monkhouse, *A Regional Geography of Western Europe*, London: Longmans, 1959

John Morris (ed.), *Domesday Book Lincolnshire (Part One)*, Chichester: Phillimore, 1986

Marc Morris, *The Anglo-Saxons: A History of the Beginnings of England*, London: Hutchinson, 2021

Richard Muir, *The Lost Villages of England*, London: Book Club Associates, 1985

Rufus Noel-Buxton, *Westminster Wader*, London: Faber & Faber, 1957

R. J. Olney, *Rural Society and County Government in Nineteenth Century Lincolnshire*, Lincoln: History of Lincolnshire Committee, 1979

Mike Osborne, *Defending Lincolnshire: A Military History from Conquest to Cold War*, Stroud: The History Press, 2010

SELECT BIBLIOGRAPHY

Frances M. Page, *The Estates of Crowland Abbey: A Study in Manorial Organisation*, London: Cambridge University Press, 1934

Roy Palmer, *A Ballad History of England: From 1588 to the Present Day*, London: Batsford, 1979

Edward Parnell, *Ghostland: In Search of a Haunted Country*, London: William Collins, 2019

Howard Peach, *Lincolnshire Curiosities*, Wimborne: Dovecote Press, 1994

Ken Pearson, *Tairtyville Talk or the Language of Kirton*, Boston: Richard Kay, 1995

Nigel Pennick, *Lost Lands and Sunken Cities*, London: Fortean Times, 1987

Niklaus Pevsner, John Harris and Nicholas Antram, *The Buildings of England: Lincolnshire*, London: Penguin, 1998

Stuart Piggott, *William Stukeley: An Eighteenth Century Antiquary*, London: Clarendon Press, 1950

David A. Price, *Love and Hate in Jamestown: John Smith, Pocahontas and the Heart of a New Nation*, London: Faber & Faber, 2004

Abraham De La Pryme, *Diary*, Durham: The Surtees Society, 1870

Francis Pryor, *Seahenge: New Discoveries in Prehistoric Britain*, London: HarperCollins, 2001

——, *The Fens: Discovering England's Ancient Depths*, London: Head of Zeus, 2019

Willingham Franklin Rawnsley, *Highways & Byways in Lincolnshire*, London: Macmillan & Co, 1914

Herbert Read (ed.), *The English Vision*, London: Eyre & Spottiswoode, 1933

Peter Rex, *The English Resistance: The Underground War Against the Normans*, Stroud: Tempus, 2004

Bechhofer Roberts, *Paul Verlaine,* London: Jarrolds, 1937

David L. Roberts, *Lincolnshire Houses*, Donington: Shaun Tyas, 2018

David N. Robinson, OBE, *The Book of the Lincolnshire Seaside*, Buckingham: Baron, 1989

——, *Lincolnshire Bricks*, Lincoln: Heritage Trust of Lincolnshire, 1999

——, and Christopher Sturman, *William Brown and the Louth Panorama*, Louth: Louth Naturalists, Antiquarian and Literary Society, 2001

A. Rogers, *A History of Lincolnshire*, Henley-on-Thames: Darwen Finlayson, 1970

Ethel H. Rudkin, *Notes on the History of Toynton All Saints and Toynton St Peter*, Burgh-le-Marsh: Old Chapel Lane Books, 1992

Peter Sawyer, *Anglo-Saxon Lincolnshire*, Lincoln: History of Lincolnshire Committee, 1998

Percy A. Scholes, *The Oxford Companion to Music*, London: Oxford University Press, 1950

A. F. Scott, *Every One a Witness: The Plantagenet Age*, London: Purnell Book Services, 1975

W. G. Sebald, *The Rings of Saturn*, London: Vintage, 2002

John Seymour, *The Coast of North-East England*, London: Collins, 1974

James Sharpe, *Dick Turpin: The Myth of the English Highwayman*, London: Profile Books, 2004

Eric N Simons, *The Reign of Edward IV*, London: Frederick Muller, 1966

Julia Skinner (ed.), *Lincolnshire: A Miscellany*, Salisbury: Identity Books, 2010

Samuel Smiles, *Lives of the Engineers: Early Engineering*, London: John Murray, 1874

John F. H. Smith (ed.), *An Important Set of William Stukeley Drawings: his houses and gardens at Holbeach, Grantham, Stamford, Kentish Town, and a series of family portraits*, Spalding: Spalding Gentlemen's Society, 2016

Dava Sobel, *Longitude*, London: Fourth Estate, 1996

Judith Spelman (ed.), *Lincolnshire Bedside Book*, Wimborne: The Dovecote Press, 2003

Stewart E. Squires, *The Lost Railways of Lincolnshire*, Ware: Castlemead Publications, 1988

J. H. Srawley, *The Story of Lincoln Minster*, London: Raphael Tuck, 1947

Stamford, *Official Town Guide*, Stamford: Dolby Brothers, 1977

David Start, *Lincolnshire From The Air*, Sleaford: Heritage Lincolnshire, 1993

SELECT BIBLIOGRAPHY

——, and Collette Hall, *Lincolnshire's Heritage*, Sleaford: Heritage Lincolnshire, 1996

F. M. Stenton, *Anglo-Saxon England*, London: Oxford University Press, 1943, my edition 1950

Richard Stone, *The River Trent*, Chichester: Phillimore, 2005

G. S. Streatfeild, *Lincolnshire and the Danes*, London: Kegan Paul, Trench & Co., 1884

Christopher Sturman (ed.), *Some Historians of Lincolnshire*, Lincoln: Society for Lincolnshire History and Archaeology, 1992

Maureen Sutton, *We Didn't Know Aught*, Stamford: Paul Watkins, 1992

——, *A Lincolnshire Calendar*, Stamford: Paul Watkins, 1997

J. E. Swaby, *A History of Louth*, London: A Brown & Sons, 1951

——, *The Marshmen*, London: A Brown & Sons, 1962

Alfred Tennyson, *Poetical Works*, London: Ward, Lock & Co., no date

Joan Thirsk, *English Peasant Farming: The Agrarian History of Lincolnshire from Tudor to Recent Times*, London: Routledge & Kegan Paul, 1957

Ian Thompson, *Julian's Bower: A Guide to the Alkborough Turf Maze*, Scunthorpe: Bluestone Books, 1999

——, *Lincolnshire Springs and Wells*, Scunthorpe: Bluestone Books, 1999

P. Thoresby Jones & J. P. Hoskins, *Stamford: The Story of Six Parish Churches*, London: British Publishing Company, 1958

Henry Thorold, *Lincolnshire*, London: Pimlico, 1996

——, *Lincolnshire Houses*, Norwich: Michael Russell, 1999

Michael Todd, *The Coritani*, London: Duckworth, 1973

Ralph Townley, *The Brides of Enderby: A Lincolnshire Childhood*, London: Century, 1988

Various authors, *Sands of Time*, North Somercotes: English Nature, 2000

Various authors, *Three Chronicles of the Reign of Edward IV*, Gloucester: Alan Sutton, 1988

Joan Varley, *The Parts of Kesteven: Studies in Law and Local Government*, Bourne: Kesteven County Council, 1974

Stephen Wade, *Lincolnshire Murders*, Stroud: The History Press, 2009

Gilbert George Walker, *Tales of a Lincolnshire Antiquary*, Sleaford: W. K. Morton & Sons, 1949

SELECT BIBLIOGRAPHY

Richard Waters, *The Lost Treasure of King John*, Lincoln: Barny Books, 2003

R. C. Wheeler (ed.), *Maps of the Witham Fens from the Thirteenth to the Nineteenth Century*, Woodbridge: The Boydell Press, 2008

J. B. Whitwell, *Roman Lincolnshire*, Lincoln: History of Lincolnshire Committee, 1970

Polly Williams, *Lincolnshire Stuff*, Louth: Louth Naturalists, Antiquarian and Literary Society, 1997

Steve Willis & Barry Holliss, *Military Airfields in the British Isles 1939 – 1945*, Sutton-in-Ashfield: Enthusiasts Publications, 1990

Beckles Willson, *The Story of Lost England*, London: George Newnes, 1902

Horace B. Woodward (ed.), *The Water Supply of Lincolnshire from Underground Sources: With Records of Sinkings and Borings*, London: The Lords Commissioners of His Majesty's Treasury, 1904

Neil R. Wright, *Lincolnshire Towns and Industry 1700-1914*, Lincoln: History of Lincolnshire Committee, 1982

Meg Wynne and J. Kendal Bourne, *The Green Lady of Thorpe Hall and Local Ghostology*, Louth: Allinson and Wilcox, 1974

Jack Yates & Henry Thorold, *Shell Guide to Lincolnshire*, London: Faber & Faber, 1965

Ann Yeates-Langley, *Lincoln: A Pictorial History*, Chichester: Phillimore, 1997

Arthur Young, *General View of the Agriculture of the County of Lincolnshire, 1813*, New York: Augustus M. Kelley, 1970

INDEX

INDEX

INDEX

INDEX

INDEX

INDEX

INDEX

Magee, John Gillespie, poet 122, 125

Magna Carta 340

Manby 121

Mannyng, Robert, monkish writer 116, 152

Manston 308

Markby 110

Market Deeping 131, 161

Market Rasen 292, 327

Marlowe, Christopher, playwright

Marshal, Sir William, 1st Earl of Pembroke 274-5

Marvell, Andrew, poet 202

Marwood, William, executioner 296

Mary Tudor, Queen of England 75, 361

Maserfield, Battle of (642) 138, 228

Mason, Martin, Quaker 293-4

Massingberd, Drayner 70

Massingberd, Henry 70

Massingberd, Lambert 70

Massingberd, Oswald 70

Mathematical Analysis of Logic, The, book by George Boole 297

Matterhorn 323

McCartney, Paul, musician 62

McKisack, May, historian 312

Medieval Warm Period 86

Mee, Arthur, writer 63

Mellery, Xavier, artist 100

Melley, George, musician 61

Melton Ross 190

Melville, Herman, writer 40

Methodism 235-8

Miller, Thomas, poet 245-6

Mill on the Floss, The, book by George Eliot 246

Monksthorpe 66

Montagu, Edward, 2nd Earl of Manchester, Parliamentary commander 291, 346

Montgomery-Massingberd, Sir Archibald, owner of Gunby 70

Montgomery-Massingberd, Lady Diana, owner of Gunby 71

Montibus, William de, teacher 269

Moore, Charles, journalist 375

Moore, Henry, sculptor 21, 22, 222

Morley, Thomas, songwriter 76

Most Pleasant History of Tom a Lincolne, The, book by Richard Johnson 152

Moulton 53, 106

Mowbray Deed, medieval title deed 229, 232

Mozart, Wolfgang Amadeus 364-5

Mumby Chapel 87

Murray, Les, poet 29

National Air Traffic Control Radar Installation 317

Nene, River 52

Nennius, writer 176

Nettleham 265

438

INDEX

INDEX

INDEX

INDEX